Albin Chaplin has written more than 3,000 limericks for this book—all new and original. The following is a sampling of the bawdy fun in store for you.

True lovers say limericks don't rile 'em;
They simply collect and compile 'em—
    The limericks of whores
    And of bastards and bores,
And virgins and those who defile 'em.

*   *   *

There was a young coed of Kent,
In matters of law eloquent.
    She told lawyers from Yale
    That her ass was for sale,
But they proved it was only for rent.

*   *   *

As he spread the old nun, Father Keating
Checked her heart to be sure it was beating,
    Then his head he did bear
    And he said a short prayer,
For he always said *Grace* before eating.

*   *   *

A young lady investor, Miss Finches,
Was observing the oil rigs and winches.
    She said, "Though its fun
    To see deep drilling done,
I am thrilled if I'm drilled for six inches."

*   *   *

There was a young lady named Tweek
Whose pussy was flabby and weak,
    But her asshole was tight
    So she cried with delight,
"I'm so glad that I married a Greek!"

*   *   *

To her date said a lady named Hewitt,
"My mother said I mustn't do it.
    She advised me against fucking
    But said nothing of sucking—
Would you mind if I licked it and blew it?"

By the Same Author

The Noble Five Hundred Limericks (Fillmore P. Noble, pseud.)
The Limerick That Has the Appeal (Fillmore P. Noble, pseud.)

3024

·DIRTY·
LIMERICKS

BY
ALBIN CHAPLIN

The Largest Compilation
of Original Limericks
Ever Published
in
ONE VOLUME

BELL PUBLISHING COMPANY
NEW YORK

Acknowledgments

I am indebted to the outstanding collector of limericks, Gershon Legman, for his many letters and constructive advice and for the inclusion of a substantial number of my limericks in *The New Limerick*.

I am also indebted to Clifford M. Crist, with whom I have corresponded for many years. Dr. Crist, who has a massive file on all available limericks, has provided me with numerous stimuli to further my own work.

The Fifth Line Society of Chicago has been another inspiration, and their creativity deserves recognition.

This 1983 edition is published by Bell Publishing Company, by arrangement with Albin Chaplin

Manufactured in the United States of America

Library of Congress Cataloging in Publication Data
Chaplin, Albin.
    3024 dirty limericks.

    Bibliography: p.
    Includes index.
    1. Limericks.   2. Bawdy poetry.   I. Title.
PN6231.L5C52   1983   811'.54   83-3749
ISBN: 0-517-413175

Designed by Brian Malloy

h   g   f   e   d   c   b   a

Contents

Introduction • vii

1 Limericks about Limericks • 1

2 Little Romances • 5

3 Organs • 58

4 Strange Intercourse • 97

5 Oral Irregularity • 118

6 Buggery • 135

7 Abuses of the Clergy • 145

8 Zoophily • 169

9 Excrement • 180

10 Gourmands • 188

11 Virginity • 198

12 Motherhood • 213

13 Prostitution • 217

14 Diseases • 259

15 Losses • 267

16 Sex Substitutes • 279

17 Assorted Eccentricities • 293

18 Weak Sisters • 370

19 Chamber of Horrors • 436

20 Addenda • 450

Bibliography • 465

Notes • 467

Index • 485

Introduction

This book is the result of twenty-five years of fascination with the limerick. The three-thousand-plus limericks contained herein are the original work of one author. The reader will, no doubt, find many familiar themes and some similarity to previously published material, but in general I have attempted to be novel in all presentations. Included in this volume are eleven limericks that have been previously published. These are limerick series that have been further embellished, and they are shown in italics. To the Fisk limerick, I have added one limerick; to The Lady of Natchez, I have added four; to The Bishop of Birmingham, I have added two; to Clyde, I have added one. I trust that my contributions will enhance these classics, but the final judgment must be left to the reader.

The humble beginnings of this volume can be traced back to the 1950s when I was first exposed to the classic Gail limerick:

> On the breasts of a lady named Gail
> There was tattooed the price of her tail,
>   And upon her behind,
>   For the sake of the blind,
> Was the same information in Braille.

This limerick has the perfect anapestic meter, excellent rhyme, free-flowing syntax, and a superb punch line—thus meeting all the requirements of a classic. For all aspiring limerick writers, this is a worthy example to emulate.

Having thoroughly digested the Gail limerick, I began to collect as many as I could find for my index file, while committing the better ones to memory. Composing at this time was out of the question. Soon I had three hundred in a card file, and then I decided to try my hand at adding to this with my own efforts. In the late 1950s I received a startling setback to my collecting when I ran across Gershon Legman's *The Limerick: 1700 Examples*. This volume was available only in France, but I was fortunate in procuring a copy from a friend and I was able to gorge myself on limericks for a few weeks. This served to whet my appetite, and I proceeded to compose in earnest with *The Limerick* as my guide. This worthy book, replete with notes, variants, index, and bibliography is highly recommended to all as the canon, for it is a genuine and inspired collection of sacred works.

In the ensuing decade I had accumulated more than five hundred limericks, which I laundered to suit the times, and I hurriedly rushed these into print in 1967 under the title of *The Noble 500 Limericks*. I soon learned to my dismay that expurgated limericks have little or no appeal, and I wrote off this effort as a total disaster, though continuing to compose limericks. By 1975 I had more than two thousand items, which I proceeded to arrange in manuscript form. Before taking any further action, I contacted Gershon Legman for his thoughts regarding publication. Gershon was very helpful, advising that the limericks be unexpurgated and suggesting that they be grouped according to chapter headings, as in *The Limerick*. Furthermore, Gerhson sent me a list of aficionados throughout the country that he advised me to contact for assistance in getting started. It was thus that I was introduced to Dr. Clifford M. Crist, who had compiled *Playboy's Book of Limericks*. I also exchanged letters with Dr. Ray A. Billington, who produced his excellent book, *Limericks Historical and Hysterical*, in April 1981. Unfortunately, Dr. Billington passed away just before his book was published—a great loss to the field. Dr. Billington refers to Dr. Crist as "that master of the medium," an honor justly deserved and earned. Dr. Crist's assistance has been invaluable to me, and his many letters have been an inspiration to produce more and better limericks.

Gershon Legman's work in limericks is unsurpassed. His incomparable collection, under the innocuous title *The Limerick*, is the result of an exhaustive research into publications of more than eighty years. The earliest date given in the sources is 1870 and the latest is 1952. The bibliography provides the reader with all the available information on the subject, while the notes section pays tribute to the numerous contributors who embellished the limericks as they orally passed them from one to another, thus enriching the folklore. No doubt *The Limerick* must have inspired many readers, for there was a renaissance in production, culminating in sufficient material for Legman to produce his second book, *The New Limerick*. Major contributors to this volume were Clifford Crist—two hundred from his originals and his *College Collection*—and myself, contributing two hundred originals. *The New Limerick* is a welcome supplement to the earlier work, since it provides the reader with an up-to-date collection spanning the last three decades, and it should be evident that composing, far from waning, is alive and vigorous.

The most prolific supplier of limericks today is the Fifth Line Society of Chicago whose members, under the cloak of anonymity, feel more at liberty to permit their minds to run rampant, unrepressed by the taboos of society. One hopes some enterprising member, spurred by the Goddess Anapesta, will take it upon himself in the near future to review and edit this marvelous collection and prepare it for publication. For a review of the annual meetings, the reader is referred to the bibliographies in *The New Limerick* and in *Limericks Historical and Hysterical*, both of which contain a sprinkling of Fifth Line Society innovations.

For those readers who are interested in limerick lore or who wish to compose, exchange, or simply to keep in touch with limerick culture, a national society has just emerged. It is known as The

Introduction

Limerick League, Inc., 1212 Ellsworth Street, Philadelphia, PA 19147. Under the guidance of Roy Warren West, a quarterly publication will be issued, commencing fall 1981. Readers are encouraged to subscribe and participate so that wit, humor, and satire in the anapestic medium will flourish. Roy W. West has authored several booklets of limericks relating to the Philadelphia scene and to the Scottish dialect.

There is no need to burden the reader here with advice on how to compose limericks, for this information can best be acquired by reviewing the excellent introductions in the books listed in the bibliography. However, I do wish at this point to review the material in this book and to disclose the most probable reasons for its existence. My work is meant to be satirical, witty, simple, humorous, and ironic. Some poems are based on material that I have heard in joke form since my early grade-school days, and it should not surprise the reader to discover that he probably heard many of these themes as "dirty jokes" in his own early years. Other items are the result of inspirations from daily contact with fellow office workers, who constantly seek to relieve monotony with excursions into humorous anecdotes. There is also the ubiquitous collection of graffiti, which has taken on new mobility with the advent of the rapid copy-machine. The news media provides a perpetual source of subject matter with reports on machinations of politicians, misbehavior of clergy, unusual court cases, capricious behavior of members of respected professions, weird sex crimes, blunders of world leaders, mismanagement, corruption, grand larceny by seemingly honest businessmen, and numerous other items with which the reader is all too familiar. The limerick honors all these! In the format of this book, I have emulated Legman's categories as presented in *The Limerick*, a work that consists mainly of collections from three major United States colleges. My work has also been influenced by that eighteenth-century master of satire, Jonathan Swift, whom I hold in high esteem.

As for the future of the limerick—who knows? There has been a resurgence in the last twenty years, undoubtedly due to the liberalization of moral codes and taboos. Limericks, long clandestine, are now exposed to the light of day, while new material is sprouting all over the country. Several organizations are prominent in the production or collection of new limericks—the Fifth Line Society, the Limerick League, and the Mohegan Folklore Society (Mohegan Community College). Legman is optimistic about the future of the limerick as we note in his book *The Limerick:* "Limericks are not only the folklore almost solely of the educated but are almost their only folklore—with the exception of jokes and tales. . . ." and from *The New Limerick:* "For good or bad, they are poetry. And they are the only kind of rhymed poetry being written today in English that has the slightest chance of survival in oral circulation. . . ."

With these thoughts I rest my case—the future looks bright.

1

Limericks about Limericks

1

To limericks some folks are adverse;
'Tis said that no odes could be worse,
    So a prudish man pondered
    And he had them all laundered,
But they all ended up as blank verse.

2

The limerick that has the appeal
Is penned by the quill that's facile
    In the sordid, grotesque,
    And in bawdy burlesque,
And contorted reports imbecile.

3

The limericks that men like the best
Are morally banned and suppressed,
    But they orally sprout
    For there's rich soil about,
And they leave all the ladies distressed.

4

The limericks that I like the best
Are those that put morals to test
    On things biological
    And matters illogical,
Which are all in a nutshell compressed.

5

When out on a date with Miss Best,
A man quoted limericks with zest.
    This disturbed the girl so,
    That she told him to go,
And she called him a bore anapest.

6

A limerick is callous and crude;
In no way must it be construed
    As a subject worth reading
    By men of fine breeding—
It's designed for the vulgar and rude.

1

7

The limericks that here are exhibited
Are bold and downright uninhibited,
　　And we warn ladies meek
　　It was only last week
They were banned and suppressed and prohibited.

8

The limerick, outlandish and garish,
May come from the whorehouse or parish,
　　And renown can ensure
　　By avoiding what's pure
And attacking the symbols folks cherish.

9

Though limericks will suit either gender,
Yet some are devised with such splendor
　　That they're far too stentorian
　　For young ladies Victorian,
Since they're not meant for ears that are tender.

10

The limerick which brings most hilarity
Is brewed with ingenious dexterity.
　　It contains an event
　　With improbable bent
And a dash of erotic vulgarity.

11

There was an old limerick so naughty
That it traveled from potty to potty
　　Reaping shameful cognition
　　By oral tradition;
It was polished and now it is haughty.

12

New limericks herein are presented—
Some simple, some bold, some demented.
　　There is here an arrangement
　　Of every derangement,
Either factual, supposed, or invented.

13

True lovers say limericks don't rile 'em;
They simply collect and compile 'em—
　　The limericks of whores
　　And bastards and bores,
And virgins and those who defile 'em.

2

14
For your limericks you never will score—
They are rotten right down to the core.
    They're abusive and crude,
    Offensive and rude—
I love them, keep telling me more.

15. ADVICE TO POETS
If you write just line one, you're a bum;
Two lines and you get a ho-hum.
    Three lines are still bad,
    And with four you're a cad,
But five gets you plaudits from some.

[16]*
It is simple to write limericks new;
You first write line one, then line two.
    Line three is no chore,
    And neither is four.
When you get to line five you are through.

[17]
Into five lines a tale you compress,
But compressing too much is a mess.

[18]
A limerick of five lines will do
But never with four, three or two.
    For three is two short—

[19]
A poet who lived in Verdun
Wrote limericks which stopped at line one.
    Since that's how it is,
    This limerick's not his.

[20]
A foreshortened limerick's not pure;
Its need to exist is obscure.
    It is very important
    That it not be fourshortened.

* *Note:* Limericks with numbers in brackets are part of a series.

[21]

The man who writes six lines, I'll bet,
Has not been located as yet,
  But I sense now and then,
  He's still wielding his pen,
And he's someone that one time I met,
A meeting I'll always regret.

[22]

A poet efficient, perplexed
Many folks, and it seems they were vexed,
  For his theme, we deplore,
  Would end at line four.
The fifth line was first for the next,
A thing that left many perplexed,
  For shortly his theme
  Would run out of steam.
Since this line must rhyme with "the next",
It soon left the poor poet vexed
  And somewhat perplexed. . . .

[23]

AspacesavingpoetnamedBliss
Thoughtnothingatallwasamiss,
  Formuchpaperhesaved,
  Buttheyjudgedhimdepraved
Whenhetriedtojamletters *likethis.*

[24]

A muddled young poet named Clyde,
In upside down writing took pride.
  The strain of this work
  Snapped his brain with a jerk!
He was hung by his heels when he died.

[25]

.front to back lines wrote poet One
.brunt the took ,abuse to exposed And
  track the on remain To
  ;back to front write must One
.dunt say I ,perverse verse write who Those

[26]

The limerick is neat and concise,
Yet crammed with delectable spice.
  There's no need for pomposity
  Or extraneous verbosity
When a four-letter word will suffice.

2

Little Romances

27
To a young man who threatened abduction
The lady imparted instruction,
    "If you're crude, you dumb ape,
    I will charge you with rape;
If you're clever, I'll call it seduction."

28
A lady with no mean ability
Was raped by a man with agility.
    She said, "You are pleasant
    But you're only a peasant,
And I'm usually raped by nobility."

29
While a lady gave Newton some action
He paused in a fit of distraction,
    "How stupid of me,
    It's so easy to see
Why action does equal reaction."

30
All women would gain more affinity
With husbands who'd love to infinity,
    And wives' troubles would pass
    If they'd struggle for ass
Just as hard as they fought for virginity.

31
When the queen dined with John Jacob Astor
She claimed he could never outlast her,
    But she failed to account
    For his intricate mount
And resources superior and vaster.

32*
A horny young lady was Babbitt;
To fuck in a car was her habit.
    On the banks of Euphrates
    She tried the *Mercedes.*
"It is better," she said, "in a *Rabbit.*"

* Note: Asterisks on limerick numbers are to alert the reader that
the limerick is discussed in the Notes section.

33

The dignified Baron of Barden
Observed the young maid in the garden
   As she wiggled her ass
   While trimming the grass,
So he fucked her and said, "Beg your pardon."

34

When dying, a fellow named Bate
Arranged to pay charges and freight
   On his brand-new Mercedes
   To be sent down to Hades,
To ensure that he'd get a hot date.

35

An agile contortionist, Beakley,
Was screwing a lady uniquely.
   In the midst of ferment
   She got twisted and bent,
So he finished his fucking obliquely.

36. MAKE PIECE—NOT WAR*

There was a young lady named Beatty,
So gorgeous and wholesome and meaty,
   That when she had a fuck
   With an ardent young buck,
She requested he sign a piece treaty.

[37]

A horny young fellow was Beatty;
He called up his girl and said, "Sweetie,
   In the place of this bickering
   I propose we start dickering;
I'll be over to sign a piece treaty."

38

When Hoover was dating Miss Beggs,
She said, when she spread out her legs,
   "I deplore, Mr. Hoover,
   Such a lengthy maneuver;
It is time for the sausage and eggs."

39

A destitute lady named Beggs
From hunger was on her last legs.
   As she walked through the city,
   The old mayor took pity
And he slipped her some sausage and eggs.

40

A novice young girl of Belgrade
Remarked as a man with her played,
    "I have never been had."
    So he took out a pad
And he noted the blunders she made.

41

A simple young lad was bereft
Of knowledge that makes a man deft.
    Said his girl, "Let me know
    When you're ready to go."
He said, "Now," and he got up and left.

42. LIKE FATHER, LIKE SON

There was an old fellow of Berne
Whose son was the cause of concern,
    For girls were perplexing;
    He knew nothing of sexing,
So they went to a whorehouse to learn.

[43]

They picked an old whore without peers;
The father fucked this one for years,
    But the son was so thrilled
    When his wants were fulfilled
That he wed the old whore, it appears.

44. TRY A DRY RUN!

A lady went out with young Bert
But he couldn't get under her skirt.
    He said, "Do you fear
    A prick?" She said, "Dear,
It isn't the prick—it's the squirt!"

45

An elderly matron named Bess
Was raped by a thief with finesse.
    She cursed the detective
    With her vilest invective
For the failure to find his address.

46

The chef de cuisine, name of Biddle,
Explained before starting to diddle,
    Why his girl he did toast:
    "For like pancakes or roast
They are good when they're hot off the griddle."

47. LISSAJOUS FIGURE*

A jungle explorer named Biggar
Was fucking a colored gold digger.
    It was just like a tonic
    With her fanny harmonic
Which traced a fine Lissajous figure.

48

A young sausage-stuffer, Miss Binks,
Stuffed sausage all day into links.
    Her nightly routine
    Was more sausage between,
And she never could catch forty winks.

49. WHERE DID HE KISS HER?

There was a young fellow named Bister
Who fucked Miss Laporte and her sister.
    When he fucked Miss Laporte
    'Twas a marathon sport,
But her sister would come when he kissed her.

50

"My stock is first class," said Miss Bloor,
"The best on the market, for sure."
    After old Merrill Lynch
    Shoved his prick in one inch
She was rated as *Standard and Poor.*

51

When my girl friend is dressed in her bonnet,
She is striking and sweet as a sonnet,
    And a thing she's concealing
    Which arouses my feeling,
But my finger I cannot put on it.

52

At Christmas each girl and each boy
Expects Santa Claus to deploy
    His fine reindeer and sled,
    Gifts and goodwill to spread,
But he spends the whole night spreading Joy.

53

A farmer who came from Bordeaux
Was screwing a lady named Jeaux.
    This young lady, so proud,
    Had too often been ploud,
And he found her a hard reaux to heaux.

54

There were two young ladies named Bower
Who screwed two young Krauts for an hour.
    Said one, "My Kraut is sweet,
    I must have a repeat."
But the other said her Kraut was sour.

55

There was a young lady named Bower
Who dwelt in an ivory tower,
    But a farmer from Perth
    Laid her flat on good earth
And proceeded with vigor to plough her.

56. QUIET PLEASE!

In the library, stuffy Miss Boyes
Was raped, but she maintained her poise.
    Though her arms waved about
    There was nary a shout—
She respected the rule against noise.

57. HATCHET MAN

The woodchopper dated Miss Brackett
And proceeded to take off his jacket.
    Her pussy felt tight
    But he said with smile bright,
He was sure without doubt he could hack it.

58

To his bride said the farmer named Brickley,
As he fondled her cunt, sprouting thickly,
 "Though it looks very nice,
 We must pack it in ice.
I don't want it to ripen too quickly."

59

In the sticks lives a lady named Bright
With a face that's a horrible fright,
 But no fellow minds that—
 She feeds gin to her cat—
And it's fun when her pussy is tight.

60. EVERY RULER HAS TWELVE INCHES

Said the Duke to the Queen, "I will bring
Great joy," and he showed her his thing.
 When the Queen viewed his gear
 She said with a sneer,
"You have not enough prick to be king."

61

A fussy young lady named Brinkage
When fucking would raise a big stinkage,
 But a simple mechanic
 Avoided a panic
By adjusting the stops on her linkage.

62

While driving, a lady named Brinker
Had turned on her left-turning blinker,
 But she waited so long
 That a man from Hong Kong
Fucked her once and then called her a stinker.

63

A novice at fucking was Brook;
He felt something starting to cook.
 He did not understand
 That feeling so grand,
So he backed off a foot for a look.

64. THE GOOD BOOK
In demand was a lady named Brook
Though she never had learned how to cook.
   It was on her divan
   That she pleased every man,
For she knew every trick in the book.

65. THE CORRECT RECIPE
From the book a young lady named Brook
Was unable to learn how to cook,
   But to fuck she was able,
   So she lay on the table
And supported her ass with the book.

66
There was a young bowler named Brophey
Who fucked a young lady named Sophie.
   Seven strikes in a row
   And it was apropos
That he give her his bowling ball trophy.

67
A well-hung young fellow was Browder;
His pecker was longer and prouder.
   When he screwed old Miss Gariepy
   Who was looking for therapy,
She no longer did need sleeping powder.

68
While fucking a fellow named Bruce
A girl made excuses profuse.
   She was late for her class,
   So she stepped on the gas
And she left him to stew in his juice.

69. ANY PORT IN A STORM
A stoical fellow named Bud
Was fucking a lady—a dud—
   And she had a bad smell,
   But he said, "What the hell,
It is better than pulling my pud."

70

There was an old fellow named Bunche
Who met an old whore with a hunch.
    No time could she take—
    It was time for a break—
So she fucked him while munching her lunch.

71

There was a young lady named Bunky
Who asked for a date from a flunky.
    He declined her because
    There's a whole set of laws
About what he could do to a monkey.

72

So spent was his lordship, Sir Burke,
No pussy could get him to perk,
    But a lady named Opal
    Came from Constantinople
And she sure put his pecker to work.

73

There was a young lady named Bustard
Who went on a date and got flustered.
    She was told that with Draper
    She could cut a fine caper,
But she found he could not cut the mustard.

74

A vigilant fireman named Byron
Extinguished the fire in a siren,
    But it smoldered and flamed
    And he sadly proclaimed
There were too many fires for his iron.

75

The premier danseur of Calais
Was carried completely away
    As he screwed Wilhelmina
    The renowned ballerina
While performing the *Swan Lake* ballet.

76

The confident man of Miss Campbell
Had offered to teach her to scramble.
    He was ready to breech her
    But the pupil turned teacher
And she left him a broken down shamble.

12

77

A lustful young trapper named Capper
Got hitched to a dapper young flapper.
    His assault was released
    Right in front of the priest,
For he did not have time to unwrap her.

78

Said the lady to old butcher Carr,
"Your sausage is not up to par."
    But his sausage went in
    Till it tickled her chin,
Which was stretching a good thing too far.

79. RECALL*

Her buttocks had started to chafe
In back of the car with young Shafe.
    It did bruise and abrade her
    And when this got to Nader
He declared all those models unsafe.

80

A clear-thinking fellow was Chape;
He married a girl like an ape.
    He said in the main
    He would never complain
As long as her cunt stayed in shape.

81

A frustrated fellow named Chase
Had nothing to say to wife Grace
    For three decades or so—
    But his family did grow
For he only was mad at her face.

82

When the Baron is faced with a choice,
At the airport he parks his Rolls-Royce,
    Then goes up in a plane
    And he fondles Miss Jane,
While slipping his joy stick to Joyce.

83

The mother of buxom Miss Claire
Discovered her secret affair.
    She admonished her child
    For her antics so wild,
"This is something we both have to share."

84

There was a young fellow named Clairwell
Who fucked his girl once and said farewell.
    He went to the door
    But she cried for some more,
So he fucked her twice more on the stairwell.

85

A carefree Lothario named Clark
At night went to spark in the park.
    He remarked, rather sprightly,
    "It's to hide what's unsightly,
For they all feel the same in the dark."

86

The engine mechanic named Clark
Picked up a young maid in the park.
    He could not get her started
    For she sputtered and farted,
Till he found the advance on her spark.

87*

"See-through fashions are fun," said old Clark.
"They fill me with vigor and spark.
    It makes life with wife Claribel
    A little more bearable,
For I always get fucked in the dark."

88

There was a young lady named Cleft
Who dated a man who was deft.
    Though she kept in full view
    What his right hand did do,
She was screwed by the one that was left.

89

Since screwing his mistress, young Cleft
Of pep for his wife was bereft.
    To allay her suspicion
    He assumed the position
And he offered what juice he had left.

90

While having with wifie coition
The hubby jumped up with cognition
    And he cried, "Oh my dear,
    I have hurt you I fear,
For I felt a slight change in position."

91
A baker who lived in Cologne
Was screwing a lady named Jogne.
When he offered her bread
She refused it and sead
She could not live by bread just alogne.

92
The chief of police in Cologne
Was dating a meter-maid, Joan.
He was slow in his sparking
So she fined him for parking
To long in her *No Parking* zone.

93
There was an old fellow named Coombs
Who rented apartments and rooms,
And the rents were reduced
For the girls he seduced,
And were free to the ones with tight wombs.

94
A lady of means was Miss Cord;
All pleasures in life she explored.
Yet this lady demure
Was in truth insecure
For wherever she went she was bored.

95
In need of a man, widow Cotter
Went to bed with a fellow named Potter.
She was no good in bed
So she said to him, "Fred,
You can finish the fuck with my daughter."

96
There was a young lady named Coulsom
Who went with her boy friend to bowl some.
She was fucked on the alley
By an old man from Bali,
And she found it nutritious and wholesome.

97
There was a young girl of Coxsaxie
Whose skirt was more mini than maxi.
She was fucked at the show
In the twenty-third row,
And once more going home in the taxi.

98

A comely young coed named Crassar
Was raped twice a day while at Vassar.
  She hoped to get peace,
  But attacks did increase
When she levied a fine for trespasser.

99

A bestial young fellow once crept
Upon an old lady who slept.
  He was husky and stout
  But she threw the man out
For his fucking was grossly inept.

100

Miss Summer was nice, thought young Cummer;
One drink and he'd have him a hummer.
  To his sorrow he found,
  After many a round,
That one swallow does not make a Summer.

101

There was an old duchess named Dag
Whose duke on occasion would lag,
  But she had a good servant
  Who was very observant—
He stepped in when his lordship did flag.

102

On going to college, Miss Dare
By mother was told to beware
  Of boys in her bed
  For this she did dread,
So Dare fucked the boys in a chair.

103

The maids joined the bride in her dash
To ride with the groom in his Nash.
  As they rode dignified,
  The groom fucked the bride,
And the bridesmaids were caught in the splash.

104

The maids joined the bride in her dash
To ride with the groom in his Nash.
  As they rode to the ferry
  The bridegroom made Mary,
And Joy, Rosie, Grace, and Miss Cash.

105
The mother advised her young daughter
To shun the conniving young plotter
    Who was after free tail,
    So she fucked with a male
If he offered some gin, scotch or water.

106
There was an old lady of Dawson
Who said to a lad, "You've a flaw, son.
    If you stay for a while
    I'll improve on your style.
You are not near as good as your pa, son."

107. THE LAW OF GRAVITY
Young Newton partook of depravity
And filled up a young lady's cavity.
    To indulge in some brevity,
    What to Newton was levity
He found was a law of some gravity.

108
There was a young girl of Detroit
Whose movements were very adroit.
    She was screwed by old Harris
    Who was just in from Paris,
But some facets he failed to exploit.

109
There was a young girl named Dewald
Who was in her bedroom appalled
    By the agile virility
    And the great capability
Of the man that she screwed that was bald.

110
An expert old lady named Dickinson
Said, "Here is where you put your prick in, son.
    Now do not drool and dribble,
    You must give these a nibble,
And get an occasional lick in, son."

111
A lady had thought to discuss
With the driver, her rape on the bus,
    Till she noticed the sign
    Which said ten dollar fine
If you raise on the bus any fuss.

112

On the beach all her parts were displayed,
But she said to her man, "I'm afraid
    It's too hot in the sun
    To have any fun."
Which was why she was made in the shade.

113

The priest told a lad to divest of it.
He said, "You must tell all the rest of it."
    So the young lad did blurt
    How he fucked Dirty Gert.
He felt good when he made a clean breast of it.

114

A man dissipated was Dougal;
He failed his relations con*j*ugal,
    So his wife sadly said,
    "Since your pecker is dead,
I'll blow *Taps* on your battered old bugle."

115

A virile young fellow of Dover
Made Mary when out in the clover.
    He was found weak and wan
    At the crack—yes—of Dawn.
He looked pale but felt Rosie all over.

116

Two eager young fellows of Dover
Made Mary when out in the clover.
    When Mary played coy
    They both jumped with Joy,
And later felt Rosie all over.

117

A man who made Mary in Dover
Had Mercy when out in the clover.
    With Joy he did jump
    Then with Ethyl did pump,
And of course, he felt Rosie all over.

118

While checking the cunt of Miss Drew,
The doctor tried one inch, then two.
    Said Miss Drew, without merriment,
    "Please forget the experiment—
You can shove in the prick and let's screw."

119
So slow was a horny old duchess
She could never keep out of men's clutches.
    She was fucked as she ran
    By a one-legged man,
Who managed to crotch her on crutches.

120
The snatch of the Countess Dumore
Was bald as the knob on the door.
    Said the Duke, in surprise,
    As he parted her thighs,
"No doubt it's because of the war."

121
There was a young girl of Dundee
Who complained that she gave too much free.
    Her beau felt a pang
    When he heard her harangue;
He lay back and said, "This one's on me."

122. BATMAN AND ROBIN*
A buxom young lady named Dunder
Said *Batman* had plenty of thunder,
    But her young sister said
    As she left the *Bat* bed,
He was not near as sharp as *Boy Wonder*.

123. DOUBLE YOUR FUN*
A *Doublemint* lady named Dunn
Had doubled her pleasure and fun—
    On a date with a lad
    She invited his dad,
For two heads were much better than one.

124
A circus stunt pilot named Dunway
Was fucking his girl on the runway.
    He received commendation
    And a standing ovation,
But he said that he knew only one way.

125*
A farmer by name of Durante
Was watching TV in his shanty
    With the picture askew;
    When his wife he did screw
She complained his performance was slanty.

126
There was a hot-rodder named Dutch
Who steered his way to his girl's hutch.
    But he said to her, "Dear,
    I can't get into gear
For it seems I can't break from your clutch."

127
A nympho young lady of Eire
Was lustful and full of desire.
    To her husband she said,
    "Would you please turn your head
While the neighbor helps put out the fire."

128
A man with his pecker erected
To fondle his dear wife elected.
    With her clit he did play
    But he found in dismay
That her pussy was not well connected.

129
There was a young coed named Esther
Who claimed that the frosh could not best her,
    But a freshman, a jester,
    With his prick he did test her,
And he fucked her for one whole semester.

130
A lady of faith was Miss Eve;
She gave her ass free, I believe,
    And the reason, she said,
    As she climbed into bed,
"It's more blessed to give than receive."

131
The noted Professor Herr Ewing
Gave coeds free lessons in screwing.
    "It's amazing," he said,
    "When they're stripped and in bed,
How so few of them know what they're doing."

132
A fellow unskilled in excesses
Was hugged and received such caresses
    When his girl held him tight
    And then kissed him good night,
That he left with residual stresses.

133. VAGINA DENTATA
Said a girl to a lad, "You excite me.
Your prick in my cunt would delight me."
    Said the novice young lad,
    "I'll not do it, by Gad,
For I fear it will come back to bite me."

134
There was an intrepid explorer
Who dated a lady named Forrer.
    He explored every cranny
    Which she had in her fanny,
But she claimed that he never did bore her.

135
An anxious young lady, so fair,
Requested her escort, young Pierre,
    To advise what he'd do
    When prepared for a screw.
"It is neither," he said, "here nor there."

136. EASY DOES IT
To the doc said the heart patient, Fife,
"Will intercourse shorten my life?"
    "Not a bit," said the doc,
    "You will suffer no shock
Just as long as you fuck with the wife."

137
There was a young lady from Fife
So gorgeous she started much strife:
    Her tight ass and proud bubby
    So inflamed one poor hubby,
He began to throw rocks at his wife.

21

138. LEFTOVERS AGAIN

There was an old fellow named Fife
Who led a lascivious life.
    When his organ was limp
    As an overboiled shrimp,
He brought home what was left to his wife.

139

A young lady investor, Miss Finches,
Was observing the oil rigs and winches.
    She said, "Though it is fun
    To see deep drilling done,
I am thrilled if I'm drilled for six inches."

140

There was a young lady named Finnegan
Who said to her man, "Pour some gin again,
    And then rest you a while
    For I fancy your style,
And I want you to put that thing in again."

141

A long-distance runner named Flanagan
Had raped an old maid and he ran again,
    But the old maid, she chased him
    And with ease she outpaced him,
For she said that she wanted that man again.

142

A wavy-haired lady named Flavey
Got more out of screwing than Davy,
    For when fucking was done
    She received half the fun,
And besides, she got all of the gravy.

143

To the doc went a lady named Flo;
Her blackheads and pimples did show.
    Said the doc, with reflection,
    "You will need an injection."
So he gave her four fucks in a row.

144

To his girl, a young fellow named Flock
Said, "Show me a fine curly lock
    Of that beautiful hair
    From between your legs bare,
And I'll show you the knob of my cock."

145. POLISH SAUSAGE
A destitute lady named Flossa
Was begging for food in Owossa.
 She appealed for some meat
 From a Pole, name of Pete,
So he slipped her his eight-inch kielbasa.

146
At the show two young ladies did focus
As Houdini presented his hocus.
 When the show was completed
 The young girls remained seated—
They were waiting, they said, for the poke us.

147. ASTRONOMY CLASS
The astronomer asked young Miss Ford
If she ever the stars had explored.
 She replied, "In the night
 I see stars clear and bright
When I lay on my back and I'm bored."

148
There was a young lady, a foreigner,
Who had an affair with the coreigner.
 When he faltered at four
 She belittled his scour,
But he managed to muster formoreigner.

149
A lady whose named is forgotten
Said her ass to Marines was verboten.
 But the G.I.'s, they vaunted
 They got all that they wanted—
It was said to the corps she was rotten.

150
There was a young lady named Forrer
Who looked for a man to restore her.
 With her spouse so inept
 She would rather he slept,
For she called him the *Great Unexplorer*.

151. A LESSON IN BREVITY

The pedantess who taught fossilology
Was fucked by the dean of brachylogy.
    She exclaimed, "You old fossil,
    You are simply colossal!"
"To be brief," he said, "this is my trilogy."

152

A noble old duchess named Foster
Had barons and dukes on her roster,
    But her best fuck, we're told,
    Was the time she was rolled
In a ditch when a drunk did accost her.

153

The duchess sneaked out by the fount
To screw in the park with the count,
    But he fucked her so bad
    That the duchess got mad
And a sermon she gave on the mount.

154

An artful young fellow named Fred
Maneuvered his girl into bed.
    When she altered her mind
    It created no bind—
He maneuvered her mother instead.

155*

A young coed freshman named Fretter
In fucking could not earn a letter,
    But when she was a soph
    She worked under a prof
And got better and better and better.

156. WHAT YE SOW, YE SHALL REAP

To his girl, a young fellow named Fred
Said, "Darling, let's both fuck in bed."
    But the lady replied,
    "Not until I'm a bride,
But I'll let you put in just the head."

[157]

So Fred dropped his pants to the floor
And over his girl he did soar,
    And his pecker he urged
    Till the head was submerged,
But her mother saw all through the door.

[158]
The mother observed with remorse
And she kicked Freddy's ass with such force
    That his prick sailed on through,
    Split the hymen in two,
And Fred blew his wad like a horse.

[159]
Though mother the marriage did thwart,
There still was bad news to report.
    To the daughter forlorn
    An infant was born;
As for Fred, he was sued for support.

[160]
The old lady's charges were filed
That her daughter by Fred was defiled.
    The facts were extruded
    And the jury concluded
That the mother had fathered the child!

161*
Epileptic cornhusker, young Fritz
Shucked corn and he shucked between fits.
    He dated Miss Bruce
    Whose bowels were loose,
So he fucked in between fits and shits.

162
"I'm beat," said a fellow named Fry,
"I can't even lick my girl's thigh.
    I don't mean to deride her
    But she's much like a spider,
For she's constantly after my fly."

163. SAFE DEPOSIT
A prominent banker of Galt
Attacked an old maid in his vault.
    She was battered and frayed
    But no charges were laid,
For his fucking was done without fault.

164
A sea-loving lady named Gast
Went out on a ship sleek and fast.
    She was fucked in her cabin
    By a sailor named Babbin,
While her panties were flown at half-mast.

165
In the circus a lady named Gaynor
Was screwed by an animal trainer,
But a sheik named Amir
Found her sex life so queer
That he spent a whole year to retrain her.

166
A short-peckered fellow named Gene
Had failed in his fucking routine.
Said his wife in dismay,
"Though I'm spread night and day,
I don't get any fun in between."

167
The landlady, kind, gentle-hearted,
Would wait till her husband departed,
Then she'd treat her new roomer
With a peak 'neath her bloomer,
Which explains how the roomer got started.

168
A simple mechanic named Giles
Succumbed to a young lady's wiles.
Though her chassis looked fair
It showed signs of great wear—
It was driven for too many miles.

169
There was a young lady of Glosting
Whose man was a dud and exhausting.
He fucked her so bad
That whene'er she was had
She needed all day for defrosting.

170
The horny old duchess of Gloucester
Would welcome all men to accost her.
She would take with no qualm
Every hairy Dick, Tom,
But only the king could exhaust her.

171
When ready for bed, Mrs. Glover
Observed as she pulled back the cover,
That her man, slipping fast,
Was expiring at last,
So she made a quick date with her lover.

172

The new secretary, Miss Gold,
Was fucking her boss young and bold.
     He was blowing his thing
     When the phone gave a ring,
So she put the young fellow on *Hold.*

173

The wife of a young man named Goozie
Had left him a little bit woozy.
     In the place of resisting
     She attempted assisting,
And he thought he was back with his floozie.

174

There was an old prophet named Gophet
Who promised two ladies named Moffat
     Untold wealth would be theirs
     If they purchased his shares;
Before long they were sharing the prophet.

175

A soft-hearted lady named Gore
Gave the G.I.'s relief from the war.
     But the anxious Marines
     Could not get in her jeans—
She was rotten, they said, to the corps.

176

A thoughtless young fellow named Gore
Forgot to buy safes at a store.
     Said his girl, "Why you lubber,
     This glove made of rubber
I am sure will be good for five more."

177

On a date with a lady, young Gore
At first thought his girl was a bore
     For her mother had said
     Don't take boys into bed,
But she fucked very well on the floor.

178

Dejected and limp was young Gorse
And his girl was left full of remorse.
     He confined his maneuvers
     For so long to *hors d'oeuvres*
That he failed when he tried the main course.

27

179
A homely old lady named Grace
Had plenty of dates at her place.
    She was classed as first rate
    For she'd greet a new date
With her dress pulled up over her face.

180
An amorous lady named Grace
Was thrilled by a passioned embrace,
    So she said to her lover,
    "Let's get under the cover."
He said, "No, I'm just out for the chase."

181. SPACE ODYSSEY
When Armstrong went out with Miss Grace,
His rocket he slipped into place.
    When she said to him, "Neil,
    Tell me—how do you feel?"
He replied he felt far out in space.

182
An artless young fellow named Grover
Had raped an old spinster of Dover.
    She admonished this youth
    For his manners uncouth
And insisted he do it all over.

183. WON'T IT SPOIL?
To his wife, said a fellow of Guelph,
"This erection is not for myself."
    But she said, "Let it wait,
    For I don't feel too great."
So his hard-on he put on the shelf.

184
At the Firemen's Convention Miss Gump
Asked a fireman to give her a jump.
    Without thinking she chose
    A young man with a hose,
When she needed a man who could pump.

185
An eager young beaver named Gump
Tried giving a fat girl a jump.
    But he failed in his screwing
    And it proved his undoing,
For he couldn't get over the hump.

28

186*
A busy old milkman named Haines
Delivered to old spinster Baynes.
    She asked, "Have you the time?"
    He said, "Yes, but it's prime,
So you'll have to hold on to the reins."

187. SMALL WORLD
There was a young fellow named Hame
Whose wife her great love did proclaim.
    When his plant moved to Rome
    There he built a new home,
But his milkman, he found, was the same.

188
An overjoyed lady named Hample
Remarked to the salesman, "You're ample."
    With a smile on his face
    He reached for his case
And said, "This one is simply a sample."

189
A boastful young fellow named Hartley
Had fucked an old dowager smartly,
    And he bragged to express
    His sexual excess,
But she claimed that he fucked her just partly.

190
Said a frustrated bride, Mrs. Hayes,
"Education on sex matters pays,
    For my groom, so untaught,
    Cannot locate my twat,
And he's asked for a couple more days."

191
A stalwart young fellow was Hearst
But the sickness he had was the worst.
    After fucking old Clausia
    He developed a nausea
And did not know which end to set first.

192
A learned old lady was Hicks
Who knew how with old men to mix.
    She dated young Steve
    Who was somewhat naive,
And she taught a new dog some old tricks.

193
So ugly a bitch was Miss Hind
That she never with man had entwined,
      But she showed up one day
      In family way,
For it seems she was fucked from behind.

194
To his wife said a fellow named Hind,
"When we fuck in the dark, it's a grind.
      Though you may get delight,
      Yet a cunt out of sight
You will find is a cunt out of mind."

195
The wife of a fellow named Hite
Said the headache she had was a fright.
      But he said, with some thought,
      "You can spread out your twat—
In your head I won't fuck you tonight."

196. CONDITIONED RESPONSE
The newlywed man of Hoboken
At first thought his darling was jokin'.
      She withdrew, not to bed,
      But the auto instead,
For the poor dear had not been housebroken.

197
The battery mechanic named Hood
Was pumping as fast as he could
      On top of his wife,
      And he said, " 'Pon my life,
An occasional discharge is good."

198*
A newlywed couple named Hooper
Had fucked themselves into a stupor.
      Some joker named Kelly
      Put glue in their jelly
But the glue that he added was *Super*.

199
There was a young lady named Hoover
Who knew not the bedroom maneuver,
      But Professor McBride
      Who in teaching took pride
Gave his wholehearted time to improve her.

200

A troubled young lady named Hoover
Rejected her young man's maneuver.
    Though she locked him outside
    This was taken in stride,
And he slipped her a fuck through the louver.

201

A young mountain lad name of Horton
Once called on his gal for some courtin'.
    She had doused with perfume
    Labeled "Hill-Billy's Doom,"
And he stood there just pantin' and snortin'.

202

The semantics professor was hot in
The midst of a fuck with Miss Cotten.
    She said, "Fucking is grand
    But I can't understand
Why the words that describe it are rotten."

203. RICH FOOD

A lady who found herself huffing
Observed that her belly was puffing.
    It was due to the gravy
    Of a cook in the navy,
And the sausage and eggs and the stuffing.

204

A thorough old doctor named Hugh
Was checking a girl for the flu.
    Though she seemed to be well
    And as sound as a bell,
When he banged her, she did not ring true.

205

Ingenious indeed was young Hugh;
His girl also cleverness knew.
    For a ride they did go
    And had three in a row
On a bicycle fashioned for two.

206*

A skilful old toolmaker Hugh
Prepared a young girl for a screw,
    But he first blued her in
    From her knees to her chin
Before thrusting his prick up her flue.

207
An expedient young fellow was Hugh;
In church he knew just what to do.
    While the priest was exhorting
    On immoral cavorting
He was fucking a nun in the pew.

208
A passionate lady named Hughes
Once cornered a lad and did choose
    To recline on his lap,
    But it caused a mishap
For she found that he had a short fuse.

209
There was a shoefitter named Hughes
Who softened a lady with booze.
    When she lay down, unwitting,
    He attempted a fitting,
But he found her too big for his shoes.

210
There was an old woodsman named Hunt
Whose pecker was solid but blunt.
    When he fucked with Miss Fraser,
    Who was sharp as a razor,
The chips flew in streams from her cunt.

211
To her boyfriend a lady named Hunt
Said, "Don't ask me to fuck, it's too blunt."
    So he said to her, "Dear,
    I need screwing, I fear.
Would you care for a prick up your cunt?"

212
A newlywed pair was incited
At tactics of airlines shortsighted.
    Their honeymoon flight
    Was canceled outright,
For they wanted to travel *United*.

213
With his finger, the able instructor
Directed a maid to conduct her
    To arrive home direct,
    But the route was suspect
For the finger was fickle and fucked her.

214
The teller said she was invincible
But the banker thought she was convincible,
    So he set down her figure
    And he proved with some rigor
That the interest negated the principle.

215
From his wife, a young fellow named Jack
Got much more than a fair share of flak.
    So he said, "You know what,
    If it weren't for your twat
I would leave you and never come back."

216
An insulting old fellow named Jack
Was berating his wife for her lack
    Of a navel and tits
    And she caused him the shits—
So she told him to get off her back.

217
In the pasture, a farmer of Jackson
Debauched an old maid name of Saxon.
    When the orgy was over
    She arose from the clover
And said, "When do you think you'll be back, son?"

218
There was a young lady named Jane
Who fucked in the park with her swain.
    They were hardy and tough
    But did not know enough
That they should have come in from the rain.

219. GOOD THINKING!
To his wife said a fellow named Jay,
"Jump in bed and we'll have us a lay."
    Said his dear wife, distraught,
    "Though my head aches a lot,
I believe that my cunt is okay."

220
While the harlot was screwing some jerk
The old landlord came in with his clerk,
    And he asked for the rent,
    But she said to the gent,
"Not right now, for I'm wrapped up in work."

221
When out with his girl friend, young Jock
His fingers slipped under her frock.
    But she said, "Not now, dear.
    Let us play it by ear."
But said Jock, "Let us play it by cock."

222
On trial was a young man named Joe
For raping and beating Miss Flo,
    But the charge was dismissed
    For the proof did exist
She was beat when she failed to let go.

223
There was a young lady named Joy
Who spread out her legs for a boy,
    Then she let out a shriek
    Which reechoed a week,
But the shriek that she let was for Joy.

224
An elderly matron named Jude
Was screwed by a man who was stewed.
    She exclaimed in disgust,
    "My old man, he's a bust;
Now I know what it's like to be screwed."

225
There was a young soldier named Kane
Who picked up a girl on the train.
    He said fucking this wench
    Was like slogging the trench
In the midst of the tropical rain.

226
The computer assisted Miss Kate
To find her a husband first rate,
    But the programmer wily
    Seduced her twice slyly
Before finding a qualified mate.

227. THE FICKLE FINGER
A naive young lady named Kate
Requested a drink from her date:
    "Just two fingers for me."
    But he poured her full three.
She was Fucked by the Finger of Fate!

[228]
Observe this young girl in a pickle;
The Finger of Fate must be fickle,
    For his love, the man swore,
    In great torrents would pour,
But the best he could do was a trickle.

229
A wary young lady named Kay
Five inches of cock took one day.
    Her lover had six
    But she told him no tricks,
For her mother said not all the way.

230
A horny young lady was Kay
Who wanted to fuck every day,
    So she gave every caller
    A *Kennedy* dollar
For providing a friend the next day.

231. SOLOMON'S CHOICE
Old women, said learned Judge Kett,
For him were the very best bet.
    They won't yell, tell or swell,
    And they fuck hard as hell,
For it may be the last one they'll get!

232
When the Queen viewed the prick of the King,
No joy to her face did it bring.
    She said in despair,
    "Try fucking my mare,
Or perhaps you can do your own thing."

233
The old stockbroker dated Miss Kline
And she said, "Is youk stock doing fine?"
    He replied, "How surprising!
    For a while it was rising,
But I think it is now in decline."

234
There was a young fellow named Knightley
So masterful, active and sprightly,
    And so adept and agile,
    That with young ladies fragile
He would give them the once-over lightly.

235

A lady named Wally we've known,
With a single cunt hair all alone
    Tied a knot neat and slick
    Around Edward's prick,
And she pulled the king right off his throne.

236

A fearful young bride name of Kreitzon
Got ready for bed with no lights on,
    And despite every plea
    She would never agree
To get into bed with no tights on.

237

The music appealed to young Lancet;
He asked if his lady could dance it.
    She danced that and some more
    For the length of the floor,
So he screwed the young lady in transit.

238

A thorough young thief named Lautrec
Once frisked an old maid from Quebec.
    He discovered no money
    But she said to him, "Honey,
Don't stop now, I will write you a check."

239

A bridegroom confused was young Lauzon;
His bride he just could not impose on,
    For she said it was lewd
    To be viewed in the nude
And she climbed into bed with her clothes on.

240

A glowing young lady of learning
In her hunt for a man was discerning.
    She had a desire
    For a man with some fire
Who would help keep the home fires burning.

241

The intelligent newlyweds, Lee,
Sensed the future had no guarantee.
    They faced life, but on guard;
    They both knew 'twould be hard,
But they knew not how long it would be.

242
A hot little twat name of Lillian
Said her pussy was worth a cool million.
    A fellow named Rand
    Who tried it, said, "Bland—
I will stick with my sexy Sicilian."

243
There was a young lady named Linning
Who, after some wining and ginning,
    Agreed to play ball
    And in bed she did crawl,
But she only was good for one inning.

244
A buxom young lady from Linz
Said, "I like ballplayers for sins.
    I like best Minnesota,
    They give more than their quota,
And I know why they call them the *Twins*."

245
A stinky old smoker was Lipe
Who smoked on a pipe that was ripe.
    A girl sniffed it one day
    And she fainted away,
So he fucked her while smoking his pipe.

246
A lively young lady named Lou
Rebuked the young man of Purdue,
    "I've had better, methinks,
    In a crypt in the Sphinx
Where the Pharaoh was quicker than you."

247
The old window washer, Luigi,
Was screwing a lady from Fiji.
    When she started to sweat
    He said, "Hold it my pet,"
And he wiped off the sweat with his squeegee.

248
There was a young lady named Lynch
Who would not give in—not an inch—
    Till a fellow named Grable
    Fucked her twice 'neath the table,
And he started it all with a pinch.

249. FIVE MORE TO GO
She screamed with great joy as young Lynch
Provided the meat in the clinch.
    She cried, "God, but you're great!"
    But he said to her, "Kate,
You have only received the first inch."

250
When Chuck asked a lady named Mabel
Why she wanted to fuck on the table,
    She replied to him, "Chuck,
    I can't cook worth a fuck,
So I fuck any place that I'm able."

251
While out with his girl, young MacBird
Some feelings erotic bestirred.
    With boldness and pluck
    He asked, "Do you fuck?"
She said, "Yes, but please don't use that word."

252
A thrifty old Scot was MacDubbers
Who looked like he'd been through the scrubbers.
    He spent nights on the benches
    Carousing with wenches,
And his days he spent patching his rubbers.

253
There was a young girl of Madras
Whose marriage was as fragile as glass,
    For her husband, sweet dove,
    Needed plenty of love,
But this bitch had a hunger for ass.

254
To her husband, old Mrs. Magoo
Said, "I'm beat and too tired to screw."
    Said her husband, discreet,
    "While I stick in the meat
Please lay still like you usually do."

255. WHICH TWIN HAS THE TONI?*
There were two young twins named Mahoney
And Tony screwed one out on Coney.
    Though this may be hearsay
    No one knows to this day
Which twin had been screwed by young Tony.

256
There was an old man named Mahooty
Who found in a whorehouse a beauty,
    But his wife was a whore
    With a room right next door;
He was torn between love and his duty.

257
There once was a luscious young maid
Who never her young man dismayed.
    It's a matter of record
    That before she was peckered
He fell down to his knees and he prayed.

258
A skillful young fucker's maneuver
Excited his girl and did move her
    To exclaim, "Oh dear Ben,
    I must come back again."
But he said "This is just the *hors d'oeuvre.*"

259
A popular lady was Marge;
Her number of suitors was large.
    One young caller polite
    Said, "Are you free tonight?"
She said, "Darling, you know I don't charge."

260
A hi-fi fanatic named Mario
Made love to a girl from Ontario.
    She was tuned to fine pitch
    Then he buggered the bitch
In 3-D, Technicolor and stereo.

261
There was a young lady named Mays,
The queen of the courts in those days.
    She was screwed by the dukes,
    The lords and the flukes,
And she left all the knights in a daze.

262
While shopping for groceries, old Max
In morals became somewhat lax.
    He was bold—stuck his neck out—
    Fucked the girl at the check-out;
She charged ten on the meat key, plus tax.

263
A dentist by name of McGavity
Was subject to fits of depravity.
    On his chair sat a maid
    And her teeth she displayed,
But he probed and he filled the wrong cavity.

264
A young astronaut named McGraw
Sailed space ships without any flaw,
    But when he tried to lay
    With his girl friend one day,
He went into a roll, pitch and yaw.

265
While out for a walk, Miss McKesson
Encountered a fellow in Essen.
    She was fucked in the park
    But he lacked drive or spark,
So she made him stop in for a lesson.

266
There was a young girl named McKinnon
Who spent so much time in her sinnin',
    She did not have an hour
    For a bath or a shower,
And she never had time to change linen.

267
A learned young girl of Milan
Said fruit has its place in God's plan,
    And the juice is divine,
    But there's nothing so fine
As the juice that you squeeze from a man.

268
There was a young lady named Minnie
Who screwed an old man from New Guinea.
    He was so big and fat
    That he broke every slat,
So now she dates men who are skinny.

269
A passionate lady named Minter
Was screwed on a park bench in winter,
    But she failed to take care
    To find one in repair,
And her fanny was pierced by a splinter.

270*
There was an old man of Montbello
Who met a young girl who said, "Hello."
   "Well, enough has been said,
   Let us both get to bed.
I'm a man of few words," he did bellow.

271
There was a fruitpicker named Mott
Who said to his girl, "You know what?
   Let's get in to some grapples
   And I'll sample your apples,
For if not, I believe they will rot."

272
There was a young farmer named Murray
Who took his girl out in a surrey.
   He said, "We are undone,
   There's no room to have fun."
She said, "Show me, for I'm from Missouri."

273
Though the nations all feared Caesar's name,
Not just war, but in love he won fame.
   Said the Queen of the Nile,
   "I admired his style,
For he saw and he conquered and came."

274
"I must give up my girl friend," said Nate.
"She demands far too much on a date.
   Although fairness is due me,
   She would much rather screw me—
If I give in one inch, she wants eight."

275
At the butcher's, a lady dressed neat
Complained of his poor grade of meat.
   His baloney, she felt,
   Was so bad that it smelt,
So he threw her the meat in the street.

276
When Joe came to visit young Nell
She convulsed in a bad, sickly spell,
   But she said to him, "Dear,
   There is nothing to fear,
For my grandmother fucks very well."

277

A devious young fellow was Neville,
Possessed of a bit of the devil.
    He screwed his girl Jill
    On the side of a hill,
Which proves he was not on the level.

278

A lady complained in New York
That she never had meat on her fork
    For the meat was priced high,
    So the butcher did sigh
As he slipped her a pound of fresh pork.

279. A COMMON AILMENT

A passionate fellow named Nicky
Found marriage to be a bit sticky.
    At the end of the week
    He was up to his peak,
But his wife merely wanted a quickie.

280

The Wrong brothers went out one night
And drank until they were both tight.
    They fucked, on this bender
    Miss Wright, the bartender,
And that's how two Wrongs made a Wright.

281*

A lad should not bellow an oath
When mother appears somewhat loath
    To let daughter stay late
    With the lad on a date,
He should simply remain and fuck both.

282

A thoughtless young maid named O'Dirk
Got soused on her way home from work.
    She slept, she had thought,
    With a prince in his yacht,
But at dawn she awoke with a jerk.

283

There was a young maid named O'Hare
Whose cunt was so juicy and rare
    That her date, if you please,
    Simply fell to his knees
And he paused for a moment of prayer.

284
While sailing his ship, Duke O'Malley
Hurt his back when he fell in the galley,
    But he got along fine
    With his old concubine
With a push and a shove from his valet.

285
A lady with hot pants in Oregon
Was screwed by a fellow named Corrigan.
    She had four on the floor
    But she wanted some more
So he fucked her four more on the floor again.

286*
An African hunter named Pace
Felt the need of a female embrace,
    So he looked for a cutie
    And he found him a beauty
With horseshit and flies on her face.

287
There was a young girl of Pagonia
Who said to her man, "I will phone ya."
    But something went wrong
    For he waited so long
That there grew from his ass a begonia.

288. LADY CHATTERLEY'S LOVER?
Said the Queen to the King, "Beg your pardon, er,
It appears that your prick needs a hardener."
    Said the King, "I'm afraid,
    If you want to get laid,
You will have to get fucked by the gardener."

289
When the sisters McGrath took the path
Which led to the new public bath,
    They were stopped in the park
    By a lad on a lark
Who indulged in the rapes of McGrath.

290
A low-priced young lady named Perkins
Would do it for peanuts or gherkins,
    But she wouldn't give in
    To a man for some sin
Till she had a good look at his workin's.

43

291. GAME FELLOW
An African hunter named Pete
Would often play *Lion* with his sweet.
    He requested she prowl
    On her knees, with a growl,
Then proceeded to throw her the meat.

292
In winter two ladies named Peters
Kept warm by their cozy gas heaters.
    Their gas price was low
    And the reason was: "So
We are screwed by the readers of meters."

293
A slovenly fellow named Phil
Assaulted a lady named Jill.
    She did not mind the rape
    Which she took in great shape;
She objected when asked to lie still.

294
A feeble old gambler named Phipps
Was sure he could take pleasure trips,
    So he bet an old whore
    He could fuck her once more,
And he won, but he cashed in his chips.

295
There was a hairdresser named Pierre
Who lavishly dressed a girl's hair.
    It was styled so romantic
    That Pierre became frantic
And he fucked her right there in her chair.

296
The tight pants which were worn by Miss Pink
Would be hard to get into, I think.
    Said Miss Pink, "It is plain
    You'll get in without strain,
But first you must buy me a drink."

297
There was a young fellow named Plum
Who cleaned up and shaved and did hum.
    It was all for his mistress
    So as not to cause distress.
For his wife he looked just like a bum.

298
There was a young lady named Plum
Who drank a whole bottle of rum.
 She thought that she spent
 The night with Lord Kent,
But next morning she woke with a bum.

299
There was a young girl of Port Hood
Who said that she would if she could.
 A young man in his prime
 Did not waste any time
For he fucked her right there where she stood.

300
A sexy young model named Prude
For artists had posed in the nude.
 Since she posed with a passion,
 This young lady of fashion,
She was oft misconstrued and got screwed.

301
There was a young lady, a Puritan,
Whose boy friend was fat, like manure a ton.
 He said, "Let's have a fuck."
 She replied, "No such luck,
I believe that I cannot endure a ton."

302
There was a young man of Purdue
Who bragged of the women he slew,
 But a nymph from De Witt
 Forced this man to admit,
"One more victory like this and I'm through."

303
In his car, a young lad of Purdue
A romance with his girl did pursue.
 He said, "Jump in the back."
 She replied, "No sir, Jack,
I would rather stay up front with you."

304
The girl that was pledged to young Pursall
Proposed how to forestall reversal.
 To avert any woes
 They removed all their clothes
And they went through a full-dress rehearsal.

305

The prominent Duchess of Pyle
Was screwed by a Hindu with style
    On the banks of Euphrates,
    And was screwed with such great ease
That she asked for a trial on the Nile.

306

While screwing a girl, Mr. Pyle
Was fucking along in great style,
    But the phone gave a ring
    So she pulled out his thing
And she put him on *Hold* for a while.

307

A horny old maid of Quebec
Was robbed and was raped by Lautrec,
    And he raped her so well
    That she said to him, "Hell,
You can fuck me again, here's a cheque."

308

Said young Marvin, "I'm for *quid pro quo*,
So a sum to my girl I'll bestow.
    Since her cunt has no wear
    There's no need for repair—
It's to rebuild her lips like *nouveau.*"

309

A bachelor fellow named Ramon
Would check before letting a dame in.
    Of a girl, he asked, "Mary,
    Do you still have your cherry?"
She said, "No, just the box that it came in."

310

There was a young lady named Rand
Who said to her man, "I demand
    That you take your hand off,
    For my clothes I must doff
As the matter is now out of hand."

311

A cunt-struck young fellow named Randitt
Decided to be a love bandit.
    When he rolled in girls' arms
    And they unleased their charms,
He found that his heart couldn't stand it.

312
A passionate fellow named Rassity
Attacked a young maid with rapacity.
    She said, "You must learn
    To await your right turn,
For at present I'm filled to capacity."

313
Said Flo to her husband, refined,
"I'm leaving, you're cruel and unkind."
    He said to her, "Flo
    I don't care if you go,
Just as long as your cunt stays behind."

314
The psychiatrist heard with reflection
While a maid gave her tale of dejection.
    He leaned back with a sigh
    As he unzipped his fly
And he slipped her some love and affection.

315
There was a young lady robust
Who thought that her date was a bust
    Till he slipped her his missile
    And her ass gave a whistle,
While the gas from his ass gave him thrust.

316
Said the bride at the church, young Miss Rousseau,
"I'm afraid I must take off my trousseau,
    For this itch is provoking—
    It needs licking or poking.
It would please me no end if you'd do so."

317
A reliable butler was Runshawn;
'Mid servants they say that this one shone,
    For he started one day
    To make old Duchess May
And was still making May while the sun shone.

318
"My honeymoon," young Stover said,
"Will last and with passion be fed."
    But you'll find, Mr. Stover,
    That the honeymoon's over
When the bride lets her first fart in bed.

319

There was a young man of Salonika
Who climbed into bed with Veronica.
    When she asked him so tender
    What great things he could render,
He played Beethoven's Suite for Harmonica.

320

A prudent young fellow named Sam
Was screwing a girl from Siam.
    He said to her, "Nellie,
    If you don't use some jelly
I am sure you will be in a jam."

321

There was an old recluse named Schartner
Who found his young lady a heartener.
    He said, "Now I can see
    How much fun it can be
When you do all these things with a partner."

322

There was a young lady named Schilling
Who said to the oil man, "I'm willing
    To engage your fine rig,
    But it looks mighty big
So forget any off-the-shore drilling."

323. STICK TO THE RECIPE

There was a young waitress named Schirring
Who started a-trembling and purring.
    Said the chef, "Are you ready?"
    She said, "No, not yet, Freddie.
I believe I would like some more stirring."

324

Thee was a young fellow named Schleft
With movements so rapid and deft,
    While his girl had her dinner
    He maneuvered it in her—
She was still in her throes when he left.

325

An ugly old maid was Miss Schmidt,
As homely as two crocks of shit,
    But her boyfriend was simple
    For he loved every pimple
And he prized every wart on her tit.

326

A sturdy young fellow named Schmidt
Was blessed with an oversize kit.
    When he took off his clothes
    His new ladyfriend froze,
But she felt it would not hurt a bit.

327

A practical sailor named Schwartz
Was looking for girls in the ports.
    He found one in Peru
    Much too ugly to screw,
So he played with her pimples and warts.

328

All evening the girl of young Shevor
Rejected his every endeavor.
    She made up with her lover
    But was sad to discover
That erections do not last forever.

329

The housewife her duty does shirk
As she jumps into bed with a smirk
    And she shows her crevasse,
    But she parcels her ass
In return for some specified work.

330. OR WAS IT A WEINER?

The butcher was fucking Miss Shore
Who lay on the butcher shop floor.
    She pondered the ceiling
    And had a strange feeling
She had felt that salami before.

331

There was a young sailor named Sinbad
Who screwed a young lady named Linbad.
    But she swears to this day
    Though she has gone astray,
She maintains that in bed she'd not been bad.

332

A darling young lady named Skinner
Felt good when she had a drop in her.
    But after Carruther
    Provided another,
She was good for a flop after dinner.

333

A hapless young coed named Slade
In a sex course could not get a grade.
    Her prof heard her confession
    That she'd fail her profession,
So he showed her how she should be made.

334

An impatient young fellow named Slatter
Was disturbed by his ladyfriend's chatter.
    He said, "Gabbing's a crime;
    I believe it is time
That we got to the root of the matter."

335

A marvelous memory had Sloan;
This trait his dear wife did bemoan,
    For he knew every cranny
    Which she had in her fanny
And could screw her right over the phone.

336

The fellow that fucked Lady Smith
Said, "You are great fun to be with;
    By the way, I am Thor."
    She said, "Me too—no more—
I'm tho thore that I hardly can pith."

337

"With my wife I'm fed up," said old Snyder.
"As a bride she was fun when astride her.
    At first, I admit,
    There was a small split,
But at present the split is much wider."

338

The housewife exposed her breasts so
She would set the old plumber aglow.
    Said the plumber at that,
    "I've no time to chew fat,
I have time just to come and to go."

339

The maiden cried out in deep sorrow,
"Now that you've defiled me, my Zorro,
    You can never deny
    That I surely must die,
So you'd better be back here tomorrow."

340

A passionate lad one time sought
A no-good young lady named Scott.
    "How much," the lad said,
    "To be no good in bed?"
She replied she'd be no good for naught.

341

A young lady who came from the South
Said she'd give her ass free to McLouth.
    He said, "Show what I'm getting."
    She replied, "Stop your fretting,
Do not look a gift horse in the mouth."

342

A sensitive girl from South Bend
At first thought her man did offend,
    For this rotten old Bart
    Let a terrible fart,
But was awfully good at the end.

343

Although John many wild seeds had sown,
He was shocked when he tried fucking Joan.
    There was room in her slue
    For a truck to drive through.
He went off—but felt strangely alone.

344

There was a young sparrow with spark
Who flew to the park in the dark.
    He came back to the nest,
    Kissed his mate and confessed
That he only went off on a lark.

345

A novice young fellow named Stan
Was screwing a whore in Milan.
    'Twas his very first venture
    In this type of adventure.
"You must face it," she said, "like a man."

346

A stately young lady named Stella
Was fucked by an agile young fella
    While she walked in the rain,
    And without any strain,
'Neath her colorful, fancy umbrella.

347

The wife of a fellow named Steve
Gave him pain and much reason to grieve.
    She taunted him so,
    Saying, "Why don't you go?"
He said, "Give me your cunt and I'll leave."

348. DRIVING LESSON

There was a young lady of Stockholm
Who took through the park a long walk home,
    And at home did arrive
    With a man who could drive—
Yes, he knew how to drive the old cock home.

349

The husband drives off down the street
To earn daily bread for his sweet,
    While his wife sets her down
    And she waits, in her gown,
For the butcher to bring her the meat.

350

There was a young fellow named Tateful
Whose wife about sex was so hateful
    That she offered him tail
    Once a month without fail,
And he fell on his knees and was grateful.

351

When Caesar stepped in the Queen's tent,
She quickly divined his intent.
    Erect and unbowed
    Straight forward he ploughed—
He saw and he conquered and went.

352

When a man placed his hand on her thigh,
The young lady remarked with a sigh,
    "You cannot have my heart."
    Said the man, "We must part,
For I did not aspire that high."

353

A drunken old servant named Thor
Attacked England's Queen on the floor.
    The scene that transpired
    By the King was admired,
While the Queen simply shouted, "Encore!"

354. ROUND PEG IN A SQUARE HOLE

When a whore stopped a man in Tobruk,
He went down on his knees for a look.
    He parted her hair,
    But her cunthole was square,
So he looked at his cock and he shook.

355

A lively young girl of Toronto
Was harder than hell to hold on to.
    It required the Lone Ranger
    With his horse and a stranger
To restrain her while fucking old Tonto.

356

In his sled Santa placed every toy,
But this action was only a ploy
    To mislead Mrs. Claus,
    And his reason—because
He was spending the night spreading Joy.

357

The King saw a girl from his tower
As pretty and sweet as a flower,
    So the first day in May
    Made her *Queen for the Day*,
But she barely was good for an hour.

358

There was a dog-lover named Towser
Whose girl was a charming arouser.
    When she asked him to state
    What he liked on their date,
He said what he liked was her schnauser.

359

Young Ivan watched Anne on the tractor
And took off his pants to distractor.
    Her position to Ivan
    Suggested connivin',
So he climbed on the tractor and factor.

360

Young lads will resort to strange tricks
To jump in the hay with young chicks.
    Even old ones will do,
    Be they black, brown or blue,
For no conscience is found in stiff pricks.

361

A deluded young man of Trieste
Was impressed by his ladyfriend's breast,
But he soon was distressed
And he lost all his zest;
She came out second best when undressed.

362

A moral young lad who was trusting
Was stopped by a girl who was lusting
For a man with a prick,
So she dropped her pants quick,
But the hole thing, he said, was disgusting.

363

There was a young lady named Tuller
Whose sex life got duller and duller,
Till she sampled the nectar
Of a rector named Hectar,
In 3-D, and in stereo, and color.

364

There was a young fellow named Tully
Who wanted to screw in the gully,
But his girl took a stand
With her feet in the sand
So that none of her clothing would sully.

365. SPRING PLANTING

The old farmer instructed Miss Tweed
How he tended the corn to grow feed.
He said, "Lay on the ground
Where I've ploughed it around,
And I'll show how I planted a seed."

366

Said a homely old maid, unrefined,
"Let us fuck!" to a man just and kind.
He replied, "For this task
You must put on a mask,
And I'll give you a fuck from behind."

367

An artist who came from Vancouver
Was raping a maid in the Louvre.
The old guard passing by
Paid no heed to her cry,
For he thought the affair would improve her.

368
The young man who was dating Miss Venus
Had some trouble erecting his penis,
    So with candor, she said,
    As she climbed into bed,
"Let's get something, my dear, straight between us."

369
When dating the pitcher, Miss Vetch
Reduced the poor man to a wretch.
    He had heeded her call
    And agreed to play ball,
But he needed a sixth-inning stretch.

370
There was a young sailor named Vetch
Who took his girl out on his ketch.
    She did learn in a thrice
    How the main brace to splice,
And came out very well in the stretch.

371. FIRST AID
A frustrated fellow was Vince;
His girl took too long to convince.
    When at last she agreed
    He could only proceed
With a roll of Scotch tape and some splints.

372
The lady next door got the votes
Of a family of goatherds named Coates,
    For she fucked with them all,
    The great grandfather tall,
And the father, the son and the goats.

373
There was a young lady named Wacker
Who claimed that no man could attack her.
    'Twas no trouble at all
    To avoid Pete and Paul,
But Graham was able to crack her.

374. BEST LAID PLANS
An eager young fellow named Wade
Was anxious to see his fair maid.
    He laid plans for the day
    But they all went astray
When he found that his plans had been laid.

375
There was a young fellow named Wage
Whose girl thought that he was the rage
    For he placed her ass hairy
    On a fat dictionary,
And had one piece of ass on each page.

376
There was a young man from the West
Who fucked with his wife with great zest.
    He discerned a slight motion
    And with tone of devotion,
"Did I hurt you?" he queried, distressed.

377
A fastidious old man of Westminster
Once dated a dubious old spinster.
    So he laundered her clean
    In his washing machine,
Where he thoroughly washed out and rinsed her.

378
There was a young fellow of Wheeling
Who jumped into bed with great feeling
    To his dear wife outspread,
    And she looked up and said,
"I believe there's some dirt on the ceiling."

379
A fellow canoeing named Whipple
Seduced an old maid with a triple.
    With his stance ornamental
    And his manner so gentle
One could scarcely observe any ripple.

380
An amorous lady named White
Went out in a Chevy one night.
    She was fucked by young Brinkage
    But she fouled up his linkage
And it gave him a pull to the right.

381
There was a young fellow named Wilford
Who married a lady of Milford.
    They were married in June,
    Not a moment too soon,
For the mass of her ass had been pilfered.

382
There was a young lady who'd wince
From lads that approached her with hints.
    She decided to gamble
    With a fellow named Campbell,
And has gamboled with everyone since.

3

Organs

383. EMISSION PROBLEM
An engine mechanic Alphonse
Looked ruefully down at his schwantz,
    For it pained when he piddled
    And it kinked when he diddled
And was lacking a motor response.

384
The crotch of a harlot Alsatian
Was largest throughout the whole nation,
    But she said the enormity
    Of her grievous deformity
Was the hazard of her occupation.

385
The lady said she was annoyed
And avoided advances by Boyd.
    When he promised her payment
    She discarded her raiment,
But Boyd was annoyed by the void.

386
A lady could not apprehend
Most sports where two people contend.
    She was much better at
    The game with the bat
Which dangles two balls at the end.

387
An old man with two pricks, from Azores,
Had one small and one big as a boar's.
    His dear wife he would stick
    With his undersize prick,
But the big was for bitches and whores.

388
There was a young girl of Baghdad
Who swore she would never be had,
    But there came an Italian
    With a prick like a stallion
And she said as she spread, "I am glad."

389
There was a young lady named Banks
Who said to her man, "Hold your pranks
    Before getting to bed,
    It has come to my head
I've forgotten to purchase some franks."

390
Before Clarence could date with Miss Barents,
He requested consent from her parents,
    So the clearance he got
    And he got in her slot,
But the clearance was too much for Clarence.

391
An intrepid explorer named Barr
Once encountered a pussy bizarre.
    Though at times he did bungle
    And got lost in the jungle,
Yet this cunt beat the jungle by far.

392
At the circus, a stunt girl Miss Barr
Displayed antics that made her a star,
    But her ride on two horses
    Heading opposite courses—
It was stretching a good thing too far.

393
There was a young lady of Barrie
Whose crotch was exceedingly hairy.
    Once her beau went to find it
    But got lost in behind it,
And when he comes out they will marry.

394
A cunt is a thing of great beauty
When viewed in the crotch of a cutie,
    But the same cunt's a bust
    And is viewed with disgust
When the lady is homely and fruity.

395
The girl who was dating young Beedle
Said his pecker was unfit to tweedle.
    But he gave her some credit
    When she showed she could thread it
Through the eye of her rug-hooking needle.

396

So big was the cunt of Miss Beggs,
There was room for two dinosaur eggs,
    But this bothered her not—
    She could tighten her twat
With ease just by crossing her legs.

397

A yogi who came from Beirut
For women he cared not a hoot,
    But he'd get an erection
    Which would stand to perfection
When a snake charmer played on his flute.

398

There was an old harlot of Belfast
Whose pussy no longer would sell fast.
    Said the King, "The whole trouble
    Is from taking pricks double.
From this the Queen's cunt went to hell fast."

399

Four breasts had the girl from Benares;
Two men would start off her affairs.
    Then a coin would be tossed
    And the young man who lost
Would retreat to reflect on the stairs.

400

There was an old fellow named Bertie
Who said as he diddled Miss Gertie,
    "I must make a confession,
    I've not seen a depression
Of this magnitude since 1930."

401

A harlot deficient was Bess;
She had nothing at all to caress.
    Her titties were small,
    She had no ass at all,
But she promised much more for much less.

402

There was a young lady named Betty
Whose hair was as dense as spaghetti,
    And her pussy was hairier,
    But this was not a barrier
For the man with an ax or machete.

403
If you ever should go on a binge
With a girl that is plump, do not cringe
    At the layers of fat
    Where her pussy is at—
You'll find benefits all 'round the fringe.

404*
A lonely old nun name of Birch
Enticed a young boy in her search.
    When she asked how he fared,
    He replied, as he stared,
"It's like singing alone in the church."

405
To her husband, a lady named Blaining
Of his shortness of prick was complaining.
    But he said to her, "Dear,
    It's your pussy, I fear,
For it looks like a ditch used for draining."

406
There was an old hooker Brazilian
Whose pussy was blue and vermilion.
    When a friend asked her why,
    She replied, somewhat wry,
"It's because of the fuckers—one million."

407
A joyful young lady named Brenda
Was born with a double pudenda.
    Men found her so rigorous
    That they had to be vigorous
Or they couldn't get on her agenda.

[408]
Another young lady named Brickley
Had hair on her crotch sprouting thickly.
    She made dates in advance
    To give suitors a chance,
For they never could find it too quickly.

409
There was an old whore name of Brown
Whose pussy could smile or could frown.
    If a fellow was bust
    It would sneer with disgust,
But it smiled if he put twenty down.

410*
There was a young lady named Brown
Who taught her vagina to clown.
    It could nibble a plumb
    And could chew Dentyne gum,
So her cunt was the freshest in town.

411
There was an old lady of Butte
With an oversize quim so hirsute
    That a flutist fell in
    And was saved by his chin,
But no person has yet found his flute.

412
In the cunt of a girl named Cahalan
You could insert a broom and a pail in.
    Said her husband, "We're through."
    And he married anew
To a girl with a space for a whale in.

413
A fisherman out from Calais
A mermaid ensnared in the bay.
    Though he searched back and front,
    He could not find a cunt,
So he sucked on her titties all day.

414
There was a young lady named Carrie
Whose crotch was exceedingly hairy.
    Her cunt was behind it
    And a man went to find it,
But got lost like a mouse on the prairie.

415
So hairy a cunt had Miss Carriere
That no man could get past the barrier,
    That is, no man but Brungle
    Who had lived in a jungle,
And he found his way through with his terrier.

416
A world-circling pussy cartel
Composed of Dupont, Ford and Shell,
    Proposed close control
    As their primary goal,
So a poor man could not get a smell.

417
There was a young lady cavernal
Who learned how to fuck with a cernal
        And to peddle her ass
        To the army top brass
Just by reading *The Ladies Home Jernal.*

418*
There was a young fellow named Chase
Who buttressed his tool with a brace.
        Now his wife does not mention
        Any bone of contention,
For their love has a much firmer base.

419
To arouse the old ruler, a chick
Tried to stiffen his cock with a lick.
        Said the ruler, "This nation
        Is in rampant inflation,
But it seems to have bypassed my prick."

420
When dating Miss Sun-Yan, young Christopher
Discovered why all men were pistopher,
        For her cunt, if you please,
        Was off ninety degrees,
And not one out of ten got the gistopher.

421*
A newlywed man raised a clamor,
For nude, his new bride had no glamor,
        But she countered, "You simp,
        You're revoltingly limp;
It's like driving a worm with a hammer."

422
There was a young sailor named Claude,
Renowned for the size of his prod.
        He attempted to lay
        An old whore in Malay
And the last words she spoke were, "My God!"

423
When Charlie removed his girl's clothes,
She was scented from head down to toes,
        But her mood was oblique,
        And her thorny critique
Made him think he was fucking a rose.

424

A bride to be proud of, had Cole,
For he felt he achieved his life's goal,
    But he cried in despair
    When he viewed her crotch bare—
Someone ate it and left a big hole.

425

A whore spent three months in confinement,
Her cunt was way out of alignment,
    And the doc did admit
    He could not help a bit,
So she peddled her ass on consignment.

426

The cunt of a lady named Cratchet
Appeared as if slashed by a hatchet.
    Though she searched every day
    Her desire to allay,
She could not find a man who would scratch it.

427

To bed went a baker of Crete
With a girl that he found on the street.
    "My God," said the baker,
    "This twat is an acre!"
So she offered her asshole petite.

428

So big was the cunt of Miss Critchit,
No man could allay what did itch it.
    She had given up hope
    Till, with tackle and rope,
An old sailor was able to stitch it.

429. CAVE MAN

There was a spelunker named Danny
Who dated a girl with a fanny
    Which contained such a maze
    That it took him ten days
To explore every nook and each cranny.

430

When out with young girls on a date,
Remain calm and be cool and sedate.
    When they badger, don't flinch—
    If you give in an inch
They'll proceed to take seven or eight.

Organs

431
While writing his music one day,
Tchaikovsky was struck with dismay,
  For his wife grabbed his balls,
  So he climbed up the walls
And composed the *Nutcracker Ballet*.

432
Cried the dumfounded groom in despair,
"My pecker will never fit there!"
  But his bride countered, "Hell,
  It should fit very well,
And with plenty left over to spare."

433
There was a young girl of Detroit
Whose pussy was very adroit.
  She could open the throat
  To be large as a moat
Or reduce it as small as a quoit.

434
On a date, the young girl will discover
Why the fireman is such a great lover,
  For the Lord only knows,
  When he reels out his hose,
How much time it will take to recover.

435
When the old maid was fucked by the doc,
She relapsed into rapturous shock,
  Then she fucked him so hard,
  He was caught off his guard,
And he fractured the bone in his cock.

436
Though she hadn't the tenth of a dollar,
An old harlot for taxis did holler.
  She tried raising her skirt
  And a cab did alert,
But he asked if she had something smaller.

437
The snatch of a lady named Doris
Was stretched as she sang in the chorus.
  Along came a baker,
  A fine donut maker,
And he fashioned her one like a torus.

438

A very small organ had Eiffel;
His approach to his girl it did stifle.
    In the nude he did jaunt
    And the law he did flaunt,
But no law does apply to a trifle.

439

Asked a man of a girl named Elaine:
"With how many men have you lain?
    I have slipped into bores
    Of some hundreds, but yours
Looks like armies have used it to train."

440

A roomy old lady named Fanchion
Was fucked by a man in her mansion.
    He said, "You have a womb
    Which is big as Grant's Tomb,
And there seems to be room for expansion."

441

The cunt doctor looks and he feels
And ponders each crotch as he kneels,
    Then he writes so obscure
    A prescription for cure,
But it seems that the wound never heals.

442

To the doctor went itchy Miss Fern,
For the itch in her cunt caused concern.
    She was strapped with a cable
    To the hospital table
And the interns all fucked her in turn.

443. EINSTEIN THEORY*

*A fencing instructor named Fisk
Was at fucking exceedingly brisk.
    So fast was his action
    The Lorentz contraction
Foreshortened his prick to a disk.*

[444]

It seems that a girl with two cunts
Had failed to find two-peckered runts,
    So she tried this instructor,
    And so quickly he fucked her
That he fucked both her pussies at once.

445
There were two old icemen named Fleckers
Whose cocks when erected were wreckers.
    They could handle their tongs
    With the ends of their dongs
And could lift blocks of ice with their peckers.

446
With muscles all rippling and flexing
The weightlifter found it perplexing.
    He had strengthened his cock
    By the lifting of rock,
But it made it quite useless for sexing.

447
The weatherman falters and flinches
When the voice on the phone is Miss Lynch's.
    She expects it to blow
    At least four in a row,
For a total of twenty-four inches.

448. THE ORGAN CONCERTO
When Bach met the organist Flo,
He noted her organ did show.
    She looked tempting to Bach
    So he pulled out his cock
And he played her a fugue with his bow.

449
The Duchess of York never flinches
When the king pats her ass and he pinches,
    For she welcomes a date
    From the head of the state;
Every ruler, she knows, has twelve inches.

450
A teacher of language, Miss Flock,
Had taught her vagina to talk,
    And it managed by rote
    An old biblical quote,
And could sing a few snatches by Bach.

451
A young lady from China named Fot
Had a cold, and a doctor she sought.
    Said the doctor, alert,
    "Will you please raise your skirt
To confirm the direction of twat."

452

By hand, an old fellow named Fred,
Tried hard to erect it in bed.
   Said his wife to the fink,
   "I do really not think
You should flog an old horse that is dead."

453

There was a young coed named Fretter
Who wrote the professor a letter,
   "Though your hot dog is fine,
   Yet for hunger like mine
The young butcher's baloney is better."

454. THE REALIST

When Rosie was dating young Fritz,
Her father was pleased, he admits.
   He said, "Fritz, you are grand,
   Would you care for her hand?"
Fritz said, "No, just her cunt and her tits."

455

A Hebrew explorer named Frost
Was screwing a harlot at cost,
   But he found her so roomy
   That he soon became gloomy
And he cried, "I am hopelessly lost!"

456

A limpid old fellow was Gene;
His cock was the deadest I've seen,
   But a doctor named Sears
   Worked for forty-two years
And he kept it alive by machine.

457

A young navy captain named Gene
Had skippered a big submarine.
   He had plunged to depths hairy
   But his plunge into Mary
Was the deepest he ever had been.

458

There was a young lady named Gimbel
Whose cunt was so supple and nimble
   She could open it wide
   So you'd stand up inside,
Or could close it as small as a thimble.

459
In his lab, an old scientist Gluck
By a novel idea was struck,
  So he worked night and day
  To improve on the lay
By inventing a cunt that would suck.

460
A rapist deflowered Miss Grace
And the jury was trying the case.
  Said His Honor, Judge Beggs,
  "You may spread out your legs;
I must see where this foul act took place."

461
There was an old Bedouin grand,
Who lived in the hot desert land,
  And though strange it may seem,
  When he had a wet dream
He awoke with a handful of sand.

462
There was a young lady named Greenery
Who slaved all day long in a beanery.
  Then she worked in a factory
  But she found it distractory
For her monkey was wrenched by machinery.

463
There was a young lady named Groatwell
Whose pussy was big as a boatwell.
  When she drew in some air
  And then tied her cunt hair,
She could jump in the water and float well.

464
The scientist sweats and he grunts
As problems anew he confronts.
  He is solving the scheme
  That God managed to dream,
Which is making pricks feel good in cunts.

465
There was a young lady named Gubb
Whose cunt was as big as a tub.
  There was room for her groom
  And a mop and a broom,
And some space for an evergreen shrub.

466

When the doctor examined Miss Gusty,
He was thrilled at her figure so busty,
 And he looked with elation
 On her pussy formation,
But he noted her asshole was rusty.

467

A cavernous lady was Gwen;
Her cunt was so big, now and then
 Her purse she would lose
 And sometimes her shoes,
And one time she lost her friend Ben.

468

There was a young barmaid named Gwen
With a cunt like the canyon called "Glen."
 She was fucked on a date
 And the man blew at eight,
And the echo was heard around ten.

469. PUT UP OR SHUT UP

To his date, a young fellow named Hame
Said, "Your cunt is too big for this game."
 But she said, with derision,
 "It should fit with precision
If your prick is as big as you claim."

470

There was an old coal miner Hamp
Who picked up a worn out old tramp.
 He examined her tunnel
 Through an oversize funnel,
And he charted the depths with his lamp.

471

An old engineer name of Hector
Had a prick with a built-in corrector,
 To correct for the mass
 And the heat of the ass
And the bore and the stroke and the vector.

472

The crotch of a girl named Hilaria
Was largest in all of Bavaria.
 Said old Baron von Bliss,
 "Der dimension, vot iss?"
"Do you want," she said, "volume or area?"

473
There was an old whore of Hong Kong
Who always attracted a throng.
    'Twas her fortune, so rare,
    To be born with a spare,
A reserve in case something went wrong.

474
There was a young fellow named Howe
Whose girl had a cunt like a sow.
    When he looked at this well
    His erected cock fell
Like the turd from the ass of a cow.

475
"Let's go to see *Jaws*," said Miss Hunt,
"A show about sharks that is blunt."
    Said her man, graciously,
    "I would much rather see
The jaws that you find in a cunt."

476. THE NEW MATH
A teacher of math named Miss Hunt
Developed a fine teaching stunt.
    She would clear up distractions
    And explain vulgar fractions
By exposing a fraction of cunt.

477. A ROSE IS A ROSE IS A ROSE
An explorer of note once did hunt
Through the masses of hair out in front
    Of Miss Stein's crotch hirsute,
    And observed, so astute
That a cunt is a cunt is a cunt.

[478]
The observant philosopher, Black,
Stuck his prick in Miss Stein from the back,
    Then he fucked her in front
    And he said of her cunt,
That a crack is a crack is a crack.

[479]
To Miss Stein, this philosopher slick
As a fucker was far, far too quick,
    So his pecker she sucked,
    And she said, "I deduct
That a prick is a prick is a prick."

480

In the violin section Miss Hunt
Rubbed her twat with her bow out in front.
      The conductor, in shock,
      Waved the knob of his cock,
And sweet music poured out of her cunt.

481

There was a young lady ill-treated
By men who would date and retreated,
      For they said, with a start,
      When her legs spread apart,
"If you call that a cunt, I will eat it!"

482*

The prick of the Shah of Iran
Was so big that all world rulers ran,
      For to save ass was smarter.
      Said a man, a bold martyr,
"Up the ass or to suck it, I can."

483

A flutist who came from Iraq
Drilled holes like a flute in his cock,
      And the ladies were thrilled
      When he tooted and trilled
A concerto by Mozart or Bach.

484

There was a geologist Jack
Who placed his dear wife on her back.
      Then he lifted her gown
      With a manifest frown,
And he studied the growth of her crack.

485

When dating a lady, young Jack
Observed that her cunt had some slack.
      With his laces he thought
      He would tighten the twat,
But he slipped and he fell through the crack.

486

There was a magician named Jack
Whose prick had an uncommon knack.
      He could fit any cunt,
      Whether fat, tall or runt,
And change color to suit white or black.

487. THE ARCHAEOLOGISTS
While digging for fossils, Miss Joan
Discovered a cunt made of stone.
    She remarked, "I conclude
    It has never been screwed.
I'll install it in place of my own."

[488]
Her new pussy was rated decorous
By a horny geologist Boris,
    And after he fucked it
    He said, "I deduct it
Is very much like brontosaurus."

489. THE LOST KINGDOM
The right-angle pecker of Jock
At first gave the ladies a shock,
    But he gained their good graces
    For it tickled the places
Which had never been touched by a cock.

[490]
There was a young lady of Crewe
Whose vagina was straight and so true
    That the navy when fighting
    Would employ it for sighting,
And at ten miles could hit a canoe.

[491]
But Jock met the lady of Crewe
And he fucked up her bore straight and true.
    Because of the kink
    The navy did sink,
And the kingdom was lost for a screw.

492
To the doc went a fellow named Jock
For his neck was as stiff as a rock.
    The able physician
    Called in a magician,
And he transferred the cramp to his cock.

493
A colorful fellow was Joe;
His prick was as black as a crow,
    So he painted it white
    But it didn't look right,
For young Joe was a Negro, you know.

494

A near-sighted fellow named Juba
Was playing a piece on his tuba,
  When across on the floor
  Without pants walked a whore,
"Say Fidel," he said, "why'd you leave Cuba?"

495

An intrepid old oilman named Jude
Told a colored whore, "Strip to the nude."
  When her clothes fell away
  He exclaimed in dismay,
"Why, it looks like a barrel of crude!"

496

A hairy young lady was Kay;
Her cunt hair grew faster than hay.
  She was fucked by a lush
  Who got lost in the brush,
And he's never been found to this day.

497. DELTA

A young lady distressed was Miss Kay,
Her smallpox had caused her dismay.
  What had been so hirsute
  Was now bald as a coot,
So she wore a triangle toupee.

498

A haggard old harlot named Keating
Encountered in life such a beating,
  She was buggered and worn
  And her asshole was torn
And her pussy was not fit for eating.

499

There was a musician named Keitel
Whose pecker learned words that were vital.
  It proposed to a twat
  Which responded, "Why not?"
And engaged in an organ recital.

500. WHORESENSE
A cautious horse-trader named Keith
Asked a whore for a look underneath,
    So she spread out her snatch
    Which he viewed with dispatch,
But rejected because of old teeth.

501
There was a young lady named Kimball
Who was so adroit and so nimble,
    She'd enlarge with impunity
    If there was opportunity,
Or contract it as small as a thimble.

502
There was a young woodsman named Kimber
Whose cock was so long and so limber
    That when brought to erection
    'Twas a work of perfection.
When it fell, all the ladies cried, "Timber!"

503
There was a young fellow of Kings
Whose pecker had sprouted some wings.
    When there blew a slight breeze
    It would take off with ease
And go off on a lark and such things.

504
There was a young lady named Kissel
Who seated her ass on a thistle.
    Though surprise was in store,
    . What surprised her much more
Was the way that her ass learned to whistle.

505
There was a young lady of Kitchener
Who had a most terrible itch in her.
    A lad offered relief
    But he ran like a thief
When he saw the great size of the ditch in her.

506
A teacher of math named Miss Kitt
Made certain her students were fit.
    She would clear up distractions
    And explain vulgar fractions
By exposing a fraction of tit.

507. DUTCH TREAT

To the doctor went Duchess van Kleering
To complain of a fault persevering—
    Through her cunt she could hear.
    Said the doctor, "Don't fear,
You will find it is mere *Cherry Heering.*"

508

The photographer, down on his knees,
Was at work on nude shots of Miss Keyes.
    He said, "Smile for the picture."
    So she opened her stricture
And her cavity smiled and said, "Cheese."

509

To the firemen's ball at Fort Knox
Came a girl with a cunt like an ox.
    It had such a bad smell
    That they hosed it down well,
Then a garbageman reached for her box.

510

In the cunt of old baroness Kropp
There was space for a broom and a mop.
    A butcher named Tucker
    Attempted to fuck her,
But he needed a ham for a prop.

511

A flat-chested lady named Krupp
With fucks from the back was fed up,
    So she tattooed her front
    Just an inch from the cunt
With advice that this side be turned up.

512

A lady who felt a great lack
Complained of an itch in her crack,
    And she said it needs scratching.
    Said a man who looked, "Patching
Would do better to take up the slack."

513

There was a young man of Lapeer
Who said to his date, "You're a dear.
    Such a lovely big breast
    Would be fun when caressed."
So she gave him her blow-up brassiere.

514
There was a young lady named Laurel
Who sinned with a man—I've no quarrel.
    But this man did the sin
    With a cock like a pin,
And a sin of this size I call moral.

515. NO LEAD IN THE PENCIL*
There was a young draftsman named Lee
Whose pecker hung down to his knee.
    He advised every maid
    That *6H* was the grade,
But they checked and they found it *6B*.

516
For screwing, a fellow of Leeds
No jelly could find for his needs,
    So he said, "What the damn,
    I'll try raspberry jam."
But his foreskin got jammed with the seeds.

517
A lonely young midget was Lew;
He met a tall girl from Peru.
    When he stood on his toes
    Her twat came to his nose.
He had someone, he said, to talk to.

518. DOUBLE OR NOTHING*
A long-peckered fellow was Lew;
When he screwed, it would double in two.
    He sincerely believed
    That he came, but was grieved
To discover he went when he blew.

519
There was a young fellow who lifted
The skirts of a lady and sifted
    Through the layers of fat
    Where her twat should be at,
But discovered her cargo had shifted.

520
There was a young lady named Liston
Whose cunt was as big as a piston,
    But an able mechanic
    Who was not one to panic
Fucked her twice with his foot and his fist in.

521

An overworked harlot was Lizzie
Who left a young man in a tizzy,
      For her pussy was bare
      And her answer was, "There
Is no grass on a street that is busy."

522

The nuns with the church cast their lots;
In God's name they have tied holy knots.
      In their manner austere
      They assembled each year
At a dinner for petrified twats.

523

A loathsome young lady named Lou
Had titties that hung to her shoe,
      And her cunt was a wow
      For it sagged like a cow,
And when fucked from behind she would moo.

524

A cautious young fellow named Lumming
Selected young girls with good plumbing.
      He advised, "When I choose 'em
      They must have a big bosom
So I plug in and hear myself coming."

525

The harlots who worked for Miss Luntz
No longer could do any stunts,
      So they spent their last years
      In the bars, drinking beers,
And comparing the size of their cunts.

526

Said the harlot to stockbroker Lynch,
"My ass is ten dollars per inch."
      Said Lynch, "You have blundered;
      That makes it two hundred,
But I won't pay a cent if you flinch."

527

A young lass offered ass to MacNeal
And her panties she dropped for a feel.
      When he saw the great wound
      He exclaimed as he swooned,
"Oh my God! Do you think it will heal?"

528
There was a young girl of Madras
Who was blessed with an oversize ass.
  When the symphony played
  Her fat ass was displayed
For enhancing the boom in the brass.

529
There once was a pretty young maid,
Hirsute to extremes, I'm afraid.
  It was somewhere behind
  But took too long to find,
So it seems she had never been made.

530
There was a young lady named Mame
Whose cunt was so big, 'twas a shame.
  She was fucked by a cleric
  With a cock like a derrick,
But between them a falling out came.

531
Said a floundering fellow named Manion,
As he fucked with his lady companion,
  "I've had better, I think,
  When I pulled on my dink
On a trip to the depths of Grand Canyon."

532
A young man indiscreet name of Manion
Had picked up a strolling companion.
  He went to her apartment
  Where he viewed her compartment
And he cried, "I have seen the Grand Canyon!"

533
The girl that was dating young Max
Proceeded to take off her slacks.
  He said, somewhat blunt,
  "It looks like your cunt
Was made by the slash of an ax."

534. HE FOUND THE RIGHT SLOT
A lover of assholes, McGirk,
Was shamed many times for his quirk,
  So a doc he became.
  Now he feels without shame
Every ass, and he's paid for his work.

[535]
But a change overcame Doc McGirk,
And a pussy would send him berserk.
  Now he tugs and he wrenches
  At the pussies of wenches
And goes off in his pants at his work.

536
Said the dentist to harlot McKay,
As he poked in her cunt with dismay,
  "Your life of depravity
  Has fucked up your cavity.
What you need is a gold crown inlay."

537
There was a young man named McLoud
Who tackled a maid that was proud.
  He emerged a bit bloody
  And disheveled and cruddy,
But his prick was erect and unbowed.

538
A buxom young girl named McLoutch
Was screwed by a man on her couch.
  He was robust and strong
  With a pecker so long
When he walked he would step on it—ouch!

539
The cunt of a girl named McLouth
Stretched right from her ass to her mouth.
  Her young boyfriend, impressed,
  Spread her arms east and west,
And he fucked from the north to the south.

540
A hardy young girl named McLouth
While taking a trip through the South
  Was accosted by Willie,
  A vulgar hillbilly,
So she gave him a bust in the mouth.

541
While choosing a girl, young McNair
Did check and select with great care
  A most fitting companion,
  But got lost in the canyon,
And fell in an abyss of despair.

542*

There was a young girl named McNurd
Whose cunt was the strangest one heard.
    It would cheep and would cluck
    And right after a fuck
It would twitter and sing like a bird.

543

So loose was the wife of young Merritt
He felt he no longer could bear it.
    As he picked up her slipper,
    He remarked not too chipper,
"This old shoe, if it fits, I will wear it."

544

The lady that dated young Mick
Was depressed by his shortness of stick,
    But it grew to such size
    That she screamed in surprise,
"Just look at the size of that P R I C K!"

545

The girl of a lip-reader, Morse,
Said "No" as a matter of course.
    Said Morse to her, "Bess,
    Please raise up your dress.
I must hear from the mouth of the horse."

546

An oversize wife had young Mort;
Her cunt was as big as a quart,
    But he managed to fuck her
    With the help of a trucker,
And a safety belt held for support.

547

There was a young fellow named Mose
Whose pecker hung down to his toes.
    When erect it stood free
    Like a solid oak tree
And attracted some termites and crows.

548

A crosseyed young lady named Mott
Was born with a right-angle twat.
    The more that you spread her
    The more it got better,
For it tightened her twat quite a lot.

549
All day the young girl from Fort Mudge
Her face filled with candy and fudge,
  And her ass was so fat,
  It went *splat* when she sat,
And nobody could get her to budge.

550
There were two young ladies of Natchez
Who'd catch a fly ball with their snatches,
  So they played for Detroit
  With their pussies adroit,
And they helped them to win all their matches.

551
A bricklayer's wife named of Nixon
Had room in her cunt for three bricks in,
  And some space for a hod
  With cement in, by God,
And she still could fit three or four pricks in.

552. THE LADY OF NATCHEZ*
There was a young lady of Natchez
Who chanced to be born with two snatches,
  And she often said, "Shit!
  Why I'd give either tit
For a man with equipment that matches."

[553]
There was a young fellow named Locke
Who was born with a two-headed cock.
  When he'd fondle the thing
  It would rise up and sing
An antiphonal chorus by Bach.

[554]
But whether these two ever met
Has not been recorded as yet.
  Still, it would be diverting
  To observe him inserting
His whang while it sang a duet.

[555]
Young Locke felt the need of God's grace
So in Natchez at church took his place.
  There he fondled his cock
  And delighted the flock
When it sang both soprano and bass.

[556]
The lady of Natchez came there
And both of her snatches did bare.
    The whole congregation
    Sang hymns with elation,
While the bishop was blessing the pair.

[557]
On the altar the lady of Natchez
Lay down to show Locke her two snatches,
    And his two-headed prod
    Sang with glory to God,
While she measured to see how it matches.

[558]
Locke plunged in his two-pronged erection.
It fit the two cunts to perfection.
    While the organist played,
    The young lady got laid,
And the bishop observed with affection.

559. THE SAGA OF CORKSCREW DICK*
A corkscrew-pricked fellow of Natchez
Tried thousands and thousands of snatches,
    But this fellow named Dick
    Found no cunt for his prick,
And he cried in despair, "Nothing matches!"

[560]
In France, a young lady named List
Had a cunt with a helical twist.
    She could not find a fit
    For her helical slit,
So she cried in remorse, "I am pissed!"

[561]
In the circus Miss List did enlist
Where she pissed with a spiraling twist.
    All the patrons convulsed
    But Miss List was repulsed,
For a fuck was the thing that she missed.

[562]
When Dick saw Miss List piss a twister,
He ran to the ring and he kissed her.
    Then he showed her his thing
    Which was coiled like a spring,
And she yelled to him, "Fuck me now, mister!"

[563]
They checked that their spirals turned right
And they faced their first fuck with delight.
   On Miss List Dick did flop
   And he spun like a top,
And their organs at last did unite.

[564]
Their screams of despair were symmetric,
And they needed assistance obstetric,
   For Dick's thread, you can guess,
   Was a standard U.S.,
But Miss List had a cunt that was metric.

[565]
Their ending was sad, we admit;
Their organs were shattered and split.
   From the force that existed
   Both their assholes were twisted
And they died amidst spirals of shit.

566
There was a young maid of New Liskeard
Who claimed she had never been friskered,
   But a man stood aghast
   When her skirt came unfast
For her pussy was worn and dewhiskered.

567
There was a young girl oriental
Whose strength lay in matters non-mental.
   When her boyfriend said, "Kit,
   Would you like a titbit?"
She said, "No, I like men who are gentle."

568
Said a man to a girl in Orillia,
"I am sure my big dong will not kill ya."
   But she showed him her size
   And he cried in surprise,
"I'm afraid my poor dong will not fill ya."

569
To the ladies, a fellow named Pakenham
Said, "Your pussies have far too much slack in 'em."
   But the ladies, chagrined,
   Said, "You big bag of wind,
It's your prick—it does not have the knack in 'em."

570
Obese was the wife of young Pat,
While he was as thin as a slat.
    But the neighbors could see
    That the two did agree,
For much time he spent chewing the fat.

571
There was a young fellow named Peak
Whose pecker had learned how to speak.
    When it screamed in the cavern
    Of the maid from the tavern,
It reechoed the best of a week.

572
An able old surgeon named Pease
Refitted worn cunts with great ease,
    But one whore was left bitter
    For he carelessly fit her,
And the damn thing hung down to her knees.

573
As the twisted old cock of Doc Perce
Was rammed in the cunt of his nurse,
    She complained—but too late—
    By a strange twist of fate
She had taken a turn for the worse.

574
A man who knew cheese to perfection
Was asked how he made his selection.
    He answered, "By Jesus,
    I sniff all the cheeses,
And I choose cheese which fosters erection."

575
A lady who came from Peru
Was proud of the magic she knew.
    After having a fuck,
    From her cunt she would pluck
Several geese and a rabbit or two.

576
A wanton old tart of Peru
Had drummed up her business anew.
    Though she lowered her rates
    To attract many dates,
It turned out her appointments fell through.

577
There was a young lady named Pickett
Whose crotch was as thick as a thicket.
    Her snatch was behind it
    But her man could not find it,
And he never was able to lick it.

578
An expert well-digger named Pflugge
Wed a girl with a cunt like a jug
    For he noted the size
    Of the hole in her thighs
Was the same as the last well he dug.

579
Said the King to the Queen, "I am pissed,
For my fist goes right in to the wrist.
    I have not fucked a whore
    With so mammoth a bore,
And loose women are high on my list."

580
There was a young couple named Pitt
Who never had argued a bit,
    But it was not all bliss,
    There was something amiss
And between them a permanent split.

581
There was a young fellow named Pitts
Whose big-breasted girl gave him fits.
    When one time he got naughty,
    She applied her karate
And she busted his jaw with her tits.

582. CASH CROP*
A man saved old twats, if you please,
And he planted an acre of these.
    They grew up soft and hairy,
    Each one topped with a cherry,
And they all smelled like limburger cheese.

583. ONE BUSHEL EQUALS FOUR PECKS
An oversize crotch had Miss Pleasure,
A cunt like a bushel—a treasure.
    When she wanted some sex
    She took four men named Pecks,
And two half-pints thrown in for good measure.

584
A girl with two snatches named Plum
Left a lad so confused, he was numb.
    What bothered him so—
    He knew where to go
But he never knew where he should come.

585
An intrepid explorer named Prater
Tried screwing a girl from Decatur.
    He was wordly and wise
    But exclaimed in surprise,
"I believe I am lost in this crater."

586
The poll-takers checked with precision
The men in an army division
    As to preference for food
    Or a girl to get screwed,
And it was, without fail, *Split Decision!*

587. GOOD DEED FOR THE DAY
Much obliged was a lady named Pyle
When a Boy Scout assisted a while,
    So she said, "In what way
    Can I brighten your day?"
He said, "Flash me a vertical smile!"

588. THE FOUNDRY CONNECTION
The widow of Baron von Rasting
Disclosed her devotion long lasting:
    "For a time I was sick
    As I missed his big prick,
But not now, since I made a bronze casting."

589
The professor emeritus, Reese,
Had a penchant for ladies obese,
    And he said, "In my lab
    I examine their flab
In the hopes I can find a new crease."

590
There was a young man of Regina
Who sampled all kinds of vagina.
    Some were fat, some were thin,
    Some were blacker than sin,
And some sideways like ladies in China.

591
A kink in her cunt had Miss Rose
Which presented a problem to those
    Who had pricks that were straight,
    But the fire chief was great,
For he fucked with a flexible hose.

592
There was an old whore from the Ruhr
Whose cunt was as big as a sewer.
    If five men got together,
    With hip boots for bad weather,
They could go on a Cook's guided tour.

593
A fellow whose background was rural
Disclosed that his organ was plural.
    He requested two maids
    Hold it up with their braids
While an artist produced a large mural.

594
There was a young man of St. Paul
Whose phallus was strangest of all,
    Like the cock of an ape
    But a helical shape,
And was topped by a cubical ball.

595
Said a helpless old fellow named Sands,
"I have lost all control of my hands.
    When I see a big tit
    I go into a fit,
For I'm partial to mammary glands."

596
A bashful young fellow was Schick;
The sight of young girls made him sick.
     Wherever they found him
     They gathered around him,
So he beat them all off with his prick.

597
The prick of a fellow named Schink
Was set in a teratoid kink,
     So he cut off the end
     Where it started to bend
And he used it for mixing his drink.

598
There was a young lady named Schink
With a crotch like the drain in the sink.
     She was fucked by young Ned
     With a loaf of rye bread
And an oversize pork sausage link.

599
There was an old barber named Schippers
Who fucked an old whore with big flippers,
     And a cunt so hirsute
     That he floundered en route,
So he sheared off the bitch with his clippers.

600. PIT STOP
Said a girl to a fruit-picker, Schmidt,
"A sweet cherry you'll find in my slit."
     Replied Schmidt, up her flue,
     "What you say may be true,
But I never have seen such a pit."

601
To the doc went a fellow named Schule
For correcting the kink in his tool.
     Said the doctor, sedate,
     "I will make your prick straight—
I'll exchange it for mine, you damn fool."

602
To a lad, an old maid name of Schust
Was exposing her twat and her bust,
     But he said, "Hide your tits,
     For they give me the shits,
And your cunt is beginning to rust."

603
A well-hung young fellow was Shaver;
He owed an old whore a small favor.
    So she said to him, "Joe,
    Take it easy and slow—
This is one fuck that I want to savor."

604
A rugged old captain named Schwartz
Carried cargoes abroad of all sorts.
    At each port he got laid
    And a mattress he made
From the cunt hairs of whores of all ports.

605
Said the tailor, while fitting Miss Schwartz,
Whose cunt was as big as two quarts,
    "I can give you a fit."
    So she answered, "No shit—
Let me see what you have in your shorts."

606
There was a young fellow named Schwartz
Who was hounded by girls of all sorts,
    Since he pleased them all good
    Like no other brand could
For his penis was studded with warts.

607
At pussies in China don't scoff
Though ninety degrees they are off.
    When Caucasians are spread
    They are wider a shred,
While in China it tightens the trough.

608
As the lady undressed before Scott
He pulled out his pecker so hot.
    She smiled with a flair
    But it didn't compare
To the smile that she had on her twat.

609
At eighty an old man named Scott
Once more a young lady had sought.
    So he caught her, it's true,
    And he knew what to do,
But his pecker, indifferent, forgot.

Organs

610

There was an old lady named Scott
Who never gave pricks any thought.
    She said, "They're a mess,
    Like the beast of Loch Ness,
But my cunt seems to like them a lot."

611

A much deformed lady named Scott
By young men was constantly sought.
    Though her cunt was distorted
    And most strangely contorted,
Men were thrilled by the twist in her twat.

612

There was a young lady named Scott
Whose cunt was as big as a yacht.
    When she died they all prayed
    But the rites were delayed
For the coffin was lost in her twat.

613

So big was the cunt of Miss Sears
That it thrilled a young man, it appears.
    In amazement he said,
    "May I stick in the head?"
She said, "Yes sir, but just to the ears."

614

A mathematician named Shaw
Examined the twat of a squaw.
    He summed the perimeter
    Plus the depth by altimeter
And he stared at the figures with awe.

615

A young man in frustration and shock
Took his tax form to H. & R. Block.
    Said old Block, "Please comply
    And unfasten your fly—
I'm afraid there's a tax on your cock."

616

The cunt of a harlot named Shutes
Was enlarged by some oversize roots.
    The last one that fucked her
    Was a railroad conductor
Who waltzed through her cunt with hip boots.

617

So big was the cunt of Miss Shutes
That she never was thrilled by men's roots,
　　But an angler named Bill
　　Gave her more than her fill
When he tromped in her cunt with hip boots.

618

When you lay a young girl on the sod,
Don't consider the size of the prod.
　　It's the way that you diddle
　　In your ladyfriend's middle
That restores her relation with God.

619

The lady from China is sought
For sideways direction of twat,
　　And the more that you spread her
　　The more it gets better,
For it tightens the pussy a lot.

620

A young Pole who was traveling in Spain
Was cut clean in two by a train.
　　The ass-half did sue
　　For a million or two.
For that was the seat of his brain.

621

He looked at her twat with a spasm,
And went into a fearful orgasm.
　　She said that her slot
　　In beauty was wrought,
But he thought it was more like a chasm.

622

While counting, a fellow named Springer
Would check off each toe and each finger,
　　And he reached twenty-one
　　With his zipper undone
By checking the knob of his dinger.

623

The cunt hair profuse of Miss Steiner
Was better than steel and much finer
　　For it fashioned a net,
　　The strongest one yet,
Which captured a whale and a liner.

624

The auto mechanic was straining
In bed with a lady named Blaining.
      He examined her snatch
      And he said with dispatch,
"I believe that your crankcase needs draining."

625

A cavernous lady was Strand;
Her cunt, without question, was grand.
      There was room for a fridge
      And four tables for bridge,
And a place for a symphony band.

626

Since men all complained that they swam in her,
A girl asked the doc to examine her,
      So he fucked her that night
      But he found she was tight
For the butcher had left a prime ham in her.

627. THE ILLUSIONIST

Said the girl who was dating a swami,
"There are times I suspect that I'm balmy.
      There can be no dispute
      That his prick is minute,
But it feels like a full-size salami."

628

There was a young lady of Thrace
Whose cunt was a cavernous place.
      When she married young Phipps,
      He stepped in to his hips,
And she took up the slack with a lace.

629

A salesgirl of perfume, Miss Tish,
Stunk bad, though her pussy she'd swish.
      Said her boss, "You must leave,
      But there's no need to grieve.
You can work as a monger of fish."

630

When the captain went out with Miss Toal,
He fell in to his knees in her hole,
      And he struggled in vain
      On the tricky terrain.
"I have foundered," he said, "on a shoal!"

631

A poorly-hung fellow was Tucker
And no good at all as a fucker,
 Yet when girls saw his root
 They agreed it was cute,
And their lips would invariably pucker.

632

A redhead approached Mr. Tuller
And showed him her crotch, which was duller.
 He exclaimed in despair,
 "What I seem to see there
Is a horse which is different in color."

633

A conductor of note named Umberto
Did what no other maestro would dare to.
 While he brandished his cock
 To the music of Bach,
He conducted the organ concerto.

634. TRY THE OTHER CHANNEL

A TV repairman undaunted
Tuned in on the lady who taunted;
 When he saw her crotch bare
 He exclaimed in despair,
"Why this can't be the channel I wanted!"

635. SAVED BY THE FORTUNATE FINGER

A Dutchman, concerned, named Vandyke,
Observed an old maid on her bike
 As she stopped for a pee,
 And he cried, knowingly,
"Oh my God, we must plug up the dike!"

636

There was a young lady named Venus
Whose man had a very small penis,
 So exceedingly small
 It was nothing at all,
So she told him, "There's nothing between us."

637
There was a young lady named Violet
Whose cunt was so small that a pilot
    Who attempted to wreck her
    Was advised that his pecker
Must pass first through the hole in an eyelet.

638. RECORD IN THE ROCKS
A noted geologist, Walt,
Once screwed a young lady of Galt.
    She said, "You are proficient,
    Is my fissure sufficient?"
But her fissure, he said, was a fault.

639
There was a young girl from the West
With tits on the back of her chest.
    Though her face was a fright
    She had dates every night
Since for dancing by far she was best.

640
On his back lay a fellow from Wheeling
While he fondled his cock with great feeling.
    On the knob of his cock
    Came a fly for a walk,
And he plastered the fly to the ceiling.

641
A lady whose head spun and whirled,
Her snatch to her lover unfurled.
    He stood back in great fright
    And cried, "God, what a sight!
I have just seen the end of the world."

642*
On TV appeared a man wise
To clear up the scandals and lies.
    Then he showed a fine trick,
    For he pulled out his prick
And he said to the nation, "Surprise!"

643. THE HIGHWAYMEN
An old Pole rode his cart through the woods
And encountered some thieving young hoods.
    Said the Pole, "Let us be
    For my daughter and me
Are poor and we carry no goods."

[644]
The thieves searched the cart and were vexed.
They found nothing, and stood there perplexed.
    Since no booty was there
    In their utter despair
The horse and the cart they annexed.

[645]
"Alas," said the Pole in dismay.
"My fortune was hid there away
    In the cart 'neath the seat
    In a hiding place neat.
Now my fortune is lost—let us pray."

[646]
The daughter said, "Father, so what.
The robbers are gone, but with naught.
    You do not have to chafe
    For your fortune is safe—
I have hidden it all in my twat."

[647]
Though left with a worthwhile resource
Yet the anguished Pole said in remorse,
    "If your mother were here
    We'd have nothing to fear.
We'd have saved both the cart and the horse."

648
A well-hung young fellow named Zeeter
Was blessed with a twelve-inch long peter.
    Said a lady, so thrilled,
    "Now my cunt will be filled!"
But young Zeeter proceeded to eat her.

4

Strange Intercourse

649

There was an explorer named Behring
Who spoke of his exploits so daring,
    "I've fucked ladies so vigorous
    That strong men found them rigorous,
And I've fucked them as dead as a herring."

650

There was an old lady named Billings
Who went to the dentist for fillings.
    But he lost all control
    And he filled the wrong hole,
So she charged him four pence and two shillings.

651

A fussy old plumber named Bokum
Would not stand for fooling or hokum.
    Before diddling a whore
    With an oversize bore,
He would carefully caulk her with oakum.

652. THE MAPMAKER

There was a topographer bold
Who fucked a fat lady, I'm told,
    And he mapped every cranny
    Which she had in her fanny,
And he fucked every wrinkle and fold.

653

A discomposed dentist named Booth
Had guzzled a jug of vermouth.
    In his chair sat a maiden
    With perfume heavy laden,
So he screwed her while pulling her tooth.

654

A careless young fellow named Boris
Tried diddling his girl in his Morris,
    But the facts we compile
    Were his car had a smile
And he never got near her clitoris.

655

An agile old butcher named Bounter
A fussy old hag did encounter.
    She complained of his quality
    Which disturbed this man's jollity,
So he threw her the meat on the counter.

656

There was a young spaceman named Brimbles
Who mounted his girl while on gimbals,
    And he marked the conclusion
    At the end of this fusion
With a crash on a pair of brass cymbals.

657. ON TOP OF OLD SMOKY

There was a young fellow named Brophey
Who won a big blue ribbon trophy
    For carousing and dancing
    And repulsive romancing
And for staying on top of old Sophie.

658. RODEO

So wild was the lady of Bruce
They tied her ass down with a noose,
    Then a cowboy named Scott
    Shoved his cock in her twat
And proceeded to cut the bonds loose.

659

The agile contortionist Burgess
Said, "Dear, I've a new way to merge us."
    They contorted a knot
    Which was drawn up so taut
That the church bells are now tolling dirges.

660

There was a young butcher named Caesar
Who froze his dead wife in the freezer.
    On the day of Yom Kippur
    He proceeded to strip her,
And he took her to bed and did tease her.

661
There was a young fellow named Caesar
Whose girl got too hot when he'd tease her.
    To resolve this dilemma
    He said, "Step this way Emma
And we'll have three or four in the freezer."

662. TAKE THE BOOK TO BED
From the sex book a fellow named Chris
Tried a stunt which his girl thought amiss,
    "I do not share your view—
    I have read the book too,
And the book was much better than this."

663
A horny young fellow named Chuck
Was challenged to prove he had pluck,
    So in utter defiance
    Of the laws known to science,
He engaged with himself in a fuck.

664. OPHTHALPHILIA
To a whore a young fellow named Clyde
Said, "I'll pay if new sex you provide."
    Her glass eye she took out
    And she said, "Without doubt
Here's a fuck that you never have tried."

[665]
He gave her the dough from his pocket
And his prick he slipped into the socket.
    Before he could blink
    She gave it a wink
And his pecker went off like a rocket.

[666]
"My God!" shouted Clyde as he blew,
"I must have me another such screw.
    For more cash I must go."
    And the harlot said, "So
I'll be keeping an eye out for you."

667
A feeble old fellow named Clyde
Was screwing his wife when he died.
    He was cold as a worm
    But his pecker was firm,
Which meant burial was not justified.

668

On the street in a hurry walked Clyde,
And he noticed a whore by his side.
    When he said, "I can't stay."
    She replied, "If you pay,
I believe I can take this in stride."

669

There was a young Vassar collegian
With exploits in sex that were legion.
    She could outlast them all
    From Berlin to St. Paul,
But she could not outlast a Norwegian.

670. INFOLONEL

There was a respected old colonel
Who screwed a young lady cavolonel.
    But she had a relapse
    And her twat did collapse,
So he noted the facts in his jolonel.

671. ASCENT TO HEAVEN

When Johnnie with mother conversed
He asked if maid Brown went feet first
    When to heaven she went
    On her upward ascent.
His mother said, "Nonsense, the worst!"

[672]

With toes pointing up and no gown,
"I'm coming, oh God!" yelled maid Brown.
    And she would have got there,
    Johnnie solemn did swear,
Except father was holding her down.

673

A wealthy old harlot named Commer
Fell dead after fucking old Palmer.
    Though her will did declare
    The last fucker would share,
Palmer lost to the wily embalmer.

674
A painter named Salvador Dali
Was stopped by a harlot in Bali,
    So he made a cheap deal
    And he fucked her, the heel,
As she hung from a post in the alley.

675
There was an old blacksmith of Danville
Who screwed two young dancers name Granville.
    He removed their sarongs
    With his hammer and tongs
And he gave them a course on his anvil.

676
"My dear," said a poet named Damatur,
"You'll find that I am not an amateur,
    So grab hold of your toes
    And I'll fuck you in prose
And then in iambic pentameter."

677
A young tightrope walker named Darius
Would fuck in a manner precarious.
    He was asked to account
    For his dangerous mount.
He replied with a smile, 'twas hilarious.

678
There was a young lady named Dee
Who wanted the late show to see,
    But her husband, though blind,
    Just had sex on his mind,
So she fucked him while watching TV.

679
The doughty old Duchess of Depter
Deserted the duke who had kept her
    To fuck with the king,
    But so tight was her thing
That he diddled the bitch with his scepter.

680
The king pinched the ass of Miss Depter
And said that in bed he'd accept her.
    She was slow to respond
    To the king's royal wand,
So he first pepped her up with his scepter.

681

A strange race of people are Dokks;
In the mountains they live with their flocks,
    And what seems most perplexing
    Is their method of sexing—
Instead of their tongues they use cocks.

682

There was a young fellow named Dorgan
Who tried to make love in his Morgan.
    The result of this madness
    Was to view with great sadness
The decline and the fall of his organ.

683. WHAT IS DONE IS DONE*

A noted composer named Dunn
A worldly young lady did stun.
    She said, "You have such feeling
    That I simply am reeling."
He remarked, "This is my *Opus One.*"

[684]

However old Dunn was not through,
He tackled this lady anew.
    She said, "Never have I
    Been so high in the sky."
Said old Dunn, "This is my *Opus Two.*"

[685]

This noted composer with glee
Then tackled his maid in a tree,
    And he fucked her with vim
    On the outermost limb,
And he said, "This is my *Opus Three.*"

[686]

He next fucked his girl on the floor;
She knew not what there was in store.
    He progressed with great feeling
    To the walls and the ceiling,
Then he gasped, "I am Dunn! *Opus Four!*"

[687]

It seems Dunn was no longer alive
But his pecker erect still had drive.
    Though devoid of all breath
    He was fucked after death,
So Dunn's posthumous opus was *Five.*

688
There was an old whore of Dundee
Who took two at one time for the fee.
In due time she was worn
But her fate did not mourn,
There was room in her cunt now for three.

689
A woodsman who lived in Dundee
Had diddled an oak tree with glee.
From the end of his cock
Came a wisp of a stalk
Which grew into a mighty oak tree.

690
There was a young fellow named Dunn
Who dated a nun just for fun,
But in bed she was dead
So he tried screwing bread
And found half a loaf better than nun.

691. THE HEAVENLY FATHER
A responsive young girl from the East
In her bed was an able artiste.
She had learned two positions
From her family physicians,
And ten more from her old parish priest.

692
Dear Rosie, the wife of young Ellis,
Fell down and she broke her pelvellis.
With a cast to her head
She was no good in bed,
So he screwed his sweet Rose on the trellis.

693
There was a canoeist named Ewing
Who took a young lady canoeing.
She was playful and chipper
As she unzipped his zipper;
This undoing canoeing meant screwing.

694
The Byrd brothers snared Sally Fern
And each of them raped her in turn,
But they ran out of breath
And she fucked them to death,
And she killed off two Byrds with one stern.

695

A learned young fucker named Ferrer
Would fuck like an unholy terror.
    No hole would he spare,
    Without or with hair,
Thus leaving no margin for error.

696

So fast was the girl of young Fletcher
That he never was able to ketch 'er.
    What accomplished the trick
    Was the time she got sick
And he buggered the bitch on the stretcher.

697. A LITTLE LIE WON'T HURT

The old woodcarver's helper, Miss Fry,
Took Pinocchio aside on the sly,
    Then she took off her clothes
    And she stuffed his big nose
In her cunt, and said, "Now tell a lie!"

698

There was a young fellow named Gaines
Whose girl gave him trouble and pains,
    So he shot the girl dead
    With a hole in the head,
And he blew his cock off in her brains.

699

The Bell Telephone man, Mr. Gold,
Was fucking a lady, so bold,
    When he heard the phone ring,
    So he pulled out his thing
And he placed the young lady on *Hold*.

700

A rugged young lady named Good
Stood up to a man in the wood.
    They could see where his knees
    Skinned the bark off the trees,
For she stood a lot more than he could.

701

There was a young fellow named Gord
Who diddled his girl in his Ford.
    Though he managed her neat
    In the front and back seat,
She claims to this day she was bored.

702. HOME ON THE RANGE
With the cook, the new butler named Grange
Indulged in his antics so strange,
    For he screwed her, the fink,
    In the fridge and the sink,
But she felt he had not found the range.

703. SHE HEARD HIM COMING
There was a young lady named Greer
Whose method of fucking was queer.
    If you asked for a whack
    At her front or her back,
She would smile and would turn a deaf ear.

704
There was an old cowboy named Hadl
Who raped an old maid from Seattle.
    She jumped on to his horse,
    To avoid him of course,
But he screwed her once more in the saddle.

705
There was a young cowgirl named Hadl
Who dated a lad from Seattle.
    She preferred not to spar
    In the back of the car;
She would much rather fuck in the saddle.

706. WITH HEART AND SOLE
There was a young lady named Hall
Who dated a shoemaker Paul.
    His last she got first
    With his tongue interspersed
And the heel finished off with his awl.

707
There was a young fellow named Hambler
Who tackled a girl in his Rambler.
    Just when things looked much brighter,
    He got fucked by the lighter,
But Hambler, of course, was a gambler.

708

In Rome a young lady named Harriet
Was roped by a man with a lariat.
    They say 'twas Ben-Hur,
    Who screwed her, the cur,
As he rode at full speed in his chariot.

709

A horny young fellow was Harris;
He dated an heiress in Paris.
    He fucked her a trifle
    On top of the Eiffel,
And he finished her off on his terrace.

710

An agile old painter named Hartley
Seduced a young lady named Bartley.
    Though he fucked with restraint
    And continued to paint,
Yet he managed to fuck her right smartly.

711

A stalwart old fellow named Hatch
Made love to a maid with dispatch.
    She was charming and merry
    But her cunt was so hairy
That he lost his toupee in her snatch.

712

If a girl will not give in an inch,
And from moral behavior won't flinch,
    And she finds it too crass
    To be fucked up the ass,
Then her armpit will do in a pinch.

713. THE JOCULAR PHILOSOPHER

A noted philosopher, jocular,
Was stopped by a harlot monocular.
    He rejected her ass
    As vulgar and crass
Till she offered him intercourse ocular.

[714]

This one-eyed old harlot named Kim,
The philosopher screwed with such vim,
    That he said, "I'll be back
    When I get some more jack."
So she kept an eye out just for him.

715
To spice up his sex life, young John
Said, "Darling, new plans I have drawn.
We will try it dog-fashion."
But she said with face ashen,
"You will never get me on the lawn."

716. THE UNKNOWN SOLDIER
A full-armored knight screwed Miss Keyser;
She said that this did not surprise her
For his act was well-meant,
But he was not a gent
For he failed to uncover his visor.

717
There was a young fellow named Kimmen
Who had a great way with the women.
He would fuck them in cars
And in parks and in bars,
And he fucked them when he went in swimmin'.

718. THE DOG SHOW
When Tichenor dated Miss Kitchener,
She came to the door with no stitch on her.
They went out on the lawn
Where he fucked her till dawn
'Fore he managed to stifle the itch in her.

[719]
A passing reporter was shook
But he took down some notes in his book.
They had used for coition
Such a fancy position
That the neighborhood dogs stopped to look.

720
An amorous WAC name of Laker
Was screwed by two chefs and a baker,
Then a bombardier, Palmer,
And the colonel's embalmer,
Then the priest and the old undertaker.

721
The learned young linguist Lautrec
Made love to a girl from Quebec,
And he kissed her, they say,
À la manière français,
And he finished her off à la Grècque.

722

In the forest a woodsman named Lee
Was fucking a whore 'gainst a tree.
> He went right through the bought hole
> And he fucked up a knothole,
So the lumber mill charged him the fee.

723. THIS WON'T HURT A BIT

There was a young lady of Linz
Who went into antics and spins
> With her Hindu ascetic
> And his counsel prophetic,
For he had her on needles and pins.

724

There was a musician named Lute
Whose girl thought that he was so cute,
> And what made him the rage
> Was he fucked her on stage
While he played a concerto for flute.

725

An agile young lady was Lynn;
For money she married old Flynn,
> But his pecker was dead
> So the young lady said,
"When I stand on my head, drop it in."

726

There was an old Scot named MacDilts
Whose girl stood high over his kilts.
> This girl was too tall
> And his bed was too small
So he screwed her while standing on stilts.

727

There was a stout Scot named MacPherson
Who cared not the sex of a person.
> He fucked Mrs. MacFee
> And her daughter Jane Lee,
And he next fucked her father and her son.

728

There was a young midget named Madder
Whose girl was as tall as a ladder.
> When he stood on his toes
> Her cunt came to his nose,
So he stood on his shoulders and had her.

729
There was a young man named Malone
Who screwed an old whore in Cologne.
He had better, he thunk,
At the time he got drunk
When he buggered a statue of stone.

730
Though she tried many men in her manor,
No man could appease old Miss Banner,
Till a plumber named Lew
Shoved a pipe up her flue,
Which he worked with a seven-foot spanner.

731. WOMEN'S LIB
When the railroad advanced Miss McCord
A new honor for women was scored.
She was made a conductor,
But so many men fucked her
She no longer will shout *All Aboard!*

732. ALL IN THE FAMILY
There was a young man named McGraw
Who had an affair with his ma.
She said, "Give me another,
You are better than brother."
He said, "No, I must save one for pa."

733
Another young man named McLure
Had thought that his sister was pure.
When he took off her panties
He cried, "Why they're auntie's,
And uncle's been in here for sure."

734
There was a young man named McNull,
Devoid of all brains and so dull,
When he found his girl dead
From a shot in the head,
He buggered the hole in her skull.

735
There was an embalmer named Moffin
Whose work kept him late very often,
For when anyone died
He took personal pride
In laying each corpse in its coffin.

736
There was a young maid of Montbello
Who thought that musicians were mellow,
But a man named Casals
Made her climb up the walls
When he buggered the bitch with his cello.

737
A scholarly fellow of Natchez
Found so many unconquered snatches
That pursuit was in vain
And he failed to make gain
Till he tackled the snatches in batches.

738
A noted biologist Nate
Developed a thought that was great.
In his lab, on their knees,
The young girls would eat peas,
And he'd throw them the meat while they ate.

739
A statue of stone that was nuder
Caught the eye of the noble King Tudor.
It looked like a whore of his
But was lacking an orifice,
So he drilled out a hole and he screwed her.

740
When John saw his girl, Miss O'Dare,
Remove her fake ass, tits and hair,
He went into a shock
As he pulled out his cock
And he fucked all the stuff in the chair.

741
There was a young girl named O'Hare
Who said she had no love to spare.
When her suitor asked why,
He was left high and dry,
And besides, 'twas a family affair.

742
There was a queer fellow of Perth
Whose antics romantic caused mirth,
For he only disported
With young ladies distorted
With unfortunate defects from birth.

743. ROYAL SCREWING
The Queen of King Louis Philippe
Would wait till the king was asleep.
    She'd sneak out on all fours
    And work out with the whores,
And then back into bed she would creep.

744
There was a young lady named Pola
Who put too much rye in her cola.
    She rode on a train
    Where she sang a refrain
And was fucked on the fourteenth gondola.

745
"It's *Pony Express*," said Miss Pound,
"A sprightly new game that I've found—
    Like *Post Office*—instead
    You must play it in bed,
And there's also more horsing around."

746
There was a young lady named Powell
Who played in a ball game in Howell.
    As she rounded each base
    All the players gave chase;
What they did on home plate was called foul.

747
To novice young typist Miss Presk,
The office appeared picturesque.
    She was struck with dismay
    To learn fixtures to stay
Were the ones that were screwed on the desk.

748
A moral old man of Racine,
Whose love life was wholesome and clean,
    Fucked his wife all these years
    With his nose and his ears,
So was never considered obscene.

749
A lass who possessed a plump rear full
Tried sex in ways diverse and cheerful,
    But a preacher named Hays
    Who did not like her ways
Proceeded to give her an earful.

750

There was an old doctor named Reese
Who was screwing a harlot in Nice,
    In the midst of it all
    He received a rush call;
He returned for the rest of the piece.

751

A lady returned with remorse
From a trip to the land of the Norse.
    It was not to her liking
    To be fucked by a Viking
Who had failed to dismount from his horse.

752

In Miami a fellow named Reuben
Did ask of his wife, "Where have you been?"
    "I was screwed," she did boast,
    "While I swam off the coast,
By a well-known and bearded old Cuban."

753

The lumberman's daughter, they say,
Appeared somewhat splintered away,
    For her motto, she said,
    When she climbed into bed,
Was to let the chips fall where they may.

754

There was a young fellow named Scott
Who failed to get in his girl's slot,
    So he said to her, "Dear,
    Let's try one in your ear,
For there's far too much wax in your twat."

755

There was a young fellow named Scringe
Who picked a fat girl for a binge.
    He preferred plump girls more,
    He found more to explore;
There were benefits all 'round the fringe.

756. HONOR AT STAKE

An old two-bit whore name of Shorter
Was engaged by an elderly porter.
    She was so much impressed
    By his vigor and zest
No one asked for or gave any quarter.

757
There was a young plumber named Simms
Who acted on impulse and whims.
  When he dated Miss Bruce
  Who was said to be loose,
He brought plenty of caulking and shims.

758
There was a young lady named Skinner
Who claimed that no young man could win her,
  But a cellist from Rio,
  With the help of a trio,
To a quartet by Handel did pin her.

759. NICOTINE COMPULSION
"You can fuck from behind," said Miss Snood.
Said her man, "I don't wish to be rude,
  Can you please tell me why?"
  Said Miss Snood, "Please comply—
I can smoke a cigar while I'm screwed."

760. A *FRIEND* INDEED!
The snatch of a girl of South Bend
Was deep and appeared without end.
  She could not get her fill
  Till a plumber named Bill
Plumbed her depths with the help of his *friend*.

761. IN SPAIN ON THE PLAIN IN THE RAIN
In a trance a young lady of Spain
Removed all her clothes on the train.
  A brave matador
  Fucked her twice on the floor,
And once on the plain in the rain.

762
A cuckolded fellow was Stein;
His dear wife for lovers did pine.
  "You are welcome," he said,
  "To take men to your bed,
But keep them the hell out of mine."

763

The doctor was able to stir
New life into nervous Miss Kerr.
 He applied all his skills
 For ten weeks to her ills,
Then she found that he should have paid her.

764

A prize-winning golfer was Stokes,
His wife taught him golf just for jokes.
 He learned golf by doing
 The same as in screwing,
Which he finished in very few strokes.

765

A horny old plumber named Stout
Engaged an old maid with a shout.
 His apprentice named Prentiss
 Fucked her non compos mentis,
And left tools of his trade strewn about.

766

Now for the young lady of Strand
The park on the beach was just grand.
 There were plenty of benches
 For young lads and their wenches,
And their fannies were out of the sand.

767

A dignified duchess named Sutter
Caused many a duke's prick to flutter,
 But the man to attract her
 Was a bum who attacked her
And he fucked her four times in the gutter.

768. PLAY BALL!

The players were irked by Miss Thatcher;
In yelling no ball fan could match her.
 She was fucked on the mound
 By the pitcher renowned,
And again on home plate by the catcher.

769

A great one for dates was Miss Thatcher
And many young fellows did snatch her.
 As a matter of fact
 She was scarcely intact
And the next one in line had to patch her.

770

When Max looked at Anne on the tractor
He pulled out his prick to distract her.
She encouraged young Max
So he pulled off his slacks,
And on top of the tractor Max Factor.

771. FASTEN SEAT BELTS!

A vacationing lady named Violet
Took a plane to a far away islet.
She slept sound in her seat
And did not feel the meat
Of the captain, the steward and pilot.

772. HERR DOG

A jungfrau by name of Von Ritter
Was bit by the old herr who smit her.
She discovered the bite
And went looking that night
For the dog of the herr who had bit her.

773

At baseball, a lady named Walls
Disturbed all the fans with her calls.
She was fucked in the bleacher
By a chemistry teacher,
Then the man with two strikes and three balls.

774

Young Sue was prepared to wed Walter;
She walked up the aisle but did falter
For her period was due,
So Walt thrust up her flue
And he fucked her in front of the altar.

775

An incestuous fellow was Watson;
He tackled his aunt in a Datsun.
For an hour he strained
Then his auntie complained,
"I'm afraid that you're in the wrong slot, son."

115

776

There was a young fellow named Watson
Who tried to make love in a Datsun.
    Said his dad, "It's no shame
    If you forfeit the game,
It just matters how well you have fought, son."

777

A fragrant old lady name Wells
Said life with no man is two hells,
    So she said, "I'll go look
    And I'll find me a schnook,
And I don't care how badly he smells."

778. MORE BLESSED TO GIVE

A charitable lady named Wertz
Exclaimed as she lifted her skirts,
    "The *United Foundation*
    Is a poor imitation
Of the way that I give till it hurts."

779

There was a young lady named Wertz
Who lay down and lifted her skirts,
    And she cried out with clarity,
    "This is strictly for charity,
You can give all you have till it hurts."

780. THE BUTCHER DONE IT

There was a young lady named Willet
Whose cunt was as big as a skillet.
    It took four pounds of ham
    And a large leg of lamb
And a length of baloney to fill it.

781

The wily old duchess of Wings
Knew all about birds, bees and things.
    She ignored all the flukes
    Like the barons and dukes,
And she fucked the Plantagenet Kings.

782
There was a young fellow named Winkle
For whom a new ray once did twinkle.
   With his wife he was bored,
   She'd been fully explored,
But he looked and he found a new wrinkle.

783. IN THE ALLEY
There was a young fellow named Yost
Who said that his girl was the most.
   She was sick and half-blind,
   In a wheelchair confined,
But was super when hung on a post.

784
A simple young lady of Ypsi
Was fucked every time she got tipsy
   By the chief of police
   And the justice of peace
And a preacher disguised as a gypsy.

785. BOIL HIM IN OIL!
There was an old chef name of Zimmer
Who had in his eye a strange glimmer.
   With his girl he did toil
   Till she came to a boil,
Then he set her aside just to simmer.

5

Oral Irregularity

786
A lady of joy and adventure
Was fucked by a pervert named Bencher.
    When he left, she had gas
    And a pain in the ass,
Till the doctor removed Bencher's denture.

787
To the doc went the lady allurin',
For her cunt was in need of some curin',
    But the doc licked her twat
    And he said, "You know what?
There is sugar, I fear, in your urine."

788
A simple young girl was beguiled
By suitors who every night dialed,
    And they smiled with delight
    When they kissed her good-night,
But the lips that they kissed never smiled.

789
A musician who went to Beirut
Picked up an old whore while enroute.
    Then he blew like a trumpet
    On the cunt of the strumpet,
While she played on his cock like a flute.

790. JUST DESSERTS
By chance, a young lady named Black
Was born with a tongue in her crack,
    Which left Pierre so distraught
    For he often licked twat,
But he never had one lick him back.

791
A boss with two assholes was Bliss;
His office routine was amiss.
    The reduced dedication
    Was because of frustration,
For they knew not which hole they should kiss.

792
A lonely old lady named Blissit
Oft dreamed of a love life illicit.
    To the milkman, she chose
    Her affair to expose,
But the best that he did was to kiss it.

793. MERIT BADGE
The busy street frightened Miss Blue,
Till Boy Scouts assisted her through.
    She asked, "Can I repay
    Your good deed for today?"
Said the leader, "A blow job will do."

794
A worldly old lady named Blugg
Was floored by an anxious young thug.
    She said to him, "Sire,
    You had better try higher
For I fear you are licking the rug."

795
A young girl that smoked heavy, Miss Bright,
Had a nicotine cunt—'twas a fright.
    A bold fellow from Wheatley
    Learned to eat it discreetly
After licking an ashtray each night.

796
On a date with his girl friend, Young Brose
Placed his head right between her big toes,
    Then went in to his chin
    Where her Kotex had been,
And he thought he was kissing a rose.

797. FAIRY EXCHANGE
While driving, two queers in Calais
Bumped into each other one day,
    So they glared nose to nose
    Then they both exchanged blows,
And they happily went on their way.

798
A dying Lothario named Castle
No longer with problems would hassle,
 So he took a last trip
 To that desolate strip
Which bridges the cunt and the asshole.

799
A lapper of cunts name of Chase
When asked by his girl friend to place
 A kiss on her cheek,
 But he said, somewhat meek,
"I can't—there's no hair on your face."

800
As a man licked the asshole of Claire
She complained in a tone of despair,
 "Will you please try the cunt?"
 And he said, with affront,
"That's a bridge I will cross when I'm there."

801
While preparing a dinner first class,
The chef felt the dishwasher's ass.
 As she spread out her feet
 He proceeded to eat,
And she said, "You are cooking with gas."

802. MISS FERN WINS ELECTION
The mayor at first felt concern
When his fate for the worse took a turn.
 He left, not dejected,
 But proud and erected—
He enjoyed being licked by Miss Fern.

803
A cocksucking lady named Conne
Explained how success could be won:
 "A profession you pick,
 Like sucking a prick,
Then sink in your teeth and hang on."

804
There was a fellow named Crassus
Whose girl was the finest of lasses.
 Once he kissed her good-night
 And her legs closed so tight
That she fractured the frames on his glasses.

805. JUICY FRUIT
When Johnny was dating Diana,
The apples he brought her began a
    Nice custom that pleased her,
    But soon Johnny teased her
Into letting her bite his banana.

806. EAT THE HOLE THING
For a novice, a young lady deft
Dropped her panties, exposing her cleft.
    She said, "Eat your fill."
    He said, "So I will,
But what do I do with what's left?"

807
The pollution inspector, so droll,
Was eating a young lady's hole.
    He ran into a fart
    And he said, with a start,
"We must fix your emission control."

808. THE BROWNNOSER
A simple young fellow, a dunce,
Cared nothing for titties and cunts,
    But he knew all the tricks
    How to satisfy pricks,
For he managed to blow two at once.

809. NO APPLES IN EDEN*
In the Garden of Eden man's fate
Was settled when Eve took the bait,
    But it wasn't an apple
    With which Eve had to grapple,
It was Adam's banana she ate.

810
An ambitious young girl of Fort Knox
Made her money by working the docks.
    There she worked without shame
    By assuming a name—
She was "Fuller" when sucking on cocks.

811

A cigar-smoking fellow named Fox
Would puff on cigars by the box.
    When asked how he started,
    He said, as he farted,
"I started by sucking on cocks."

812. I THOUGHT YOU'D NEVER ASK

To the doctor went old Mr. Frick,
And the nurse said, "Lie down, you look sick.
    "Tell me, what can I do
    Till the doc can see you?"
So he asked her to suck on his prick.

813

A lady of fashion, Miss Glick,
Was asked why she never was sick.
    She replied with reflection,
    "I suck cocks for complexion,
And there's vitamin D in a prick."

814

The fear, said a nurse named Miss Glock,
Of drowning would send her in shock.
    It was known to all folk
    She could not swim a stroke,
But was often found down on the doc.

815. SAVE FACE

To her boyfriend, a lady named Grace
Said her cunthole had rags set in place.
    Said her boyfriend, so grave,
    "Though your cunt we can't save,
You can still find a way to save face."

816

A grisly appearance had Grace
With pustules all over the place.
    She married young Pierre,
    Who said, "I don't care
For I will not be kissing her face."

817

In the cunt of a lady named Grace
By some freak, there a tongue grew in place.
 A lad spread out her thicket
 And he got down to lick it,
But the cunt licked him first in the face.

818

A happy old hooker named Grace
Once sponsored a cunt-lapping race.
 It was hard for beginners
 To tell who were the winners;
There were cunt hairs all over the place.

819

A decrepit old harlot was Grace,
And her cunt was a filthy disgrace,
 But she still made a buck
 Whether planned or by luck,
Since she took a good fuck in the face.

820

A girl had a problem of gravity—
She was born with no vaginal cavity.
 She was no good for fucking
 But was expert on sucking,
And superior for asshole depravity.

821. STRANGE TAIL*

There was a young fairy named Gray
Who dated a Lesbian one day.
 They agreed that they knew
 Who'd do what, how, to who,
But they could not agree who should pay.

822. HOLY DAY

There was a young lady named Grunday
Who fucked every day except Sunday,
 When she rested her box
 By sucking on cocks,
For the Lord's Day must not be a fun day.

823
A determined old harlot named Gwen
Said success comes to those with the yen.
    If at first you proceed
    And you fail to suck seed,
Then by all means you suck, suck again.

824. COCKSICKLE*
A lollipop maker named Hans
Fulfilled every young lady's wants.
    He made candy so slick
    With a head red and thick,
And he flavored it just like a schwantz.

825
There was an old fellow named Hicks
Who dated a girl from the sticks.
    Though they fought over straws
    It was not a lost cause,
For he said he got in a few licks.

826
A practical fellow was Hicks;
On dates he engaged crosseyed chicks.
    He said, "They're no trouble—
    I'm glad they see double,
For they suck what they think is two pricks."

827
There was a queer fellow named Hollow;
In glory one day he did wallow,
    For he chewed a big pecker,
    An enlarged double-decker,
But he found it was too hard to swallow.

828
To the dentist, a fellow named Huff
Showed his teeth, which were worn and so rough.
    "From the wear and the tear,"
    Said the dentist, "I swear
That the cunts which you eat are too tough."

829
An ingenious old fucker named Hunt
Refined the Pinocchio stunt.
    From behind on a lass,
    With his nose up her ass,
He extended his tongue up her cunt.

830
A girl of great height was Miss Hunt;
Her man was a very small runt.
 When in front he did face her
 And reached up to embrace her,
He was faced with a faceful of cunt.

831
There was an old harlot named Hutch;
The price that she charged was not much,
 Yet she knew every action
 Which would give satisfaction,
And was expert on blow jobs and such.

832
There was a young fellow named Jack
Who ate his girl's snatch from the back.
 He developed the art
 Of avoiding a fart,
But got hit in the face with the flak.

833. MAN'S BEST FRIEND
When Johnny was dating Miss Jean,
He complained of her cunt which was green
 And all covered with mold,
 But he soon was consoled—
She got Fido to lick it off clean.

834
A young circus midget named Joe
Was looking for whores in Bordeaux,
 But Joe was demeaned
 When a queer intervened
And he gave little Joe a low blow.

835
At a party one evening in June
They were playing a game, *Hide the Prune.*
 It was hidden by Claire
 But nobody knew where,
Till her pussy was kissed by a coon.

836
To the doc went a lady named Kate,
Her oversize shape to abate.
 Said the doctor, "By chance
 I've some fruit in my pants—
This banana will gain you no weight."

837

A fuck-tax was passed by old Keating
But a check proved the tax self-defeating.
    There was no tax collected
    By collectors dejected,
For the men switched from fucking to eating.

838. NOT HUNGRY

Coming home late at night, Mr. Keaton
Did appear to his wife somewhat beaten.
    She lay down on the bed
    And her pussy she spread,
But he said he had already eaten.

839

While the dentist was drilling young Keith
His assistant reached down underneath
    And she sucked on his cock.
    He went off in a shock,
But felt nothing at all in his teeth.

840

There was a young Scotsman named Keith
Who said to his girl on the heath,
    "What I'd like, Miss MacLouth,
    Is a bust in the mouth."
But she gave him a crack in the teeth.

841

A cautious young fellow named Keith
After feeling a whore underneath
    Said, "Your twat's like a ditch!
    Better suck me, you bitch,
But first you must take out your teeth."

842

The ugly old girl friend of Keith
Was blessed with a poor set of teeth.
    But Keith didn't care
    For her pussy had hair,
And mostly he kissed underneath.

843

An invention produced by young Keith
Was for men that licked girls underneath,
    A most handy device
    Which he sold at low price
For removing the cunt hairs from teeth.

Oral Irregularity

844

"The man that I want," said Miss Kell,
"Will buy dinner and drinks for a spell,
 And with little persuasion
 He will snatch on occasion
A sweet kiss and vice versa as well."

845

A cocksucking lady named Koppers
Had chewed on some oversize whoppers.
 When she sampled the whang
 Of a fellow named Chang,
The fucking thing stuck in her choppers.

846

In Washington, Madam LaBlunt
For her whorehouse prepared a new stunt.
 On her opening day
 She wore a bouquet
While the president ate the first cunt.

847

A teacher of note named Miss Laurel
Taught classes in sex that were moral.
 There were tests through the year
 Which were written, I hear,
But the final exam, it was oral.

848. TONGUE LASHING

A major in language, Miss Lee,
Attended a school in *Paris*
 So she'd master the tongue,
 But she said with head hung,
"I'm afraid that the tongue mastered me."

849. THAT'S THE WAY IT IS IN SWEDEN*

Though the butler proceeded to lick,
He failed to erect the King's prick.
 Said the butler, "Your Majesty—
 Indeed, what a travesty!
How come that my ass does the trick?"

850

A cautious young lady named Liskers
Proclaimed that she only would risk hers
    For a man who was true.
    One man came—not to screw—
But he planted a kiss on her whiskers.

851

There was a young fellow named Lunt
Whose girl had no teeth out in front.
    He said, "I don't miss 'em,
    Her lips, I don't kiss 'em
For mostly I'm kissing her cunt."

852

A man with two tongues name of Luntz
In speaking performed fancy stunts.
    On a flute he could trill
    While he sang with great skill,
Or could lick on two pussies at once.

853

The English professor, MacMeech,
Was fondling a girl on the beach.
    She said, "Shall we fuck?"
    But he said to her, "Suck—
For *fuck* is a figure of speech."

854. LET THEM EAT CAKE

The Queen a new law once did make—
Of pussy no man could partake.
    So the poor did entreat,
    "Tell us, what can we eat?"
Said the Queen, "You can always eat steak."

855

There was a young fellow named Mason
Whose spectacles needed replacin',
    For he lit up a match
    To observe a fine snatch,
But he slipped and fell down with his face in.

856

"Let's try sixty-nine," said McLouth.
"I'll face to the north, you the south."
    So she sucked on his pride,
    But the fucking guy lied
When he said he'd not come in her mouth.

857
To Keith said a girl named McLouth,
"Be nice to us girls from the south,
    Or you'll get, my dear Keith,
    A crack in the teeth."
So he gave her a paste in the mouth.

858
To a lad, a young girl named McLure
Showed her pussy, so sweet and so pure.
    "There's no hair!" the man cried,
    And the young girl, replied,
"It's for licking, it's not quite mature."

859
There was a young fellow named Mellin,
And this is the story they're tellin',
    He spelt cunt with a "k"
    And his reason was, "Say,
I'm much better at eatin' than spellin'."

860
A talented artist named Merritt
Was painting a nude in his garret,
    And he said, with great lust,
    "I must wolf it, I must,
For I fear I can no longer bear it."

861
A stylish young fellow named Nash
Was sporting a gorgeous moustache,
    So his steady girl, Kate,
    Said, "No longer we'll date."
For it roughed up her thighs with a rash.

862
There was a young fellow named Nate
Who went to his girl for a date,
    But her parents were there
    So he sucked off the pair,
Then he cornholed the daughter first rate.

863
A popular athlete was Pete,
A winner who gave fans a treat.
    It was rumored in town
    That he often went down,
But he never went down in defeat.

864
To the lab went the cunt of Miss Phipps;
From whoring she cashed in her chips.
 It was pilfered en route
 By a mailman hirsute,
Who got chancres and sores on the lips.

865
A man and his wife name of Pickett
Had boarded the train with no ticket.
 This made the conductor
 So mad that he fucked her,
And when through he forced Pickett to lick it.

866
At tennis, when playing Miss Pict,
All men were outsmarted and tricked.
 Though she won every day,
 Yet in truth she did say,
 At the end of the day she was licked.

867
A despairing young lady named Plum
Called a fellow and said, "I am glum.
 You don't come when I call."
 But he said, "Not at all,
If you blow the meat whistle, I'll come."

868
A clean-thinking fellow named Potts
Would not entertain evil thoughts,
 So he went everyplace
 With a mask on his face
For concealing his tongue which licked twats.

869
When the Queen asked the King if he'd prick it,
He spent too little time in her thicket.
 The Queen moaned in despair
 For the itch was still there.
Said the King, "Call the Pope—he will lick it."

870
Two fairies got married with pride;
They took all the jibes in good stride,
 But they faced with some fright
 A dilemma that night,
So they flipped to see who'd be the bride.

871

The doctor examined Miss Queen,
The dirtiest whore he had seen.
    He exclaimed, "I have not
    Seen so dirty a twat.
Hold still while I first lick it clean."

872

The new mayor to all did reveal
What was for her cunt the best deal.
    She chose for variety
    The Limerick Society,
For their tongues were adept and facile.

873

When out on a date, Mr. Riffer
Got down on his lady to sniff her.
    When she felt his limp meat,
    She said, "Better you eat,
For a prick is no good 'less it's stiffer."

874

A lady of learning named Roma
Learned much while at school in Tacoma.
    Her instructor had sucked her
    And her principal fucked her
For a *Summa Cum Laude* diploma.

875

Said a fag to a queer named Salome,
"If you think you're so good, simply show me."
    Said the queer, "Why you prick, you,
    I will deck you and dick you
Long before you can throw me and blow me."

876

A stork is a bird, so they say,
Which brings in nine months and a day
    A bundle of joy,
    An infant so coy—
But a swallow keeps babies away.

877

While the dentist was drilling young Schick,
His assistant, so comely and slick,
    Was sucking his cock.
    His tooth felt no shock
But he blew with a pain in his prick.

878*

An ingenious inventor named Schlock
Inventions produced, 'round the clock.
    "Ideas," he said,
    "Will come to my head
When a lady is sucking my cock."

879

A homely young fellow named Schwartz
Was cherished by girls of all sorts.
    He had ears, so I'm told,
    That were easy to hold
And his tongue simply bristled with warts.

880

A Salvation chick named Miss Scott
To save souls of drunkards had sought.
    A drunk in the ditch
    Said, "Help me, you bitch."
So she gave him a lick of her twat.

881

Down the street walking backward went Sears
With his cock hanging out, it appears.
    Said a lady in shock,
    "You're exposing your cock!"
But he said he was trolling for queers.

882

The high price of stamps made one sick,
But the Postal Department was quick,
    And new heights they attained
    With a stamp which contained
A cunt that was pleasure to lick.

883

An old social worker named Shutes
Worked hard to assist prostitutes.
    He spent his last years
    With fairies and queers,
Enjoying the labors of fruits.

884

Said a lady, "How much do I suffer
When my husband, the miserable duffer,
    Eats the crotch in my thigh,
    And when I ask him why,
He says eating an asshole is tougher."

885

A good wife must be thoughtful and sweet
And if husband is late, be discreet.
    Although dinner is cold
    There is no need to scold,
For perhaps somewhere else he did eat.

886

As she sucked on his pecker so sweet,
Said Hines, "What a wonderful treat!"
    She said, "It's not luck,
    For I learned how to suck
By watching the lions gobbling meat."

887

There was a young fellow named Thomas
Who said to his girl, "Let us calm us.
    When the times comes, we'll marry."
    But she was not too wary;
All she got was a lick and a promise.

888

There was a young fellow of Thrace
Who went to his ladyfriend's place.
    She complained, "I am wore
    And my cunt is too sore,
But I'm good for a fuck in the face."

889

A wealthy old midget, Miss Tuck,
Disclosed how she met with good luck.
    She had yawned in a crowd
    Near a man who was proud—
It was there her first low blow was struck.

890. THE SNAKE BITE

A snake bit a fellow named Trout
On the end of his cock, and no doubt
    He would die, but by luck
    His friend said he'd suck,
But more than the poison came out.

[891]

"Keep sucking," said Trout to the guy.
"You can get it all out, if you try."
    Said his friend, in a huff,
    As he swallowed the stuff,
"You son of a bitch, you can die."

892

There once was a zealous old Turk
Who drove all the ladies berserk.
 It was not with his prick
 Which was three inches thick,
But his tongue which he worked with a jerk.

893

A lady, naive and unknowing,
Asked a fellow how long he was going
 To nibble and lick
 While she fondled his prick.
He said until juices start flowing.

894

A harlot was thoroughly vexed
By a man who had left her perplexed.
 In his sordid adventures
 He had lost both his dentures
Which surprised the old man who was next.

895

"When I'm kissing," said Evelyn Waugh,
"It's the cunt of my sister-in-law.
 As my eyes close up tight
 I will hug with delight,
And I dream it is George Bernard Shaw."

896

There was a young fellow named Wise;
The beard that he grew was a prize,
 But his dear wife was pained
 And she loudly complained,
For it terribly scratched up her thighs.

897. DON'T LOSE THE ELECTION

Said a whore to the loser, "Don't yak, son.
I will treat you just like I do Jackson.
 While you're running in front
 You can lick at my cunt—
While you're losing, you lick at the back, son."

6
Buggery

898
The bugger does not make amends;
His action he staunchly defends.
   His approach, though posterior,
   Without doubt is superior
For enlarging the circle of friends.

899. SEPARATE THE MEN FROM THE BOYS
The Grecians are famed for fine art
And buildings and stone work so smart.
   They distinguish with poise
   The young men from the boys,
And use crowbars to keep them apart.

900
There was an old Baron of Basle
Who buggered the Queen in her castle.
   He said to her, "Queen,
   It remains to be seen
If your cunt is as good as your asshole."

901
There was a young fellow named Beard
Whose father's behavior was weird.
   He left home at sixteen
   Never more to be seen;
He did not like the way he was reared.

902
On a trip was the girl of young Beecher
And he was not able to reach her,
   So on Sunday at church
   He conducted research
And proceeded to cornhole the preacher.

903*
There was a young man of Belgrade
Who dated a girl somewhat frayed.
   She said to him, "Jack,
   Try the hole in the back,
For the front one is badly decayed."

904. TURN THE OTHER CHEEK

A frustrated lady of Berne
Had problems that caused her concern
    For she married a Greek
    Who male partners did seek,
And she knew not which way she should turn.

905

There were two young brothers named Bowles
Who buggered each other like moles.
    You could join in their sport
    If you were the right sort;
They rejected the types with two holes.

906. TIME SHARING

To his bride said the groom, Mr. Bowles,
"In your life you will find many shoals.
    To avoid any bind,
    It is best, you will find,
That we give equal time to all holes."

907

The disc jockey said to his bride,
On observing her cunt spread out wide,
    "It appears by the record
    That too oft you've been peckered,
So perhaps we can play the back side."

908

A flat-chested lady named Brown
Was fucked in the ass by some clown,
    So she tattooed her back
    In event of attack
With advice that this side be placed down.

909

A man with a girl named Carruther
Were sure that they'd love one another.
    She dated this Greek
    For a month and a week,
But he first threw the meat to her brother.

910

To a whore said a man named Carruthers,
"I would like to fuck one of your brothers.
    When I want a good screw,
    An old cunt will not do.
I don't travel in ruts made by others."

911. WHEN IN ROME . . .
The pope in his wisdom first class
Advised all the bishops en masse,
     The approved contraceptive
     To which he was receptive
Was fucking the wife up the ass.

912
Best man at the wedding was Clyde;
He had an affair with the bride,
     And the bridesmaids were next,
     But they all were perplexed
When he hustled the groom for a ride.

913
There was an old preacher named Cole
Who did what was good for the soul:
     Pederasty, his game,
     Which he did without shame.
He was good, so they say, on the hole.

914
There was a young lady of Cretchmore
Who found that her asshole would fetch more.
     To her utter dismay
     When she cornholed all day
Both her pussy and asshole would retch more.

915
When St. Peter was fitting young David
With his halo, he ranted and ravèd
     About David's fine ass,
     So said David, "Alas,
Not just father I find is depravèd."

916
A nearsighted fellow named Fender
Said, "Pardner, I think I surrender.
     I've had more than enough
     As the going is tough
And I fear that you are the wrong gender."

917. THE FRUSTRATED BRIDE
The bride to the groom did express
Her sad tale of woe and distress,
     "I've had men in my bed."
     But the groom simply said,
"I have also had men, I confess."

[918]
"Oh dear," said the bride with concern,
"A problem is here I discern.
    It's a bit of a bind
    And it boggles the mind,
For I don't know which way I should turn."

919
On a date with a lad went Miss Flo;
She was asked for a fuck, but said, "No,
    You can go second class,
    Shove your prick up my ass—
I am saving my cunt for my beau."

920
There was a blind fellow named Fretter
Who found the cunt hole with his setter.
    He could tell the right slot
    By the twitch of the twat,
But he claimed that the asshole was better.

921
There were two young brothers named Frood
Who only each other they wooed.
    Though their love was intense
    It was full of suspense
For they never knew which would get screwed.

922
While screwing a harlot, old Gimp
Discovered the bitch falling limp.
    She got sick halfway through
    And began to turn blue,
So he finished the piece with the pimp.

923
The mother was chastising Hammer
For getting behind in his grammar,
    But said Hammer, "I'd rather
    Get it into Grandfather,
And if Grammer don't like it, why damn her."

924. TWO QUEER IRISHMEN
There is a young fellow named Harold
Who oft with two Irishmen carolled.
    He finds them theatric
    For Fitzgerald Fitzpatrick
As well as Fitzpatrick Fitzgerald.

925

There was a queer fellow named Hector
Who sought an affair with the rector.
 What he put in the male
 Got him five years in jail
When picked up by the postal inspector.

926. NAVY SPORT

New sailors on ships have high hope;
Old salts show them how to tie rope,
 And they show them the games
 With the fanciful names,
And they teach them to play *Drop the Soap*.

927. POLITICAL PATRONAGE

"I'm indebted to all," said old Humphrey,
"So I'll offer you whiskey and rum free.
 For my ass there will be
 A most reasonable fee,
And for those without cash, you can thumb free."

928

The noble old Shah of Iran
Said, "Women from courts we must ban,
 For they haven't the clutch
 Or the velvety touch
Of the orifice found in a man."

929

A thoughtful old fellow named Keaton
Observed that his whore was moth-eaten,
 But this man was sagacious
 And he found it more gracious
To depart from the path that was beaten.

930

A fairy who came from Khartoum
Faced life in the depths of deep gloom,
 And he moaned in despair
 That he could not be there
When the Saviour was laid in his tomb.

931
We hail the wise prince of the Kurd
Who fucking dog-fashion preferred.
    He found much more fitting
    The hole used for shitting,
Though he risked an occasional turd.

932
A sordid old whore from Lapeer
Was fucked in the ass from the rear,
    And her pussy smelled sweeter
    For there issued a peter
Which had lodged in her crotch for a year.

933
The chef was an avid young learner;
The maid said his acts did concern her.
    She perceived he had class
    And was cooking with gas,
But she asked him to try the front burner.

934
With Persians, a lady named Lee
Went on a libidinous spree,
    She said, "Heavens above,
    Why the way they make love!
I find that it's all Greek to me."

935. FAMILY AFFAIR
There was a young fellow named Lister
Who said to his dad, "Call me Mister.
    Though I'm just twenty-two,
    I am better than you,
For I've just fucked my mother and sister."

[936]
Though father was somewhat perplexed
He did not appear to be vexed.
    He said, "You can have mother
    Since I've just fucked your brother,
Now prepare, for your asshole is next."

937
To the doctor went old lady Linkter
And he plunged up her asshole and dinked her.
    When she had a conniption
    He explained this prescription
Was not cheap, but was good for the sphincter.

938
A lady was trapped in Madras
In a door that revolved, made of glass.
    By its very construction
    She was saved from destruction,
But was fucked twenty times up the ass.

939. ROYAL BIRTH
While in France, England's King, hunting males,
Fucked a man in the ass in Marseilles.
    When the man shit a turd
    Said the King, " 'Pon my word,
I will christen this turd *Prince of Wales.*"

940
There was a cornholer named Max
Who assholes preferred over cracks
    Since the cock was intended
    For the asshole upended,
Or it would have been shaped like an ax.

941
There was an old bastard named Mott,
By the vilest of fates he was wrought:
    He was born of skulduggery,
    And a product of buggery—
He was born through the ass, not the twat.

942
To his dad said a lad name of Neals,
"I'm aware how a piece of ass feels,
    For I've had my first screw,
    And I'll have some more, too,
Just as soon as my orifice heals."

943
The emperor sat in his palace
Complacently fondling his phallus,
    When he spied the fat ass
    Of the bishop at mass,
So he buggered him twice with his chalice.

944. SHORT-TERM DEPOSIT
A banker, hardpressed, name of Paul,
The handwriting saw on the wall.
    He was broke and demented,
    So his asshole he rented,
With a charge for an early withdrawal.

945
There was a young lady named Plum;
It seems she was smarter than some,
    For when periods were due
    She said, "Don't use my flue,
For a change you can come up my bum."

946. TRUE FRIEND
A companion, sincere and refined,
Is the Persian, the best you will find.
    To the bittermost end
    He remains a staunch friend
Who will not leave his buddy's behind.

947
The smelly old girl friend of Schink
Had a crotch with a terrible stink,
    But he cared not a rap,
    He just turned on the tap
And he buggered the bitch in the sink.

948
With Ernest, Frank stood in high score—
Outspoken, sincere to the core.
    Upon this you could bank:
    Although Ernest was frank,
Yet Frank was in Ernest much more.

949
There was a young man named Sebastian
Who had for his bride a suggestion,
    "Though I'll try for a day
    In the regular way,
We must look at both sides of the question."

950
There was an old fellow of Skokie
Who spent a long time in the poky.
    He spent so many years
    In his cell with some queers
That his asshole was charred and was smoky.

951
She spoke in a tone that was sternest,
"The trouble within me now churnest.
   I know why I was spurned,
   For when my back was turned
I discovered my love was in Ernest."

952. BARGAIN HUNTER
To the harlot, the old chimney sweeper
Complained that her prices were steeper.
   Said the harlot, nonplussed,
   "If for bargains you lust
You will find that the back hole is cheaper."

953
A young Harvard man, sweet and tender,
Went out with some queers on a bender.
   He came back in two days
   In a sexual haze,
And no longer too sure of his gender.

954
There was a young lady named Tweek
Whose pussy was flabby and weak,
   But her asshole was tight
   So she cried with delight,
"I'm so glad that I married a Greek!"

955
There was a young maid unaware,
Who married a sheepherder fair,
   And he said, somewhat gruff,
   "You must learn how to stuff
Both your feet in the hip boots I wear."

956
A sixty-year codger of Wapping
Had figured his wife was worth swapping
   For three maids young and bold
   Who were twenty years old,
And he buggered them all without stopping.

957
There was a young fellow named Watson
Who buggered his girl in a Datsun,
   But he lost this mad scramble
   And his car was a shamble,
And his epitaph said "Well You've Fought, Son."

958
Said the bride on the night of the wedding,
To the groom, as she smoothed out the bedding,
    "Please step out here in front
    And I'll show you my cunt.
I don't like the way your prick is heading."

959
A newlywed lady named White
Said, "Husband, you are not too bright.
    You are not near as slick
    As my dear old dad, Nick."
So he buggered them both the same night.

7

Abuses of the Clergy

960
A collection of stories absurd
Is known as the Lord's Holy Word,
    But a much better use
    For the Good Book abstruse
Would be cleaning up splatters of turd.

961
The wealth of the Pope needs accounting—
He adds to world woes that are mounting
    As he goes to his hoard
    Where his bullion is stored
And there daily he blesses those counting.

962
A nun with a pious affinity
From priests took a course in divinity.
    They were fun to work under
    But it caused her to wonder
If that's how she lost her virginity.

963
There was an old harlot Alsatian
Whose house was the best in the nation.
    An old bishop of yore
    Who loved piece and not war,
Kissed a twat at the house consecration.

964
The whore to the Pope did appeal,
"Save my soul—before Christ I will kneel."
    Said the Pope to the whore,
    "You may go—sin no more.
But be sure when you fuck it's for real."

965
When the bishop's prick failed, it appears
That the nuns were beset with great fears.
    Fifty harlots from Dallas
    And the Queen from her palace
Attended the wake and shed tears.

966

The bishop engaged an assortment
Of hustlers for ribald disportment.
    He observed, "Though I'm thrilled
    By their antics so skilled,
I must censor their vulgar deportment."

967

There was a young lady named Astor
Who first fucked the lads who were faster,
    And then business men
    And the young lads again,
Then the rabbi, the priest and the pastor.

968

There was a young nun name of Babbitt;
No priest had got into her habit,
    Until old Bishop Bart
    Threw her off with a fart
And was in just as quick as a rabbit.

969. BAD HABIT

Said the playful young priest name of Babbitt,
"If I toss you the ball, will you grab it?"
    Said the nun with a smile,
    "I will play for a while,
If you do not get into the habit."

970

A theology student named Baird
Was asked how in courses he fared.
    He said he was screening
    The words with no meaning,
And was expert in double-talk squared.

971

A horny old bishop named Bart
Made buggery a very fine art.
    He performed so superior
    At the papal posterior
That the Pope had no time for a fart.

972. CHEMICAL PEACEFARE
The chemists are working like beasts
Fomenting solutions like yeasts
    To make sprays for the bugs,
    Politicians and thugs,
And a spray to get rid of all priests.

973
The bishop who came from Berlin
Had a cock that was longer than sin.
    When he fucked his nun, Grace,
    It came out through her face
And it splattered all over his chin.

974. THE BISHOP OF BIRMINGHAM*
There were two young ladies of Birmingham,
And this is the story concerning 'em:
    They lifted the frock
    And they tickled the cock
Of the Bishop engaged in confirming 'em.

[975]
But the Bishop was nobody's fool;
He'd been to a fine public school.
    He lowered his britches
    And he skizzled those bitches
With his eight-inch Episcopal tool.

[976]
Then up spoke the lady of Kew,
Who mocked as the Bishop withdrew,
    "The vicar is quicker
    And thicker and slicker,
And he's longer and stronger than you."

[977]
Said the Bishop, "My dear girl, take care.
You were taken, it seems, unaware.
    The vicar's protrusion
    Is but an illusion—
A fake phallus inflated with air."

[978]
All was seen by a nun from the choir,
And it filled her with lust and desire,
    So her habit she lifted—
    But the Bishop, well-gifted,
Took one look and he pulled on his wire.

[979]
It is true that the Bishop of Birmingham
Had diddled these girls while confirming 'em,
For he took down his pants
'Mid liturgical chants,
And released the Episcopal sperm in 'em.

[980]
The clergy of Birmingham last heard
That their broad-minded Bishop got plastered.
The occasion was this:
He was told by a miss
He'd begot an Episcopal bastard.

[981]
But this Bishop did nothing amiss
In conducting these lasses to bliss.
May the Church ne'er unfrock
His Episcopal cock,
But preserve it—a relic to kiss.

982
There was an old bishop named Birch
Who never for women did search.
When the girls came to mass
He would finger their ass
And he fucked all the good ones in church.

983
Each Sunday a harlot named Birch
Was roused by the sermon at church.
The old priest and his choir
Would remove her attire
And proceed to conduct their research.

984. THE RESTORATION
A frustrated bishop was Blaining;
On nuns he was no longer gaining,
So to better his scores
He relinquished his whores,
And from cornholing priests was refraining.

[985]
The artful old priest of North Junction
Corrected the bishop's dysfunction.
Now it's nuns on the grass
And old priests up the ass,
And he fucks without fear or compunction.

986

For the bishop, a nun name of Block
Showed her cunt when she lifted her frock,
    But the bishop drew back,
    "What an unholy crack!
I would much rather play with my cock!"

987

To replenish each Parish Poor Box,
The cardinals held secret talks.
    By Papal Decree,
    For a nominal fee,
Each bishop should suck forty cocks.

988

There was a young fellow named Brechtly
Who said to the preacher, abjectly,
    "Your blessing won't cure."
    But the priest said, "I'm sure
It would work if you used it correctly."

989

A joyful young lady named Brenda
Was born with a double pudenda.
    An old bishop named Lew
    Split his pecker in two
And he fucked her in his hacienda.

990

There was a young lady named Brenda
Who went to the priest's hacienda.
    This old priest was no slouch;
    She had four on the couch
And was not even on the agenda.

991

The fearless old Bishop of Brest
Put his faith in the Lord to the test.
    In the apse he fucked whores
    Who had chancres and sores,
But first they were sprinkled and blessed.

992. CONVERTER CONVERTED

A twat-licking priest name of Bright
Licked twats up and down with delight.
    He was sent overseas
    To convert the Chinese—
Now he licks from the left to the right.

149

993*
A queer missionary named Cavage
Attempted to ravage a savage,
    But the savage was wily,
    He reversed himself slyly
And the savage old Cavage did ravage.

994
"Poor drunk," said a Salvation chick,
"Your choice for the faith must be quick.
    'Twas for you Jesus died."
    But the drunkard replied,
"I did not even know he was sick."

995
A lady of North Chesapeake
Advice from the bishop did seek,
    But he said her pudenda
    Was not on the agenda,
So he scheduled her Thursday next week.

996
An unwary nun named Christine
Walked into the Chapel Sistine
    And there had a shenanigan
    With His Eminence, Brannigan;
Now Christine is no longer pristine.

997
The Pope in regalia first class
Kissed the cunt of a nun from Madras.
    He judged her fair slit
    To be hairy and fit,
So smoke signals poured from his ass.

998. NOW WE KNOW!
The vilest of priests are collected,
Then bishops, archbishops selected.
    From the worst of this scum
    All the cardinals come,
And the Pope from the dregs is elected.

999. NO DIDDLING FOR FUN
Said the Pope, "It's my studied conclusion,
We must clear up the fucking confusion.
    May God's Will be done—
    No fucking for fun!
Every fuck should result in a fusion."

1000. THE BEST PART
As Graham for God madly dashes,
His mind is disturbed by strange flashes.
    He believes, when he dies,
    Like the Phoenix he'll rise,
But his asshole will rise from the ashes.

1001
The Pope spoke on moral decay,
With a nun to exhibit the lay:
    "Lay the bitch on her back—
    Shove your prick up her crack;
By God, there is no other way!"

1002
A rabbi magician of Deever
Could hoodwink the sharpest perceiver,
    For the tricks he could do
    With a foreskin or two
Would surprise the devoutest believer.

1003. RUSSIAN ROULETTE*
Said the Pope, "Contraceptives won't do,
And abortions are sinful things too.
    But there's no need to fret—
    Just use *Rhythm Roulette.*
If you don't want a family, don't screw."

1004
A pious old preacher named Dockery
Put sanctified water in crockery,
    Then he sprinkled the floor
    Where he screwed an old whore
And thus of her profession made mockery.

1005
The man from Basilican Dome
Brought humor to many a home.
    They all gathered to hear
    And by millions to cheer
The great double-talk artist from Rome.

1006
A bashful young preacher, a Druid,
Would run from a nun when pursuèd.
    One kissed him with zest
    Which left him distressed,
And he lost all his seminal fluid.

1007
There was an old bishop named Dunn
Who screwed an old lady for fun.
    Then he wrote her a letter—
    Said her daughter was better
And her mother was second to nun.

1008
The priest lives a good life on earth
While providing a heavenly berth
    At a price for his flock.
    They grow thin as a stalk
While his belly increases in girth.

1009
There was an old slut from the East,
A slovenly foul-smelling beast,
    And so utterly sordid
    That she'd never been boarded,
Except twice by the new parish priest.

1010
There were two young nuns named Elias;
Said one, "I think we are too pious.
    There's a ship in the port,
    We must join in the sport.
Let us see if two sailors will buy us."

1011
The world on a new course embarks—
Let bishops clean toilets in parks,
    And the all-holy Pope
    Should be strung from a rope,
And the cardinals thrown to the sharks.

1012
The bishop no more could endure
The whores on the banks of the Ruhr
    For their cunts were depressing,
    So he gave them a blessing
And the Pope checked each one to be sure.

1013
The discerning old Bishop of Ewing
Observed that his nun had tattooing
    So loathsome and crass
    On her belly and ass
That he wore his dark glasses while screwing.

1014
Now what can a person expect
From people who think they're select,
    And who spend their time drumming
    Jesus Christ's second coming,
When the first one, you'll find, is suspect.

1015
While out for a walk in the fall
The young priest said, "Let's jump that wall
    And we'll each screw a nun."
    but the old priest said, "Son,
Let us walk to the gate and fuck all."

1016
A talented lady named Ferrer
Made love like an unholy terror.
    She met old Father Beecher
    Who was able to reach her,
And he showed that her ways were in error.

1017
A lecherous preacher named Ferrer
Left a nun with a feeling of terror,
    For her belly did swell,
    But he said, "What the hell,
It is merely a clerical error."

1018
John Paul in regalia so fit
Went to Poland to visit a bit.
    His dear land he had missed
    So the good earth he kissed
Where a canine had thoughtfully shit.

1019

There was an old bishop named Fitches
Who ripped off his gown and his britches.
　　With his prick at full length
　　He cried, "God give me strength!"
And he fucked all the saints in their niches.

1020

By the bishop the lady was floored
And her faith in the Lord was restored.
　　Into heaven they went
　　As the two of them spent
A few moments of joy with the Lord.

1021. THE DELINQUENT PREACHER

There was an old harlot named Foster
Who searched for the preacher who crossed her.
　　She requested he pay
　　But his answer was, "Nay,
As a whore you are just an impostor."

[1022]

She called the old preacher a roach
And said that he needed a coach
　　For he'd never be bishop
　　Till he larned how to dish up
A more varied and charming approach.

1023

The horny old bishop of Franktum
Invaded the Pope's inner sanctum
　　Where he beat it to metre
　　'Neath the Dome of St. Peter,
Then he buggered the Pope and he thanked 'im.

1024

There was an old bishop of Franktum
Who checked all the nuns and he ranked 'em
　　As to depth of the twat,
　　Whether cold or how hot,
And the way that they fucked in his sanctum.

1025

In the abbey, a monk name of Fred
Every day would take nuns to his bed.
　　But the nuns did relent
　　On the advent of Lent,
So he cornholed the bishop instead.

1026
There sat a disconsolate friar—
His balls were inflamed with desire,
    For his cock was his pride
    And would not be denied,
So he brought up some lads from the choir.

1027*
The stuffy old Bishop of Galt, he
Was licking a nun that was faulty.
    He said, "Lord, bless my soul!
    So deep is this hole,
I find that the water is salty."

1028
A wily old bishop was Gastard;
New tricks for the Pope he had mastered.
    He checked the Pope's gas
    With his prick up his ass,
But the pope was a bastard and passed turd.

1029
There was an old priest named Geraint;
By the Pope he was made a great saint.
    When he lifted his frock
    He put reins on his cock
And he fucked all the nuns with restraint.

1030
There was a young girl of Gibraltar
Who was to be wed to Sir Walter,
    But old Father McCulpit
    Fucked her twice in the pulpit
As he read her a psalm from his psalter.

1031
The monk at the calendar glances,
Then he picks out a nun and he prances
    With his head bowed in prayer
    To a niche in his lair
And in his retreat makes advances.

1032
There was an old nun name of Gore
Whose cunt was all festered and sore.
    Since she needed some jack
    She sewed tits on her back
And she set herself up as a whore.

1033

There was a young lady named Gression
Who went to the church for confession.
>> She was felt as she knelt
>> By the Bishop of Gelt,
Who confessed to a serious transgression.

1034

For Graham the populace grieves,
And their bosom collectively heaves.
>> For the way people live—
>> It is blessed to give—
But poor Graham, he only receives.

1035. UNMISSIONARY POSITION

An old missionary named Hagan
Once had an affair with a pagan.
>> He was forced to declare,
>> "This unchristian affair
Makes me think that my wife's been renegin'."

1036

There was a young nun name of Hunt
Who swore in her manner so blunt
>> That she lived like a saint,
>> But her lies were so quaint—
You could tell by the wear on her cunt.

1037

A lecherous preacher named Hurd
Some doubts in a young maiden stirred
>> As he patted her rear;
>> She had nothing to fear,
For he solemnly gave her his word.

1038

In the crypt an old priest named Ignatius
Was fucking a Sister flirtatious.
>> He said, "I have often
>> Fucked nuns on a coffin,
But never has one been so spacious."

1039

To the faithful Pope Pius implored
That in heaven they'll get their reward,
>> Then he pulled out his cock
>> And he said to his flock,
"Believe ye in me and the Lord."

1040
There was a young preacher Italian
Who fucked an old harlot named Galion.
    He was so far transported
    By her antics contorted,
That he gave her his holy medallion.

1041. LEFTOVERS FROM STATUES
A sculptor of note name of Jacques
Carved a beautiful tree out of rock.
    'Twas a moral design
    And the Pope liked it fine,
For he hid every leaf with a cock.

1042
There was an old whore of North Junction
Who fucked without any compunction,
    And her fucking went fine
    Till a quarter of nine
When she had a most serious malfunction.

[1043]
She was having a fanciful bout
While she screwed with a preacher devout,
    But his horny old knob
    Was as rough as a cob
And he twisted her twat inside out.

1044
There was an old preacher named Jock,
The best that they ever did clock.
    He was so slick and fast
    That the nuns were aghast;
He wore nothing at all 'neath his frock.

1045
As he spread an old nun, Father Keating
Checked her heart to be sure it was beating,
    Then his head he did bare
    And he said a short prayer,
For he always said *Grace* before eating.

1046
There was an old bishop of Kent
Who never screwed nuns during Lent.
    He said this motivation
    Was from sheer exaltation,
But in truth his resources were spent.

157

1047

There was a young girl of Kentucky
Who said to her man, "You are lucky;
　　I've been out on a binge
　　With the Dean of St. Inge,
And I'm still full of pep and feel fucky."

1048. UNHOLY TRINITY

At the church stood the Bishop von Krepp;
He was eating a nun on the step,
　　While the Pope in a rage,
　　And belying his age,
Fucked the Bishop with vigor and pep.

1049

A novice young priest of Lahore
Saw nuns in the convent galore.
　　He climbed in and defiled one
　　But she was such a wild one
That he stayed to defile her some more.

1050

An old missionary named Lee
Was fucking baboons in a tree.
　　An explorer named Cy
　　Who was passing nearby
Hollered, "Throw in a few fucks for me!"

1051

Said the preacher to prospector Lee,
"You're a sinner, it's quite plain to see.
　　For your own good, I vow,
　　I will save your soul now,
But your ass, I will save it for me."

1052

To the cunt show went old Father Lee
But he could not afford the high fee,
　　So he said in despair,
　　As his ass he did bare,
"I will look at my asshole for free."

1053. PENITENCE
At confession a fellow named Locke
Described to the priest in great shock
    How a cunt he had sucked.
    Said the priest, "I deduct,
For your sin you must suck on my cock."

1054
A big-hearted preacher was Locke;
He won the respect of his flock.
    If a lady discreet
    Let him suck on her teat,
She could suck on the knob of his cock.

1055. UNDER A PALM TREE
The horny old bishop of Lundy,
While itching for ass, sipped burgundy.
    But no nun would consent
    For the period of Lent,
So he palmed it by hand on Palm Sunday.

1056
The lecherous preacher, so lusting,
Entraps the young ladies, so trusting.
    In the Lord's Holy Name
    He teaches them shame,
And that pleasure and joy are disgusting.

1057
There once was a pretty young maid
Who went to the church and there prayed
    Right in front of the priest,
    But he leered like a beast,
And this sweet little maid was betrayed.

1058. PACKAGE DEAL
With a nun lay old Father McKesser,
He proceeded to hug and undress her.
    He said, "Be without fear
    For the good Lord is here,
And I will be your Father Confessor."

1059. CASH DEAL

To preachers, a fellow named Meyers
Said, "Use your own blessings, my sires."
    But they answered, "You'll find
    They are only designed
To be properly used by the buyers."

1060. THE FICKLE FINGER OF FAITH

With his finger, the pious priest Mickel
To confession did beckon Miss Schickel.
    She observed and obeyed
    And she promptly got laid,
So the finger of faith turned out fickle.

1061

A polluted young nun from the mission
Got pregnant and found herself wishin'
    That she'd not gone so far
    With the priest in his car
Till controls were installed on emission.

1062

"Too much," said the priest from the mission,
"For viewing the cunt exhibition."
    So he looked with dejection
    At his asshole reflection,
And he thus saved the price of admission.

1063

When dealing with matters numerical,
Avoid interferences clerical,
    For the preacher's phantasm
    Is a mental orgasm
Which results in solutions chimerical.

1064

There was an old monk named O'Hunt
Who showed a young nun a new stunt.
    On the banks of the Shannon
    He attacked with his cannon,
But she withstood the brunt with her cunt.

1065

The pope in profoundest oration
Disclosed the Grand Scheme of Creation.
    He declared that the soul
    Is conceived in a hole
In the midst of orgasmic vibration.

1066
A rotten old harlot of Oregon
Had thought to be pure to the core again.
　　She sought help from some priests,
　　But they fucked her, the beasts—
She was glad to be back as a whore again.

1067
Miss Master said no man outclassed her;
The pastor, past master, surpassed her.
　　When the pastor had passed her
　　His disaster came faster,
The past master became the passed pastor.

1068
There was an old priest name of Parches
Who took all the nuns out on marches.
　　From a brisk walk around
　　They returned safe and sound,
Then he screwed three or four 'neath the arches.

1069
A priest with facade of great piety
Admonished a maid's impropriety,
　　Then at length he expounded
　　How her life should be rounded,
And he showed her new ways for variety.

1070
After failing the bishop, the Pope
Looked down at his cock without hope.
　　It would no longer rise
　　And he said, "I surmise
That I'm now at the end of my rope."

1071. SHADES OF ONAN
The Pope gave his final position
To those who indulge in coition:
　　"The union is best
　　When by priest it is blest,
And be sure you don't ground your emission."

1072
A simple young lady named Post
Liked Bishop O'Malley the most.
　　When he plunged in his knob
　　She felt such a throb
That she swore she was fucked by the *Ghost*.

161

1073
There once was a neophyte priest
Attending a holy day feast.
    In a trance he went forth
    With his asshole to north
While the nob of his dong pointed east.

1074
There was a young lady professional
Who went to the priest for confessional.
    She confessed to her deeds,
    He professed to his needs,
So they merged in a cubical sessional.

1075. THE CUSTODIAN OF THE FAITH*
The preacher my soul will protect
And my morals he seeks to correct.
    As clean living he preaches
    In my trousers he reaches
To be certain my prick's not erect.

1076
After mass, an old preacher so quaint
On his knees he prayed long to his saint,
    Then he ate twenty cunts,
    Four or five more than once,
Yet from hunger he fell in a faint.

1077
John Paul felt a pang of remorse,
So he set for his Poland a course.
    There he kissed the good earth
    Of the land of his birth,
But ran into the turd of a horse.

1078
The pious old Cardinal Rory
Seduced an old prostitute hoary
    And devoid of all wit,
    But he had to admit
She was good as the Pope in his glory.

1079
The eminent Cardinal Royster
Seduced an old nun in the cloister.
    He said, "Lord bless my soul,
    I have struck a dry hole;
Why, the assholes of popes are much moister."

1080
The capable Bishop of Royster
Was fucking a nun in the cloister,
  But he soon did lament
  And he left her, unspent,
For he felt that she could have been moister.

1081
To the priest a young girl of St. Claire
Her sinful behavior did bare.
  Her wretched confession
  Made such an impression
That he fucked her while kneeling in prayer.

1082
The pompous old Dean of St. Inge
Seduced a fat nun on a binge.
  He was hailed into court
  But he said of his sport,
There were benefits all 'round the fringe.

1083
The pious old priest of St. Moak
Damnation and hell did evoke
  On the sinners that whored
  And broke faith with the Lord;
He went off in his pants as he spoke.

1084
A horny old bishop named Schleft
Plunged his prick in a worn-out nun's cleft,
  But her cunt was so spacious
  That he said, "Goodness gracious!
For a moment I thought you had left."

1085
There was a young lady named Scott
Whose cunt was so terribly hot
  That ten bishops of Rome
  And the Pope's private gnome
Failed to quench the hot flame in her twat.

1086. A FURTHER STUDY OF FURTHER
    STUDY*
Said the Pope, as he read from the Scroll,
While he fondled the Archbishop's hole,
  "We must have further study,
  And then more further study,
And then study some more birth control."

1087
The bishops were tighter than sin
So Cardinal Horst of Berlin
    Kept a jar 'neath his frock
    With some grease for his cock
And a shoe horn to ease himself in.

1088
On the balcony stood the Pope slick
To display to the faithful a trick.
    Every Christmas and Easter
    He would show them his keester,
But today he would show them his prick.

1089
The pious old preacher named Smuts
Rejected the nun of St. Klutz
    When she asked for a screw
    For he said, "If I do
I'm afraid I will pop off my nuts."

1090
A comely young medium, Miss Snaith,
Conjured for the preacher a wraith.
    When she tripped and fell over
    With his finger he drove her;
She was fucked by the finger of faith.

1091. BARGAIN HUNTER
At confession a fellow named Spence
Described his cock-sucking offence.
    Said the priest, "For your wrong
    You must suck on my dong,
But I only will pay fifty cents."

1092
At confession the prostitute spilt
How her fortune on fucking was built.
    Through a hole in the lattice
    The old priest fucked her, gratis,
Which diminished her feelings of guilt.

1093
The rotund old preacher had started
To pray for the dear and departed.
    As he wheezed and knelt down
    He was squeezed by his gown,
So he parted his cheeks and he farted.

1094. COROLLARY
While at stool the old bishop was straining,
He developed a thought entertaining.
    He had proof by the ton
    That a whore could be nun
Without further instruction or training.

[1095]
In answer, the priest of North Junction
Remarked without fear or compunction,
    He had proofs by the score
    That a nun could be whore
Without training or further instruction.

1096
To the Pope, said the Bishop of Strand,
"I've a birth control method so grand.
    The solution, I fear,
    May not be very clear,
But I have it right here in my hand."

1097. STUDY PERIOD
In the Chapel Sistine, old nun Tealing
Described all the frescoes with feeling,
    Which much pleased an old visitor,
    And she told the inquisitor
That when floored, she would study the ceiling.

1098*
For Spellman they've gathered in throngs;
He's gone to the place he belongs.
    If we scale all the heights
    We can't hold enough rites
To atone for his dastardly wrongs.

1099
Said the preacher to naive Miss Todd,
"Your ass you must lay on the sod.
    Take this bible and pray,
    And you'll feel right away
The magnificent scepter of God."

1100*
To the church went the Bishop of Thrace
Where he knelt at the altar with Grace,
    But Miss Grace, who was smart,
    Stood with feet spread apart,
For like Frenchmen, he fucked with his face.

165

1101

Two nuns who were walking the town
Were stopped by a man in a gown.
> They said, "You cannot buy us
> Even if you're Pope Pius."
He said, "That's who I am, so lay down."

1102

The bishop was asked why he tripped
With a nun to the depths of the crypt.
> He replied, "They collapse
> If they're fucked in the apse,
And when fucked in the nave, some have flipped."

1103

There was an old preacher named Tuckem
Who liked little girls and would suck 'em,
> But when cunts were hirsute
> They would tickle his snoot,
So when cunts were hirsute he would fuck 'em.

1104

There were two young ladies of Twickenham
Who asked an old priest to try stickin' 'em,
> But the priest held high mass,
> Put a bib on each ass,
And proceeded with eating and lickin' em.

1105

By the Thames lay the Bishop of Twickenham;
He was straddling a lad and was sticking him.
> But the main thing concering him
> Was the Bishop of Birmingham
Who talked only of pussies and licking 'em.

1106

The girls at the parish of Twickenham
Said the use of foul language did sicken 'em.
> Said the bishop, so pensive,
> "If you find cunts offensive,
Then be sure that you don't stick a prick in 'em."

1107

The venerable Bishop of Twickenham
His youth spent on assholes and sticking 'em.
> After years had elapsed
> His poor prick—it collapsed—
Now his thoughts are on pussies and licking 'em.

1108
A witless young girl of Vancouver
Was vague about bedroom maneuver,
    So her Sunday School teacher
    Made an effort to reach her,
And with faith persevered to improve her.

1109
There was a young girl of Verdun
Who studied to be a good nun.
    It's a matter of history
    That she fucked the consistory
And by bishops the Pope was outdone.

1110
The priest makes an offer vicarial:
Good life in the afterworld aerial.
    And his motto: Don't Sin.
    He gets fat—you get thin.
You will get for your pains, decent burial.

1111
There was an old preacher named Walter
Who read to two nuns from his psalter.
    He seduced novice Destry
    On a chair in the vestry,
And the other he fucked on the altar.

1112
At the church the new preacher of Wheeling
Gave the girls an oration with feeling.
    When he showed them his dong
    Over ten inches long,
All the bells in the church started peeling.

1113
A priest who sniffed panties, named West
His obsession defended with zest.
    This pursuit, he did claim,
    Although not the best game,
Yet in truth it was next to the best.

1114
So large was the hole of Miss Willet,
There was no young man who could fill it.
    She was fucked by a friar
    With a carnal desire,
But he first stuffed her cunt with a skillet.

1115

"I say," said the Bishop of Woking,
"This matter I fear is provoking,
 For the Duchess of Tweekly
 Has her periods twice weekly,
Which leaves me no period for poking."

1116

Said the Bishop of Bonne, " 'Pon my word,
When eating a cunt, it's absurd
 To draw back or to flinch
 For you're clear a full inch
If you come face to face with a turd."

8
Zoophily

1117

There was a young maid acrobatic
Who said in her manner emphatic
    That her best kind of sex
    Was to screw her dog Rex
While she stood on her head in the attic.

1118

There was a horse fancier Adair;
His love with his horse he did share.
    Now he wasn't a queer
    As at first may appear,
For the horse that he loved was a mare.

1119

A man had his maiden agog
And was ready to slip her the log,
    But her dog interfered
    And a crisis appeared,
So he first threw some meat to the dog.

1120

A dog that could speak, once began
To stay from his home for a span.
    Said his trainer, irate,
    "Tell me why are you late?"
Said the dog, "I've been fucking the man."

1121

There was a horse trader named Benny
Who traded his wife for a jenny
    That no louder did bray
    And she made a good lay,
And he claimed that she cost not a penny.

1122

In the movie, the cowboy named Brady
Would look with disdain on Miss Sadie.
    As we all are aware
    He went off on his mare,
Which is what he preferred to a lady.

1123

No fellow could fuck with Miss Bright
For it seems that her cunt was too tight,
     So she called her retriever
     Who sniffed on her beaver,
And he licked on her pussy all night.

1124

A girl who loved pets was Miss Bunky;
She married a vapid young flunky.
     With her dogs he would fiddle
     And her sheep he would diddle,
But he never would play with her monkey.

1125. DOG DAYS

There was a young girl of Calais
Who had seven dogs to display.
     All their names were unique—
     After days of the week,
And she said every dog had his day.

1126

A wistful young lady named Carr
Divulged her perversions bizarre:
     "Though this may sound preposterous,
     I have fucked a rhinosterous,
But the unicorn's better by far."

1127

The dog that we label first class
Is one that won't shit on the grass,
     And he will not be cursed
     If he licks your face first
Before licking his way through his ass.

1128

A circus stunt girl of Decatur
Performed as a crocodile ate her.
     But a skeptic did smile,
     "It was no crocodile,
It was simply a large alligator."

1129. THE BIRDWATCHER

The birdwatcher looks in despair
As birds 'round him fuck everywhere.
    Though he strains through his glasses
    For a view of their asses,
Yet he cannot see what goes in where.

1130

There was a young man named Ducharme
Who spent his whole life on a farm.
    He made love then and now
    To a sheep or a cow,
But he never did girls any harm.

1131

At confession a man from the East
His perversions disclosed to the priest.
    After two drinks, he said,
    He'd take girls to his bed—
After four, 'twas a four-legged beast.

1132

A fisherman queer name of Fife
Preferred screwing fish to his wife.
    Though he wrote a report
    On the fish-screwing sport,
He did not have a porpoise in life.

1133

There was a young lady named Fleegle
Who had an affair with her beagle.
    But she could not have sinned
    For he ran out of wind,
And therefore this act was not legal.

1134

A lonely old maid name of Flock
Was given advice by the doc,
    "Since you're fearful of men
    It must be a dog, then,
And be sure that he has a big cock."

1135

A thoughtless old harlot was Fogg;
It seems that her mind slipped a cog,
    For when business was slack
    She slipped out in the back
Where they say that she put on the dog.

1136

A rapist attacked spinster Fogg
Who was taking her dog for a jog.
    She was left with disgust
    For this man filled with lust,
For it seems he fucked only her dog.

1137

There were two young shepherds named Fox
Renowned for the size of their cocks.
    When at home, in bad weather,
    They would both fuck together—
In nice weather they fucked with their flocks.

1138

There was a sheepherder named Fretter
Who said of his wife, "I'll forget her.
    Though there's much to be said
    For a lady in bed,
I must say that a sheep is much better."

1139*

There was an old lady named Fretter
Who screwed every week with her setter.
    With oleo she greased her
    From Christmas to Easter,
Till she found that real butter was better.

1140

A stalwart young fellow named Galion
Was given the Pervert's Medallion,
    For he buggered a cow
    As he stood on a sow,
While he sucked off a Percheron stallion.

1141

An eminent lady named Galions
Was screwed by a bull and two stallions,
    Then a St. Bernard dog
    And a fine Polish hog,
And a host of assorted rapscallions.

1142

A lonely old trapper named Goggs
Would hunt in the muskeg and bogs.
    He had huskies and sled
    But no woman to wed,
And in time this man went to the dogs.

1143
In bed climbed the dog of Miss Grogg;
This put her young man in a fog.
	When he said to her, "Darling,
	Tell me, why are you snarling?"
She said, "Why are you fucking the dog?"

1144
A skilful young surgeon named Grogg
The pussy removed from a hog.
	In a whore 'twas installed
	And the men said, enthralled,
"This is better than fucking the dog."

1145
An inveterate smoker named Hamal
Was asked had he sampled a *Camel.*
	He replied that he had
	And it wasn't too bad,
But the sheep was a much better mammal.

1146. THE SON LEARNETH
To his son, explained father so harried,
As at intercourse two canines parried,
	"They have learned a fine trick,
	For the one dog is sick,
And it's thus that the sick dog is carried."

1147
The son these fine points did amass
As he watched the two dogs on the grass,
	And he said, "I'm dismayed—
	If you give a friend aid,
He will give you a fuck in the ass."

1148
At the zoo a young fellow named Heeper
Asked the price of a screw from the keeper.
	Said the keeper, "A gnu
	Will be ten bucks a screw,
But the rhino and camel are cheaper."

1149
There was a young lady named Hensley
Who put on a smoker intensely;
	What she did was a shocker
	With her cute little cocker
Who appeared to enjoy it immensely.

1150. THE FREELOADER

There was an old harlot inept
Who broke down one day and she wept,
    For she slept like a log
    And could not catch the dog
Who was eating her snatch while she slept.

1151

While out on the farm, Mr. Jay
Saw a lad fucking pigs in the hay.
    Said Jay, "Why you brat!
    Tell me who taught you that?
Stand back and I'll show you the way."

1152. MOTHER HUBBARD

For Bowser, a lady named Joan
Bent over to pick up a bone,
    But she met with disaster
    For her Bowser was faster,
And he had a big bone of his own.

1153

When Dan and his lady friend kissed
Her Dobermann could not resist
    To get in some licks too
    So when time came to screw
The old bitch was put first on the list.

1154. UNTIL DEATH DO YOU PART

The sheepherder came with his knife
To slaughter a sheep for his wife.
    Said the sheep, "Why you freak,
    It was only last week
That you promised to love me for life."

1155. PUPPY LOVE

On trial was a young man named Krupp
Who raped an old maid and her pup.
    But he stated in court
    That this low, bestial sport
Was a friendship he tried to work up.

1156
There was an old priest of Lapeer;
A pious old man and austere.
    He recited a psalm
    Which would keep the sheep calm
While he buggered the beasts from the rear.

1157
There was a young man of Lapeer,
Renowned as a fine engineer.
    He invented a kit
    So the sheep wouldn't shit
While he made an approach from the rear.

1158
A cute animal trainer, Miss Lee,
Taught her poodle to speak fluently.
    When a man did abduct her
    And he floored her and fucked her,
Said her dog, in tears, "What about me?"

1159
A Montreal madam named Lillian
Had opened an Expo pavilion.
    Six harlots worked there
    With a dog for a spare,
And their clients were over a million.

1160
A prudish young lady named Lynd
Made claims that she never had sinned.
    Her affair with her beagle
    Was considered not legal
For he quit when he ran out of wind.

1161
A dog screwed a lady named Madder
Who stooped as she worked near a ladder.
    'Twas the neighbor's Great Dane
    But her search was in vain
For a hair of the dog that just had her.

1162
Since men were disturbing to Marge
She lived all alone on a barge
    In pure sanctimony
    With naught but a pony,
But they say that his pecker was large.

1163

"This plot," said old farmer McGraw,
"I hold in great reverence and awe,
    For my first piece of ass
    I had here on the grass,
While her mother stood near and said 'Baa.' "

1164

To the madam said old man McNish,
"A fuck that is novel I wish.
    I've fucked sheep, goat and gnu,
    And a jackrabbit too.
Tell me, what do you have in a fish?"

1165

There was a young girl of Milan
Who never had fucked with a man,
    But she fucked in a bog
    With a St. Bernard dog,
A pig and an orang-utan.

1166

Said the smelly old stableman, Morse,
"There's a place for young ladies, of course—
    Not in bed, I declare,
    For they'll never compare
To inserting a cock in a horse."

1167

A fearless young cowboy was Morse;
For women he had no remorse.
    He cared not a whit
    For a cunt or a tit,
He simply went off on his horse.

1168

Said the Saviour to Samuel, "Please note
There is blood of some sort on my coat.
    To the gullible, Sam,
    'Tis the blood of a lamb,
But in truth I was fucking a goat."

1169. AT THE ZOO

At the zoo an old keeper named Phelps
From the lioness seized her two whelps,
    Then he buggered the pair
    And he said, "I declare
They are good, but I can't stand their yelps."

[1170]
His twin brother, a keeper named Mel,
Shoved his prick in a skunk and said, "Hell,
      It is better than scroon
      An old yak or racoon,
But you have to get used to the smell."

1171
There was an old fellow named Pine
Who traded his wife for a swine.
      He remarked with a giggle
      That he got far more wriggle,
And even the dead ones were fine.

1172
Said a girl who was laid 'neath the pines,
"You give a great fuck, Mr. Hines."
      He said, "At the zoo
      I learned how to screw
By throwing the meat to the lions."

1173. VIRGIN WOOL IS FASTER
If you want virgin wool, you must plan
And the flock you must carefully scan.
      Shear the sheep that are fleet
      Which are quick on their feet
And run faster than sheepherders can.

1174
There was a young fellow named Radwan
Whose wife was a mean and a bad one.
      He could stand all the slog
      Making love to a dog,
But he could not make love to a mad one.

1175
There was a young lady named Rote
Who dated a goat-herd of note.
      Though her plan was to marry
      Yet her plans did miscarry
When she found he was getting her goat.

1176
A harlot who came from St. Paul
Was raped by six men in the hall,
      Then sucked off by a dog
      And a prize-winning hog,
But she stayed and she outfucked them all.

1177
While screwing a lamb, sheep-herd Sam
Was seen, but did not give a damn.
    He did not run in fright
    And he said, "I just might
As well hang for a sheep as a lamb."

1178
There was a sheepherder named Sam
Who studied the girls of Miss Pam.
    When he viewed all her hags
    He cried, "Who'd buy these bags?
I would rather be back with my lamb."

1179
If garments of wool clog my sheep,
I set them aside in a heap.
    Let the winter winds blow
    As sheep-fucking I go,
Though the snow may be ever so deep.

1180. CHRISTMAS PARTY
At Christmas a lady named Thrasher
With three drinks got bolder and brasher,
    For she screwed Santa Claus
    And next without pause
She had Donner and Blitzen and Dasher.

1181
Said an old sausage stuffer, Miss Toni,
While stuffing the prick of a pony,
    "When young and much leaner
    I could stuff a small wiener,
But now I can stuff a baloney."

1182
The miner, it seems, undertook
To fucking his mule by the brook.
    He said, "Bless my hide;
    I'd make her my bride,
If only she knew how to cook."

1183
There was a sheepherder named Veep
Affected by sickness called *Gleep*.
    He would run out of gas
    From the lead in his ass,
And he got it from buggering the sheep.

178

1184
"When I'm back in the next life," said Watt,
"A dog's life would be a good lot.
   I would search every day
   And I'd find me a stray,
And I'd sniff on her asshole and twat."

1185*
Nine doctors told poll-taker West
That Camels for them were the best.
   The tenth doctor benign
   Said, "Though camels are fine,
Yet I still feel that women are best."

9

Excrement

1186*
To ride on a tiger's absurd—
I solemnly give you my word—
    For I rode on a tiger
    On the banks of the Niger,
And I found I was changed to a turd.

1187*
When Bert at his job did arrive
A stench in his pants came alive.
    Remarked Jimmy, "My word,
    Though it smells like a turd,
We will call it *Chanel No. 5.*"

1188
At the wedding, so nervous was Bart
That he pissed in his pants at the start.
    When the priest spoke his bit,
    He proceeded to shit,
And the nuptials were sealed with a fart.

1189
The OSHA inspector named Bart
A rectum observed, split apart,
    So he wrote a directive:
    "On The Asshole Protective,"
Which depicted the shape of a fart.

1190
The sparrow and horse have begun
A friendship that's second to none.
    This is proof, I submit,
    That if one can eat shit,
Then two can live cheaply as one.

1191
The ambassador Hermann von Bliss
Said, "Something, I fear, is amiss.
    The terms I projected
    By the Queen were rejected,
For she farted and said, "Here's a kiss."

Excrement

1192

There was a young lady of Butte
Who thought that her fart was so cute,
    But a man in despair
    Was left gasping for air
For a week after sniffing the brute.

1193

At a contest for farting in Butte
A lady's mutation was cute.
    It won a diploma
    For fetid aroma
When three judges were felled by the brute.

1194

At a meeting appeared old man Carter,
He let a big fart as a starter.
    Then he talked for a spell
    But no person could tell
The orifice which was the smarter.

1195

So glib with his tongue was old Carter
No man with his mouth appeared smarter,
    And what issued, ethereal,
    From that venthole sphincterial,
Transcended the farter from Sparta.

1196

To the doctor went old lady Castle,
And he stuffed up her ass with a tassel.
    When she asked him the reason,
    He replied, amidst wheezin'
"I have plugged up the leak in your ass'le."

1197

The farter from Sparta had class,
And many awards did amass,
    But a fellow named Carter
    Was a much better farter
Who could whistle a tune with his ass.

1198

In the pew the old Duchess of Corning
Let a fart without noises adorning.
    Said the bishop, with poise,
    "Please incorporate noise—
It would help if you gave me a warning."

181

1199

A sorry young fellow was Dan;
He smelt like an old garbage can.
   He remarked, so morose,
   "I was standing too close
When the feces was flang at the fan."

1200*

Though Gable was well disciplined,
With Vivien he farted and grinned.
   The farting left Vivien
   In a state of oblivion,
So Vivien was *Gone With The Wind.*

1201

When the bride let a terrible fart,
The bridegroom jumped back with a start.
   He said the profusion
   Of this fetid effusion
Was fouler than yesterday's tart.

1202*

The farmer his horses had haltered
And went to the privy, but faltered.
   When he lost all control
   He fell into the hole,
And he found that his future was altered.

1203

A bridge-playing lady, Miss Harte,
Proceeded her cheeks both to part,
   And she tried to pass gas
   But a turd she did pass
Which finessed her right out of a fart.

1204

There was a young lady named Hartz,
Well-known for her wind-breaking arts.
   She produced such a noise
   That she won, with great poise,
An Olympic medallion for farts.

1205

There were two young twins name of Hartz
Exactly alike in all parts.
   No one knew which was who,
   But their mother, she knew.
She could tell them apart by their farts.

1206
A chemist inventor named Hartz
Stopped odors from underarm parts,
    And he's now on the brink
    Of producing a drink
Which imparts a fine flavor to farts.

1207
The dignified Duchess of Howell
Examined the turd from her bowel,
    And she said, rather miffed,
    That she never had sniffed
An odor so fetid and foul.

1208
In his septic tank fell Mr. Hurd,
And his wife fell in too, how absurd.
    In their will they had stated
    That they should be cremated,
But it seems that they both were interred.

1209
A mathematician named Hurd
Did prove, if you shit a square turd,
    That the pain and the strain
    Will effuse through the brain,
And your vision is apt to be blurred.

1210
A limburger lover was Keyes;
His wife said to him, "Charlie, please,
    When you open that cheese-jar
    Shove a plug up your beezbar,
For I can't tell your farts from that cheese."

1211
There was a food faddist named Keynes
Who only ate carrots and beans.
    At night on the prowl
    He could see like an owl,
But he farted all day in his jeans.

1212
While lost in deep thought, Dr. Krantz
Emerged from his lab in a trance.
    To the toilet he went
    But forgot his intent,
And imprudently shit in his pants.

1213
A gifted musician named Lorne
Was jammed in the ass with a horn.
    He ate beans and got started
    And the whole night he farted
And blew taps right from midnight till morn.

1214
A flatulent lady was Mame;
Her delicate farts won her fame,
    But her husband, the shit,
    Was devoid of all wit
For to him all her farts smelt the same.

1215
A flatulent whore name of Mame
Broke wind without feelings of shame.
    Her farts were so rotten
    They were never forgotten,
For she honored each fart with a name.

1216
From the fart that was let by McNair,
The doc was left gasping for air.
    Between panting and wheezes
    Said the doctor, "By Jesus,
We must send you to heavy repair."

1217
There was a young fellow named Mel
Who had such a terrible smell,
    When he walked, you'd see where,
    From the crud which was there
That would hang in the air for a spell.

1218
There was an old farter named Mel
Who claimed that his farts had no smell.
    The doc checked his ass—
    Got a whiff of his gas—
And concluded Mel's nose went to hell.

1219
There was an old monk monasterial
Whose farts were so pure and ethereal
    That a panel of judges
    Passed wind on the smudges
And they judged him Olympic material.

1220
There was an old fellow named Newman
Whose wife was left angry and fumin'.
   He was told to take care
   Where he vented his air,
But to air, he said stoutly, was human.

1221
The gourmets in dining take part
And together enjoy the chef's art.
   But farting is fun,
   So when eating is done
They should gather together to fart.

1222
The doctor examined the parts
Of a sickly old fellow named Hartz,
   And he said, "I can't see
   What your illness can be,
For you're letting some fine healthy farts."

1223
There was an old lady named Pitt
Whose dog was large, healthy and fit.
   All the neighbors did fear
   If she wandered too near
When she took her dog out for a shit.

1224*
A farter who lived in Rangoon
With his asshole could blow a fine tune.
   He played with perfection
   A Mozart selection
By farting the part for bassoon.

1225
A confident fellow was Ray,
He smiled and broke wind and was gay,
   But his smile turned out sickly
   And he left rather quickly
For he shit and he said, "Not my day."

1226. COMPATIBILITY
There's no need to live in remorse
For two can live cheaply, of course.
   Choose a partner with care
   And you'll sing, I declare,
Like the sparrow who shares with the horse.

1227

There was a smart fellow named Retwun
Who laughed a big laugh as he let one,
  Then he smiled at the blast
  But his smile did not last
For the fart that he let was a wet one.

1228

In Tacoma a lady named Roma
Let a fart with such fetid aroma
  That her panties corroded
  And her asshole eroded,
But it won her a fine arts diploma.

1229

So loud was the farting of Scheering
That he had to fart in a clearing.
  As he phoned in Duluth
  He did fart in a booth,
And he never recovered his hearing.

1230

The gourmets at dinner all sit
Enjoying the food fine and fit.
  But excreting is fun,
  So when dinner is done
They should gather together to shit.

1231

A man turned his head to the sky
And said, as a bird flew on high:
  "This manifestation
  Is God's great creation!"
But the bird dropped a turd in his eye.

1232*

The asshole's exceedingly smart—
It is tuned to a fine state of art.
  It can blow a sweet tune
  Or can blast a monsoon,
Or distinguish a turd from a fart.

1233

There was a young fellow who started
To fuck with Miss Cash, but she farted.
  He said, "I'm a fool.
  Her farts foul my tool."
So the fool and Miss Cash were soon parted.

1234
In the heart of a lady there stirred
A joy for which there was no word.
    As the feeling progressed
    She farted with zest,
And thoughtfully dropped a fat turd.

1235
An old fortuneteller, Miss Toole
Would ride into town on her mule,
    And your fortune she scanned,
    Not by reading your hand,
But by pondering the twist in your stool.

1236
There was a young boxer two-fisted;
Too long in the game he persisted.
    He received such a clout
    That his ass was knocked out
And his turds came out warped and some twisted.

1237*
There was a young lady of Wheatley
Who perfumed herself so discreetly.
    From her head to her toes
    She offended no nose,
But her rectum, alas, smelled less sweetly.

1238
There was a young lady named Wigger
Who ate like a bird for her figure.
    From the size of her turd
    I'm afraid that the bird
Was an elephant bird or much bigger.

10
Gourmands

1239
An intrepid old man of Azores
Engaged one of the dirtiest whores.
    In her twat was a blight
    Which he licked with delight,
And he fucked all her festering sores.

1240
At a contest for bakers, Chef Bart
Took first with his prizewinning tart.
    He embellished it nice
    With snot, shit and spice,
And he topped it by whipping a fart.

1241
Two cannibals out in Bengal
Were eating a preacher named Paul.
    "How's it going there, Fred?"
    Said the man at the head.
Said the other, "I'm having a ball."

[1242]
The first fellow stood up aghast,
Observing his comrade's repast.
    "Slow down," he said, "Fred,
    For I'm still at the head.
I'm afraid that you're eating too fast."

1243
There was a cocksucker named Bentley,
Renowned for his art prominently.
    It was quite an adventure
    For he took out his denture
And he beat with his gums very gently.

1244
When Jane viewed the prod of young Bert,
She cried, "Oh my God, will it hurt?"
    But Bert lit a match
    And ignited her snatch
And went down for the flaming dessert.

1245. BY THE EARS
A comely young lady named Bricker
With men was decidedly slicker,
    For she knew how to tease 'em
    And the tricks that would please 'em,
And knew how to hold on to her licker.

1246
As they rode to the top, Mr. Brown
Slipped his prick 'neath the young lady's gown.
    When they reached the top floor
    She requested some more,
So she asked if he'd like to go down.

1247
A pedantic old teacher, Miss Brown,
Brought class to the young lads in town.
    She taught Pierre to aspire
    To seek things that were higher,
But Pierre, he did fail and went down.

1248
To her boyfriend a lady named Brown
Remarked that her mother did frown
    On screwing when dated,
    So the young lady stated
That the best she could do was go down.

1249
The clues were examined with care—
The body, the bones and the hair.
    The sleuth did surmise
    That the lady's demise
Was due to a lion or to Pierre.

1250
There was a young fellow named Case
Who entered a cunt-lapping race.
    He licked his way clean
    Through Number Thirteen,
But he slipped and got pissed in the face.

1251
The TV all people confronts
With food-selling gimmicks and stunts,
    And they peddle with passion
    The low-caloried ration,
But they never show men eating cunts.

1252
Ten men who were shipwrecked connived
To find food until searchers arrived.
    Nine had morals and pride
    And these poor fellows died,
But the cocksucker, Pierre, he survived.

1253
A sea-loving girl of Decatur
Went out to the sea on a freighter.
    On her very first date
    She was ate by the mate,
But the captain was first man to mate her.

1254
When Flynn kissed a girl, he kissed deep
And left her collapsed in a heap.
    This he learned in Australia
    By sniffing the dahlia
And biting the balls off the sheep.

1255
There was a musician named Drife
Who knew how to live a good life,
    For he buggered Veronica
    While he played his harmonica,
And he ate her while playing his fife.

1256
An eater of pussy was Durham;
His wife had a mind she would cure him.
    She spread limburger cheese
    On her pussy and knees,
And she figured that this would deter him.

[1257]
But he was a man of great pride;
He took all of this in good stride.
    Since the flavor was right
    He ate her that night
With crackers and beer by his side.

1258
There was an old butcher out East
Who cut off men's peckers deceased.
    They were tied with fine braids
    And sold to old maids—
It's amazing how business increased.

1259
She opened his zipper to feel it
And his trousers fell down to reveal it.
    She said, "I must eat
    This banana so sweet,
But first I believe I should peel it."

1260
A sensible, stalwart young fellow
Went into a third-class bordello
    Where he ordered four whores
    All with chancres and sores,
And he ate them like strawberry Jell-O.

1261
There was a pipe-smoker named Flock
Who puffed on his pipe 'round the clock.
    Though his girl friend did miss him
    Yet she hated to kiss him;
She would much rather suck on his cock.

1262
To her man, said a lady named Frood,
"Your manners are uncouth and crude.
    Though you gobble your dinner
    Like a famished muleskinner,
Don't you gobble my snatch like your food."

1263
For busy young typist, Miss Fry,
Advancement no boss could deny.
    To the top she did climb
    Just by coming on time
And by eating her lunch on the fly.

1264
A merry fruit-picker of Gary
Was thrilled when he tried Mary's cherry
    On the day before Christmas
    On the Panama Isthmus,
So he shared his banana with Mary.

1265
So busy a lawyer was Gene
He passed up his wife's fine cuisine,
    But his wife, so sedate,
    Painted cunts on his plate,
And now daily he licks his plate clean.

1266
"I'm wearing my Kotex," said Gert,
"So you can't stick your prick 'neath my skirt."
    Said her boyfriend, "So what,
    I can still eat your twat,
And the Kotex I'll have for dessert."

1267
The butcher's apprentice, Miss Gossage,
Observed on her cunt a green moss edge.
    Said the doctor, "How quaint,
    From a man's meat it ain't,
And it tastes just like smoked liver sausage."

1268
When making banana cake, Joel
Put fruit and two eggs in the hole
    'Tween two legs and proceeded
    To cream nicely as needed,
And he finished by licking the bowl.

1269
To Harry, a lady named Kibbel
Remarked, "I'm not prone here to quibble.
    If you spread my limbs, Harry,
    You can have a sweet cherry,
And your hairy banana I'll nibble."

1270
While licking the ass of King Kivel
The duchess came out with some drivel.
    She ran into a turd
    And she said a bad word,
So he told her to keep her tongue civil.

1271
As he entered the lift, Mr. Kropp
Was aroused and his pecker did pop
    Through his fly, and was felt
    By a young lady svelte—
She went down as they rode to the top.

1272
To the druggist, a man of Lapeer
Said, "You've cunts made of rubber, I hear."
    Said the druggist, "We do.
    Shall I wrap one for you?"
He said, "No, I will eat it right here."

1273
A gourmet type fellow named Linus
Was expert at eating vaginas,
　　But he made a bad slip
　　And ate one that did drip,
And contracted a bad case of sinus.

1274
On his girl a young gourmet named Lissing
Put whipped cream on where she was pissing,
　　And on this spot hairy
　　He added a cherry,
For that was the thing that was missing.

1275
If you lose all your teeth through bad luck,
You must meet your sad fate with great pluck.
　　When you face your next treat,
　　Do not flinch or retreat—
If you find you can't chew, you must suck.

1276
There was a food faddist named Luntz
Whose theory on foods brought forth grunts,
　　For his treatise complete
　　Showed you are what you eat,
Which is obvious, for some men are cunts.

1277
A fortune awaits the bold man
Who knows how this business to plan:
　　He will step out in front
　　With a foam rubber cunt
Which will sell in a vacuum-sealed can.

1278. DAIRY TREAT
The dairy bar waitress named Mary
Was all out of milk for young Harry,
　　So she stripped her brassiere
　　And said, "Harry, come here,
You can get it direct from the dairy."

1279
Some men have a taste hard to match;
The feeblest excuses they'll hatch.
　　They will raise a big stink
　　For a hair in their drink,
But think nothing of eating a snatch.

1280
A meat packing plant out in Natchez
Sold hot dogs in increasing batches.
    Though small, they would rise
    And would double in size
When stuffed in the counter girls' snatches.

1281
In a meat plant a butcher named Nick
Introduced a cost-saving plan slick:
    A new hot dog treat,
    More taste and less meat,
Which he found after sucking a prick.

1282*
While dining, a fellow named Nick
In his stew found an elephant's prick.
    Said the waiter, "Don't hunt,
    Someone just found a cunt;
If you're nice he might give you a lick."

1283
There was a young man named O'Dare
Who maintained his teeth in repair.
    After eating a snack
    He would brush front and back,
But the brush that he used was for hair.

1284
There was an old fellow named Papp
Who cared not for women a rap.
    His profoundest delight
    Was achieved on the night
That he gobbled a joint with the clap.

1285
There was a twat-licker named Parr
Who sometimes with assholes would spar.
    One hole he did lick
    With shit an inch thick—
He had gone, it seems, one bridge too far.

1286
A moral young lady named Pease
Stuffed her pussy with lunch meat and cheese.
    A man took her to bed
    And he ate it with bread
And he said, "Pass the beer, if you please."

1287*
There was a young gourmet named Pete
Who gave a fair maiden a treat
 While he ate at the "Y,"
 So she said to the guy,
"Do you mind if I smoke while you eat?"

1288
In a meat packing plant, butcher Pete
Implemented a savings plan neat.
 After sucking a prick
 An idea came quick—
Bigger hot dogs he made with less meat.

1289
While painting his model, old Pete
Observed how she spread out her feet
 To expose her vagina.
 So he said, "Angelina,
I must go to the kitchen to eat."

1290
A newlywed man of Racine
Made fucking a daily routine.
 Many times he would lay
 Through the night and the day,
And his dinner he ate in between.

1291. TOCCATA FOR ORGAN
When Bach strayed too far, he repented,
For hunger pangs gnawed and tormented.
 By luck passed a maid
 And her crotch she displayed
And thus was the Bach's lunch invented.

1292
From the office came newlywed Scott
While upstairs his wife waited, distraught,
 And when he got inside,
 Down the handrail she'd slide
To prepare him a meal that was hot.

1293
While dozing, a fellow named Scott
Had illusions of eating a twat,
 But when he arose
 He was picking his nose,
And he found himself eating the snot.

1294

There was a young fellow named Scott
Who found the great thrill that he sought.
  A whore was festooned
  With sores, and she swooned,
So he ate all the scabs off her twat.

1295

When purchasing cheese, Mr. Scott
Would examine with care the whole lot.
  He would make a selection
  When he got an erection
From the cheeses which smelled like a twat.

1296

A Japanese girl cooked some squid
And made a fine meal for young Sid.
  She said no one could beat it
  And she begged him to eat it,
So he got on his knees and he did.

1297

The vending machine made by Steiner
Made profits from New York to China.
  A dime got you Cokes,
  And a quarter bought smokes;
For a buck you could eat a vagina.

1298

The aroma of well-heated stew
Was praised by the head of the zoo.
  He fished from the back
  The balls of a yak,
And also a phallus or two.

1299

While the waitress was serving the tray,
She was flashing her cunt such a way
  That a diner named Bert
  Said, "I'll eat for dessert
A fresh cherry split à la toupee."

1300

At the whorehouse, old handyman Watts
Would make up the customers' cots,
  And when harlots were through,
  Just for something to do,
He would lick out their assholes and twats.

1301. BOX LUNCH?
A careless young bride name of White
The dinner had burned in a fright.
Soon her husband was due
And she cried in a stew,
"I wonder what he'll eat tonight?"

1302
A girl that loved cooking, Miss Wise,
Made a meal that would win a first prize.
She invited young Hunt
But he first ate her cunt,
Then her asshole and all her French fries.

11

Virginity

1303
A fervent young lad set aflame
An elderly spinster named Mame,
    So she took out her pad
    And she said to him, "Lad,
Tell me what is the name of this game?"

1304
There was an old maid of Algiers
Who was raped by two young cavaliers.
    She had never been screwed
    But knew how to be lewd;
She had practiced the motions for years.

1305
There was an old lady aloof
Who thought that old Rufe was a spoof.
    To his penthouse she went
    With this harmless old gent,
But old Rufe on the roof gave her proof.

1306
An elderly lady aloof
Gave a ride to a lad as a spoof.
    He ravished her neat
    In the front and back seat
And he buggered her twice on the roof.

1307
There was a young lady named Astor
Who claimed that no man was her master.
    She had a long drink
    With a fellow named Brink,
And by Brink she was led to disaster.

1308
An elderly spinster suspicious
Was raped by a man that was vicious.
    She came out of a faint
    To file a complaint,
But she said the whole thing was delicious.

1309
There was a young fellow named Baker
Who had an affair with a Quaker.
　　The things she partook
　　Were not in the Good Book,
But he never was able to shake her.

1310
A furnace repairman named Bates
Examined a spinster named Yates.
　　He thrust up her flue
　　Like the chimney sweeps do
And the clinkers he cleaned from her grates.

1311
There was a young girl of Beirut
Who swore she had never been put.
　　She said on her honor
　　No hand laid upon her,
But it looked like some man laid his foot.

1312
There was a young fellow named Ben
Who raped an old maid in her den.
　　It was three weeks of hell
　　'Fore she felt very well.
She said, "When can we do it again?"

1313
A frigid old lady named Bogg
Had a pussy as cold as a frog.
　　A man with dispatch
　　Lit a flame in her snatch
When he slipped her a heat-warming log.

1314
An adamant lady named Boker
Had claimed that no fellow could stoke her.
　　She was stoked by the iron
　　Of a fireman named Byron
And he stoked her so well it did choke her.

1315
A lonely old lady named Boyd
Of charm and allure was devoid,
　　So her search was in vain
　　For a man to ease pain
Who would help her to fill up the void.

1316

A frigid young lady named Bryce
Thought sex was a low form of vice
   Till she met Captain Baker
   Who had sailed an icebreaker,
And he ploughed a wide path through the ice.

1317

A happy young bridegroom was Cass,
Much pleased that his bride was first class.
   She was virgin and true
   And her cunt was brand new,
For she took all her fucks up the ass.

1318

A ravaged old spinster did chafe
Till officers caught rapist Rafe.
   They threw him in jail
   But the spinster made bail.
"Thank God," she exclaimed, "that you're safe!"

1319

By luck an old spinster named Chape
Recorded the sounds of her rape,
   All the grunting and wheezing
   And the sighs and the squeezing,
And she now has his pants all on tape.

1320. SLOW LEARNER

While out for a walk, old Miss Clark
Was savagely raped in the dark,
   But her neighbors discerned
   That no lesson was learned,
For she takes the same path through the park.

1321

When Mary went out to the coast
She'd write to her mother and boast
   She behaved very well,
   But her belly did swell
And she swears she was fucked by the Ghost.

1322

A young man raped a lady named Cole
And it tickled her heart and her soul,
   So she ran home and said
   To her dear husband Fred,
"All these years we have used the wrong hole!"

1323. THE CURE FOR DEPRESSION

A lady depressed was Miss Crockett;
Each eye was sunk deep in its socket.
    Said the doctor, "I'm sure
    I can find you a cure,
And I have it right here in my pocket."

[1324]

In his pocket she placed her hand bony
And she said to the doctor, "You phony,
    Can this shriveled-up weiner
    Reconstruct my demeanor?"
But it grew to a full-length baloney.

[1325]

"Lie down," said the doc to Miss Crockett,
"I wish to examine your socket."
    Then he spread her legs wide
    And got on for the ride,
And he blasted away like a rocket.

[1326]

Soon Miss Crockett's depression was gone;
With a light that was bright her eyes shone.
    The baloney was in
    All the way to her chin,
And he fucked her right through until dawn.

[1327]

The doctor then gave her advice—
One treatment would never suffice.
    To insure some protection,
    A baloney injection
She must take every week, once or twice.

[1328]

After having this wonderful tilt
Miss Crockett had feelings of guilt,
    So she went to a priest
    Who was hung like a beast
And he straightened her out 'neath the quilt.

1329. LOOK FOR THE BEST

Advice from a spinster named Crowe,
Be wary of places you go,
    Since man, you will find,
    Has rape on his mind,
And it's best to be raped by a pro.

1330
There was a young lady of Dallas
Who never knew what was a phallus,
    So a fellow named Broder
    Took his pants off and showed her,
And she took it in stride without malice.

1331
A young engineer did debase
A hardy young virgin of Thrace.
    He got into her crevice
    With a lever and clevis
And a crowbar beside, just in case.

1332
To the doc went a maid in dejection;
He examined her twat with reflection.
    "What you need is a screw
    For that pussy brand new.
I'll prescribe you some love and erection."

1333
A simple young lady, devout,
While screwing a lad, had some doubt.
    Though she whined of the sin
    When he dared put it in,
She said shame if he dared take it out.

1334
A visit was paid to the Dr.
By a grouchy old spinster, Miss Pr.
    She lay on the couch
    And no longer did grouch
For the Dr. unfr. and fr.

1335
A moral young girl from the East
Rejected a cunt-struck young beast.
    She'd avoid an affair
    And her cross she did bear
Till her fuck-hole was blest by the priest.

1336
A lady depressed was Miss Finches;
She'd been in too many tight pinches.
    Said the doctor, "You'll find
    I've a cure for your bind.
I will sink in my shaft for six inches."

1337
A simple old spinster named Fitches
Was raped by two mean sons of bitches
 While she knitted a sweater,
 But her pussy felt better
And she never dropped more than two stitches.

1338
There was an old lady who flipped
And lived all alone in a crypt,
 All because flies she hated
 With a hate unbated,
Until one day a fly she unzipped.

1339
A frigid young lady named Fox
Resisted young men of all walks,
 But what thawed out her body
 Was a double hot toddy
Which was followed by two on the rocks.

1340. TAKE MEDICINE WEEKLY
There was an old lady of France
Who said to the doctor, "Perchance,
 Can you cure my depression?"
He said, "Yes, in one session,
And the cure is right here in my pants."

[1341]
Said the maid after taking the cure,
"Depressions I cannot endure.
 Just for added protection
 I will need an injection
Every week without fail to be sure."

1342
There was an old spinster named Frances
Who hoped for improper advances,
 So she went on the pier
 Without pants or brassiere—
There was no need to take any chances.

1343
There was an old maid name of Frick
Who said to the doc she was sick.
 The doc was no slouch;
 He said, "Lay on the couch."
And he cured her complaint with his prick.

1344

In courtrooms the ladies all gaped
At trials where the rapist escaped
　　But was caught and then judged,
　　And the spinsters begrudged
The most fortunate girl who was raped.

1345

A misinformed lady was Gertie;
She had her first fuck at age thirty.
　　So she said, "It is clear
　　That my mother was queer,
For she told me that fucking was dirty."

1346

The noted psychologist Gluck
Observed that some ladies were stuck
　　In the depths of depression,
　　So with learned discretion
He taught the old bitches to fuck.

1347. WITH THE FIRE HOSE

A spinster left burning with grief
Had been partially raped by a thief.
　　By a matter of luck
　　She observed a fire truck,
And the flame was put out by the chief.

1348

A happy young bridegroom was Hadley
And in love with his bride very madly,
　　For she married, in fact,
　　With her cherry intact,
But her asshole was worn very badly.

1349. THE UNSEAMLY SEAMSTRESS

In a bind was a seamstress of Hasting—
She spent her time sewing and basting.
　　It was needles to say
　　She did not mend her way,
Sew it seams that her hole life was wasting.

1350
A nervous and flustered Miss Hewitt
Was given advice by Doc Bluett,
    "Take these birth control pills,
    Which are not for your ills,
But what goes with these pills will sure do it."

1351
There was an old maid of Hoboken
Who sued an attacker outspoken
    Who had threatened to rape her,
    But he robbed and escaped her,
Hence his verbal agreement was broken.

1352
An unprincipled fellow was Jack;
On a spinster he leashed an attack,
    But the spinster was calm
    And she said with aplomb,
"I'll be ready whenever you're back."

1353
A hardy old spinster named Jane
Was raped by a man on the train.
    She enjoyed it so much
    He could scarce break her clutch,
So he fought his way free with his cane.

1354
In Lachine lived an old maid named Jean;
She was raped as she passed a ravine.
    She was left much deranged
    For her will was arranged
To construct more ravines in Lachine.

1355. TAT FOR TIT
There was a young man in a jeep
Who raped an old maid name of Heep.
    He was raped the next day
    By Miss Heep, who did say,
"What ye sow, my young lad, ye shall reap."

1356
The doctor, for old spinster Kieful,
Prescribed a young man for life gleeful.
    By the druggist 'twas filled
    And Miss Kieful was thrilled;
She came running right back for a refill.

1357
Returning home late, old Miss Knight
Would shiver and shake with great fright,
 Not from fear that some man
 Would attack as she ran,
But from fear that perhaps no man might.

1358. KNIGHTLIGHT
Attacked was a lady named Knight;
Her plight was soon changed to delight.
 She was screwed in the dark
 By a man who had spark,
And that is where Knight saw the light.

1359
A gentle old lady named Krauss
Was robbed and debauched by a louse,
 Which brought forth tears galore
 From the spinster next door,
For she knew that she bought the wrong house.

1360
A cautious young lady named Kropp
Used a cork in her cunt for a stop,
 But she caused undue strain
 When she drank some champagne,
And was fucked when a man heard it pop.

1361
There was an old spinster named Lakme
Who prayed to the Lord, "You must back me.
 You did not give me features
 To attract the men creatures;
You must help some young lad to attack me."

1362
There was an old lady of Lissing
Who discovered what she had been missing.
 She was fucked on the sod
 And she cried: "Oh, my God!
All these years it was just used for pissing!"

1363. NOT TOO LONG
A moral young lady named Lynn
Rejected an offer to sin,
　　But she said, when young Decker
　　Slipped her one foot of pecker,
"Let it stay for a while, since it's in."

1364
A pious old maid name of Lord
Was gored by a man in a Ford.
　　She recited a psalm
　　With such stoical calm
That they say she appeared to be bored.

1365
A frigid young wife had MacFogg;
In bed she was known as a dog.
　　She learned nothing from bees,
　　But she had studied trees,
For she learned how to sleep like a log.

1366
There was a young girl named MacNeal
Whose panties were fashioned of steel,
　　For diverting the thrust
　　Of a thumb filled with lust,
And deflecting an unwanted feel.

1367
There was a young girl of Madrid
Who said that she'd never been rid.
　　When an old steamboat oiler
　　One fine day did despoil her,
She said, "You must undo what you did."

1368
A lad selling lewd magazines
Encountered a lady of means.
　　She claimed strong moral fiber
　　But became a subscriber
When he once penetrated her jeans.

1369
A lustful young fellow named Mattis
Seduced an old maid through the lattice.
　　She offered to pay
　　But his answer was nay;
He insisted the first one be gratis.

1370
There was an old maid name of Minnie
Who chanced to observe a lad skinny
　　As he beat on his meat,
　　So she said, "Come in, sweet;
That is love's labor lost, you dumb ninny."

1371
There was a young fellow named Mott
Who raped an old maid in her cot.
　　He was soon out of action
　　As he lost by a fraction,
For she gave it as good as she got.

1372
There was an old maid named O'Keefe
Who feared that some handsome young thief
　　Would steal into her shack
　　For a vicious attack—
When it came she felt blessed relief.

1373
There was a young man of Ostend
Who raped an old maid from South Bend.
　　She was just halfway through
　　When he bid her adieu,
But she made him stay right to the end.

1374. PERHAPS IN A HAYSTACK
The doctor examined Miss Pask;
He took the old spinster to task.
　　He said, "What I'm thinking
　　You will have to stop drinking,
For you'll not find a prick in a flask."

1375
A sordid young fellow named Peak
Once ravaged a spinster antique.
　　Before he could flee
　　He was forced to agree
That he'd ravage her once every week.

1376
A TV repairman named Peak
Was called by two sisters antique.
　　He repaired their resistors
　　Then he screwed the two sisters,
So they asked for repairs every week.

1377
A lady infused with persistence
Encountered from men much resistance.
    Though she raised up her dress
    To invite a caress,
Not a finger was raised in assistance.

1378
There was a young fellow named Pratt
Who fucked an old maid in her flat.
    She admonished the youth
    For his manners uncouth
And his failure to take off his hat.

1379
There was an old virgin of Preakness
Who lived in a sad state of bleakness.
    In her moral behavior
    She was strong as the Savior,
But her strength was of course her great weakness.

1380
A highly-strung lady named Proctor
Was checked by the doc who unfrocked her.
    He said, "You're in great shape."
    She said, "Don't stop, you ape!
It's a man I need now, not a doctor."

1381
How to handle a man in Quebec
Was revealed by old spinster Lautrec.
    "The use of my knack
    Will not thwart an attack,
But my method will hold it in check."

1382. THE CHERRY PICKER
A maid with a cherry was Richters,
Forlorn because no one had nichters,
    So she climbed up a tree
    Where the cherries would bee;
A mechanical picker then pichters.

1383
There was an old lady named Rideout
Whose pussy had never been tried out.
    It took the same shape
    As a plum or a grape
Which had lain in the sun until dried out.

1384

A lady with fine cheeks was Rootes;
Her leotards warded off brutes,
    For she put them on double
    And she kept out of trouble,
But she farted and blew off her boots.

1385

A lady whom fate had made rootless
Had pride, though she often went bootless.
    Self-respect made her wary,
    And she treasured her cherry,
But her efforts to save it were fruitless.

1386

A spinster who came from the Ruhr
Was grasped by a vulgar young boor.
    This detestable varmint
    Unfastened her garment,
But she found he was just a voyeur.

1387

The noted psychiatrist Schick
Discovered old maids were not sick
    When they came for advice,
    So he charged a small price
And he cured all their ills with his prick.

1388

The rapist a young lady seized
And inward his pecker he eased.
    He said, "Bear it and grin,
    For when it's fully in
I am sure you will not be displeased."

1389

There was a young lady named Seward
Who claimed she had never been skewered,
    Till the time she was trapped in
    The hold by the captain,
And was fucked by the purser and steward.

1390

A lad once subjected to shame
A pious old spinster named Mame.
    'Twas a shock, we all know;
    She now rocks to and fro
And she stares at his pants in a frame.

1391
There sat an old maid name of Shirley;
She stared at a relic, so surly—
 A balloon in a frame
 From a young lad who came,
But he left a few moments too early.

1392
There were two old maids who were sisters,
And they never had dealings with misters.
 A repairman, undaunted,
 Gave them both what they wanted,
But first he replaced their resistors.

1393
A vulgar and loathsome young slob
Defiled an old spinster named Cobb.
 She called for some help
 To lay hands on this whelp
For he hadn't completed his job.

1394
There was an old lady named Smither;
It seems that no man had fun with her
 Till a tailor named Clem
 Lifted up on her hem,
And Miss Smither was left in a dither.

1395
When ravished, a spinster named Sperling
Was left with head spinning and whirling.
 She was taken aback
 By this beastly attack,
But she said the performance was sterling.

1396
A hasty young man, quick and spry,
Once fucked an old maid and did fly.
 She called him a vulture
 Devoid of all culture
For his failure to kiss her goodbye.

1397. THE VIRGIN FOREST
To the forest primeval went Spurgeon,
For within him he felt a deep urgin'.
 There he fucked up a sapling
 With which he was grappling,
And the forest no longer was virgin.

1398
There was an old lady named Tudor
Who saw in her house an intruder.
    With an armful of loot
    He attempted to scoot,
But she raped him for she was much shrewder.

1399
The panties of old spinster Tweek
Dropped down in a mishap unique
    At a twat exhibition—
    It was judged mint condition
And it won the first prize for antique.

1400. AN EYE FOR AN EYE
A lad with a fine virtuosity
Debauched an old maid with ferocity.
    When the maid did recover
    She said, "Where is my lover,
For the law does permit reciprocity."

1401
A young mountain climber named Weeks
Loved virgins with oversize cheeks,
    For he loved to explore
    Where no man was before,
And he romped in the valleys and peaks.

12
Motherhood

1402. KNIGHT LIFE
The bulge up in front was apparent
Which made the young maid incoherent.
    She explained a bad day
    Was the cause of dismay,
But the truth was a knight had been errant.

1403
A careless young girl of Bangkok
Was nailed by old carpenter Brock,
    And it left her distressed
    For in time she was blessed
With a sliver, a chip off the block.

1404. FINGER-LICKIN' GOOD
A pregnant young lady named Blake
Was certain she made no mistake.
    "I held on to his dinger
    While he stuck in his finger,
At least while I lay there awake."

1405
A cautious young lady of Butte
The value of pills did dispute.
    One day in her garret
    She played with a carrot,
But this harmless relation bore fruit.

1406. ASP IN THE ALFALFA
In Hawaii a lady named Cass
Had a belly that swelled up a mass.
    At a dance, she did blurt,
    When she wore a grass skirt
She encountered a snake in the grass.

1407
Because of her careless consortion
Her belly was out of proportion.
    Though she had gone astray
    It was only part way,
So she asked for a partial abortion.

1408
A lady proceeded to curse
Her child with his antics perverse.
    "He's brought nothing but shame
    And he's sullied my name,
And the fuck that he came from was worse."

1409
There was a young lady demure
Who messed up her shapely contour,
    And she sadly did mention
    That an ounce of prevention
Would have given her five pounds of cure.

1410
A girl thought it wise to divulge
The reason her belly did bulge:
    "It is not pie and cheese
    Which expands my chemise,
I suspect it's the sport I indulge."

1411. THE BUTLER DONE IT!
When Mary's new baby was due
She confessed to her mother she knew
    That the chef was to blame,
    And her mother said, "Shame,
I'm afraid that he's your father too."

1412
A pregnant young lady named Kant
Was asked who had been her gallant.
    "When it's wild oats you sow
    Tell me how can you know
Which seed grew which singular plant?"

1413
A family of twenty had Kelly.
When asked why, he replied, what the hell he
    Came home and was fed,
    Then with wife went to bed,
And they spent their time belly to belly.

1414
A family of twenty had Kelly
For he never used condoms or jelly.
    When they asked, what's the score,
    He replied, "I'd have more,
But my wife never bathes and is smelly."

1415
A negligent lady named Lyriad
Had talents so diverse and myriad
    But she will be a momma
    For mistakes she made,
And she says it's the end of her.

1416
Efficiency expert McGraff
Thought nine months for birth was a laugh.
    He emerged from seclusion
    With his studied conclusion,
That two men would reduce it to half.

1417
A pregnant young lady named Nettie
Could blame either John, Joe or Freddie,
    Or it could have been Thackeray,
    Or from Aaron to Zachary,
For her mother said, "You can't go steady."

1418
There was a young girl from New York
Who plugged up her cunt with a cork
    From a fifth of champagne
    Which she drank with disdain;
When it popped it was heard by the stork.

1419
A half-wit young fellow named Newt
Was thought by relations as cute.
    He went over to auntie's
    And got into her panties
And this harmless relation bore fruit.

1420
A very large family had Peaks,
And he sat in remorse for some weeks.
    When asked why, he replied,
    "Godnose that I've tried,
But the condom I use has some leaks."

1421
An order religious of Perth
Attracted young ladies of worth.
    They found the baptismal
    A rite not too dismal,
But the postulants often gave birth.

1422. IT WAS ONE-TOOTH RHEE
A popular lady named Ritter
Found many young fellows that fit her.
    When her belly was swelling
    There was no way of telling
Which tooth in the buzz saw had hit her.

1423
A seamstress divulged midst her sobbin'
She'd been pricked by a tailor named Robin.
    The results of her sins
    Were some needles and pins
And some red and white thread on a bobbin.

1424
A female lion tamer of York
Would tackle a lion with a fork,
    And she held him at bay
    Without fear or dismay,
But she never could hold off a stork.

13
Prostitution

1425
A madam of no mean ability
Developed a fine new facility
    For outcasts discarded
    And the mental retarded
And those in the prime of senility.

1426
A wretched old whore of Algiers
Was judged in the court by her peers,
    But the jury dismissed her
    For the foreman had kissed her,
And the judge was a month in arrears.

1427
There was a young lady all-fired—
To be a great whore she desired,
    But her crotch was perfidious
    And so gruesome and hideous
That men dextrous bogged down and got mired.

1428
The preacher this point must allow—
His head to the harlot must bow,
    For she works hard in bed,
    There to earn daily bread,
And it's earned by the sweat of her brow.

1429
The madam who came from the Andes
Had rooms of fine girls that were dandies,
    And some girls in a ward
    If that's all you'd afford,
And some girls in a room for the standees.

1430. MAFIA RECALLS 2000 GIRLS
Old Nader one time was appalled
On finding his harlot was bald.
    Said old Nader, "I think
    I will raise a big stink."
And the whores that were bald were recalled.

1431
A sturdy old harlot named Astor
Was fucked by a gent who outclassed her.
    She found the old codge
    Was head of the lodge
And she knew why they called him *Grand Master*.

1432
A whore who much trade did attract
Fell dead in the midst of a pact.
    Twenty men with no hitch
    Paid for screwing the bitch
Before anyone noticed the fact.

1433
The harlot that's smarter avoids
Disaster of work stoppage voids
    From a pregnancy lapse
    Or a case of the claps
By insuring her pussy with Lloyds.

1434. WILL BE BACK FOR LUNCH
An overworked harlot named Baird
Remarked to the next man who stared,
    "You are shit out of luck
    For right after this fuck
I must go get my pussy repaired."

1435
A busy old harlot named Banks
Had died in the mist of her pranks.
    She was thrown twenty dollars
    By the last of her callers;
She revived long enough to say, "Thanks."

1436
A harlot was charged by old Barger;
She claimed that his charge did enlarge her.
    Barger griped at the charge
    Charged by old harlot Marge,
But she claimed that his charge was much larger.

1437
There was a young fellow named Bart
Who picked up a flatulent tart.
    Though she lacked fucking skill
    Yet she gave him a thrill
By producing an exquisite fart.

1438
A bulgy old harlot was Bassett;
Her *derrière* was her finest asset.
 She was fucked by old Pierre
 Who explored everywhere,
But he failed to exploit every facet.

1439. THIN ICE!
A sporting old harlot named Bates
For athletes devalued her rates.
 She took on the team manly
 Who had won the Cup Stanley,
But she asked them to take off their skates.

1440
The richest old whore in Bengal
For rajahs was ready on call,
 But a Hindu from Delhi
 Claimed he laid on her belly
When her house was a hole in the wall.

1441. AU MONTRÉAL
A thoughtless old man name of Beque
Was raping a whore in Québeque.
 She complained in dismay,
 "I'm a whore—you must pay."
So when finished, he wrote her a cheque.

1442
There was an old whore of Berlin,
As rare as an old violin.
 She was not a bit sloppy
 With her fine carbon copy
Of the thing called *Original Sin.*

1443
A harlot who worked at Bernice's
Collected her things in valises.
 Said old madam Bernice,
 "Won't you stay for a piece?"
She said, "No, I am going to pieces."

219

1444. WORK YOUR WAY UP
The story is told of young Bess
Which is one of great trial and duress.
    She lay flat on her back
    And she peddled her crack
To achieve the top rung of success.

1445
A homely streetwalker named Bess
Would walk till her feet were a mess.
    Now she's great fun to meet
    For she walks on the street
With her face covered up by her dress.

1446. FIVE MORE MINUTES
While fucking a whore, Mr. Binks
Observed that she died from some kinks
    Which her cunt did invade.
    But said Binks, "Since I've paid,
I will fuck the old bitch till she stinks."

1447. ALWAYS ON A SUNDAY
A church-going harlot was Birch;
Her record no man could besmirch.
    Through nine pieces she'd writhe,
    Then avoided the tithe
By donating the tenth to the church.

1448
A hapless young lady named Black
In poverty lived in a shack,
    So she took to the street
    To get back on her feet,
But she found herself flat on her back.

1449
There was an old harlot named Blake
Whose price made a young sailor quake.
    He had thought to complain,
    But he found in the main
That she gave all the lads a fair shake.

1450
A hardy old harlot named Blanding
Had found that her work was demanding
    Due to obstacles hidden.
    Though she was once bedridden
Her position of late was good standing.

1451
An able young harlot named Bobby
Was asked by a man in the lobby
    If her husband did moan
    When she took her work home;
She said, "Yes, but my work is my hobby."

1452
A lady of joy, young and bold,
Offered ass to a man for some gold.
    The man was beguiled
    By her warmth as she smiled,
But the ass that she sold was ice-cold.

1453
A worn-out old harlot was Boocher;
Her cunt was in need of a suture,
    But she knew fucking well
    That her asshole would sell,
So she had no concern for the future.

1454
The daily routine was a bore
For a lady who managed a store.
    With her business depressed
    She was somewhat distressed,
So she joined the *Piece Corps* and made more.

1455
A hard-pressed young lady was Bounting;
Her debts were beyond all accounting.
    She thought pay for coition
    Would improve her position,
But she found that her problems were mounting.

1456
A versatile harlot named Breech
Ten methods of fucking did teach,
    But a man in a bind
    Could not make up his mind,
So he tried a small portion of each.

1457
There was an old madam named Bryce
Whose school for young harlots was nice.
 While the ladies did learn
 How to handle their stern
They were fucked for a very low price.

1458
A cagy old madam named Bryce
Was ready for all in a thrice.
 She never ran short
 Of girls for the sport,
For she kept a few hot ones on ice.

1459
There was an old harlot named Bryce
Who tried a new business device.
 For the fathers who came
 She kept prices the same,
But their sons were let in for half price.

1460*
An artful old madam named Bunce
In business was nobody's dunce.
 She invited all jokers
 To her excellent smokers
Where she showed them some fine cunning stunts.

1461
While screwing a harlot named Bunny,
A lad told bad jokes he thought funny,
 But the whore had some pride
 For she threw him outside
And she cursed him and gave back his money.

1462
A hapless young lady named Burke
Had failed in her search for some work.
 A profession was offered
 By a pimp name of Crawford,
And she launched her career with a jerk.

1463
A whore on the railroad, Miss Burrage,
The overtime screw would discourage.
 A conductor named Tiding
 Fucked too long on the siding,
So she charged the old fellow demurrage.

1464
There was a young fellow of Butte
Who differed with a prostitute
 As to what he should pay,
 So she met him halfway
And said, "Sir, I'm not prone to dispute."

1465
A dying old harlot of Butte
Had logic one cannot refute.
 When a man offered five
 The old whore came alive
And she said, "I'm not prone to dispute."

1466. WAR AND PIECE
Old Hitler in fits of caprice
The mad dogs of war did release,
 But madam McAdams
 Collected her madams
And leased out the pussies of piece.

1467
A whore by the name of Carruther
Was rough on the one as the other.
 If a lad pulled a blooper
 She would swear like a trooper,
And then set him aright like a mother.

1468
A whore ran a wild place in Chester;
An officer came to arrest her.
 The warrant he waved
 Was for action depraved,
But he thought it was best that he test her.

1469. PIECE AT HOME
There was a young prostitute chubby
Whose work left her sweaty and grubby,
 But this sensible girlie
 Every day would leave early
For she saved the last piece for her hubby.

1470. BETTER THAN SNIFFING GLUE
A man short of cash name of Cliff
Told a whore that her price was too stiff,
    And he asked how much fuck
    He could get for a buck,
So she told him she'd give him a sniff.

1471
The unionized whores of Miss Clift
Would fuck all day long without rift,
    But the girl fucking Hugh
    Disengaged halfway through,
And gave up at the end of her shift.

1472
A drowning old harlot named Clive
Was pulled from the lake half alive.
    On reviving she spoke
    She could not swim a stroke,
But she swore that she knew every dive.

1473. POSTHASTE
A feeble old whore on the coast
Low prices for sailors would boast.
    She was too weak to lay
    In the regular way,
So was fucked as she hung on a post.

1474
An old business man had compassion
While screwing a whore that was ashen.
    He said, "If you've ambition
    I've a better position."
But she said she preferred it dog-fashion.

1475
An impatient old harlot of Corning
To her husband presented a warning:
    "Get your ass out of bed,
    I must earn daily bread,
So do not oversleep in the morning."

1476
There was an old harlot of Cottam
Whose business picked up in the autumn.
    She managed to keep
    On top of the heap
For she did a fine job on the bottom.

1477
A thrifty old harlot was Cotter;
She put a small price on her daughter.
        When a man stayed all day
        The old harlot said, "Say,
You have rented my daughter, not bought her."

1478
The liquor of naive young Cotter
Was soaked up by whores like a blotter.
        They drank only straight drinks,
        So said Cotter, "Methinks
You can lead whores to drink, but not water."

1479
"Your price—is it firm?" said young Croft,
While fondling her ass in the loft.
        She said, "Why you worm,
        It's got to be firm;
It will never go in if it's soft."

1480
An agile old harlot named Cruse
Was making a deal with some Jews.
        She contorted her slot
        To create a new twat—
An or'fice they could not refuse.

1481
"When you buy ass from me," said Miss Curry,
"There is no need to fret or to worry.
        I can give you a lay
        Which will last you all day,
Or a quickie for men in a hurry."

1482
A selective old madam was Dades;
She instructed her skilful young maids
        To give fine fucking sessions
        To the men of professions,
But they only should jack off all trades.

1483
"We're here," said two harlots of Daucus,
"To tour through the White House so raucous,
        For we have an obsession
        To see Congress in session,
And to see if the Senate will caucus."

1484
There was an old whore name of Dawes
Who put on a show for a cause.
    She went into a frenzy
    With a man named Mackenzie
Then she paused for a while for applause.

1485
In the ward lay a harlot half dead,
Confined by a blow on the head.
    In a week she felt well
    To get up, but said, "Hell,
I make more when I lay there in bed."

1486
There was an old whore of Decatur
In matters of finance first rater.
    If your cash went for chow,
    She said, "Why not fuck now
And pay for the goods sometime later."

1487
For men who were lacking defrayment
The harlot would not strip her raiment,
    But she took a deposit
    For a feel in the closet
And the rest on receipt of full payment.

1488
A dignified harlot of Dimmage
Would caution each man in the scrimmage
    There'd be less of a bind
    If they acted refined
So that no one would fuck up her image.

1489
A thrifty old harlot discerned
Small savings were not to be spurned.
    From her callers, so many,
    She'd request one more penny,
For each penny she saved was one earned.

1490. DOUBLE JEOPARDY
There was a streetwalker discreet
Who would not cut her price for a treat,
    For she said prices low
    Would not bring enough dough,
And she'd find herself out on the street.

1491
A lad caused a harlot distraction;
His passion put her out of action.
　　She requested he pay
　　Five more dollars that day
For she felt that there was an infraction.

1492
The pious old harlot named Dix,
Each time, before turning her tricks,
　　On her knees she would pray
　　To gain strength for the lay,
Then she thanked the Good Lord for stiff pricks.

1493
At the brothel, a man from Djibouti
Took his pick of the harlots, a cutie.
　　But the madam said, "Nay,
　　For the union rules say
You will have to take age before beauty."

1494
There was an old madam named Douglas—
The floors in her house were all rugless,
　　And what passed off as beds
　　Were but tatters and shreds
But she claimed that her harlots were bugless.

1495
A horny old man of Dubuque
Made a deal with a harlot, a fluke,
　　But her cunt was so foul
　　That he said, with a scowl,
"Tell me, where is your pisspot to puke?"

1496
There was a streetwalker named Duckworth
Whose ass was not even one fuck worth.
　　She offered young Clive
　　Her ass for a five,
But all he could take was one buck worth.

1497
A loose-fitting whore of Dundee
Had tits that hung down to her knee.
　　They were tied in a knot
　　And stuffed into her twat—
Now she gives a tight fuck but can't pee.

1498. AUSTRALIAN?
A girl strapped for cash named Miss Dunder
Had so many debts, it's a wonder.
　　She divulged in confession
　　That she tried the profession,
But could not work her way from down under.

1499. COUPON DEAL
A businesslike harlot named Draper
Presented an unusual caper,
　　And what made it so nice,
　　You could get it half-price
If you brought in her ad from the paper.

1500
A careless young fellow named Dreyoss
Had screwed an old harlot in Laos.
　　There he left such a mess
　　That she cried in distress,
"Tell me who will take care of this chaos?"

1501
A madam of East Middlesex
Was sued by an old man named Tex
　　For her hindrance to scores
　　Of young men to be whores,
And he ended her bias towards sex.

1502
To a whore a young fellow named Elliot
Said, "Dear, can I stay on your belly yet?"
　　She said, "Sir, you have gall.
　　I've ten drunks in the hall,
And I still have to fuck Father Kelly yet."

1503. COOL RECEPTION
An old hoar had her business embossed
On a card, and a man did accost.
　　He exclaimed, "What the hell,
　　You cannot even spell!"
Said the hoar, "It's because of the frost."

228

1504
When the harlot a man did entice,
He agreed and exposed his device.
　　As it dropped to his feet
　　She exclaimed, "What a meat!
Just for you I will lower the price."

1505
A wily old harlot was Ewing;
The cash in her bank kept accruing.
　　No taxes were paid
　　On the money she made
And she gave Uncle Sam a big screwing.

1506
A well-worn old trollop was Fairless,
Her pussy was shabby and hairless,
　　But she said, "You can see
　　It's for others, not me,
And besides when it's dark I could care less."

1507
There was a young sailor named Farber
Who screwed the old whore at the harbor,
　　But this young buccaneer
　　Wore a muff on each ear
For she gave him more talk than the barber.

1508
There was a young varlet named Farlet
Who laughed as he raped harlot Scarlet,
　　But his efforts lacked lustre
　　And he died in a fluster
With the laugh on the face of the harlot.

1509
There was a young plumber named Fenchter
Who wrenched an old whore and he benched her.
　　She went into a panic,
　　But there came a mechanic—
With a twist of the wrist he unwrenched her.

1510
While checking her cash, madam Fern
Found counterfeit bills from young Bern.
　　Though she ran up the stair
　　He was already there
At the point where there was no return.

1511

The harlot from old madam Fern's
Had such a great time with young Burns,
And she found him so gay
That she asked him to stay
Until all of the harlots took turns.

1512

A timer was used by Miss Fitch;
She timed all the men and got rich.
An old-timer named Joe
Fucked her ten in a row
When he found her asleep at the switch.

1513. COUNTERCLOCKWISE

A sailor went out on a fling
And screwed an old whore name of King.
He had no cash to pay
So she made the lad stay
Until he had undone the whole thing.

1514

A post-office clerk named Miss Flounce
Had titties with plenty of bounce.
It was frank up her ass
But her cunt was first class—
It was thirty-one cents for each ounce.

1515

A novice young harlot of Flushing
Enjoyed all the rushing and mushing,
Till the wear and the tear
Gave her naught but despair,
And she found that the work load was crushing.

1516

A hefty old harlot named Flynn
Was fat and as ugly as sin,
But she cried in defiance,
"I can take no new clients,
For I fear I am spread far too thin."

1517

There was an old man somewhat foggy
Who fucked an old harlot so scroggy
That he asked the old hag
To put some in a bag
And he took a piece home to his doggy.

1518
A sordid old whore of Fort Meyer
Was screwed for two bucks and no higher,
    But her faults were correctible
    And she now is respectable,
For the price of her ass is much higher.

1519
While walking, a fellow named French
Was stopped on the street by a wench.
    He said, "Come to my room,
    But bring some perfume—
You need something to cover the stench."

1520
A squalid old whore name of Funks
Would fuck only junkies and drunks,
    But her daughter prodigious
    Was profoundly religious
And consorted with friars and monks.

1521
The old miner inserted a funnel
In the cunt of a whore named Miss Bunnel.
    Then he shouted with glee
    And he said, "I can see
There's a light at the end of the tunnel!"

1522
A harlot did not think it funny
To hear the bad jokes of young Tunney.
    "I have never" she said,
    "Heard such filth on my bed."
She got up and refunded his money.

1523
A non-union harlot named Furze
Would urge union men on with spurs,
    And she speeded seduction
    With her in-line production,
While ignoring the jibes and the slurs.

1524
In the house of a madam named Gail
Was presented her annual sale.
    She bestowed a free piece
    To the Chief of Police,
And the Mayor was next without fail.

1525
There was an old whore name of Gail
Who bailed an old man out of jail.
    By a strange stroke of fate
    He became head of state,
So he made her the head of all tail.

1526
To the butcher, a lady named Gail
Made it clear that she charged for her tail.
    But he said, with reflection,
    "I can make no exception—
You will find all my sausage for sale."

1527
It appears the Machine Age was gaining
On the whores of a madam named Blaining.
    The machines could fuck faster
    And new tricks they did master,
So the whores were sent out for retraining.

1528
A practical madam was Garrity;
The brothel she ran was a rarity.
    She ran newspaper ads
    At half-price for young lads,
And was open on weekends for charity.

1529
A haggard old bitch name of Gleek
Was forty-five years past her peak,
    But her profits did soar
    And she made more and more
For the thing that she sold was antique.

1530
A seasoned old harlot named Gleason
Remarked, "No young lad outdoes me, son."
    But so long did one stay
    That the harlot said, "Say,
Don't you think we should stop for a pee, son?"

1531
There was an old strumpet named Glim
Who went to the gym to keep trim.
    There was nothing mysterious
    For this matter was serious;
Making love as a business is grim.

1532
At the doctor's, a whore name of Glover
When checked for her health did discover
      A run-down condition,
      So said her physician,
"You must stay out of bed to recover."

1533
A shabby old harlot sold goods
To forgers, embezzlers and hoods,
      To old judges and preachers,
      And to Sunday School teachers,
And she fucked them all good in the woods.

1534
There was an old lady with gout
Whose balance of cash was in doubt.
      She resorted to whoring
      Where the prices were soaring,
But a malpractice suit forced her out.

1535. PENALTY FOR EARLY WITHDRAWAL!
"By the minute I charge," said Miss Grange,
"And five bucks is the usual range."
      But the way one man reckoned,
      Is he blew in one second,
So he gave her a dime and got change.

1536
A battered old harlot named Greer
Decided to quit her career.
      From a fuck she arose
      With her hand at her nose.
"I have had it," she said, "up to here."

1537
Young Joe, who was not in the groove,
Could not get the whore to approve,
      So she let little Joe
      Fuck her twice in a row
For she felt there was room to improve.

[1538]
But when the old harlot fucked Ben
She cried out, "Oh Lord!" and "Amen!"
      For this man was so learned
      That the tables were turned,
And she payed him to do it again.

1539. ELECTRONIC AGE
Said a man to the madam, Miss Grout:
"Do you have any free whores about?"
    The old madam serene
    Checked her monitor screen—
"There's a trucker," she said, "pulling out."

1540
A religious old madam was Grunday,
For on one day each week she had nun day,
    And her business did peak
    At the end of the week
When she made it a *Father and Son* day.

1541
There was an old whore name of Gudget
Who said to a man, "Don't begrudge it.
    If you come each week thrice
    I will lower the price."
He said, "No, I must live on a budget."

1542. SELF-SERVICE
An old man with a dollar, in Guelph,
Asked a whore by the name of Miss Schelf,
    "Have you any cheap fucks?"
    But the harlot said, "Shucks,
Save your buck—you can do it yourself."

1543
An overage harlot from Guelph
Worked hard to improve on herself.
    She had her cheeks shifted
    And her face she had lifted;
She cared not to be laid on the shelf.

1544
A worn-out old harlot named Hatch
Asked a tailor to try out her snatch.
    He said, "I will fuck it,
    But first I must tuck it,
And secure it in place with a patch."

Prostitution

1545. y = f(x)
An old mathematician named Hearst
Picked a harlot to fuck with—the worst.
    By a quick calculation
    He deduced this relation
Was a function of age and of thirst.

1546
The whore that was picked up by Hearst
Looked so badly worn that he cursed,
    So he asked her how long
    She'd been taking the dong.
"I've just started," she said, "you're the first."

1547
There was an old harlot named Heather
Whose pussy was tougher than leather.
    She would peddle her meat
    On the neighborhood street,
And was handy in all kinds of weather.

1548
When visiting harlots, old Herm
For early appointments was firm.
    He was somewhat aghast
    At the time he was last,
For the bird that was last got the sperm.

1549
A whore went to old Dr. Hubbell
To cure on her cunt a bad bubble.
    He repaired that and more
    On this slimy old whore,
So she gave him a fuck for his trouble.

1550
An old madam, retired, name of Hunt
In her manner so forthright and blunt,
    All her memoirs collected
    In a volume respected,
And she proofread the book with her cunt.

1551. TEN, NINE, EIGHT . . .
A vice cop one time did inveigle
To trap a young lad with whore Beagle.
    But the lad turned eighteen
    As he blew his nuts clean,
So his climaxing action was legal.

1552. STRATOCRUISER

In flight a young hostess named Jane
Improved on her pay with no strain,
    But she peddled no meat
    Below ten thousand feet,
For she worked on a much higher plane.

1553

There was an old whore name of Jane
Who made a fast buck with no strain.
    She had twenty, one hour,
    And she said in the shower,
"I've been riding the old gravy train."

1554. COUNTERPLOY

Sin fighters with banners of Jesus
Showed films on venereal diseases,
    But a madam named Stoker
    Stole a march with a smoker,
Where she offered free pinches and squeezes.

1555. PUT OUT A FEELER

A cautious old fucker was Jewett;
He said to a harlot, "I'll do it
    If at first you expose
    What's between your big toes,
For I know what I want when I view it."

1556

There was a streetwalker, Miss Jones,
Who felt a deep chill in her bones.
    She performed for humanity
    Interspiced with profanity,
And the whole night was pierced with her groans.

1557

In the church an old trollop named Kay
Knelt her down in a reverent way.
    Said the preacher with gravity,
    "You are saved from depravity."
But she said, "It's for piece that I pray."

1558
While skiing, a harlot named Kay
Her leg broke a very bad way,
    But could still fuck as fast
    With her leg in a cast
As the girls they are hiring today.

1559
Miss Jane ran a whorehouse in Kent;
She asked no advance, not a cent.
    In most business we know
    It is pay *as you go,*
But with Jane it was pay *as you went.*

1560. SMART-ASS LAWYERS
There was a young coed of Kent,
In matters of law eloquent.
    She told lawyers from Yale
    That her ass was for sale,
But they proved it was only for rent.

1561
A man screwed a harlot in Kent
And his credit card he did present.
    He was billed in a flash,
    But for those who paid cash
They got discounts of twenty percent.

1562
There was a young girl of Key West
Who claimed that her ass was the best.
    There were forty marines
    Who were still in their teens
Who agreed, for they all took the test.

1563
A sailor who came from the Keys
Had ploughed through the heaviest seas
    And survived every one,
    But a harlot named Dunn
Left him wobbly and weak in the knees.

1564
"The pros who play ball," said whore Kiefer,
"I find them at fucking much briefer."
    But a batter named Pat
    Gave her such a fuck that
She had to call in a reliefer.

1565. ONE FEEL IS WORTH A THOUSAND PICTURES

There was a streetwalker of Kiel
Who offered some fun to MacNeal.
  With some words she did tease him
  And showed pictures to please him,
But he said, "I get more from one feel."

1566

A particular lady of Kitchener
Would welcome old men who were ritchener.
  By the bed, near the closet
  Was a box for deposit,
For each buck you could feel a new twitchener.

1567

A girl short of cash was Miss Kitty;
She drove a sand truck for the city,
  And at night she would work
  For old madam McGirk,
But the clients complained she was gritty.

1568

There was a young madam named Kline
Who always kept prices in line.
  She did not deal with tramps,
  She gave S & H Stamps,
And she charged just a buck ninety-nine.

1569. NO CARRYING CHARGES

Let's give credit to old harlot Klutz
For the way she sold ass—it took guts.
  With her added refinement
  You could fuck on consignment,
And could pay after blowing your nuts.

1570

A scrupulous whore name of Koppers
Would cater to opulent shoppers,
  But she said, "I confess
  That in times of distress
My asshole's for tradesmen and paupers."

1571

A professional lady named Kropps
Was expert in pulling all stops.
  When Dunn slipped a disc
  He called her a risk,
But Bradstreet still rated her tops.

1572
A hungry young lady was Krupp;
She often had nothing to sup,
    So she took to the street
    And established a beat,
And her business is now picking up.

1573
There was a young cocksman named Krupp
Who was by a harlot keyed up.
    As he zipped in great style
    He outstripped her a mile,
Then he paused so that she could catch up.

1574
A whore who turned nun, felt a lack
And sought out her old madam's shack.
    Said the madam, Miss Hood,
    "Have you come back for good?"
She said, "No, it's for evil I'm back."

1575
At Macy's worked harlot LaFarge;
Her fucking department was large.
    When it came time to pay
    The old harlot would say,
"Shall I make this a *Cash* or a *Charge?*"

1576
A sordid old whore from Lahore
Would fuck till her asshole was sore,
    And her cunt was more hairy
    Than the sweet Virgin Mary,
And she never got pregnant, what's more.

1577. THE DAY OF THE MOURNING
There was an old whore of Lapeer
Esteemed by all men, and so dear
    That when she passed away
    They all gathered to pray,
And the mourners had one on the bier.

[1578]
The passing of old harlot Krauss
Was reason for more men to grouse.
    Her remains were displayed
    On the roof, and all prayed,
Then the mourners had one on the house.

1579
When a gentleman wants to be laid
Let reason his actions pervade.
    From amongst the profession
    He must choose with discretion,
Lest he's stuck with a whore that's decayed.

1580
For Pickett, a madam named Larket
Provided a place he could park it,
    And then she told Pickett
    To pick up a ticket
Like customers at the meat market.

1581
The girls of old madam LeClaire
Were sadly in need of repair.
    A great many had snatches
    That were covered with patches,
And some were devoid of all hair.

1582
There was an old harlot named Lemann
Who fancied all sailors were he-men.
    When a ship came to port
    She would open for sport,
And she closed when they ran out of seamen.

1583
In Hong Kong a Texan named Lew
Was looking for ladies to screw.
    Said the madam, Miss Chang,
    After feeling his whang,
"My girls have small cunts, so take two."

1584
"The price," said the whore from Livonia,
"Is fifty, and I'll have to phone ya."
    Said the fellow named Reese,
    "I just came for a piece,
And I really do not want to own ya."

1585
There was an old madam named Lize
Who carried some fine merchandise.
    You could view her collection
    And not make a selection
Till you sampled a couple for size.

1586. TAIL OF SORROW*
A sorry old fellow named Lorne
Was fucking a harlot forlorn.
 When she told him her fears
 He welled up with tears
And he wished he had never been born.

1587. ANNUAL CHARGE 18%
There was a young lady of Lucknow
Who said, "If you don't have a buck now
 Then your credit is fine,
 Simply sign on this line.
You can always pay later and fuck now."

1588
A hard-up old harlot of Lucknow
Remarked, "If you don't have a buck now
 And you fancy my crater
 You can pay sometime later,
And I'll give you one half of the fuck now."

1589
A peglegged lady named Lunt
Could always sell plenty of cunt.
 It was not by deceit
 That she peddled her meat,
But by putting her best leg out front.

1590
A thrifty old whore was Miss Lynch
Who never from business would flinch.
 But one day she said, "Shit,
 I am rich, I will quit.
I no longer can feel any pinch."

1591
No cash to buy ass had MacDuff;
Said the whore with a laugh, "That is tough."
 To him trousers she threw
 As she bid him adieu.
"You can have one," she said, "on the cuff."

1592
At the whorehouse, Explorer MacFrost
Picked a harlot, the lowest in cost.
 But the cunt of the Miss
 Was a dismal abyss,
And he fell through the crack and got lost.

1593

A miserly man named MacGregor
Scrimped so that he looked like a beggar,
 And at madam MacLoozie
 He would get a cheap floozy
Which she saved him, the one-eyed peglegger.

1594. UNION RULES

A union official, MacLout,
Was having a fine fucking bout.
 Twenty fucks in a row
 And the harlot said, "Joe,
Remember—it's thirty and out."

1595. INFLATION

To the call-girl went horny young Mahler,
But her price made the poor fellow holler,
 So he said, "I would pay
 The high buck for a lay
If your pussy would shrink like the dollar."

1596

An ingenious old harlot named Mallory
Had managed to earn a fine salary.
 She got nothing from screwers
 But she did charge the viewers,
And she daily would fill up the gallery.

1597

A worn-out old harlot named Mame
Attempted her youth to reclaim.
 An old surgeon, Doc Gillian,
 Made her look like a million,
But the men found her frame was the same.

1598

To the whore on the farm went young Matthews,
And through chickens and pigs did the path use,
 For the lad did not think.
 Said the harlot, "You stink!
I'm afraid that I first have to bath youse."

1599

At the whorehouse, geologist Max
The patience of harlots did tax.
 Every crotch he laid bare
 And examined with care,
Then rejected for faults in the cracks.

1600
An outstanding whore named McCord
A great many firsts in life scored.
    She went into a frenzy
    With Sir William MacKenzie
And received a posthumous award.

1601. BORED MEMBER
There was an old whore named McCord
Who received a most fitting award.
    At a harlots' convention
    She received the top mention,
For a member was she, of the bored.

1602. TEACH 'EM OR LEARN 'EM
With a harlot, Professor McHugh
Was fumbling his way through a screw.
    With a learned rendition
    He explained his position,
So she learned the old fuck how to screw.

1603. EMISSION PROBLEM
An old harlot inept named McLure,
Sold five thousand fucks that were poor.
    But complaints did her in
    And she paid for her sin,
Since a recall she had to endure.

1604
The harlots of madam McNair
Disturbed an old man debonair.
    He remarked, with great poise,
    He could stand all the noise,
But some twats were in need of repair.

1605. OCEAN VOYAGE
There was an old harlot named Measick
Who thought that she never would be sick,
    But one time she got wrapped in
    A long bout with the captain,
And she ended up terribly seasick.

1606. MIND YOUR P'S AND Q'S

A studious harlot was Metters
Who always was screwed by her betters.
　　She'd collect B.V.D.'s
　　From well-known Ph.D.'s;
She was truly a lady of letters.

1607

Said a whore to a fellow named Meyer,
"It is fifty for fucking me, sire."
　　"I'll save money," he swore,
　　So he married the whore,
But he found that the price was now higher.

1608

A practical fellow named Mickey
With harlots was careful and picky.
　　He refused to take Lizzy
　　Who was always so busy,
For he found her to be a bit sticky.

1609. WEAR A MASK

A sporting old whore of Milwaukee
Thought athletes knew best how to jockey.
　　When a Black Hawk, a runt,
　　Rammed a puck up her cunt,
She said, "I do not go for this hockey!"

1610

A worn-out old whore of Mobile
Installed a new cunt made of steel.
　　Now her fucking was painless,
　　But it should have been stainless
For the rust ran in streaks to her heel.

1611. TRAVEL FIRST CLASS

In Scotland far out on the moor,
As shown in Cook's travel brochure,
　　Lives a harlot named Fitch
　　With her niche for the rich
And her asshole for those that are poor.

1612. A MATTER OF DEGREE
If a girl charges fifty or more,
She's rotten, they say, to the core.
    Then strange though it seem,
    Take the other extreme—
If her price is too cheap, she's a whore.

1613. THE LOANER
A wily old whore of Mt. Blanc
  Did not miss a chance for a franc.
    When a man could not pay
    She would find him a way
To establish a loan at the bank.

1614. SUSPICION IN QUESTION
A pious old preacher named Mort
Deplored all the ladies of sport.
    He rebuked a young maid
    Who was plying her trade
For not having a means of support.

[1615]
The harlot, whose name was Miss Bodim,
Had not thought to taunt or to goad him.
    She advised Preacher Mort
    She had means of support,
And she lowered her panties and showed him.

1616. FAIRNESS DOCTRINE
A state-controlled brothel in Natchez
Was ruled by Fair Practice dispatches.
    You would get, by priorities,
    Worn out whores from minorities,
Or old harlots with handicapped snatches.

1617. THE PATRIOT
A flag-waving harlot with nerve
Her country in two wars did serve.
    In the trenches up front
    With her cunt took the brunt,
And she wiggled her asshole with verve.

1618
A harlot who came from the Nile
Had patents for fucking, worthwhile,
    And no whore could get laid
    Until premiums were paid,
For she sued if they copied her style.

1619. WORLD WAR II VICTIM
A whore who survived Occupation
Was freed by U.S. Liberation,
    But she wore out her ass
    With the army top brass
So she sued and received reparation.

1620
A way to spur business occurred
To thoughtful old madam McNurd.
    She attracted new trade
    And the boys had it made
When she offered two sterns for each bird.

1621
A detective by name of O'Connor
Made raids on a house of dishonor.
    With his timing precise
    He caught girls in his vise;
One was caught with the goods right upon her.

1622
Said the priest to a harlot, O'Keefe,
"Your response to the faith is too brief."
    She replied, "By comparison,
    A well-overhung Saracen
Will do more to enhance my belief."

1623
There was an old whore of Orleans
Who knew how to pull in the greens,
    For she screwed the flotilla
    Which was based at Manila
While she still was a girl in her teens.

1624
A hustling old madam named Park
Provided young girls who had spark.
    She gave drinks up to three,
    Turkey sandwiches free,
And a choice between light meat or dark.

1625
A wealthy whoremonger named Paul
Disclosed how he managed it all.
    He began it in Thrace
    And his very first place
Was at best just a hole in the wall.

1626. CONSUMERS REPORTS
You will find that the house of Pauline
Is where critical men will convene.
    In the month of July
    She was rated *Best Buy*
In a nationwide-known magazine.

1627. TIT FOR TAT
The madam advised Mr. Perkins
That she thoroughly scrutinized gherkins,
    But he would not expose
    In between his big toes
Till she likewise displayed her own workin's.

1628
The State meat inspector named Pete
Worked evenings for madam LaFitte,
    Where he checked every twat
    For decay or for rot,
And he passed on each customer's meat.

1629. THE SHOW MUST GO ON
Disillusioned and baffled was Phil
When he found that his harlot was ill.
    He had paid her the cost
    But it all was not lost,
For she farted and puked with great skill.

1630
In the cunt of a dead whore named Phipp
Was installed a new silicon chip,
    So the feedback from sensors
    Went to coils and condensers,
And she fucked with new vigor and zip.

1631. IS THERE A CHOICE?

To a whore a young fellow named Pitt
Complained that her crotch was not fit,
    For her cunt had no wool;
    Said the whore, affable,
"Did you come here to fuck or to knit?"

1632

There was a young lady named Pitt
Who did what she thought right and fit,
    And great wealth did amass
    From her saleable ass,
For it's no use on gold mines to sit.

1633. THE JOLLY GREEN GIANT*

A harlot with crotch muscles pliant
Was asked by a promising client
    Could he pay her the fees
    In fresh carrots and peas;
He was jolly and green and a giant.

1634

A musical harlot was Polly;
Her students found classes were jolly.
    She taught the legato,
    The rapid staccato,
And crescendo one needs for finale.

1635

There was an old harlot named Post
Who was by a man so engrossed
    That she paid him the fee,
    For undoubtedly he
Was the master and therefore the host.

1636. THE DRIVE-IN

There was an old madam named Potts
Whose house was the finest of spots.
    With your car you'd arrive in,
    Take one out to the drive-in,
But could not take her out of the lots.

Prostitution

1637
Said the priest, on our knees we must pray
For the cunts of old whores that decay.
    At one time it was free,
    Then they charged a large fee,
And they now cannot give it away.

1638
Of the madam, a fellow named Prentiss
Requested one non compos mentis.
    "They're all busy," she said,
    "Sucking cocks that are dead.
Would you care to select an apprentice?"

1639
There was a young lady named Pryor
Who said to a gentleman, "Sire,
    Do not feed me that rot,
    I am not to be bought;
If you must know, I'm only for hire."

1640
A worn-out old harlot named Pyle
Got back into whoring with guile.
    She took off for a week
    And returned to her peak—
All she did was sit tight for a while.

1641
A despondent old fellow named Pyle
Sought the madam to cheer him a while.
    But the madam, so shrewd,
    Showed her ladies all nude,
And he picked one whose twat had a smile.

1642
There was an old harlot so quaint—
Her profession she managed to taint,
    For she offered much more
    Than was right for a whore,
Which confirms that she had no restraint.

1643. AU CANADA
A hardy old whore of Quebec
At the end of the day was a wreck
    From the moans and the trials
    Of old farts with the piles
And from bastards that breathed down her neck.

1644
A scrubby old whore of Racine
Invited a lad of sixteen
　　Every week to have three
　　And she charged him no fee,
For she said a new broom will sweep clean.

1645
There was an old madam named Rainey,
Adept in her business and brainy.
　　She charged ten bucks or more
　　For a seasoned old whore,
But a dollar would get you a trainee.

1646
A harlot who lived in Rangoon
Fucked Hindus from morning to noon,
　　But the rest of the day
　　Was the time to make hay,
For she fucked a whole British platoon.

1647
In the bed of a harlot of Rome
Was placed a concealed metronome.
　　In a manner discreet
　　She would step up the beat,
Thus increasing the pay she took home.

1648. SOUTHERN HOSPITALITY
A Bible-Belt whore of St. Claire
Gave service beyond all compare.
　　She sang hymns of devotion
　　Which brought tears of emotion,
And she opened each piece with a prayer.

1649. TAIL OF GLOOM
A gloomy old whore of St. Claire
Was fucked by a man debonair.
　　She told sad tales of woe
　　Which depressed the man so,
That he plunged in a slough of despair.

1650
A businesslike whore of St. Paul
Was asked by a fellow with gall,
      "For a five will you deal?"
      So she gave him a feel
And said, "Do it yourself in the hall."

1651
A call-girl who came from St. Paul
Described how she made a good haul.
      "Follow through in the grind,
      Stay in front, not behind,
And be sure that your eye's on the ball."

1652
There was an old whore of St. Paul
Who gave lessons to lads in the hall.
      Her motto was plain,
      There was much they could gain,
For before one can walk one must crawl.

1653. HARDY CANUCK
A harlot from Saskatchewan
Was struck by a truck which sped on.
      Though her asshole was tore
      She continued to whore,
For she said that the show must go on.

1654
An irascible whore of Savoy
Said that lads who were young gave no joy.
      "When a job must be done,
      Whether serious or fun,
Send a man," she said, "don't send a boy."

1655
A meticulous madam named Sax
Proceeded to fill out her tax.
      She deducted the wear
      On each buxom *derrière*,
And she charged off the wrinkles and cracks.

1656. TOP BILLING
There was a young fellow named Schiller;
The harlot he screwed was a thriller.
    'Twas an overmatched flop
    For she came out on top,
Which left Schiller no choice but to bill her.

1657
A clever young harlot named Scott
Knew how to make gentlemen hot.
    On the streets she'd solicit
    In her manner explicit,
And she'd hand you her card with her twat.

1658. CONSUMERS REPORTS
There was an old harlot named Shield
Who never to critics did yield.
    She settled all rumors
    With *Approved by Consumers,*
And her rating was best in her field.

1659
While walking alone on the shore
A man found a very nice whore,
    Or so the man thought
    Till he plunged in her twat,
And he found there was sand in her bore.

1660
There was an old harlot named Shutes
Who said to G.I.'s, "Don't be brutes.
    You are welcome around
    To your old stamping ground,
But please take off those big hobnailed boots."

1661
A lonely old maid name of Skilling
Proposed to sell ass for a shilling.
    Said a man, "Why so low?"
    She replied, "You must know,
There's a hole in my life that needs filling."

1662. CRACKS GROUND AIRPLANE
Fifty harlots attired in their slacks
For a meeting in L.A. made tracks.
    Their DC-10 flight
    Was canceled outright,
For the airplane had too many cracks.

1663. COME AGAIN
A bearded old fellow out slumming
Excited a girl with his thumbing.
    He divulged he was Christ
    And the girl was enticed,
And he thrilled her with his second coming.

1664. EQUAL RIGHTS
In her state-approved whorehouse, Miss Smutches
Was trapped by the *Fair Practice* clutches.
    She was forced by priorities
    To use whores from minorities,
And old handicapped cripples on crutches.

1665
A DC-10 trip bound for Spain
For 200 whores was in vain.
    Said the F-double-A,
    "You are grounded today—
There are too many cracks on the plane."

1666. METRIC SCREW
An old British harlot named Spence
Would lay down for shillings and pence,
    But the coinage was changed
    And it left her deranged,
For in decimals she was too dense.

1667
A good business head had Miss Spence;
With niceties she did dispense.
    A private named Steve
    Could not get any leave,
So she screwed him on top of the fence.

1668

A harlot one day on a spree
Was fucked by one hundred and three.
    She complained she was beat,
    But a man on the street
Said, "There's plenty of cunt there for me."

1669. COLD CUTS FOR COLD CUTS

A lady of joy on the street
Was stopped by a butcher discreet,
    For this man was beguiled
    By her warmth as she smiled,
But she sold him a cold cut of meat.

1670

A harlot, picked up on the street,
Was charged with dispensing her meat.
    She remarked in defense
    That she meant no offence,
And she offered the jury a treat.

1671

An inquisitive harlot named Strensall—
After sampling the plumber's utensil,
    To a factory went she
    There determined to see
How the lead is put into a pencil.

1672

A harlot once healthy and strong
For years had been taking the prong.
    She was ill for a year
    Then resumed her career,
But she found the road back hard and long.

1673

A simple young fellow was Stubby;
The harlot he married was grubby.
    "Every day," he said, "Shirley,
    You must leave your work early
And save the last piece for your hubby."

1674

When John licked a harlot named Susie,
He slobbered all over the floozie,
    So she said to him, "John,
    Let's go out on the lawn,
And I'll show you how dogs lick my coozie."

1675
There was an old harlot named Swincombe,
So good that she even had kin come.
    On the income she made
    There were no taxes paid,
For the income she made was all *sincome*.

1676. WASTE NOT, WANT NOT
The brothel was cleaned to good taste
By sweeper McBridle in haste,
    For when harlots were idle
    They were screwed by McBridle
As he hated to see so much waste.

1677
A low-priced old harlot of Thrace
Enticed a young man to her place,
    But he said to her, "Nellie,
    You must lay on your belly,
For I can't stand to look at your face."

1678
A capable harlot named Thresher
Worked hard all day long and felt fresher.
    All her clients were fat
    But she didn't mind that,
For she said she worked best under pressure.

1679. FAIR SHAKE
There was an old whore of Tobruk
Who kept her accounts in a book,
    And this may sound bizarre,
    But her best day by far
Was the time that with ague she shook.

1680
A lady who worked many towns
Was kidded one day by some clowns.
    They wanted to know
    How her business did go;
She said that it had ups and downs.

1681. AT THE NURSING HOME

A soft-hearted whore named Miss Tuckem
Would take on poor cripples and fuck 'em,
    And those lame, halt and blind,
    And in wheelchairs confined—
If they needed a blow-job, she'd suck 'em.

1682

There was an old madam named Tuckers
Who simplified matters for fuckers.
    She equipped all her dives
    With a room for the wives,
And young lads with their dads received suckers.

1683

The broken-down harlot named Tweek
Was thirty years over her peak.
    She was fast nearing death
    But she had a faint breath,
So was kept on the job one more week.

1684

A despondent old fellow of Twinning
Sought to bolster his image by sinning.
    The old madam showed whores
    And said, "Pick one, she's yours."
So he picked one whose pussy was grinning.

1685

An elderly harlot of Twitting
Received an award upon quitting—
    Well-preserved in a crock
    Was an elephant's cock—
And she said the award was most fitting.

1686

A brothel inspector, undaunting,
Did check on the girls who were flaunting
    The rules that were set
    By the council that met.
His report: "They were laid and found wanting."

1687

For work the old harlot undressed
And fucked a young man with great zest.
    From the strain she expired
    But her cohorts admired,
For to die in the harness was best.

1688. HONORABLE DISCHARGE
By harlots the novice is vexed,
And often he stands there, perplexed.
    She goes through the motion
    Of utter devotion,
Then discharges him, shouting, "Who's next?"

1689
Small breasts had the harlot of Wales
But profits were high on her sales.
    She was tried and confined
    For the jury did find
It was fraudulent use of the males.

1690
The Yellow Page ad of whore Wallace
For lonely young men had some solace:
    "If you can't come to us
    We'll get girls on the bus—
They can be at your place if you call us."

1691
When hunting for harlots, young Watson
Asked a whore to get into his Datsun.
    She examined his prick
    And said, "Better you lick,
And be sure that you lick the right slot, son."

1692
A sordid old harlot named Weiss
A bearded old man did entice.
    Between panting and wheezes
    He maintained he was Jesus,
So she let the old bastard come twice.

1693
Complained an old harlot named Wertz:
"My business of late badly hurts.
    At times it is slow—
    Men come and they go—
And sometimes they come in big spurts."

1694
An aged old whore from the West
Could still give a fuck with great zest.
    Though her asshole was loose
    And her cunt had no juice,
She still managed by keeping a breast.

1695. EARTHQUAKE REGION

A geologist searching the West
Met a whore whom he tackled with zest.
    Every year with his staff
    He showed plots on his graph,
To observe how her crack had progressed.

1696

There was an old harlot named Whaling
Who drummed up new business by mailing.
    She removed all her clothes
    And the men that she chose
Were invited to view the unveiling.

1697

There was an old whore, Winifred,
Who redid her room gold and red,
    She received much acclaim,
    But the reason men came
Was to view her new spread on the bed.

1698

There was an old madam named Wise
Who offered some very good buys—
    From the ten dollar girls
    Who were plump and with curls,
To the fifty-cent pieces with flies.

14

Diseases

1699. METROPOLITAN OPERA STAR*
When her fistula drained in her ano
She would scream from the pain and guano.
    Said old Bing, "Do not fret,
    You can sing at the Met
As a coloratura soprano."

1700
Three ladies out shopping, named Babbs,
Were screwed coming home in their cabs.
    One came home with some hams,
    And the second with clams,
And third one came home with the crabs.

1701*
A careless young girl of Baghdad
Divulged why diseases she had.
    She had no time to marry
    Every Tom, Dick and Harry,
And she said that she wanted it bad.

1702
There was an old whore of Belgrade
Whose chancres had left her dismayed.
    She sought help from Doc Gray
    But had no cash to pay,
So she offered her service in trade.

1703
To the doc went a lady named Bliss—
She had pemphigus sores where she'd piss.
    After treating all year,
    Said the doc, "Do not fear,
For it soon will be ready to kiss."

1704*
A gentleman friend of Miss Boyle,
Imbued with desire to despoil,
    Was advised that the gentry
    Should employ the rear entry,
For the front was commencing to spoil.

1705. THE 4-D'S*
If bargains are what you are buying,
A madam all kinds is supplying,
    She has some with Disease,
    And some Dead, if you please,
And some wretches Disabled or Dying.

1706
A canny old fellow of Chester
Advised a young girl he could best her,
    And he did for a while
    But he soon lost his smile,
For his pecker proceeded to fester.

1707. INTRIGUED BY NOVELTY
A grimy old harlot of Chester
Stunk bad and no man would request her.
    She got back in the groove
    And the lodge did approve
When she offered a sore that did fester.

1708
A thrifty old lady, so chubby,
Was saving her cunt for a hubby.
    But too long she had tarried
    And the man that she married
Complained that her cunt was too grubby.

1709
A sickly young fellow named Claude
Fell down in a faint on the sod.
    He divulged it was true,
    He had caught Asian flu,
The disease which one gets from a broad.

1710
A jealous old fellow of Corning
Suspected his wife of suborning.
    He said, "I smell a rat."
    And his wife answered, "Drat,
I will douche the first thing in the morning."

1711
While shopping, a fellow from Cottam
Observed some fine fish and he bought 'em.
    Said the clerk, young Miss Babbs,
    "Would you care for some crabs?"
He said, "Thanks, but I already got 'em."

1712
There was a young tourist named Cotton
Whose travels would not be forgotten.
     On a trip to Berlin
     He enjoyed all his sin,
But in Denmark he found something rotten.

1713. GONORRHEA OF THE BIG TOE*
To tickle a girl with his foot
Was fun for the man from Beirut.
     Said the doctor, "Now Joe,
     This disease on your toe,
Tell me where has your big toe been put?"

1714
Since his girl had the clap, Mr. Fritz
Decided the rear hole to blitz,
     Thus avoiding the pox
     Which infested her box,
But his pecker has now got the shits.

1715
A charming young lady named Gail
Was having her first piece of tail,
     And this girl, sweet and pure,
     Felt completely secure
With her scabby old scrofulous male.

1716
A conniving young fellow named Gus
Had raped an old maid on the bus.
     Though he bragged of his pluck
     And the way that he struck,
What he struck was a pocket of pus.

1717
A grimy young fellow was Gus;
His pecker was slimy with pus.
     But his girl friend was grimier
     And her pussy was slimier,
So she never created a fuss.

1718
A simple young fellow named Hame
Had syph and the clap—what a shame!
     Was it sister or brother,
     Or perhaps his dear mother,
Or one of those whores he should blame?

1719
There was a young fellow named Hap
Who caught a bad case of the clap.
     His turds ended up square—
     There was no taper there—
And his asshole would shut with a snap.

1720*
When illness struck wretched old Haver,
The doctors convened to palaver.
     They concluded the answer
     Was to keep his good cancer
And to toss out his rotten cadaver.

1721
When he dropped down his trousers, young Hearst
His foul prick he exposed, 'twas the worst.
     Said the harlot discreet,
     "What a foul-looking meat.
I believe I must suck it off first."

1722
At a dinner for whores in Hoboken
The waiter, well-hung, started pokin'.
     He ran into a batch
     With the clap in their snatch,
And found four with their hymens not broken.

1723
A carless young lady named Hussey
In fucking was not the least fussy.
     She was screwed by a cabbie
     Whose pecker was scabby,
And now Hussey's pussy is pussy.

1724. NOTHING FROM DENMARK?
There was an old tourist named Kapps
Who traced out his trip on his maps.
     He discovered that Tiflis
     Was the place he got syphilis,
And in London was where he caught claps.

1725
A lonely old maid name of Kate
Had trouble in finding a date.
     An old man who was stiff
     Took a sniff of her quiff
And said, "Kate, I'm afraid it's too late!"

1726
There was an old lady named Kay
Who bragged, in her off-handed way,
> There was life where she peed,
> And the doctor agreed,
For he gave her a bug-killing spray.

1727
There was a young fellow named Kline
Who caught his first crab at age nine.
> It is sad to relate
> It could not find a mate
And it withered away on the vine.

1728
To the doc went a whore name of Lancet
For her pussy was raunchy and rancid.
> As he pulled out his prick,
> Said the doc, "It looks sick,
And it smells pretty bad, but I'll chance it."

1729
The cunt doctor, Ephram Q. Luntz,
Was expert at transforming cunts.
> He healed chancres and sores
> In the foulest of whores,
And approved them by licking them once.

1730
There was an old whore named McFink
Whose pussy was rotten, I think.
> She was fucked for an hour
> By old Cardinal Bower,
For that's all he could take of the stink.

1731
Fine girls had old madam McLure,
Nine nine point nine nine percent pure,
> But a fellow named Vance
> Picked the wrong one by chance,
And it took him a year for the cure.

1732
For a walk in the park went Miss Minter;
A man had a thought to imprint her.
> On this fine day in fall
> She was fucked near the wall,
But she showed him where crabs spend the winter.

1733
A young female boxer was Nell,
But her pussy was raunchy as hell.
    She was always the victor
    Since no one had licked her,
For no one could get past the smell.

1734
An incredible harlot was Nellie,
Repugnant, foul-spoken and smelly,
    But she owes her success
    To an adman's finesse
For the ad space she sold on her belly.

1735
A filthy old lady named Patch
A fellow enticed with her snatch.
    He bent over to puke
    And he said, "What a fluke!
By hand I must run off a batch."

1736
The girl that was picked up by Pease
Advised him she knew how to please,
    "As you plainly can see
    There are no flies on me."
But he found there were plenty of fleas.

1737. THE HEALER*
Somoza to U.S. came quick
With pustular sores on his prick.
    Said a bigwig, bemused,
    "Do not look so confused—
I have cured them much worse with one lick."

1738
Old Nader was cut to the quick;
His whore with a full house was sick,
    So he campaigned the jails
    For the scrofulous quails
And he tested them all with his prick.

1739. LOOK BEFORE YOU PLUNGE
A mortified fellow named Ray
Complained to the madam one day,
   "All your girls are Grade B,
   Some have pox, I can see,
And I came here expecting Grade A."

[1740]
The madam, a seasoned old whore,
Replied, "You buy meat at the store
   That's derived from 4-D's,
   Which were Dead, had Disease,
Were Disabled or Dying, what's more."

1741
A forthright young fellow named Rinky
In a pussy inserted his pinkie,
   Then his finger he sniffed
   And he said, somewhat miffed,
"I don't fuck with a twat that is stinky."

1742
There was a young fellow named Scotten
Who figured that ass should be boughten,
   But he soon changed his mind
   At the time he did find
That the last one he bought was all rotten.

1743
A philosopher, walking the shore,
Was ignoring the pleas of a whore,
   But he said he would screw
   If she had something new,
So she offered a festering sore.

1744
There was a young fellow named Shorty
Who thought of himself as quite sporty,
   But the girls that he laid
   Were all sadly dismayed,
For chancres and clap were his forte.

1745. MATTER RESOLVED

A thoughtful young fellow named Slatter
Had fucked an old whore name of Hatter.
    She was slimy with pus
    But he raised not a fuss,
And he just made the best of the matter.

1746

There was a young lady of Stottam
Who itched and she scratched at her bottom.
    She said, "As I feared,
    He had crabs in his beard;
This must be the reason I caught 'em."

1747

A malodorous girl of Tacoma
Had a twat with such fetid aroma,
    That when Pierre went to lick it
    He fell down in her thicket,
And he never came out of the coma.

1748

The president knows all the tricks
How the world's major problems to fix.
    He invites the world's scum
    To convene—so they come,
And he sucks on their pustular pricks.

1749

Said a man to a harlot, "I wish you
Would wipe off your cunt with this tissue."
    But her pussy still leaked
    And she said, somewhat piqued,
"Please do not make a point of the issue."

15

Losses

1750
There was an old whore of Algiers
Who found the whole lodge in arrears,
    So she threatened to sue
    For the payments past due,
Or she'd cut off their peckers with shears.

1751
A simple young lady alluring
Thought the ditch-digger's cock was enduring,
    But the rigger's was bigger,
    And he fucked with such vigor
That her asshole was torn from its mooring.

1752
A hardy young lady named Annabel
Was terribly frayed by old Hannibal,
    But it did not compare
    To the wear and the tear
At the time she was ate by a cannibal.

1753
The surgeon applied his skilled arts
Assembling sex parts per his charts
    Which he put in his bag
    For a worn-out old hag,
And her hole was made up of the parts.

1754
There was a contortionist Bach
Who tried a new twist with Miss Flock,
    But he slipped on some shit
    And her nipple he bit
And she bit off the end of his cock.

1755
While having some tail, Mr. Baird
Was asked by his maid how he fared.
    He said, "Fit as a fiddle
    But the next time we diddle
I suggest that you have it repaired."

1756
On sick leave was old harlot Barrett;
She took some time out to repair it.
    Since the madam was short
    She returned to the sport,
Where she just had to grin and to bear it.

1757
There was a young girl of Belgrade
With teeth in her snatch where she played.
    An old dentist named Block
    Lost the end of his cock
As he probed for the tooth that decayed.

1758
A widow who lived in Berlin
Cut the cock off her dead husband Flynn.
    Up his dead ass she shoved it
    And she said, "He'd have loved it!
It's the only hole it's not been in."

1759
A gourmet with doubts was beset
When he climbed into bed with Annette.
    As he viewed her crotch bare
    He exclaimed in despair,
"I'm afraid that this pussy's been et."

1760
For a ball, a young lady named Bess
Got dressed in a newspaper dress.
    She got close to a joker,
    A most careless young smoker,
And he burned her sport section, no less.

1761. THE COUNTDOWN
Worn so bad was the cunt of Miss Bliss,
That she found it a strain just to piss.
    Said old Doctor McBounter
    As he started to mount her,
"You have thirteen fucks left after this."

1762
A skilful young surgeon named Bragg
The vagina removed from a hag.
    She recouped for a while
    And she said, with a smile,
"Now the pussy is out of the bag."

1763
A surgeon who hailed from Cape Horn
Had rebuilt a cock that was worn,
  But his climaxing feat
  Was replacing the meat
On a snatch that was tattered and torn.

1764
To the doc for repairs went whore Cappy
And the surgeon's remarks made her happy,
  "There will be no delay,
  I will start right away,
And I'll see the affair is made snappy."

1765
A worried young bridegroom named Carson
Observed his bride had every farce on.
  He was not shook a bit
  By her wig and false tit,
But he asked that she should keep her arse on.

1766
A skilful inventor named Cass
Made a plucker for chickens first class.
  But it seems, and we quote 'im,
  The machine seized his scrotum
And it plucked every hair from his ass.

1767
In the woods a young man took a crap
Directly on top of a trap.
  Though this may sound absurd,
  The fall of his turd
Caught his balls in the trap with a snap.

1768
There was an old harlot named Cushing;
Her trade for long years she kept pushing.
  She had so many scrapes
  With all manner of apes
That she needed a pussy rebushing.

1769
There was a young fellow named Dag
Who built a machine that would shag.
  On the twenty-fifth stroke
  The connecting rod broke
And it ripped out the balls from his bag.

1770
A deceptive young lady named Dare
Removed her fake tits, ass and hair,
 But her boyfriend was slick
 For he pulled out his prick
And he fucked all the stuff in the chair.

1771
The bridegroom observed his bride dear
Remove her fake tits, teeth and gear,
 So he said, with a grunt,
 "When you get to the cunt
You can toss the damn thing over here."

1772
Said the doctor with fingers so deft,
As he probed in an old lady's cleft,
 "From the wear, I would say,
 It's eroding away,
And you only have fourteen fucks left."

1773
There was a young lad of Defiance
Who valued advances of science.
 On account of the frost
 His pecker was lost,
And he fucked with a plastic appliance.

1774. BEARD THE LION
A cunt-lapping man of Dundee
Arose from the crotch of Miss Lee.
 As he fondled his chin
 He said with a grin,
"Tell me, where did I get this goatee?"

1775. A MATTER OF SEMANTICS
In Japan a young Yank with elation
Asked a whore for a new sex creation.
 But he went into shock
 When she bit off his cock,
For the meaning was lost in translation.

1776
There was a young fellow enduring
Who screwed a young lady alluring.
    He was hung like a horse
    And he fucked with such force
That her asshole was torn from its mooring.

1777
A worn-out old harlot named Ewing
Remained in her business of screwing
    With her pussy brand-new
    Which she fastened with glue,
But it could not withstand a shampooing.

1778
There was a young lady named Fabia
With hooks on the flaps of her labia.
    She was fucked by young Flynn
    But she ripped his foreskin,
And she laughed and said, "How does this grab ya?"

1779. TRANSPLANT
The harlot said, "Look, let us face it,
We're forced by this work to debase it;
    But with medical knowledge
    That they learn now in college,
It is simple enough to replace it."

1780
There was an old seamstress forlorn,
Whose asshole was weathered and worn.
    She so oft had been needled
    That she wheezed and she wheedled,
And her pussy was tattered and torn.

1781. MALPRACTICE
There was a young surgeon named Fox
Who built for a whore a new box.
    Through his lack of discretion
    She did lose her profession
For it failed to accommodate cocks.

1782
In the war a young soldier named Fred
Was bombed and he lost half his head,
    And his legs were a fright
    But he smiled with delight,
For his pecker still hung by a thread.

1783
In Japan a young GI named Goff
Fucked a whore with an ill-smelling trough.
    The bitch was a dud
    With the Japanese crud,
And his pecker turned black and fell off.

1784
From a madam, a fellow named Gore
Selected her lowest priced whore.
    When he gave her a goose
    Her right titty came loose
And her pussy dropped down to the floor.

1785*
There was a young sailor named Gore
Who danced till his asshole was sore.
    On his cutlass he slipped
    And his scrotum was ripped
And his testicles dropped to the floor.

1786
A skilful young surgeon named Gore
Gained fame that would last evermore,
    For he rebuilt a twat
    By drawing it taut
And was known as the friend of the whore.

1787
At the port a young sailor named Gore
Picked up a loose woman, a whore.
    To his utter dismay
    Both her tits fell away
And her pussy dropped down to the floor.

1788
A dim-witted fellow of Gosham
Took out both his ballocks to wash 'em.
    Said his wife to him, "Jack,
    If you don't put them back
I'll step on the buggers and squash 'em."

1789
A discomposed lady of Guelph
Would daily assemble herself
    With her wig, a glass eye,
    Her peg leg all awry,
And her cunt which she kept on the shelf.

1790. TROPHIES OF A FORMER LOVE
A sadistic young lady named Hicks
Abducted young men with sly tricks.
    She cut off their balls
    Which she hung on the walls,
And made door handles out of their pricks.

[1791]
It seems that one day she got reckless
With a midget, well-hung, name of Beckless.
    He fucked her, the runt,
    Then he cut out her cunt,
Which he hung on a gold-plated necklace.

[1792]
She met an old butler named Springer
And she marveled his oversize dinger.
    But this crafty old vassal—
    He cut out her ass'le
And he made him a ring for his finger.

1793
There was a young surgeon named Hartz,
An expert in surgical arts.
    He could fashion a patch
    To recover a snatch,
Or make cocks with replaceable parts.

1794*
There was an old scientist, Hill,
Who swallowed a nuclear pill.
    The reaction corroded
    His balls, which exploded,
And his asshole was found in Brazil.

1795
There was a sharecropper named Hopper
Whose organs were caught in a chopper.
    His gonads were tangled
    And his pecker was mangled
Till it looked like a truncated stopper.

1796*
An ingenious old chemist named Hugh
Brought some hope to the faltering screw.
    He concocted one day
    A new vaginal spray
Which made worn-out old cunts smell like new.

1797
With a whore, a frail fellow named Jay
Did not notice, while fucking away,
    That his cock broke in two.
    A cuntlapper named Lew
Had it sent back by mail the next day.

1798
There was a young soldier named Jock
Who was bombed as he worked on the dock.
    Though he lost every limb
    Yet his life was not grim;
He could still drive his car with his cock.

1799
A venturesome fellow named Jock
Picked up a loose girl in Iraq.
    Due to moral decay
    Her right tit fell away,
And her pussy came off on his cock.

1800
When Bobby played tennis with King,
His racket he rammed up her thing,
    But the smash that she threw
    Turned Bobby's balls blue,
And his prick he now wears in a sling.

1801
There was a young fellow named Kissel
Whose asshole was ripped by a missile.
    It was mended with strips
    Which they took from his lips,
And now through his ass he can whistle.

1802
A careless young fellow named Kline
Was fucking a whore serpentine.
    In the midst of her throes
    She bit off his nose.
He thanked God it was not sixty-nine.

1803
The bride of a man of Lapeer,
Removed her fake tits, teeth and gear,
    So he said with a frown
    As her panties came down,
"When you get to the cunt, throw it here."

1804
The well-hung young milkman McGivery,
While taking his horse to the livery,
    In the groin got a kick,
    And it made him so sick
For the smart did impede his delivery.

1805
A toothsome young lady named Morse
Had teeth in her snatch like a horse.
    If a man was obscene
    She would bite it off clean,
But good fuckers feared nothing, of course.

1806
There was a young sailor of Munich
Who carried a sword 'neath his tunic.
    The fandango he tried
    And he severed his pride;
Now the sailor from Munich's a eunich.

1807
A golfer who came from Nantucket
Protected his balls with a bucket,
    For one time, thoughtlessly,
    He set one on a tee
And he drove it a mile when he struck it.

1808
When her dear husband died, Mrs. Newt
Was sad, 'cause she missed the old coot,
    So she cut off his balls,
    Which she hung on the walls,
And his prick she made into a flute.

1809
A statue de-nutter named Newt
Thought statues with no nuts were cute,
    But his efforts did fizzle
    When he slipped with his chisel
And he severed his prick at the root.

1810

A fetish for fish had old Newt
And for women he cared not a hoot,
    But he met with frustration
    When he fucked a crustacean,
For it snapped off his prick at the root.

1811

A young apple-grower named Pease
Grew apples so fine on his trees.
    He took some to the fair
    In his thin underwear,
And two of his apples did freeze.

1812

A thalidomide baby was Pete;
He was born with his arms incomplete,
    But he did not lament
    This most tragic event,
He could still beat his meat with his feet.

1813

A sorry young soldier was Pete;
Some shrapnel had blown off his meat,
    And his arms were just stumps
    But he still got his lumps,
For he managed to fuck with his feet.

1814

There was an old widow who raised
The sheet on her dead man and praised
    What she sucked on for years,
    Then she cropped it with shears,
For she wanted to sample it braised.

1815

There was a young lady of Rheims
Who took on the soldiers in teams.
    Ten thousand discharges
    And some bayonet charges
And her ass fell apart at the seams.

1816. HORSE TALE

There was a young butcher named Spicer
Whose pecker got caught in the slicer.
    As it dropped from the root
    He could only salute,
And the whole thing could not be conciser.

[1817]
He met an old sailor named Pete
Who knew how to splice a rope neat,
    So he cut off the cock
    Of a horse of fine stock
And he asked him to splice on three feet.

[1818]
When Spicer attempted to lay
He held it erect and did say,
    "Are you ready to test?"
    But was sadly depressed
For his pecker dropped down and said, "Neigh."

1819. RAPER RAPPED
To fend off a rapist, Miss Scott
Applied her karate, well-taught.
    She ripped out his bum
    With her finger and thumb,
And she strangled his cock with her twat.

1820
"Well now," said the dentist named Shutes,
"I'm ready, hang onto your boots."
    With efforts protracted
    The tooth was extracted,
But his balls were torn out with the roots.

1821. HUNG UP
So thrilled was a fellow named Spence
When the widow next door cried, "Come hence,"
    That he leaped like a deer
    So the fence he would clear,
But his scrotum hung up on the fence.

1822
While hunting, some buckshot hit Springer
And some of it passed through his dinger.
    When he pissed, spray would shoot
    Through the holes like a flute,
Till a flutist taught Springer to finger.

1823
A sterling old maid name of Symes
With her counterfeit cunt had good times.
    She cashed in on the porters
    Whom she conned in her quarters,
And she fucked them for nickels and dimes.

1824
While cutting up meat, butcher Tedder
Fell down with his cock in the shredder.
    It came out like chopped veal,
    But in time it did heal,
And he said it went off a lot better.

1825
There was a young fireman named Tinder
Who saved an old lady and pinned her,
    Then he fucked her all day—
    When the smoke cleared away
His pecker was burned to a cinder.

1826
A broken-down harlot did tremble
When violently fucked by young Kemble.
    He said, "Let's have another."
    But she said, "Hold it, brother,
For my cunt I must now reassemble."

1827
A battered old whore with a worn hole
Was put on the street with her torn hole,
    But her ass was not worn
    So she sold it for corn,
And it got to be known as the corn hole.

1828
There was a young student of Yale
Whose features were sickly and pale.
    He was caught in a frost
    And his balls were both lost,
And his pecker was battered by hail.

16

Sex Substitutes

1829
There was a steamfitter Akeem
Who fitted his pipe, in his dream,
    Into twenty fair lasses
    And he wore out their asses;
When he woke he had blown all his steam.

1830. SELF-SERVICE
A man with himself made alliance—
Shoved his cock up his ass in defiance,
    And he mocked every moral
    Whether written or oral,
And defied every law known to science.

1831. SIX TO A PACK
Said the butcher's apprentice, Miss Banks,
To the butcher, "Enough of your pranks.
    As a fucker you're fair,
    But you cannot compare
To a package of *Swift's Premium Franks.*"

1832
A horny young fellow named Barm
Was miffed by his date who lacked charm.
    He was more than annoyed
    By her crotch null and void,
So he buggered the pit in her arm.

1833
Through the window a spinster named Barrett
Observed a lad beating his carrot,
    So she yelled, with arms crossed,
    "This is love's labor lost!
Why don't you come in and we'll share it?"

1834
There was a young lady named Bayer
Who took off her clothes for the mayor,
      Then she said to the fink,
      "I am ready, I think."
Said the mayor, "I'm just a surveyor."

1835
A fancy young man of Belgrade
Sex parts of both sexes displayed.
      He made short disposition
      Of this deviant condition
When he showed that he could be self-made.

1836
There was a young man of Belgrade
Who dreamt of a game that he played
      Where he chased a fair lass
      And he pounced on her ass;
He awoke and he found the bed made.

1837. CONDITIONED RESPONSE
There was an old fellow named Bert
Whose wife wore her bedclothes to flirt,
      So it turned out one day
      When his wife was away
He successfully fucked her nightshirt.

1838
An eager young beaver named Brickley
Engaged an old whore that was sickly,
      But she started to puke,
      So he said, "What a fluke!"
And he finished by jacking off quickly.

1839
To Olympics went queer Mr. Burke,
For he loved to see athletes at work.
      There the whole day he spent
      At his favored event
Which was watching the snatch and the jerk.

1840
The prick of a fellow named Chase
Got hard while his girl friend said *Grace*.
      So he tried for a fuck
      But got stuck in the duck
And blew stuffing all over the place.

1841
Miss Fern did attach to the churn
A dildoe, and started to turn
    The cream into butter
    With nary a flutter;
When the butter was made, so was Fern.

1842
A moral young lady of Clyde
In righteous behaviour took pride,
    So they made her a shunt
    Which bypassed her cunt—
Now she fucks through a hole in her side.

1843
Inventive, ingenious young Clyde
Produced a Mechanical Bride.
    Without fear or compunction
    It performed every function
While a permanent virgin beside.

1844
A beggar who alleys did comb
Accosted a harlot in Rome.
    With a passioned appeal
    He requested a feel;
She said charity starts right at home.

1845. THE LABOR OF LOVE
A lovely fiancée had Croylett,
But his morals said: "Do not despoil it!"
    So when love and desire
    Welled up like hot fire,
He would flush every drop down the toilet.

1846. STRAIGHT SHOOTER
To a girl that he met at a dance
Jack made an improper advance.
    He was so much impressed
    When this girl acquiesced,
That his rifle went off in his pants.

1847

There was an old madam distressed
From business depressed like the rest.
    It was sad and pathetic
    Till she used girls synthetic,
With their pussies replaced on request.

1848. WOMEN'S LIB

The female reporter, Miss Dix,
Used all of her wiles and her tricks
    To get news, I presume,
    In the men's locker room,
Where she fondled the winning team's pricks.

1849

The noted philosopher, Drew,
Two dancers observed in a stew.
    His studied conclusion:
    Although not quite a fusion,
A dance is a vertical screw.

1850. SNUFF ADDICT

While sneezing, a lady named Duff
Had orgasmic throes quite enough.
    Said a friend, "Don't ignore it.
    You must do something for it."
She said, "All that I take is some snuff."

1851

A man who had talents elastic
Had fashioned a penis from plastic.
    He could twirl and could spin it
    And reload in one minute;
It went off in a manner fantastic.

1852. JUST FOR THE DAY

To hardship the doctor's enured;
He stands before patients assured.
    Not one does suspect
    His illness abject—
One look at a cunt and he's cured.

1853. GESUNDHEIT!

A girl with high morals, Miss Ewing,
Said sex would not be her undoing.
      She felt good when she sneezed
      And it left her so pleased
That she used it in place of a screwing.

1854. AMEND THE CONSTITUTION

Our Congressmen we can't excuse,
For morals and trust they abuse.
      To get out of this fix
      Elect men with no pricks,
So their office they cannot misuse.

1855. MASS PRODUCTION

On a crankshaft a madam named Frank
Tied cunts to each rod for a prank.
      Then she lined up the men
      Who to fuck had a yen
And she fucked them by turning a crank.

1856. NOCTURNAL COMMISSION

There was a young fellow named Freeman
Who had a delightful time dreamin'
      How the harem he raped
      While the sheik stood and gaped;
He awoke with a handful of semen.

1857. MR. GOODWRENCH

There was an old harlot named French
Who spent a whole week on the bench.
      She'd been fucked in her manor
      By a man with a spanner
And it gave her, she said, a bad wrench.

1858. HAIR RESTORER

A distracted young mother named Frommes
Spent her time in the church singing psalms,
      For her son, keen and bright,
      Suffered loss in his sight,
And had hair growing thick on his palms.

1859

There was a cunt painter, Geraint,
Who pondered his paint bucket quaint.
    Then he said, "I declare
    That the cunts came from there,
So he blew in his bucket of paint.

1860

While walking, a fellow named Glick
Was stopped by a shapely young chick.
    He complained, "I declare
    I have no cash to spare.
If you pay me, I'll give you a lick."

1861. INDIAN ROPE TRICK

A man from the Cape of Good Hope
With women no longer could cope,
    So to India he went
    With his tool badly bent,
Where he studied the trick with the rope.

1862

The priest from the Cape of Good Hope
Was tolling the bell for the pope.
    On the twenty-fifth bong
    The rope caught his dong,
And the priest was tolled off by the rope.

1863

While shopping, a fellow named Gore
Saw manikins dressed in a store.
    Their attire was improper
    Which aroused the old shopper,
So he fucked three or four on the floor.

1864

There was a young cowgirl named Harriet;
A cowpoke she caught with a lariat.
    He was playing a game
    And she said to him, "Shame,
I've a much better place you can bury it."

1865

If you're mailing a letter in haste
Since you haven't a moment to waste,
    But you've had a mishap
    For you can't seal the flap,
Then by hand you can work up some paste.

13

1866
Man learned to burn timber to heat with
And he fashioned utensils to eat with.
　　Though his brain he has grooved
　　He has never improved
On the hand that he uses to beat with.

1867
To her date said a lady named Hewitt,
"My mother said I mustn't do it.
　　She advised against fucking
　　But said nothing of sucking—
Would you mind if I licked it and blew it?"

1868. EARLY BIRD
A spritely young lady named Joan
Invited a lad on the phone
　　To rush right over there,
　　But he cried in despair,
"It's too late—I have sinned all alone!"

1869. MAIL ORDER DEAL
At Sears, a young fellow named Jock
Bought a foam rubber cunt for his cock.
　　It was easy to wash it,
　　In a sink he would slosh it—
No expenses, complaints, stink or schlock.

1870
In his jet plane a pilot named Jock
Raced west and was beating the clock.
　　When the date line was crossed,
　　The race—it was lost—
So he sat down and beat on his cock.

1871. PREMATURE COPULATION
A novice young fellow with Kate
Presumed he was doing first rate.
　　When Kate remarked, "Flynn,
　　Let's indulge in some sin."
"Oh my goodness," cried Flynn, "it's too late!"

1872. THE SNERD
A bicycle buff name of Keats
Watched the girls doing bicycle feats,
    And right after they raced
    He ran over in haste
To sniff at the bicycle seats.

1873
The girl that was dated by Kelly
Was repugnant, misshapen and smelly,
    But in spite of her flaws
    It was not a lost cause,
For he played with the bulge on her belly.

1874. ROYAL SCREWING
The Queen got in bed with the King,
Prepared for a fine royal fling.
    But the King, so sedate,
    First her pussy he ate,
Then proceeded to do his own thing.

1875
A feeble old fellow named Kregg
Was fucking a whore with one leg.
    He could not make the grade
    And the whore was dismayed,
So she finished herself with her peg.

1876
A moral young girl of Lapeer
Held righteous behaviour so dear
    That she made her a shunt
    Which would bypass her cunt—
Now she fucks through a hole in her ear.

1877
A rugged old lumberman Lee
Wed a one-legged maid of Dundee,
    For he saw by the grain
    That her peg did contain
The knothole he fucked in a tree.

1878. LUMBER LOVER
A botany student named Lee
Fell madly in love with a tree,
    So each knothole with care
    He embellished with hair
And he went on a mad fucking spree.

1879. BUT ONLY GOD CAN MAKE A TREE
A tree-loving skeptic named Lee
Seduced a grown tree with esprit,
    And in triumph did shout
    That he too without doubt
Was proficient in making a tree.

1880
A lecherous salesman named Leith
Would always feel girls underneath.
    The young ladies down south
    Game him busts in the mouth,
While up north he got cracks in the teeth.

1881. 2.54 CM
A virtuous lady named Lynch
From decency never would flinch.
    She professed morals sound
    And she held to her ground,
And she never gave in but an inch.

1882
An old abstract painter, MacNeal,
Was painting a pussy so real
    That while he was painting
    From desire he was fainting,
And he blew on the canvas, the heel.

1883
An old engineer named McCawdel
Said women would fiddle and dawdle,
    So two days out of three
    In his lab he would be
Where he screwed a mechanical model.

1884
A heavy old smoker McLure
Did reek like the slime in a sewer.
    When he took a plane flight
    His wife missed him that night,
So she slept with a pile of manure.

1885
The crusading knight Sir McWade
Great courage and vigor displayed.
   He collected his forces,
   Some on foot, some on horses,
And embarked on a panty crusade.

1886
When a simple old maid named Moncrieff
Saw Apollo in stone, dressed so brief,
   She exclaimed in dismay,
   "He would be a great lay—
Tell me, how did he fuck with a leaf?"

1887
There were two young ladies named Pakenham
Who often let Harry and Jack in 'em,
   And when they were through,
   For something to do,
They would finger their cunts and start whackin' 'em.

1888
There were two young brothers named Pakenham
Intrigued by the way girls were stackin' 'em.
   But a girl got them hot
   By exposing her twat,
So they unzipped their flies to start whackin' 'em.

1889. BACK TO THE DRAWING BOARD
For a lad, an old surgeon named Patch
Reconstructed a pecker from scratch.
   When he felt through his pocket
   It would blow like a rocket,
But it failed to go off in a snatch.

1890
A bicycle buff name of Pete
Would cycle each day with his sweet,
   Then he'd send her away
   And the rest of the day
He would sniff at the bicycle seat.

1891. ONCE A YEAR DOWN THE CHIMNEY
At Christmas a lady named Plum
Presented her bare-naked bum
    And asked Santa to fuck,
    But old Santa said, "Yuck,
Down the chimney I've already come."

1892
A husband deprived was young Rand;
His wife took a most stubborn stand,
    For she doled out his pleasure
    Every month a small measure.
He fell madly in love with his hand.

1893
A simple young lady named Randall
Could not find a man with a handle,
    So she played a game shallow
    With a short piece of tallow,
But this game, it was not worth the candle.

1894
In the dark a young fellow named River
A fuck to his wife did deliver,
    But after he came,
    He said, "It's the same
As fucking a pound of warm liver."

1895
To the doc went a lady named Reepie;
Her eyes and her nose were all weepy.
    Said the doctor serene,
    "Your asshole looks clean,
Now let's have a look at your peepee."

1896
A moral young lady named Rose
For men would not take off her clothes.
    She rejected men's pricks
    And she got all her kicks
By farting and blowing her nose.

1897
There was a young lady named Schickel
Who lay on her back for a nickel,
    And when she was through,
    For something to do,
She would fuck with a kosher dill pickle.

1898
A newlywed fellow named Schickel
Attempted his darling to tickle.
>   He could not touch her teats
>   While she pickled her beets,
Which left Schickel to beat on his pickle.

1899
There was a blind fellow named Scott
Who one day a ladyfriend sought.
>   As he made an advance
>   He went off in his pants
When his cane felt the twitch in her twat.

1900
An agile young man of Seattle
Found fucking in rowboats a battle.
>   He tried screwing canoeing
>   But this proved his undoing,
So he finished his girl with his paddle.

1901
When Peter was dating Miss Shirley
He pulled out his pecker so burly.
>   As she opened her chasm
>   He went into orgasm,
And he came just before prematurely.

1902. REQUEST FOR REFUND
A bargaining fellow named Sid
Was pricing a girl in Madrid.
>   After setting a fee,
>   Said the girl, "Come with me."
He replied, "It's too late, I just did."

1903
An amorous fellow named Slade
Had dreams of a wild escapade
>   Where he had in pursuit
>   A young virgin, so cute—
He awoke and he found the bed made.

1904
Said the daughter to mother, "Some slick
Put his hand in my panties real quick
>   And he fondled my twat,
>   But I fixed the young snot
When I fondled the knob of his dick."

1905
A versatile girl from the South
Of erogenous zones had no drouth.
    When she opened her chasm
    She would have an orgasm
If she said a bad word with her mouth.

1906
A lonely old maid name of Springer
Was thrilled by the plumber's big dinger.
    She said, "A man's root
    Has no substitute—
It is better by far than *Stink-Finger.*

1907
While fucking, a fellow named Springer
Observed a relapse in his dinger.
    He was just halfway through
    When it doubled in two,
So he finished the fuck with his finger.

1908. REACH OUT AND TOUCH SOMEONE
In order to earn some subsistence
A couple led separate existence.
    They had duplicates made
    By the best in the trade,
And each other they screwed at long distance.

1909
There was a jack-offer of Thrace
Who jacked off his cock in a race.
    As the sperm from it poured
    Like a rocket it soared
And established a first into space.

1910. THE LAST HURRAH
To death jumped a harlot of Thrace;
Ten stories she jumped into space.
    She fell square with her hole
    On a telephone pole
And she died with a smile on her face.

1911. LEARN THE ROPES
The puppeteer's helper, Miss Tuppet,
Was madly in love with a puppet,
    So she said, "Puppeteer,
    Can you pull some strings dear,
And instruct my young puppet to up it?"

1912
"My poor back," said a man, "I did twist it,
And my sex life—for years I have missed it."
    The doc's nurse, young in years,
    Heard his story in tears,
So she stood on her head and he kissed it.

1913
A man who vacationed in Vail
Had thought he would find easy tail,
    But the girls were too slick—
    They avoided his prick—
So he brought home his cream in a pail.

1914
Intrepid inventor Von Gluck
Proceeded with skill and great pluck
    To make females ersatz
    With replaceable twats
That were cheaper and easy to fuck.

1915
There was a blind fellow named Wayne
Who picked up a whore with no strain.
    Up an alley they went
    But the poor fellow spent
When her twat twitched the end of his cane.

1916. THE CEILING WAS PLASTERED
An old abstract painter of Wheeling
Was painting a cunt on the ceiling.
    The cunt was so real
    An urge he did feel,
And he blew on the ceiling with feeling.

17
Assorted Eccentricities

1917
Provoked was old Sheik Abdul-Hissun;
His eunichs he started dismissin'.
　　He knew someone had crept
　　Where his harem had slept,
For last night he felt one piece was missin'.

1918. NONPRODUCTIVE
There was a young lady abject;
Her talents she did misdirect.
　　In her manner vandalic
　　She destroyed symbols phallic,
And demolished what man did erect.

1919. THE FIVE-LETTER WORD
This tale may be somewhat absurd
But this is the story I heard—
　　When a cunt learned to speak
　　It said, "Mouth!" with a shriek,
Which to cunts is the dirtiest word.

1920. WHY NOT SAY "NO. 2?"
Said the boss to his man, "I admit
That obedience from vassals is fit,
　　But it's somewhat absurd
　　To be straining at turd
Every time that I chance to say *Shit.*"

1921. THE VOTER
The voting machine I admire;
It registers tallies entire
　　By the pull of a lever,
　　But it would be more clever
If you voted by pulling a wire.

[1922]
But what about women? They'd rail—
Of this method they could not avail,
　　Nor could men old and sick,
　　But they could do the trick
By dropping their turds in a pail.

[1923]
The voting machine in Nantucket
Broke down when a mad voter struck it,
But the voters did rally
And completed the tally
By dropping their turds in a bucket.

1924
The girl that was caught by Akeem
Was threatened with rape, but her theme
Gave him cause for despair
For she said, "I declare
If you badly perform, I will scream."

1925. A SIGN OF GOOD BREEDING
When Schmidt dated well-bred Miss Alice
They went to the new movie palace.
She said to him, "Schmidt,
You can play with my tit
If you let me hang onto your phallus."

1926. ALGERIAN GAME
When you go to a town in Algiers
You will find that the girls have no fears.
When they're pinched in the ass
They will lay in the grass,
And they'll take off their pants and brassieres.

[1927]
"Not so," said a fellow named Sears,
"I've been to a town in Algiers.
They don't wear any pants
As do ladies in France,
And they wouldn't be seen in brassieres."

1928
The brown-noser, Joe, did amass
A great many points, but alas,
When his boss died of flu
They interred poor Joe too,
For Joe's nose was stuck firm in his ass.

1929. THE DISSIDENT

The toy makers started anew
With weapons of war as they do,
    But one man, we must mention,
    Went against the convention
By inventing a doll that would screw.

1930. ENERGY HINT

When energy crises arise,
We'll scrimp like the cook sage and wise
    Who connected her ass
    To her stove which burned gas,
And exploited her farts to bake pies.

1931. PLAYING HER CARDS

An avid bridge player astute
Observed his opponent so cute
    As she raised up her dress
    To promote a finesse,
But he noted it was not hirsute.

1932. CHRIS & GEORGE*

When Christine was George one fine autumn,
A great many ladies had sought 'im.
    Where he was once on top
    He has turned a full flop,
And she now spends her time on the bottom.

1933. NOW WE KNOW!

The scientist boldly averred,
After he and his cohorts conferred:
    Politicians en masse
    Get their start through the ass,
And are born as a twelve-inch long turd.

1934

While boating, a man of Azores
Switched harlots and tripped over oars.
    He fell out and he drowned;
    It was thus that he found
In midstream is no place to change whores.

1935. LOST CHORD LOCATED
With his rooster near by, J. S. Bach
On his organ would play 'round the clock.
    He was playing, so bored,
    When he struck the *Lost Chord,*
Which he found with the help of his cock.

1936
Hard at work on the job was young Baird;
He was asked by a friend how he fared.
    He replied, "At a loss—
    I've been reamed by the boss,
And I felt that his nails were not pared."

1937. THE JAPANESE TOUCH
There was an old planner named Banner
Who planned to seduce a Japanner.
    Though he tried it for days
    He could not get a raise
From his pecker which hung in this manner.

[1938]
The girl from Japan, so discreet,
Decided to give him a treat,
    So she lay down in bed
    While he stood with legs spread,
And she gave him a kiss on his meat.

1939
There once were two cooks from Barbados
Who dated two buxom tomatoes.
    After lengthy maneuvers
    They said, "That's the *hors d'oeuvres;*
Now prepare for the meat and potatoes."

1940*
For the doctor, Miss Snavely laid bare
Her hoarse throat, and he looked in with care.
    He remarked to her, gravely,
    "My opinion, Miss Snavely,
Is your cunt is in need of repair."

1941. FIRST THINGS FIRST
By the side of the road stood Miss Barr;
Her battery was not up to par.
    Said a driver named Gump,
    "Can I give you a jump?"
She said, "Yes, if you first start my car."

1942
There was an old lady named Barrett
Who lived all alone in a garret.
    It was said she was cute
    And she dated a fruit,
But the fact is she dated a carrot.

1943
There was an old spinster named Barrett
Who lived all alone in a garret.
    She was screwed by a cripple
    Who gave her a triple,
So she gave him the *Order of Merit*.

1944
An amorous fellow named Bart
Was pressing his girl to his heart.
    She remarked in a daze,
    "Will you love me always?"
He said, "Yes, tell me how shall we start?"

1945
A noted old chemist named Bayer
Was lauded at lunch by the mayor.
    They all asked to be shown
    How he made the hormone;
He replied, he neglected to pay her.

1946
A women's lib lady, Miss Beggs,
Resolved to advance a few pegs,
    So she wore a man's pants
    And she took a man's stance,
But she piddled all over her legs.

1947. SPEND WISELY
Some people there are with a bent
To save every dime and red cent,
    But this rule does not stick
    To a pussy or prick
Which feel better whenever they're spent.

1948
A bashful and speechless Bernice
Would not let a man touch her crease.
  Said her shrink, "You're too meek;
  You should learn how to speak,
Or forever you must hold your piece."

1949. WRITE UP CITATION
The OSHA Inspector named Bert
With an oversize lady did flirt.
  He got on for a lay
  But her violent display
Made him fall off the bitch and get hurt.

1950. TAKE THE FULL COURSE
There was a young lady named Bessie
Who welcomed the chef, neat and dressy.
  She did not mind his meat
  For she found it a treat,
But she felt that his gravy was messy.

1951
An uptight young lady named Bierley
Who valued her morals so dearly,
  Had her sex, so I hear,
  Only once every year,
And she strained her vagina severely.

1952
While playing at chess, Mr. Bing
Was fondling the knob on his thing.
  He displayed such delight
  As he checked with his knight
That he blew as he mated the king.

1953. SHADES OF MALTHUS
Ten billion on earth without bitchin'
Say experts, and life will enrichen.
  There is food, they agree,
  But the experts don't see
That we may have to shit in the kitchen.

1954. COUNTER PROPOSAL*
A computer programmer, Miss Black
Fell in love with her new UNIVAC.
 She had hopes to get laid
 So her cunt she displayed,
But it counted the hairs on her crack.

1955. BATS IN THE BELFRY
A pervese old fellow named Blaine
Spoke only of whores he had lain,
 So when he was dead
 They opened his head,
And the cunts flew in streams from his brain.

1956
A moral young fellow was Bliss,
So pure he would not even kiss.
 He took care not to touch
 Any ass, cunt or such,
And used tongs when he stood up to piss.

1957. LIMBURGER CHEESE SOUP
The chef de cuisine Monsieur Blunt
For a new recipe once did hunt.
 His soup of perfection
 Gave men an erection,
So he labeled it *Broth de la Cunt.*

1958. $\frac{y}{x} = f(\frac{p}{c})$
A mathematician named Blunt
For years an equation did hunt
 To prove that good sex
 Was not y over x,
But a function of prick over cunt.

1959
On vacation, three men young and bold
Left their wives to go hunting, I'm told.
 They could not sleep at night
 But their guide set them right
When he gave each a hairbrush to hold.

1960
There was a professor named Borum
Who taught all the lads with decorum
How young girls to exploit
With the movement adroit,
And how best to make love and explore 'em.

1961. NOISE POLLUTION
In his lab sits old scientist Boyes
And his knowledge and skill he deploys
To reduce wear and tear
On the asshole so fair,
By extracting from farts all the noise.

1962
There was a young lady named [
Who raised such a hideous racket
Over one missing.
But her reasons were myriad
For she took the wrong pill from her packet.

1963. CAVEAT EMPTOR
The ten-spot donated by Breech
Was counterfeit, said Father Meech.
But said Breech, "You will find
It won't cause any bind;
It's as good as the stuff that you preach."

[1964]
The preacher then screwed harlot Belle
And gave her the ten for the spell.
When she said it was bad,
He complained to her, "Gad,
It's as good as the ass that you sell."

[1965]
The harlot the doctor then sought;
He gave her an all-purpose shot.
He complained of the ten,
But the harlot said, "Ben,
It's as good as the shot that I got."

[1966]
The doctor paid old lawyer Dave
For help on how taxes to save.
    The bad ten from the doc
    Gave the lawyer a shock,
But was good as advice which he gave.

[1967]
The lawyer then gave a donation
To one who sought vote approbation.
    Said the man, "You're a fraud."
    But the lawyer said, "God,
It's much more than your help to the nation."

[1968]
There's a moral for all, we can tell.
Let The Buyer Beware may sound swell,
    But when buyers of trash
    Can use counterfeit cash,
Let the seller beware just as well.

1969. DEEP SIX
In the lab a young lady of Brest
Took a full inch of cock in a test.
    In a minute or two
    She exclaimed, "That will do!
Now provide me the rest with some zest."

1970. THE FOOTMAN
For the foot-doc, a fellow named Brent
His pecker exposed, badly bent.
    "That's no foot!" said the doc,
    But Brent claimed that his cock
Was exactly twelve inches extent.

1971
There was a young lady named Bright
Who said to the butcher polite,
    "Have you beef hearts today?"
    But the butcher said, "Nay,
Try these beans, they will be farts tonight."

1972. SEMANTIC LESSON

The word *fuck* to Miss Babbitt would bring
Her resentful remarks by the string.
    But in bed young Miss Babbitt
    Would indulge like a rabbit,
For she hated the word, not the thing.

1973. LOOK THE OTHER WAY

In the dark a young lady named Brook
A fuck from her dear husband took.
    She said to him, "Bertie,
    This business is dirty,
So I really cannot bear to look."

1974. THE FRUSTRATED RAPEE

A horny old spinster named Brook
Was undressed in the park by a crook.
    She said, "Fuck if you will;
    I'll lie perfectly still."
But he said he just wanted to look.

1975. FURTHER STUDY REQUIRED

On some bishops, a scientist, Brown,
Plastered butter in front on each gown,
    Then he threw a full score
    From the fortieth floor,
And they hit with the buttered side down.

1976. THE FORKING KNIGHT

While watching a chess match, Miss Bryce
Was trapped in a chess master's vise.
    No one envied her plight—
    She was forked by a knight,
And a bishop who mated her twice.

1977

The toy makers make the fast buck
With weapons of war and such muck,
    But one man we should mention
    Did oppose the convention
By inventing a doll that would fuck.

1978
The office brown-noser named Bunky
Would claim he was nobody's flunky.
 When the chips were all down
 His proboscis was brown
And there hung many strands which were gunky.

1979
There was a young fellow named Burl
Who married an African girl.
 Although she had a hole
 Which was blacker than coal,
To a Negro it looked like a pearl.

1980. GOLFER ENGULFED
A beautiful drive made by Byron
Went straight for the hole of a siren.
 He did not see the trap
 And got caught in the crap,
But got out with his number nine iron.

1981
There was a musician Calhoun
Who played on the flute and bassoon,
 But most of his life
 He had strife with his wife,
Since his organ was way out of tune.

1982
A hot little twat name of Carson
Was fondling the knob of the parson.
 Soon he burned with desire
 But her cunt quenched the fire
Before he could charge her with arson.

1983
There was a young lady named Carson
Who wiggled her ass near the parson.
 Her performance extraneous
 Caused combustion spontaneous,
So the parson charged Carson with arsin'.

1984
A nicotine addict was Cass;
When smoking, he'd do it first class.
 Through three fags he would leer,
 Stuck a pipe in each ear,
And he shoved a cigar up his ass.

1985
There was a young wrestler named Castle
Who practiced a new way to rassle.
    As he tried a new twist
    He slipped with his wrist
And was found with his head up his asshole.

1986. NUCLEAR POWER PLANT
A scientist struggled with charts,
Mixing beans and uranium in tarts.
    Politicians would feed
    And a plant would proceed
To perform on plutonium-rich farts.

1987
In Zurich old clockmaker Chase
Improved on the clock commonplace.
    He made one of fine brass
    With two feet and an ass
In the place of two hands and a face.

1988
For ladies who aim for clothes chic,
Beware of the tailor so slick.
    Since he's careless, it's said,
    With his needle and thread,
You must keep a sharp eye for his prick.

1989
A song was composed by young Chuck
But the lyrics ran into bad luck.
    Though devoid of all flaws
    It fell short just because
Of the title: *With Love You Don't Fuck.*

1990
"What is worse," said a lady named Claire,
"A new baby, or tooth to repair?"
    Said the dentist, refined,
    "Would you make up your mind,
For I wish to position the chair."

1991
There was a young fellow named Clark
Who cared not with whom he did spark.
    In his mind was no doubt
    For when lights were put out
All the cats felt the same in the dark.

1992. UNION ADVANCES*
For the union the rules were first class
As the leaders new terms did amass.
    Though a man could still sit
    And take time for a shit,
He did not have to wipe his own ass.

1993*
Here is some advice that's first class
Applying to doctors en masse—
    They should swans emulate
    And their stock will inflate;
They should all shove their bills up their ass.

1994
One can't always head up the class;
Some men will lose out, some surpass.
    If by chance you lose face,
    Take defeat with some grace—
It is better than losing your ass.

1995
An impotent recluse named Clif
For years had no pussy to sniff.
    Now to death he was freezing
    But he found it was pleasing,
For he died with his cock firm and stiff.

1996. APRIL FOOL!
A well-hung old midget named Clyde
Dressed up as a boy and he cried.
    He said, "Lady, help me
    For I want to go pee."
When she pulled out his PRICK, the girl died.

1997
A stoical fellow named Clyde
Revealed why he took on a bride,
    For he needed a spouse
    To take care of the house,
As he got all his screwing outside.

1998
A soldier who came from the coast
Of prowess in fighting did boast.
    He feared no man or beast
    Except bishop or priest,
For the man who feared God he feared most.

1999
A butcher who lived in Cologne
The shape of young girls did bemoan.
 He said, "Give me a honky
 Who is big, fat and chunky—
I like plenty of meat on the bone."

2000
In the fog a young man of Cologne
Took a walk in the park all alone.
 From out of the fog
 Came a slut, a real dog,
And he figured he'd throw her a bone.

2001
With his lot man has not been contented;
By compulsion to change he's tormented.
 At improvement he strains,
 But the screw still remains
Just as good as it first was invented.

2002
For the farmer worked handyman Cotter;
He dug a new well to get water.
 He hauled in the hay,
 Got the chickens to lay,
And the bleeding he stopped in his daughter.

2003
While serving a beer, young Miss Cumbo
Met up with a patron—a dumbo—
 Who asked, "Do you ferk?"
 So she clobbered the jerk
With a swing of her jugs, which were jumbo.

2004
The cat in the rocket was curled
And out into space it was hurled.
 Its owner, Miss May,
 In truth now could say
That her pussy was out of this world.

2005*
The old architect stated in Dallas,
"The church steeple is naught but a phallus."
 But the word he did pick
 Is the steeple's a *Prick*,
And he said this without any malice.

2006. HONORABLE ENTERPRISE
A noted inventor named Dan
Proceeded according to plan
 To construct a device
 At a moderate price
For deflecting the shit from the fan.

2007. WHERE THERE IS SMOKE
A hot little number, Miss Danius,
Had screwed many men miscellaneous.
 When a friend did inquire
 Why men set her on fire,
Her combustion, she said, was spontaneous.

2008
A mathematician named Dare
Could issue a turd that was square,
 Then he tried an ejection
 With a rhombus trisection—
I believe that he's still straining there.

2009
The patient lay down as if dead.
Said the surgeon, "My knife I'll imbed
 And the brain will be saved
 For this patient depraved."
And the cunts flew in streams from his head.

2010
A virgin is tender and dear,
But much like a bubble, I fear.
 The virgin and bubble
 Each face the same trouble,
For a prick will make both disappear.

2011
While crossing the street, Mr. Decker
Was struck by a fast-moving wrecker.
 Though his face was all fuzz
 They could tell who he was
By the wart on the end of his pecker.

2012
Beneath his piano, young Deever
Discovered his dying retriever.
 Sometime later that day
 He met greater dismay—
'Neath his organ he found a dead beaver.

2013
There sat an old recluse dejected;
His pecker for years had defected.
    Now to death he was freezing
    But he found it so pleasing,
For his prick was now firm and erected.

2014
Though chess gives some people delight,
For some it has nothing but fright.
    It's for queers advocated
    For the king can be mated
By the bishop, the pawn or the knight.

2015
By wives many men are demented,
Deceived and abused and tormented,
    So I say, men, beware,
    And avoid this despair—
Why own the damn thing, you can rent it.

2016
There was a collector named Dintage
Who checked every coin for its mintage.
    His paintings were rare
    And selected with care
And the ladies he screwed were all vintage.

2017
The boldness that I now discover
In *Playboy*—I may not recover,
    For they show pubic hair—
    But I fear they don't dare
To display a bouquet on the cover.

2018. TOSS OFF THE COVERS
New laws did lawmakers discover
Affecting a girl and her lover.
    The decree now made clear
    What was done in great fear
Need no longer be done under cover.

2019. IL DUCE*
Since our leader has not been discreet
A payment we have that is neat:
    We'll hang the poor wreck,
    But not by the neck—
He must hang by the balls—of the feet.

2020. THE FLAT-CHESTED HARLOT
A whore who had not used discretion
To the doctor explained her depression.
    Her complaints, she did mention,
    Were arising from tension,
But to him it looked more like compression.

2021. WOMAN ELECTED AS MAYOR!*
Once a mayor, he's now in disgrace—
The Machine failed to give him first place.
    His defeat by a dame
    Caused such feelings of shame
That a cunt he no longer can face.

[2022]
The damage was more than first feared—
His head may not ever be cleared.
    Just consider his plight,
    Now he shrinks with great fright
When he faces a man with a beard.

2023*
A lad with his life was disgusted
And he wished that his dad had not lusted,
    But it wasn't the lust,
    For his dad put his trust
In a rubber so worn that it busted.

2024
If the size of her nose is distressing,
I suggest, while the lady's undressing,
    That you cover her nose
    With her panties or hose
Before starting the pussy caressing.

2025
The faithful that followed old Dodd
Disrobed when he gave them the nod.
    Then they sang many hymns
    And they locked all their limbs,
And together they shouted, "Oh God!"

2026
There was a young lady named Donna
Who never said, no I don't wanna,
    For one day out of three
    She would take LSD
And on weekends she smoked marijuana.

2027
So famous a singer was Dotty
Devotees would make her life knotty.
    To give time to the shriekers
    And the autograph seekers
She would sign as she sat on the potty.

2028
What man needs at home is a drudge
Who never from housework will budge,
    And a mistress so spicing
    For providing the icing
Made of marshmallow, chocolate and fudge.

2029
A typist who hailed from Duluth
Was canned for her language uncouth,
    But she called her boss Clyde
    A cocksucker who lied,
For the shit that he told was untruth.

2030
On a date with a girl, a young Easterner
Had thought he would have a fine feast on her.
    When came time for the ride
    'Twas like Jekyll and Hyde—
He had roused a most hideous beast in her.

2031. BELL THE PUSSY
There was a young lady named Eleanor
Whose husband had tied a small beleanor
    So that he could divine
    When she got out of line,
For a great many man had raised heleanor.

2032. CONDITIONED REFLEX
The White Russian general embarks
To pick up some whores in the parks.
    One exposes her crack
    But the general draws back—
It reminds him too much of Karl Marx.

2033. LOOKING FOR THE SOLUTION
The Congress itself does ensconce
To study in depth a response
    For a nation that's ill,
    But they dip in the till
While the president beats on his schwantz.

2034. THE SQUARE ROOT OF EWING
A mathematician was Ewing—
His cock was in need of renewing,
    But for years he got by
    With his formula sly,
Which was using a square root for screwing.

2035
At the office, a fellow named Ewing,
His boss out of work he was screwing.
    On the toilet he'd sit
    Simply taking a shit,
For there he knew what he was doing.

2036. FIXING THE BLAME
In a heart-to-heart talk mother faced
Her daughter and said, "Remain chaste,
    For a boy can bring shame
    Which would sully our name.
If a boy lays on you, I'm disgraced."

[2037]
When the daughter went out with Carruther
His entreaties to fuck she did smother,
    But she said, "Please lay down,
    I'll get on with no gown."
And she thus did disgrace the boy's mother.

2038. THE HAND JOB

Said the recluse, "My nerve, it seems, fails me.
To fuck with a young lady pales me,
    But my balls start to swell
    And my prick's hard as hell,
So I've got to get rid of what ails me."

2039. THE VOICE OF EXPERIENCE

While taking a walk in the fall
Two bulls saw some cows in the kraal.
    Said the young bull, "Let's run
    And we'll each fuck us one."
Said the old bull, "Let's walk and fuck all."

2040. DON'T HORSE AROUND

Young ladies on bikes can ride far
And their status with men is at par,
    But when ladies ride straddle
    On an old Western saddle
It is stretching a good thing too far.

2041. THE FUEL CRISIS

For fuel our man looks near and far—
He is funding a program bizarre:
    With beans as a fuel
    And his asshole a tool,
Blasting farts for propelling his car.

2042

Great beauty possessed young Miss Fenster;
The lads that all whistled incensed her,
    And she made it quite hard
    For those not on their guard,
But not one of them held it against her.

2043. TEST TICKLE

Some women are fun, some are fickle;
By some you'll be left in a pickle.
    Put them all to a test,
    Get the one who laughs best,
And the test that is best—a test tickle.

2044
So moral and righteous was Field
To temptation he never would yield.
    Sometime later in life
    He procured him a wife,
But he found that his sperm had congealed.

2045. DIVORCE
A horny young fellow named Fitch
Engaged an old whore for his itch,
    But he blew on the floor
    As he felt for her bore,
So said, "Give me my cash back, you bitch!"

2046. NAILED
The queen from attackers once flew
And cried when her horse dropped a shoe,
    "Oh, my kingdom will fail
    For the want of a nail!"
But the kingdom was saved for a screw.

2047. ILL WIND
There was a young lady named Flo
Who said that she wanted to know
    Did bassoonist Herr Klauth
    Make that noise through his mouth?
The conductor cried, "God, I hope so!"

2048
A lady from Budapest, Florrie,
Went out in a dory with Cory.
    He got into her drawers
    While she pulled on the oars,
And he said it was all hunky-dory.

2049
Advice to young ladies that foam
When husbands have started to roam:
    You'll find men do not care
    To seek love everywhere
When they get a good screwing at home.

2050. SOAP OPERA
When Proctor entrapped her and focked her
She soon had to call for the doctor.
> So the moral, they say,
> If you're going to play,
It is best not to Gamble with Proctor.

2051
A noted tree surgeon named Fogg
Developed a tree that could jog,
> But the tree, fully grown,
> Had a mind of its own,
For it ran out and pissed on a dog.

2052
A learned young lady named Fong
Learned all about men in Hong Kong.
> She defined the word *penis:*
> "There is nothing between us,"
And a *prick:* "Something twelve inches long."

2053. ALL CAME ON TIME
A venturesome lady named Ford
A first on the railroad had scored,
> She was made a conductor
> But so many men fucked her
She no longer will shout "All Aboard!"

2054
There was an old fellow from Fordham
Who said, "We must thank God for whoredom.
> It's a matter not trifling,
> For some wives are so stifling
That their men would be soon dead of boredom."

2055
The coed put on her best form
When serving champagne in the dorm.
> She asked a lad, "Chuck,
> Would you like some *Cold Duck?*"
He said, "No, just some pussy that's warm."

2056
When you take the young girls to the forum
You must act with restraint and decorum.
> In your speech be discreet
> And your dress must be neat;
It will do you no good if you bore 'em.

2057
A frigid old Duchess named Foster
Was fucked by the Grand Duke of Gloucester.
    She was fucked by this pro
    For ten weeks in a row,
As it took all that time to defrost her.

2058
The language of English, I've found,
With many fine words does abound,
    Like *Fuck, Fart,* and *Shit,*
    Hairy Cunt, Prick, and *Tit,*
And they all have a most pleasant sound.

2059. A STUDY IN BROWN
When Bartok composed Opus Four
His asshole felt tender and sore,
    And he shit everywhere
    But no paper was there,
So he wiped off his ass with the score.

[2060]
The chambermaid, old Mrs. Burke,
Had dried up the score with a smirk.
    The critics depraved,
    They shouted and raved,
And proclaimed it a masterful work.

2061. BOXING FANS
A well-built young girl of Fort Knox
Was rugged and strong as an ox.
    When she wrestled, fans booed
    For her wrestling was crude,
But they all loved to look at her box.

2062. DOWN ON THE FARM
The pastors berated Miss Fox
For corrupting the men in their flocks.
    Said the winsome young charmer,
    "I'm a mere poultry farmer
Since I spend all my time raising cocks."

2063. CACHE CROP
There was a young lady named Fox
Who planted an acre of cocks.
They grew up firm and strong,
Over twelve inches long,
And she stuffed them all into her box.

2064
There was an old seamstress named Fran
Who screamed as her sewing began.
She was pricked by the bobbin
And she said 'midst her sobbin',
"I would rather be pricked by a man."

2065
There is an old cook freckle-faced,
Who never allows any waste.
She cooks carrots and pees
In one pot, if you please,
And it really is not in bad taste.

2066. THE PATRIOTS
At a bar in Japan, GI Frank
Became bolder as more sake he drank.
He disclosed with great zest
A tattoo on his chest,
"Take a look at this flag, I'm a Yank!"

[2067]
This action so brash did not please
A buxom young maid, Japanese.
She uncovered, nonplussed,
Both her titties robust,
And she said with restraint, "Nipponese!"

2068
A stoical husband named Fred
Would fuck with his hat on his head,
Then he'd rise up undressed
With his hand on his chest
Out of simple respect for the dead.

2069. BAD BLOOD
A perverse old fellow was Fred
Ever since his poor pecker went dead.
His blood red and thick
Had once nourished his prick,
Now it flowed unrestrained through his head.

2070
The cunt of the wife of old Fred
Was dying—till *Playboy* she read.
    It opened a shunt
    From her head to her cunt,
And now she fucks better in bed.

2071. PRICE OF LIBERATION
If a woman must really be free
And with men hold her place equally,
    She must wear up in front
    A man's fly at her cunt,
And must learn how to stand up to pee.

2072
The lady who went to Doc Fretter
Was asked to remove pants and sweater.
    He injected some plasma
    To take care of her asthma,
But it just made her pussy feel better.

2073
There was a young lady named Fretter
Whose man was a wondrous go-getter.
    Though she found that relations
    With this man were sensations,
Her relations' relations were better.

2074. BOWLER'S HEADACHE
When he bowled, a young fellow named Fritz
Gave his team a bad case of the fits,
    For he left 10 and 4
    Standing up on the floor.
"I'm accustomed," he said, "to bad splits."

2075
A frustrated lady named Fritz
Alone in her rocking chair knits.
    She knows not what is missing—
    But it's used just for pissing,
While there on a gold mine she sits.

2076

An old mountain climber named Frost
Engaged a fat whore at low cost.
   With his pitons and rope
   He was scaling her slope
But he slipped through her crack and got lost.

2077. B.Z.: BEFORE ZIPPERS

To thwart a young robber, Miss Fry
Exposed her bare breast to the guy,
   But her ploy was in vain
   For the poor girl was slain
By the buttons that burst from his fly.

2078

A baby was born to Miss Gellicut,
Delivered by means of a belly cut.
   After sewing the patch
   The doc tickled her snatch.
She awoke and exclaimed, "You're indelicate."

2079

There was a young fellow named Gelling
Who kept all the girls from his dwelling,
   For if girls came too near
   To this non-cavalier,
He complained that his pecker was swelling.

2080

There was a young fellow named Gene
Who first picked his asshole quite clean.
   He next picked his toes
   And lastly his nose
And he never did wash in between.

2081

A foul-mouthed young fellow was Gene,
Rebuked for his language obscene;
   But the foul words he knew
   Were too utterly few,
And he used many words that were clean.

2082

While grinding his meat, butcher Girk
Lost his balance because of a quirk.
   He fell into the hopper
   With his ass in the chopper,
And he thus got behind in his work.

2083
A brothel inspector named Giles
Took data from whores for his files.
    He counted each stroke
    And the depth of the poke
And recorded the number of miles.

2084
To the doctor went old Mrs. Glitz
For she had a bad case of the shits.
    But old Doctor Pitman
    Was strictly a tit man,
And he asked her, "Please show me your tits."

2085
The old archaeologist Gluck
Discovered by stupid good luck
    When he sucked 'neath the tummy
    Of an old Egypt mummy
It was better by far than a fuck.

2086. FASHION GIRL
At a contest, a lady named Gog
Took part in a quiz dialogue.
    Asked what fashions she knew,
    She replied she knew two—
One was *Paris*, the other was *dog*.

2087. KEYHOLE SYNDROME
A forgetful professor was Gore;
His actions his wife would abhor.
    He caused nothing but strife
    When he slammed his dear wife
And proceeded to fuck with the door.

2088
At the sperm bank, a lady named Gore
Used her wiles to attract many more.
    When she raised up her dress
    With ingenious finesse,
The depositors came by the score.

2089
The blood of a miner named Gorth
Was loaded with iron—one fourth,
    So his prick when erected
    By the poles was affected,
And he only could fuck facing north.

2090
There was an old pilgrim named Goss
Who walked to the shrine with a cross.
    For so long he went forth
    With his face to the north
That his pecker was covered with moss.

2091
The home of a lady named Grace
Did prompt a libidinous race.
    Just the experts could see
    Who the winners would be—
They were fucking all over the place.

2092
There was a young lady named Grace
Who made for the john in a race.
    When she saw on the wall
    The handwriting and all,
She knew she was in the wrong place.

2093. NEW MATH
There was an old bastard named Grimes
Who bragged of his sexual crimes:
    One in bed with his whore,
    Sixty-nine on the floor—
For a total of seventy times.

2094. TRY THE LIONS
There was a young lady named Gubb
Whose man was a dud and did flub.
    She said, "I declare
    I'm not getting my share;
Let us meet with a rotary club."

2095
There was a queer fellow of Guelph
Who kept an odd game on the shelf,
    Played like chess—but no Queen—
    And some thought it obscene
For the King could mate only himself.

2096. BOTANICAL INTERLUDE
John showed his fine plants to whore Gulcher;
She sneered, "Pour a drink for me, vulture."
   So said John, "I do think
   You can lead whores to drink
But you cannot lead a horticulture."

2097. DISQUALIFIED
A playful young fellow was Gump
Who cherished his ladyfriend's rump.
   "Let's play *Leapfrog*," he said,
   So she lowered her head,
But he never completed the jump.

2098
A sorry young fellow was Hame,
Surrounded by gloom and deep shame.
   He felt life was ending
   And doom was impending,
So he crawled in the cunt whence he came.

2099
The wife her dear man does harass
By saying, when time comes for ass,
   "You did not cut the lawn."
   But she never says, "John,
Let us fuck," when it's time to mow grass.

2100
Outdoors the young lady of Harrow
Adhered to the path straight and narrow,
   But she'd fuck in her flat
   At the drop of a hat;
Oh my goodness, there goes a sombrero.

2101. CUCKOO BIRD
A rabid young fellow named Haskett
Was angry and blew out a gasket.
   From a madam named Shores
   He demanded four whores;
He would not put his eggs in one basket.

2102
A fastidious hairdresser named Hatch
Prepared a girl's hair with dispatch.
    It looked neat and so prim
    That she asked him to trim
The hair on her pussy to match.

2103
A frustrated butcher named Hearst
Concluded that girls were accursed,
    So he fucked the first nine
    Who were standing in line,
And he finished the rest with his wurst.

2104
A butcher first-class name of Hearst
In slicing fine steaks was well-versed,
    But many a crony
    Preferred his baloney,
While some said his best was his wurst.

2105
A young gynecologist, Heep,
Worked long and he often lost sleep,
    For he had an obsession
    To improve his profession,
And his hand in a good thing to keep.

2106. SANCTIFIED SOUP
A moral old fellow named Hicks
From alphabet soup got his kicks.
    He said, "Waiter, make sure
    What you bring me is pure.
Remove all the *SHIT*'s, *CUNT*'s and *PRICK*'s."

2107*
There was a pipe-smoker named Hicks
Who from smoking new brands got his kicks.
    He prepared a fine blend
    Which won many a friend—
A horseshit and cherry pie mix.

2108. SHORTCOMING
An obedient young lady named Hinches
Was not bad at all in the clinches.
    Her ma she'd obey,
    Not to go all the way,
So for years she took only five inches.

2109
There was a young fellow named Hiram
Whose wife was a nymph and would tire 'im,
    So he hired simply scads
    Of unwary young lads;
When they failed to produce he would fire 'em.

2110
When Bartok composed his new hit,
A dog on the score took a shit.
    The notes were displayed
    And the orchestra played—
It did not hurt the music a bit.

2111
An able masseur of Hong Kong
Massaging one time did prolong
    On buxom Miss Mabel
    Who reclined on the table,
But the way that he rubbed her was wrong.

2112
An acrobat lady named Hope
Gave a show for the king and the pope.
    She performed on stiff pricks
    And she did far more tricks
Than a monkey could do on a rope.

2113
A girl with her soul full of hope
Prepared with her beau to elope.
    She climbed in the tub
    To get a good scrub,
But came out with her hole full of soap.

2114
A sweet and dear lady named Huck
Fell flat on her face in the muck.
    There was no one in sight
    To observe her sad plight,
So she screamed in disgust, "What the fuck!"

2115
There was a young golfer named Huff
Who had an affair with Miss Duff.
   He should have thought twice
   For he hooked a bad slice
And he found himself out in the rough.

2116
The noted biologist Hugh
Taught rabbits to dance and to do
   Many tricks very well
   At the sound of a bell,
So the rabbits taught Hugh how to screw.

2117
There was a ball-player named Hunt
Who was struck in the face with a bunt.
   They managed to save
   The poor man from the grave
But his face ended up like a cunt.

2118
There was an old woodsman named Hunt
Who implanted his ax handle blunt
   In the cunt of Miss Fraser
   Who was sharp as a razor,
And the chips flew in streams from her cunt.

2119. COME FORTH
A fearless old hunter named Hurd
Once tackled a lion—how absurd!
   Though he fought with great zest
   He came—not second best—
But it seems that he came a poor turd.

2120
To college went able young Hurd;
The parents felt they had not erred.
   When they asked him what knowledge
   He received while at college,
He replied with a four-letter word.

2121
There was a young fellow named Hutch
Who never did get very much,
   For it took him a year
   To get going in gear,
And he always was slipping his clutch.

2122
A lady depressed and ill-lucked
By hoodlums was ravaged and fucked.
    Said her lawyer, "Disgrace!
    It's an open, shut case,
But the crime we must now reconstruct."

2123
Some people have faulty impressions
Concerning young maids' indiscretions.
    If the truth must be known
    The record has shown
They are learning their future professions.

2124
A lady who was not inhibited
Her asshole and pussy exhibited
    To all manner of jokers
    Who attended her smokers,
But young lads without dads were prohibited.

2125
An agile young fräulein of Innsbruck
It seems very lightly her sins took.
    She stood ten men in line,
    Screwed them one at a time,
And then two at a time she ten twins took.

2126. BEAUTY CONTEST
For the contest, the judge did instruct
That the beauties at first must be fucked,
    Then proceed to compare
    For the orifice wear,
And for holes that are worn, points deduct.

2127
From the train, a young soldier named Jack
Said goodbye, as he leaned out to smack
    The lips of his chick,
    But the train took off quick
And he kissed a cow's ass down the track.

2128

A despondent young fellow was Jack;
He suffered through life a great lack.
    He knew whence he came
    And felt a great shame,
So he looked for a way to go back.

2129

A novice young fellow named Jack
The knowledge of fucking did lack.
    An old maid tried to teach him
    But she never could reach him,
For it seems that he fell through the crack.

2130. LEAF AND BULL STORY

A sculptor of note name of Jacques
A beautiful tree carved in rock.
    It was stately and fine
    And a moral design,
For he hid every leaf with a cock.

2131

A simple old lady named Jane
Was ravished and beat with a cane.
    She recovered at length
    And regained all her strength,
And she searched for the same man in vain.

2132

A novice young hostess named Jane
Was fucked as she flew in a plane.
    She remarked with a sigh,
    "It was fun, I felt high,
And I think I will try it again."

2133. THE STARGAZER

To his wife said astronomer Janus,
"Much renown in the world we will gain us
    When I publish my paper
    On the ungodly vapor
And the rings I have seen on Uranus."

2134
The man who writes *fuck* is a jerk;
He's suspected of having a quirk.
 But the doctor is great
 For he writes *copulate*,
And is paid very well for his work.

2135. NEIN!
A near-sighted lady was Kate
Who learned to discern rather late.
 She played with her toys
 With the girls and the boys,
But she knew not her sex until ate.

2136. WEATHER WATCH
The weatherman dated Miss Kay—
Eight inches she got in the hay.
 Though her pussy was sore
 She requested some more,
So she got one more inch the next day.

2137
A suspicious young fellow was Kelter;
His wife did behave or he'd belt her.
 Every day to be sure
 That she kept herself pure,
He extended her legs and he smelt her.

2138
There was an old miser of Kent
Who saved every nickel and cent.
 He would save everything
 Even pieces of string,
But felt good when his pecker was spent.

2139
"A prick," said the lady of Kent,
"Must be rigid and not badly bent.
 Richard's qualification
 Is the best in the nation—
As a prick he's one hundred percent."

2140

A noble young prince of Khartoum
Was laid all too soon in his tomb.
    The sage pedagogues
    Said he went to the dogs,
But the pussies had led him to doom.

2141. THE UNDOING

A fearful young lady named Kippers
Stood in fear of small dogs that were nippers,
    And in fright she would shake
    At the sight of a snake,
But she feared not the snakes behind zippers.

2142

The biologist, Hermann von Klatsch
A novel idea did hatch.
    He would transplant the gene
    Which caused scratching obscene
To a place much more decent to scratch.

2143

There was an old harlot named Klotz
Who was famed as the hottest of twats.
    When they buried the bitch
    All the graves had an itch,
And their stones blew all over the plots.

2144

When Greeley was fucking Miss Klutz,
She said, as he plunged in his putz,
    "Do you love me, dear Greeley?"
    He answered, "Not really,
I just wanted to blow off my nuts."

2145. POPLAR FELLOW

A virtuous lady was Koppler
Who claimed that no young man could topple 'er,
    But a woodsman named Max
    Came along with his ax
And he felled her like felling a poplar.

2146
In love with his work was old Kropp;
A whorehouse he cleaned with a mop.
 He liked this job best
 And he worked with great zest
For he loved to hear harlots talk shop.

2147
So artless and simple was Kubik,
So innocent, sweet and cherubic,
 That he never would dare
 To consider one hair
Of a matter suspected as pubic.

2148
A biology teacher, Miss Kudents,
Taught sex to the boys with great prudence.
 When came the finale
 She went out in the alley
And was fucked by the *A* and *B* students.

2149
There was a young fellow named Kurtew
Who shamelessly showed off his virtue.
 When the young ladies screamed
 He remarked, as he beamed,
"Why there's nothing in here that can hurt you!"

2150. RIGHT HOLE—WRONG PEG
A destitute lady named Laker
Accosted and fucked with a Quaker.
 When she asked him for bread
 He smiled sadly and said,
"If it's bread that you want, fuck a baker."

2151
In temples lived two horny lamas.
They left to chase girls in pajamas,
 But girls in pajamas
 Run faster than lamas
So they're back in their temples with traumas.

2152. OUTHOUSE HONOR
Some names will be famed through the land
And some will be writ in the sand,
    But we'll view names of fools
    While we strain at our stools
Just as long as the shithouse walls stand.

2153
To Washington went Miss Latrobe,
And by Congress was asked to disrobe.
    By the Congress respected
    She there was subjected
To a thorough Congressional Probe.

2154
A young social worker named Lear
Was counseling whores in Lapeer.
    The things that one whore did
    Were so utterly sordid
That he worked to improve her all year.

2155. THE CHIRPING ZIPPER
To lovers' lane one night went Lear
And he walked in the dark with his dear.
    She said, "Hear all those crickets
    As they chirp in the thickets."
"Those are zippers," he said, "that you hear."

2156
By passion one must not be led
Lest it lead to the loss of one's head.
    If a man be discreet
    He should not get his meat
At the place that he earns daily bread.

2157
To a fancy dress ball went young Lee,
He was dressed to appear like a tree.
    He was met at the ball
    By some dogs in the hall
And they gathered around him to pee.

2158. TEA DRINKER
A simple young fellow named Lee
Flew *TWA* to Dundee.
　　When the hostess did say,
　　"Coffee *TWA?*"
He said, "No, just *TWAT.*"

2159
There was a young lady named Leedy
Who disliked the army, indeedy.
　　She sampled the major
　　But this man did enrage her,
And she said that his colonel was seedy.

2160
There was a young man named Levant
Whose girl on a date said, "I can't,
　　For my eyes have big bags on
　　And I now have the rags on,
But I think you'll do fine with my aunt."

2161. DEAD RIGHT!
The old archaeologist, Lew,
Remarked to his wife, "We are through,
　　For a mummy I've fucked
　　And from this I deduct
That a mummy moves quicker than you."

2162
A clumsy young fellow named Linnet
Had something go wrong every minute.
　　His girl had some doubt
　　And she soon threw him out
For fear he would get his foot in it.

2163
A lovable lady of Linz
Just loved to indulge in her sins.
　　She deplored the great lack
　　Of a two-pronged attack,
And she often wished that she were twins.

2164. BLACK FRIDAY

A redheaded lady named Lize
Sat down and she parted her thighs.
    When a man saw her crack
    He exclaimed, "Why, it's black!"
But the color was due to the flies.

2165

The professor emeritus Lloyd
New methods of teaching deployed.
    He taught students obscenities
    And other amenities,
So they knew all the words to avoid.

2166

An heirloom was found by young Lorne,
A condom all battered and torn.
    He said, "Father was dull
    With no brains in his skull,
Or I surely would not have been born."

2167. SMART FELLER

For new energy Carter is looking
And the best brains in science he's booking.
    They will study their charts
    To devise richer farts
As a fuel source for heating and cooking.

2168. ONE EMBRACE = ONE BILLION WORDS

A serious young fellow of Lourdes
Concluded that talk was for birds,
    For no word will replace
    What the eye can embrace,
And a picture's worth one thousand words.

[2169]

Pedantic Professor MacNeal
A learned remark did reveal—
    Although pictures do please,
    Yet one thousand of these
Will not match what one gets from a feel.

[2170]
However, a fellow named Chase
Remarked that though feels have their place,
    Yet his thinking reveals
    It takes one thousand feels
Just to equal a fucking embrace.

2171
A marriage is not simply luck;
If you plan you will never be stuck.
    At first, what you do
    Is learn how to screw,
And later you learn how to fuck.

2172. CLEAN LIVER
A cautious young fellow named Luntz
Was hailed by a grimy whore once,
    But he said to her, "Gertie,
    Although fucking is dirty,
I fuck only the cleanest of cunts."

2173
While screwing her boyfriend, Miss Lutz
Said, "Smoking while screwing takes guts.
    I don't mind you smoking
    While diddling and poking,
But don't use my asshole for butts."

2174
"I was raped," said the lady of Lyme—
The trial, said the judge, would take time.
    In his chambers he went
    With the lady, and spent
Some time reconstructing the crime.

2175
There was a young seamstress named Lyriad
Whose talents were diverse and myriad.
    She'd do math, punctuate,
    She could sew and mend straight,
And she never missed even one period.

2176
Said the pope to a girl named MacAllister,
"I doubt if you can make my phallus stir."
    But she showed that in Texas
    With her bare solar plexus
She could make every phallus in Dallas stir.

2177. SINCERE LIP SERVICE?
To the doctor complained old MacMaddit,
"When my prick gets too hard, I have had it.
    This erection's a curse."
    Said the doc's helpful nurse,
"Would you mind if I took a crack at it?"

2178
Said a man to his girl, Miss MacNurd,
"What's the good word today, have you heard?"
    "The good word for today
    Will be *legs*," she did say,
"And it's time that you spread the good word."

2179
A magician who lived in Madras
Ingenious new tricks did amass.
    As he tried a new twist
    He slipped with his wrist
And he vanished right up his own ass.

2180
Of a feeble old man of Madras
It was said that his youth soon would pass.
    He said, "This is absurd;
    Please examine my turd—
I use *Ivory Soap* on my ass."

2181. RECTAL EMPHYSEMA
A smoking old man of Madras,
Whose jaw was cut off by some glass,
    Continued to smoke
    But no longer did choke,
For he learned how to smoke with his ass.

2182. FEAR OF PLEASURE
A simple young lady named Mame
Had no one but mother to blame.
    She was taught morals dear,
    So she fucked in great fear,
And enjoyed it so much, but in shame.

2183
There was an old actress named Mape,
A victim of sadistic rape.
    She said, "Come in the den
    And we'll do it again,
For I want to record this on tape."

2184
When Hays hired the typist, Miss May,
He found to his utter dismay
    She could not type a bit
    And was not worth a shit,
So he stroked on her pussy all day.

2185
There was a young man named McCarty
Who ate too much beans and felt farty.
    With his ass he played trumpet
    While he fucked an old strumpet,
And was known as the life of the party.

2186. ASHTRAYPHILIA
For years a young man named McGraw
Fucked a girl that smoked heavy, Miss Shaw.
    From this smoking and sex
    A conditioned reflex
Made him blow when an ashtray he saw.

2187
There was a young man named McLoud
Who fought with his arguments loud,
    And he claimed right along
    He could never do wrong;
When he shit in his pants, he was proud.

2188
There was a young man named McLouth
Who learned fine traditions down South.
    When some numbskull saw fit
    On some soap to write *shit*,
Young McLouth washed the soap with his mouth.

2189
A frustrated man was McNair,
He could not get in his Corvair,
    But he managed to squeeze
    In with relative ease
After lining the doorway with hair.

2190
The wife of a fellow named Mel
Was struck with a bad, sickly spell.
    Sometime later that day
    He attempted a lay,
But her cunt was not working too well.

2191. PETER PRINCIPLE*
While looking for fossils six meters
From basilican altars, Prof. Jeeters
    Claimed to find relics quaint—
    Holy bones of a saint—
But the bones that he found were all peters.

2192
An aging old golf pro named Meyer
At teaching young girls took a flyer.
    Every day he was seen
    Playing games on the green
Where his hole-in-one average was higher.

2193. THE TRANSFORMATION
A fanciful fellow named Milt
Was completely redone and rebuilt.
    Said his girl, "Let's partake
    Just for good old times' sake."
But he said, "That's not how I'm now built."

2194
A famed discus thrower named Molder
Attempted to toss a small boulder,
    But he slipped on a cob
    And he grasped his own knob
And he threw himself over his shoulder.

2195
The pompous old Duchess Moncrieff
Perturbed with her pious belief,
    Went out for a walk
    With her dog, round the block,
And she covered his cock with a leaf.

2196
There was an old man of Mongolia
Who suffered a strange melancholia.
    He sat for long hours
    And thought just of flowers,
Till there grew from his ass a magnolia.

2197
There was a brown-noser named Moses
Who chanced to be born with two noses.
    He could elicit grunts
    From two bosses at once,
And for this he got bouquets of roses.

2198
There was a young bowler named Motch
Whose grip was amazing to watch,
    But the girls were dismayed
    At the time he displayed
His bowling ball grip on their crotch.

2199
A man of refinement was Motch;
No date with his girl would he botch.
    When he noticed her plight
    From her panties too tight,
He would pull them with grace from her crotch.

2200
A man screwed his wife and her mother,
Her sisters, her aunts and grandmother.
    On his prick he put glasses
    And he said, "Look for asses,
To be sure we have missed nothing, brother."

2201. THE PRUDE
A lad with a saintly motivity
Declined all immoral festivity.
    In his manner pontificate
    He said, "I've no certificate
To indulge in this type of activity."

2202
A comely young lady named Mott
A drink from the bartender sought.
    And she said to him, "Bruce,
    Can you give me some juice?"
So he asked her to spread out her twat.

2203
There once was a minor musician
Who screwed in the major tradition.
    He appeared to be finished
    But returned with diminished
Then augmented the seventh position.

2204. SPENT DOCTOR
To his wife said the doctor of Natchez,
"All day I've checked twats in big batches.
    I am too beat to lay
    So I can't fuck today,
And I'm fed up with looking at snatches."

[2205]
Said the doctor's dear wife, Mrs. Dix,
"I will work as your nurse, just for kicks.
    Send the men to the back
    Where I'll show them my crack,
And perhaps I can fondle their pricks."

2206. THE FLOCKING
There was an old artist named Nate
Whose paintings were flocked and were great.
    As he fingered his cock
    He fell down in the flock,
And was flocked by the finger of fate.

2207. USE A BULLHORN
In the park an old maid with a need,
On her whistle for rape did proceed
    To blow hard—but she cursed
    Till her lungs fairly burst,
For no gentleman paid any heed.

2208
To the lawyer, a lady named Newsome
Gave the facts on her rape by a twosome.
    Said the lawyer, " 'Nough said,
    Let us both get to bed
And review all the details so gruesome."

2209. MÉNAGE À TROIS
A maker of condoms was Newsome,
And the one he designed was quite gruesome.
　　It seemed strangely confused
　　But was meant to be used
By three people instead of a twosome.

2210. TONGUE-TIED KEEPER
There was a zoo keeper named Nick—
A nasty disease made him sick.
　　Though there was a time where
　　He could lick any bear,
He no longer a pussy could lick.

2211. IN THE DARK
A CIA spy name of Nick
Would not give his girl friend a lick.
　　He kept his prick hidden
　　And to look was forbidden,
For he fucked with a classified prick.

2212
To the vet went a fellow named Nixon—
His dog and his cat needed fixin'.
　　He said, "Fix the wife, too,
　　For she has a loose screw,
And her cunt has had too many pricks in."

2213. NO CONCEPTION
In poverty folks with brains numb
Exist in the depths of the slum.
　　There they increase like vermin
　　And they cannot determine
From where in the fuck babies come.

2214. VIP ORGIES
Armed conflict would be obsolete
If leaders would end their deceit.
　　They should offer, so merry,
　　Not the hatchet to bury,
But should offer to bury the meat.

339

2215. WAIT NINE MONTHS
A suspicious old man named O'Dare
Examined his wife's pubic hair,
But he sneezed in her twat
And he found he could not
Tell the snot from the sperm that was there.

2216
An actress by name of O'Hart
In movies had made a grand start
Just by getting to know
Who was running the show,
And she often was made for the part.

2217. URGE TO PROPAGATE
There was an old botanist, Pace,
Who grew cunts in a pot at his place.
When they ripened, he'd pluck 'em,
And he'd eat them or fuck 'em—
They were simpler to grow than to chase.

2218. THE HARDY SCOTSMAN
A curious young lady named Pam
Stopped a Scotsman and said to him. "Sam.
Anything worn 'neath that skirt?"
But the Scot did assert,
"It's as good as it ever was, ma'am."

2219. POTLICKER
For men that are not up to par,
Be bold, and in life you will star.
There's no need to get flustered
If you can't cut the mustard,
You'll do fine if you just lick the jar.

2220
A purse-snatching lady named Patch
On failing a purse to detach
Cried aloud with a curse,
"I cannot snatch a purse
But I know that I can purse a snatch."

2221
To his son, said a fellow named Patterson,
"When dating young girls, pick them fatter, son."
    So his son dated one
    That was over a ton.
"Step aside," said his dad. "Let me at her, son."

2222
A couple once met at Cape Pearl,
They both wore hair long in a swirl.
    They got married of course,
    But they got a divorce,
For each figured that he got the girl.

2223
The alphabet soup made by Pease
Was flavored with spices and cheese.
    It was served with liturgy
    To old men of the clergy,
But he took out the *C U N T*'s.

2224
There was an old harlot of Peking,
Uncouth in a manner of speaking.
    This sordid old bitch
    Had been rolled in a ditch,
But she blushed when a man saw her leaking.

2225
A singles club opened in Perth;
Of women there sure was no dearth.
    A lawyer named Sawyer
    Took his share through the foyer
And he fucked them four deep on the earth.

2226
The old hamburg-maker named Pete
Came home every day somewhat beat.
    His wife itched for a lay,
    But he said, "Not today—
All day I've been plunging the meat."

2227
There was an old rabbi named Phipps
Who circumcised babies with snips,
    But the government frowned
    And his goods did impound
For he failed to pay tax on his tips.

2228
A dependable fellow named Phipps
Worked hard at his job drilling strips,
 And more points did amass
 With a broom up his ass,
For while working, he swept up the chips.

2229. THE DELTA AFFAIR
There was a hairdresser named Pierre
Who dressed a girl's hair in his chair,
 And he dressed it so nice
 For a nominal price
That she asked him to dress her affair.

[2230]
So Pierre with a feeling of bliss
Went to work on the cunt of this miss,
 And he dressed it so fine
 With his skilful design,
That it reached out and gave him a kiss.

2231
The ingenious inventor Von Phlitte
All mankind did well benefit.
 This redoubtable man
 Invented a fan
Which could not be hit by the shit.

2232
A pious old fellow named Pitt
Would never say *cunt*, *twat* or *slit*.
 To avoid controversy,
 He would beg the Lord's mercy
Whenever he sat for a shit.

2233. CANIS NOBILIS
A breeder of dogs, somewhat plastered,
A chastity belt for dogs mastered,
 A device to ensure
 That the breeds would be pure,
And no son of a bitch was a bastard.

2234. THE TRANSPLANTS
For a lady, a surgeon named Polk
Switched her cunt and her mouth as a joke.
    It was not all amiss—
    She was more fun to kiss,
But she raised up her dress when she spoke.

[2235]
She married a fellow named Frick
Whose mouth had been switched with his prick.
    There was no sixty-nine
    But they got along fine
When they found ninety-six did the trick.

2236
The King on a stamp was portrayed—
Not his face—but his ass was displayed,
    So the subjects en masse
    Could all lick on his ass,
And thus homage by all would be paid.

2237
A horny old fellow was Potter,
Who joined with a swing club, the rotter.
    Since his dear wife was dead
    He took with him instead
His buxom and cute teen-age daughter.

2238. THE QUEER DOCTOR
To the doctor went poor Mrs. Potts;
The pain in her pussy hurt lots.
    Said old Doctor McLouth,
    "Let me look in your mouth,
For I'm fed up with looking at twats."

2239
At the movies I pay a good price
To enjoy all the pussies so nice,
    But the doctor, so gay,
    Looks at pussies all day,
And he charges ten bucks for advice.

2240
The president, bursting with pride,
Made public his energy guide:
    Do not fuck in great haste—
    There is far too much waste.
Fuck slow as you lay on your side.

2241
When John fucked a girl from Purdue,
Tim would wait till his brother was through,
    Then Tim licked the paste
    For he relished the taste
Of a cunt where another man blew.

2242
In France old King Louis Quatorze
His ministers gathered indoors.
    He did want, it appears,
    An Old Home for the queers,
And a subsidy plan for the whores.

2243
Invented by Louis Quatorze
Were finest of sports for indoors.
    He would bugger the pope
    As he hung from a rope,
And the bishops he fucked on all fours.

2244
There was a young fellow named Raft
Amazed at the size of aircraft.
    To Japan he was going
    On a flight on a Boeing
With two whorehouses fore and one aft.

2245
Attached to his mother was Rand,
She catered to every demand,
    And she stood by his side
    When he fucked with his bride;
She was there to hold on to his hand.

2246. THE MAYOR'S WIFE
The lady removed all her raiment
And took on young men for defrayment
    Of her new domicile
    And she said with a smile,
"One more fuck and I'll have the down payment."

[2247]
No longer did she have to roam,
The streets and the alleys to comb.
    Though her price was now higher
    She had many a buyer,
And she soon bought a much larger home.

[2248]
She proudly condoned her caprice;
From rentals it gave her release.
   She revealed, without guilt,
   How her new house was built,
She explained it was built piece by piece.

[2249]
Her thoughts being geared to expansion
She shored up her ass with a stanchion
   She kicked out cajolers
   And decrepit bung-holers,
And she moved to the town's finest mansion.

[2250]
She still was the sordid purveyor
Who catered to those who would pay her.
   But it all went for naught,
   She deserved what she got
When she married His Honor, the Mayor.

2251. THE COPROLITE*
Two diggers of fossils stood rapt
As wondrous new relics they mapped.
   Said one, " 'Pon my word,
   It's a fossilized turd
Where some creep in the crypt crept and crapped."

[2252]
The other man said as he stooped,
"I think that we both have been duped.
   No creep ever slipped
   And crapped in the crypt,
But a pup in the pit popped and pooped."

2253
There was a proud girl of Ravenna
Who rode in a car in Vienna
   With a man dignified;
   They came back from the ride
With her panties strung from the antenna.

2254
A young gynecologist Ray,
Had a hard-on at work through the day,
   But at home it subsided—
   Left his wife unprovided,
For his pecker was too soft to lay.

2255
When Kay left her boyfriend named Ray,
He looked high and low through the day.
    He got down on his knees
    And he begged his friends, "Please,
Let me know when and if you see Kay."

2256
A drunken old sailor named Reese
Raised hell with a madam from Nice.
    He was told to keep quiet
    But he started a riot
And was jailed for disturbing the piece.

2257
A lady went biking with Reichert
And later complained that the hike hurt.
    He said, "A good lay
    Makes the pain go away."
But she said in her crotch was a bike hurt.

2258
Discovered by Newton's resources
And set down in all college courses:
    If the body you date
    Has a motionless state
You must rub it with external forces.

2259
Team captain was young swimmer Restroke;
He practiced before all the rest woke.
    He practiced the crawl,
    The backstroke and all,
And at night he perfected his breast stroke.

2260. THE COUNTRY DOCTOR
To the girl said old Dr. von Rickchurr,
"Mitt your fingers please spread out your stricture.
    To find vy iss sore
    I must shtudy zum more,
And for diss, I need full-color picture."

2261*
VW's will give a cheap ride,
Say owners with chests puffed with pride,
    But they've run out of pranks
    To get tigers in tanks,
Or to try to get pussy inside.

2262
A well-hung musician named Riggs
Was climbing a fig tree for figs.
  But all was not well—
  On his organ he fell
And he sounded like E. Power Biggs.

2263
There was an old fogey named Rinnish
Whose memory did fade and diminish,
  For in bed with a date,
  Though he started first rate,
He forgot what to do at the finish.

2264
An aged old fellow named Ripley,
Disabled and known to be cripply,
  Fucked a girl in his attic
  In a manner fanatic,
And, *Believe It or Not*, fucked her triply.

2265. DO IT FOR FUN
Give no help to poor people that roam
Seeking food as the alleys they comb.
  It is courting disaster
  For they multiply faster
And they'll fuck you right out of your home.

2266
A partisan lady named Roarch
For G.O.P. carried the torch.
  She stopped at the flat
  Of an old Democrat
And was fucked 'fore she got off his porch.

2267. COX SUCCORED
Young Cox, in despair, on the rocks,
Received aid from the parish *Poor Box*.
  Said the Pope, much impressed,
  "May this parish be blest
For providing the succor for Cox."

2268
In front of the fireplace sat Rose;
She needed to thaw out her toes.
    It was thirty below
    Where she fucked in the snow,
And her pussy was fucking near froze.

2269
When Grover fucked old harlot Rose,
A problem she had to dispose,
    So she said to him, "Grover,
    I believe I'll turn over—
I can't stand the way you pick your nose."

2270
There was a young lady rotund
For whom no young fellow had gunned,
    For on going to bed
    She appeared to be dead
And she slept like an ox that was stunned.

2271
At the beach, a big show-off named Rube
On each arm held a girl on a tube.
    A detractor came near
    And he said, with a sneer,
"Would you look at the dolls on that boob!"

2272
There was a young juggler named Ruggling
Who attempted coition while juggling,
    And today in my dreams
    I can still her his screams
And his tormented cries and his struggling.

2273. CURE FOR HOMESICKNESS
A man far from home name of Russell
Engaged a young maid for a tussle.
    "I am homesick," he said,
    "So lay down as if dead,
And do not move a tit or a muscle."

2274
A wily old codger named Ryerson
Advised a young lad, "Don't you buy her, son,
    Till you see by the bore
    That you've got a good whore
And you've taken a minute to try her, son."

2275
To the doc went the whore of St. Anne's,
And her visit fit into his plans.
    He checked her cirrhosis
    By means of hypnosis,
Then he reamed out her twat with his glans.

2276
The whore from the parish St. Giles
Retired amidst plaudits and smiles.
    When she figured each poke
    At three inches per stroke,
Her cunt had some ten thousand miles.

2277
A bulbous young lady named Sands
Resisted a fellow's demands.
    When he started to claw
    She busted his jaw
With a swing of her mammary glands.

2278
A simple young lady named Sasso
Would polish her pussy with Brasso.
    The reason, I trust—
    To eliminate rust
Which ran in long streaks from her ass-o.

2279
A maid should avoid any scandal
And with caution take what she can handle.
    If she oft takes the shaft
    From the fore and the aft
Both ends will be burned by the candle.

2280. SAFETY PLAY
Said the young gynecologist Schick
As he probed in the crotch of a chick,
    "I am through, please relax,
    You can put on your slacks,
And you'd better let go of my prick."

2281
There was a free-loader named Schroeder
Who dated a girl and did load her
    With the essence of brew—
    His intent was to screw,
But he failed for she had a bad odor.

349

2282
A simple young lady named Schust
From her mother had learned not to lust.
    She married 'midst fears,
    And for thirty-five years
She fucked in great shame and disgust.

2283
The rooster, as well known in science,
Rules the barnyard by clucking defiance,
    Whereas lawyers in courts
    Are working at torts,
And their time is spent fucking de clients.

2284
If a man gives no thought to the score
And carelessly picks up a whore,
    And he lacks self-control,
    He'll end up in the hole
For twenty-five dollars or more.

2285
There was a nosepicker named Scott
Who said, as he dug out some snot,
    "There are things that are grand
    When you do them by hand,
But they're better when done with a twat."

2286
When problems arose, Mr. Scott
All day with great effort gave thought,
    But with simple precision
    He would make a decision
When he came face to face with a twat.

2287. WHAT! NO HEADACHE?
When his wife passed away, Mr. Scott
Said a true-to-life posture he sought,
    So he laid her to rest
    With one hand 'cross her chest
And the other hand over her twat.

2288
To the doctor went old Mrs. Scott,
For the pain in her chest hurt a lot.
    Said the doctor, so wise,
    "Please spread out your thighs,
And let's have a look at your twat."

2289
The magazine publisher, Scott,
Found his sales were increasing a lot
  When he showed pictures lewd
  Of young girls in the nude
Which were sprayed with the odor of twat.

2290
A perfume inspector was Scott,
At work he sniffed perfumes a lot.
  At the end of the day
  He would come home and say,
"You can't beat the odor of twat."

2291
There was a cheese-maker named Scott
Who found the new flavor he sought.
  When he took his first sniff
  His pecker got stiff,
So he labeled it *Essence of Twat.*

2292. CHEESE DIP
The author proclaimed in his script
How man over kisses has flipped,
  But there's nothing so fine
  As the feeling divine
When the prick in the pussy is dipped.

2293. CRIME IS RAMPANT
To make the whole nation secure
Of crime, we must make ourselves pure,
  Which is just as absurd
  As to look for the turd
Of a horse in a pile of manure.

2294
There was a young lady named Sentry
Who claimed to be raped by some gentry.
  But the judge said, "Dismissed,"
  For he looked where she pissed
And saw no sign of forcible entry.

2295. LOVE IS A 4-LETTER WORD

Old ladies who suffered in shame
Were cleansed of their guilt and their blame
    By a shrink name of Scott
    Who said, "Fear not the twat,
For to love and to fuck are the same."

2296

Out shopping went lonely Miss Shore
To buy her a book at the store.
    She did not seek a book
    Which explained how to cook,
But a book to bring wolves to her door.

2297

From her husband, a lady named Shore
Asked for money, each week more and more.
    To get sex he must pay
    So he said in dismay,
"You are naught but an overpriced whore."

2298

There was a young fellow who'd shove
His finger in cunts to make love.
    Since his prick was not lewd
    It hung out and was viewed,
While his finger was hid in a glove.

2299

A musical fellow was Shrife
Who played on the organ and fife.
    At age forty-nine
    On his fife he played fine
But his organ lacked lustre and life.

2300

For ladies inherently sick
There's a cure that will sure do the trick:
    A few hours of soaking
    And some fine friendly poking
From the nearest available prick.

2301

When atom bombs fill up the sky,
You must give it the old college try.
    Say a prayer, if you please,
    Put your head 'tween your knees
And start kissing your asshole goodbye!

2302. STOCKBROKER'S ADVICE
Investment in sex would be sin,
Advised the old stockbroker, Flynn.
    If it's growth stock you hunt,
    Stay away from the cunt,
For you never get out what went in.

2303
Since porno is no longer sin
In Denmark, their movies are in.
    They will make one first class
    Where a man licks dog's ass
And where Lassie will fuck Rin Tin Tin.

2304
In Britain a harlot named Skillings
Sold ass for a crown and nine shillings,
    But she failed to adapt
    To new coins, and was trapped;
She no longer could make out her billings.

2305
There was an old harlot named Skillings
Who went to the dentist for fillings.
    In a fit of depravity
    He filled the wrong cavity,
So each cancelled the other one's billings.

2306
A destitute trapper was Skinner;
His catch was so poor he got thinner.
    He set off in pursuit
    Of the beaver hirsute
To provide him with warmth and a dinner.

2307
A man of great honor named Skinner
Said, "Mr. O'Connor, you sinner,
    You will soon be a goner.
    What is better than honor?"
Said O'Connor, "What's better is in 'er."

2308
A particular fellow named Slatter
Would never choose girls that were fatter.
    He chose those that were thin
    For it went further in
And it lessened the chances of splatter.

2309
An avid cheese lover named Smitty
Ate limburger cheese that was shitty,
    But his darling wife Jane
    Shoved it all down the drain
And she stunk up the sewers in the city.

2310
Great sculptors attired in smocks
Nude statues created from rocks,
    But their names are forgotten—
    We recall just the rotten
Old bishops who knocked off their cocks.

2311
Said the doctor, while checking Miss Sommer,
"Your urine may tell why you're glummer."
    So she stooped to the floor
    And she pissed like a whore.
"What you need," said the doc, "is a plumber."

2312
The life of a queen must be sordid;
It's news every time that she's boarded.
    Every groan, every grunt,
    Every twitch of her cunt,
Every fart that she lets is recorded.

2313*
The *NFL Cheerleaders* sought
To improve on their image and lot.
    Said Rozelle, in a fit,
    "You can show tits a bit,
But thou shalt not display any twat."

2314
To men traveling down in the South,
Of women you'll find there's no drouth,
    But it's best to be wary
    For there are some contrary,
And you might get a bust in the mouth.

2315
To his wife, said a hunter named Speers,
"I am leaving to hunt for some deers."
    If his grammar was poor,
    This his wife could endure,
But it left her with doubts and some feers.

2316
A TV repairman named Spencer
Concocted a fucking dispenser,
But a fucker did prove
If you're not in the groove,
When you blow, you will blow a condenser.

2317
An over-fucked fellow named Springer
Had lost all the life in his dinger,
So he fucked with his nose
And by twiddling his toes,
And sometimes he fucked with his finger.

2318
If your family is small, you will star,
And trips you can take, near and far.
It is not simple luck,
Just make sure you don't fuck
Yourself out of a seat in your car.

2319
Our leader asked Science to start
A project so dear to his heart—
They must work with persistence
To determine the distance
That a car can be moved with a fart.

2320
On earth man has made a poor start;
In pollution he's put soul and heart,
But in Congress, their goal
Is to plug every hole—
Man will soon need a license to fart.

2321
A girl that smoked heavy, Miss Stott,
Went out on a date with a Scot.
"I don't mind," he said, "Grace,
If you smoke with your face,
But remove that cigar from your twat."

2322
A legless old lady of Strand
Was raped by a rotter named Rand,
But the judge set him free
For he said, "I can see
She has no leg on where she can stand."

2323

A rugged old tomcat of Strand
Once took a young polecat in hand.
    He did limit his playing
    And he backed away saying,
"I've enjoyed about all I can stand."

2324

There was an old alchemist, Strensall,
Who studied his chamber utensil.
    His conclusion, sincere,
    Was an egg in your beer
Could be used to put lead in your pencil.

2325

Der vas ein jung feller of Stuttgart
Who haben in life a fine gutt start.
    Ven he vas a boy littler
    He saluted, "Heil Hitler!"
And vud end his salute mit ein gutt fart.

2326

A discerning young fellow named Sy
Paused to look at a young maiden's thigh,
    And he said with a grunt,
    "There is more to a cunt
Than you ever can see with an eye."

2327

The doctor good manners is taught
And he gives every statement due thought.
    To a lady he'll say,
    "How's your throat feel today?"
But he never will ask, "How's your twat?"

2328

Astronomers sat with nerves taut,
Their telescopes trained on one spot
    On the girl from Madras
    For a view of her ass
And a total eclipse of her twat.

2329

The Royalty gathered for tea
And to honor the new Holy See.
    Between belching and farts
    They discussed the fine arts,
Then they went on a mad fucking spree.

2330
To conserve gas supplies, Carter's team
Proceeded to work at full steam,
    So they mixed gas and farts
    In exact equal parts,
But they failed in this half-farted scheme.

2331*
There was an old man named U Thant
Who stated, "The thing that I want
    Is for Dow to make jelly
    To be used 'neath the belly,
And the *Pill* should be made by Dupont."

2332
I notice that *Playboy* has thought
That cunt hair won't leave folks distraught,
    So they've shown a bouquet;
    But I wait for the day
When the cover displays a full twat.

2333
A Scout helped a lady go through
A busy street crossing in Kew.
    She said, "Can I repay
    Your good deed for today?"
Said the Boy Scout, "Just give me a screw."

2334
Some men will not turn down their thumbs
On any young lady that comes,
    But prefer girls religious
    For their wants are prodigious
And their heads are as empty as drums.

2335. OUT-OF-DATE WIRING
A man of his dear wife was tired;
It seems that her sex life expired,
    So he switched her, at forty,
    For two twenties, so sporty,
But he was for two-twenty not wired.

2336
Mechanics are putting on tires
And firemen are putting out fires.
    While butchers discreet
    Are beating their meat,
Electricians are pulling their wires.

2337
There was a young lady named Titehouse
Who lived all alone in a lighthouse.
    She had an obsession
    To see Congress in session
But was fucked on her way through the White House.

2338
The prices they're charging today
For douches and jellies and spray
    May be too fucking high,
    But the chemist knows why—
If it's fucking you want, you must pay.

2339
A basso profundo named Totum
Tried singing the *Largo Factotum*.
    When he sang *Figaro*
    The notes were so low
That he rattled his balls in his scrotum.

2340
If life on this earth is a treasure
And man is to treasure his leisure,
    He must plan each new birth
    Lest he plague the whole earth;
He must do far more fucking for pleasure.

2341
While the chef was preparing a treat,
The waitress stood by so discreet.
    When she asked, "What is love?"
    He said, "Heavens above!
It is when I am basting my meat!"

2342. FLY THE FLAG
In the forest serene there grew one tree
Which had knotholes that made it a fun tree.
    A lone ranger came by
    And he unzipped his fly,
And said, "What can I do for my cunt tree?"

2343. PROPORTIONAL OBSCENITY
A learned old justice of Trent
Defined what obscenity meant.
　　He found *Duck* was not clean,
　　But three-quarters obscene,
And *Fudge* was foul forty percent.

2344
The doctors have learned all the tricks,
The ear, nose and throat how to fix,
　　And for ten bucks a grunt
　　They will look at a cunt,
And make fortunes from assholes and pricks.

2345. MUSH!
To Alaska went worn-out old Tucker
To gain back his strength as a trucker.
　　He expended his wealth
　　To recover his health
And he came back a strong husky fucker.

2346. CLEAR SAILING
A shipwrecked young sailor named Tudder
Tied his shirt to his prick for a scudder.
　　When the mast was erected
　　His course he directed
With his thumb up his ass for a rudder.

2347. CURE FOR THE COMMON COLD
There was a young fellow named Tunney;
The cold that he had was not funny.
　　He could barely endure it
　　So he thought he would cure it
With a hot roll in bed and with honey.

2348. WHETHER REPORT
An anxious young lady named Tunney
Called weatherman Jones and said, "Honey,
　　Tell me what is the weather,
　　And please let me know whether
It will be fourteen inches or Sonny."

2349*
Said the spiral vice-president, Twist,
Who never a buck could resist,
    "I'll eat shit off the slit
    Or perhaps off a tit,
Just as long as my asshole is kissed."

2350
A lady depressed name of Twitting
Despairingly works at her knitting.
    The excitement is missing
    For it's used just for pissing—
She knows not on a gold mine she's sitting.

2351
A novice young man unaware,
Had chosen a girl sweet and fair.
    What he thought he would treasure
    As the seat of his pleasure
Became the abyss of despair.

2352. GAME TRY
The hunter of game, unobtrusive,
Prepared all his rifles exclusive
    To pursue the big cat
    In his wild habitat,
While his son stalked the pussy elusive.

2353. GIVE TILL IT HURTS
A fund-raising man of Utrecht
Solicited clients select.
    "Would you give, Mr. Hayward,
    To the girls who are wayward?"
He replied, "I have given direct."

2354. FOR SHAME!
An ESP expert named Vance
Was walking the street, and by chance,
    When he read a girl's mind
    Was disgusted to find
That she'd like to get into his pants.

2355
Asked the waitress of customer Vance,
"Some cream in your coffee, perchance?"
    Said Vance, "If you do,
    I will slip you a screw
And a load of my cream in your pants."

2356. WHAT KIND OF HUSBAND ARE YOU?
When the husband by chance comes in view
And discovers his wife in a screw
    With some gentleman friend
    With a hairy ass end,
Tell me what does the dear husband do?

[2357]
He does not make a wild exhibition
As one would suppose from tradition.
    Observation contends
    That his action depends
On the nature of his disposition.

[2358]
The husband polite will consent
Not to stop this outrageous event.
    With culture and class
    He pats the man's ass,
And says, "Please don't withdraw till you've spent."

[2359]
The husband who's funny will pass
On tiptoe behind to harass.
    In the midst of the screw
    To the fucker says, "Boo!"
While with feathers he tickles his ass.

[2360]
The husband considerate can cope
With problems of much greater scope.
    He waits in full view
    Till the fucker is through,
Then he offers him towels and soap.

[2361]
The good-natured man unperplexed
Will wait till the couple have sexed,
    For he favors a screw
    Where another man blew,
And he gracefully says, "I am next."

[2362]
The husband who's formal will greet
The pair in a manner discreet.
    He will wait till they spend,
    Then his hand he'll extend
And the fucker he'll formally meet.

[2363]
The husband who's just will prepare
To sit while he watches the pair.
    He will show no emotion
    While he notes the man's motion
To be certain his fucking is fair.

[2364]
The husband conceited installs
Himself by the fucker who sprawls,
    And he watches discreet
    While he plunges the meat,
And he sneers at the size of his balls.

[2365]
The husband suspicious will grunt
As he watches his wife take the brunt
    Of a fuck with her lover,
    Then he raises the cover
And he says to his wife, "Wash your cunt."

[2366]
The husband refined will not scowl
At observing this fucking act foul.
    If the ass of her lover
    Is not under the cover,
He will cover that ass with a towel.

[2367]
The husband that's cautious will bend
To observe how his wife fucks her friend.
    If he sees that the lubber
    Has not put on a rubber,
He'll request that he pull out to spend.

[2368]
The husband inept says, "What luck!"
As he watches the cuntlapper suck
    On his wife's hairy cunt,
    And he notes every grunt
In the hope he can learn how to fuck.

[2369]
The excitable husband in shock
Upon the two fuckers will gawk,
    Then he'll sit in a chair
    With his feet in the air,
And he'll play until off goes his cock.

[2370]
The acquisitive husband won't stew;
He will wait till the fucker is through.
    He will offer the rotter
    A cloth, soap and water,
And present him a bill for the screw.

[2371]
If a gourmet observes a man stick it
'Twixt the legs of his wife in her thicket,
    He will let the man blow
    And he'll say to him, "Joe,
Will you please step aside while I lick it?"

[2372]
If the husband is shy and he flushes
His wife and her lover, he rushes
    To extinguish the light
    For he can't stand the sight,
And no one must see that he blushes.

[2373]
A cynical husband would stare
As he viewed the young fucker prepare
    For a mad fucking spree
    And he'd say, "I can't see
How any young fellow could care."

[2374]
The husband who's prompt, in would dash
While his wife and her friend fucked so brash.
    He would unzip his fly
    Grasp the man by the thigh,
And he'd bugger the guy in a flash.

2375
The British with heads full of vapours
Are nurtured on most stupid capours.
    When her Highness feels fit
    For a fart or a shit
It is plastered in all daily papours.

2376
So short was the girl of young Visser
He knelt on his knees just to kiss her.
    When she stood on her toes
    The end of her nose
Would come to the knob of his pisser.

2377. ARCHIMEDES PRINCIPLE
Archimedes while dipped to his waist
Tried to screw with a mermaid in haste,
    But he failed to account
    For his weight in his mount
Which did equal the water displaced.

2378*
A thrifty young fellow was Walls;
He took his girl out to the Falls.
    Said his girl, "I do think
    I would like a nice drink."
So he gave her the sweat off his balls.

2379
An old patternmaker named Warbocks
Once screwed an old whore on a core box,
    And after a flyer
    On top of a dryer,
She stayed home for a week with a sore box.

2380. CHRISTMAS TAIL
"Do not fuck with the deer," Santa warns,
For the day that he did, he still mourns.
    He had thought to fuck Blitzen
    For he felt that it fits in,
But he hung by the balls on his horns.

2381. THE PURIFIER
While eating his dinner, young Welch
Was helpless the smokers to squelch,
    So with smoke everywhere
    He made pure the foul air
With a healthy big fart and a belch.

2382. REGIMEN FOR LONGEVITY
A maid who was trim but well-fed
Explained how her weight had been shed.
　　Every night without fail
　　Her intake she'd curtail
To a sausage and two eggs in bed.

2383
There was a young girl from the West
Who looked like a queen when she dressed.
　　On a date she would wear
　　Fake tits and false hair,
And she'd shave all the hair off her chest.

2384. OR WAS IT VICE VERSA?
There was a professor named Whithouse
Who lived in a fine and a fit house.
　　Reader's Digest he kept
　　In his room where he slept,
And *Playboy* he kept in the shithouse.

2385*
There was a cheesemaker named Whithouse
Who lived in a fine and a fit house.
　　To make limburger cheese
　　For this man was a breeze.
He took two pails of milk to the shithouse.

2386
Said a fearful young lady named Whitney,
"No more will I ride on a jitney;
　　I was squeezed out of shape
　　By a man bent on rape,
And the jitney I left with a bit knee."

2387. A FITTING RESPONSE
While shopping for rubbers, young Wise
Was asked by the lady, "What size?"
　　He replied, "I'm not sure."
　　Said the lady demure,
"I will check—slip your prick in my thighs."

[2388]
So Wise slipped his prick in her twat.
"Size seven," she said, and he bought
　　A dozen or two,
　　Then he told his friend Lew
What a wonderful bargain he got.

[2389]
So Lew, by the lady unwitting,
Was checked, but he blew before quitting.
        When she asked him how many,
        Came the answer, "Not any,
For I simply came in for a fitting."

2390. THE FLYCATCHER
There was a young lady named Wise
Who claimed that her cunt ws a prize,
        And she fooled many men
        For they all came again,
But she never, but never fooled flies.

2391. THE WAX JOB*
While waxing her car, young Miss Wise
By Simon was caught in surprise.
        He lifted her gown
        And her panties dropped down—
She was trapped by those big *Simoniz*.

2392. THERMOGENESIS
When fucking, a lady of Woking
Reacted so fast to the poking
        That her relative motion
        Induced heat and commotion,
And her asshole and cunt started smoking.

2393
There was a young lady named Wood
Who claimed she was misunderstood.
        They said she was bad,
        But this made her so mad
For in bed all men said she was good.

2394
There was a young lady named Wong
Whose cunt hair was thick and so strong
        That workmen were able
        To fashion a cable
For constructing a bridge a mile long.

2395
The bearded old whore of Woodhaven
Was ugly and crude and unshaven,
    And she peddled her hole
    Just to miners of coal,
For her pussy was black as a raven.

2396. A PHALLUSOPHICAL DISSERTATION
The learned philosophers wrangle,
Exploring each facet and angle,
    And their brains they have wrecked
    Seeking cause and effect
Of the factors affecting the dangle.

[2397]
"It's needless for your tongues to wag;
The answer," said one, "is the hag.
    Though I may sound contrary
    The erection will vary
Just inverse to the sag of the bag."

[2398]
The cardinal held his cock bare
As he blew off a shot in the air,
    And he said, "I surmise
    That the pecker will rise
Direct as the square of the hair."

[2399]
A lawyer with knowledge replete
Provocative thought did repeat
    On the matters affecting
    And the cause of erecting—
It was mainly the heat of the meat.

[2400]
The doctor said sadly, "Alas,
The data that I did amass—
    And I have all the poop—
    What contributes to droop
Is most surely the mass of the ass."

[2401]
The pensive judge rose from the bench
And read from a treatise in French:
    "Your pecker will dangle
    At a vertical angle
If you tackle a wench with a stench."

[2402]
Said the bishop, "I have here the scoop
That causes the pecker to droop.
    The rot in the twat
    With peril is fraught
And your pecker will never recoup."

[2403]
The pontiff, so learned and wise,
Said seldom would he show surprise,
    But it softened his meat
    And he beat a retreat
When he ran into flies in the thighs.

[2404]
Said the senator, pausing to think,
"It is seldom from cunt I will shrink.
    What gives me a fit
    Is shit on the slit,
And it causes my pecker to sink."

[2405]
The preacher, obliged by his duty,
Told all, as he scratched on a cootie.
    His prick, he confessed,
    Was never depressed
By the beauty he saw in a cutie.

2406
I have eaten good dinners for years;
For the specials of chefs, give three cheers.
    But nothing can beat
    This delectable treat:
My head in a cunt to the ears.

2407. THE QUADRINITY?
Old Mary, it seems, has a yen
To play with a candle; not men.
    She'll be raised to the Trinity
    By the Blessed Divinity
If she shows she can do it again.

2408. SINCOME TAX
To a whore said a tax man named Zend,
"On the sinful diversion you vend
    An assessment you'll pay."
    Said the whore, in dismay,
"You have syntax I don't comprehend."

18
Weak Sisters

2409. CAMEL MEETS STRAW
To his camel, said Arab Abdu,
"Take this straw and this drink—it's for you."
    Said the camel, "Alack,
    This straw broke my back,
So I think I will break it in two."

2410
Non-smokers who foul air abhor
Must all make their voices heard more.
    They must learn the fine art
    Of the exquisite fart
And to gracefully spit on the floor.

2411. EQUIVALENT ORIFICE IN TERRA FIRMA
The earth with strange folk does abound
Who think the earth's flat and not round,
    And it seems they cannot
    Tell I'm sure you know what
From a hole which you find in the ground.

2412. DON'T ELECT HIM TO OFFICE!
The world in all types does abound;
Some fit in square holes, some in round.
    Some in storms sail a boat,
    While some men, you will note,
In fair weather will drive boats aground.

2413. GRAVITY OBSERVED
The schoolbooks with theories abound
How Newton had gravity found.
    Now it wasn't the apple
    Which his mind had to grapple
But the frolicking pair on the ground.

2414*
The smokers with tongues acrobatic
On their right to smoke are dogmatic
    For tobacco is grand,
    But thalidomide's banned
For thalidomide's much more dramatic.

2415. WATT'S COOKING
Men vary in rates they acquire
New thoughts to fulfil their desire.
    By exertion of wit
    Some men atoms have split,
While in Watts some have learned about fire.

2416. MAN THE INVENTOR
As new concepts began to accrue,
So with scarcity man was all through.
    He invented the lever
    And the wheel—no doubt clever—
But too bad he's in debt for the screw.

2417. APPROPRIATE EMBLEM
As a symbol of note, we admit
The eagle is worthy and fit,
    But for principles narrow
    Much preferred is the sparrow
Who sings with great joy and eats shit.

2418
If health is the thing you adore,
This logic will better your score:
    Since an apple a day
    Keeps the doctor away—
Two apples keeps two from the door.

2419*
An astronaut, trained and adroit,
The frontiers of space did exploit.
    He could walk with disdain
    On the moon's bleak terrain,
But could not walk the streets of Detroit.

2420. THE BOOB TUBE
When speaking of facts that affront,
The TV must take the whole brunt.
    It's no wonder tubes blow
    And the screen fills with snow
After facing the boobs out in front.

2421. PUNKTUATION
The ' sits all aglow
As high as a [can go
    Looking down at the trash
    Like the - and –
And it sneers at the , below.

2422
A newlywed girl with allurance
Admired her young groom with assurance
    As he prayed by the bed.
    "Is it guidance?" she said.
He said, "No, I just pray for endurance."

2423
My life has appealing allurance;
I feel that I have the endurance.
    I could make my employment
    The pursuit of enjoyment
But I cannot afford the insurance.

2424
The item I find that annoys
Which causes me loss of my poise,
    Is to see now and then
    A department of men
Which is run by good scouts—namely boys.

2425. AGGRANDIZEMENT
The wealth of a man we appraise,
By viewing his antics and ways.
    One can tell he has riches
    By the way that he bitches
And complains of the taxes he pays.

2426. THE HORSEMAN KNEW HER
The horses have finer aroma
Than cars that gas man into coma.
    We've proved feces en masse
    Of equus callabas
Non-conducive to vile carcinoma.

2427*
There was a young lady named Astor
Whose husband was shot by a blaster,
    But she was not too shook
    For she wrote a fat book
And made capital out of disaster.

2428
A man who would not be attacked,
To critics would firmly react.
    In his trousers he erred
    And the subject was bared,
But he strongly defended his act.

2429
A terrible toothache had Backshun;
It drove him to fits of distraction.
    A dentist named Lee
    Pulled it so painlessly
That he asked for another extraction.

2430
Said the teacher to young Master Bacon,
"Your grammar's so bad, I am shaken."
    Said young Bacon, "What gall!
    It is not bad at all—
I don't think that your point is well took."

2431
There was a young lady named Barr
Who carried her smoking too far.
    Her dilemma she cursed
    For while baby she nursed
He blew rings with a stinking cigar.

2432
On a date with a girl, Mr. Barr
Lit up a cigar in the car,
    But his girl friend, Miss Grace,
    She pissed full in his face,
And she put out the stinking cigar.

2433
"Our bankers," observed Mr. Bart,
"As servants do play a fine part.
    They give thoughtful advice
    And make great sacrifice,
And they all have our interest at heart."

2434
There was an old fellow named Bart
Who bought a new cart very smart.
    Though his cart did obsess him
    It did not full possess him,
Since his horse he still put 'fore the cart.

2435
An obstinate smoker named Bart
Would smoke till it troubled his heart.
    He said, in a huff,
    As he took his last puff,
"I will smoke until death do us part."

2436
When dying, a fellow named Bate
Arranged to pay charges and freight
    On his brand-new Mercedes
    To be sent down to Hades
To ensure that he'd get a hot date.

2437
When borrowing money, young Beach
Signed papers beyond his arms' reach.
    He signed three notes in triplicate,
    One more in sequiplicate,
And he signed three more copies of each.

2438
There was a young fellow named Beakley
Who managed at first a tri-weekly,
    Then he tried with some care
    A try-weekly affair;
Before long he was doomed to try weakly.

2439. USE A FLAWSWATTER*
Our Congress meets daily because
We live in a land full of flaws,
    But they rattle and prate
    In a lengthy debate
And their blunders become our new laws.

2440

The forest that's virgin began
With Nature preparing the plan
    To produce stately trees
    Midst a sweet scented breeze,
Untrod by the crude hand of man.

2441

At the Louvre a workman began
To crate Venus to take to Milan,
    But he slipped and he fell
    And the statue as well—
'Twas the landing of Venus on Man.

2442

There was an old man of Belle River
Who rode in an old-fashioned flivver,
    But to crank it took force
    So he purchased a horse,
And it wasn't so hard on his liver.

2443. THE RECTAL BALLPOINT PEN

To write a prescription, Doc Ben
Looked into his coat once again.
    When he found a thermometer
    He was heard a kilometer,
"Tell me what silly ass has my pen?"

2444. THE WILL OF THE PEEPLE

There was an old fellow named Bennett;
They made him the head of the senate.
    On proposed legislation
    Which was good for the nation
He made sure all the votes were again' it.

2445

The vending machines trapped Miss Beth,
And left her devoid of all breath.
    She bought coffee and cokes,
    And parking and smokes;
They nickled and dimed her to death.

2446
We live in a world that bewilders;
Inventors for death get our guilders,
    For society shuns
    Intellectual ones.
Those who work to destroy are called builders.

2447
A slow-moving fellow named Bickly
Appeared to be haggard and sickly.
    He at work was not well
    Till at five rang the bell,
Then amazingly Bickly moved quickly.

2448
There was an old banker named Bierce
Whose heart was like flint—hard to pierce.
    But a fly that was trapped
    In a web and was wrapped,
Brought tears to his eyes something fierce.

2449
A musical wrestler named Binks
Would knot all his rivals in kinks.
    As he played his accordion
    Someone slipped him a Gordian,
So he stands now on one hand and stinks.

2450
The milkman did not care a bit
When cold spells his milk truck did hit.
    Though the bottles did shatter
    He said, "It's no matter,
I don't cry over milk that is split."

2451
There was an old lady named Blake
Who never her man did forsake.
    Through foul weather and fair
    He was free from despair
For she pointed out every mistake.

2452. THE PERMANENT TRAINEE
A technology victim was Blaining
On whom the machine age was gaining.
    Though new skills he did master
    The machines learned much faster
And he spent his whole life in retraining.

2453
The turbine designed by young Blair
Won prizes at every World's Fair.
      It was driven by gases
      From political asses
Who continuously spouted hot air.

2454. VIRGINS IN THE FOREST
The ladies spend hours of bliss
In forests that hide every kiss,
      And no prying eye sees
      What occurs midst the trees,
So the forest's prime evil is this.

2455
Man's life on this earth is all blotches
As more and more projects he botches.
      Since man started his climb
      From the primordial slime
It appears that he's slipped a few notches.

2456
While driving, a fellow named Bonctor
Observed a young lady and honked her,
      But she failed to respond
      To this gay vagabond,
So he came and he saw and he conked her.

2457. STONES FROM A BLUDDE
The crud that Bludde had in his bones
Was taken in stride by Doc Jones,
      But what gave Jones despair
      Was Bludde's kidney repair,
And extracting from Bludde all the stones.

2458
A base-looking fellow named Bostick
Was asked why his manner was caustic.
      He replied with some guile
      And an acidy smile,
"The gum that I chew makes my jaw stick."

377

2459. FEAROPHOBIA

A fearful young lady named Bostick
Was asked if her fears made her caustic.
    She said, "Mother fears God,
    And I fear this is odd,
For my father, I fear, is agnostic."

2460

The wife of an old man named Boyce
Was struck with the loss of her voice.
    Divine help he did seek
    For one day of each week,
And the rest of the week he'd rejoice.

2461. PHONETIC LESSON

The use of a , or [
Will put word or phrase in a packet (comma)
    But the , (comma) it (apostrophe)s known (comma)
    Can get by all alone (comma)
Where the [needs one more to back it (semicolon
    bracket) (period)

[2462]

The use of a comma or bracket
Will put word or phrase in a packet,
    But the comma, it's known,
    Can get by all alone,
Where the bracket ([) needs one more to back it (:]).

2463. DO YOUR SPADE WORK

In his heart, a card-sharper named Boyle
Had presumed a young girl to despoil.
    His deception was quelled
    Till a diamond she held,
Then she had him according to Hoyle.

2464. THE SILOS ARE READY

Said the Indian chief to his braves,
From the way that the White Man behaves
    We will get back our plains
    Very soon without pains,
Whereas he will be back in his caves.

2465. THE NUTHOUSE*

When idiots by chance have been bred
They need to be cared for and fed.
    Though asylums are there
    It costs money for care,
So we send them to Congress instead.

2466

There was an old fellow named Breethaus
Who lived in a fine and a neat house,
    And a ghost lived therein
    Who was neat as a pin,
For he kept all his sheets in the sheethouse.

2467

Fine meats had the butcher of Brest
And buyers were duly impressed,
    But the ladies confessed
    They were mostly obsessed
With his wurst which they found to be best.

2468

Good fortune had smiled on young Bret;
No longer did he have to fret.
    After searching around
    A job he had found,
Which meant he could go into debt.

2469

A clever young fellow named Bricker
Made cigarettes longer and thicker.
    His improved filter pore
    Gave enjoyment much more,
And the cancer was king-size and quicker.

2470

There was a young fellow named Brickley,
Insipid and haggard and sickly.
    But his wife was not meek
    With her manly physique,
For the hair on her chest sprouted thickly.

2471

A famous smart feller named Bright
Outsmarted all fellers in sight.
    He progressed with his guile
    To the top of the pile,
And felt smart as a smart feller might.

2472. WHAT, NO WAR? START ONE!

A general remarked with smile brightening,
"I never feared thunder or lightning,
　　And a war, as you see,
　　Has no horrors for me,
But the prospect of peace I find frightening."

2473*

The fire chief we have is a bright one;
He has studied the fire and can fight one,
　　But the mayor, so brief,
　　Said, "We need a new chief;
What we need is a man who can light one."

2474

Said the chemist, "I'm now at the brink
Of creating a stench that I think
　　Suits a man in a car
　　Who smokes pipe or cigar,
And who wishes to live in a stink."

2475*

The scientists thoughtfully brood
As famines on earth are renewed.
　　They seek to allay
　　Food shortage some day
By conversion of feces to food.

2476*

There was a young fellow named Browder
Who puffed out his chest and was prouder.
　　In his mind he was right
　　For he won every fight,
And he won for his reasons were louder.

2477

A thoughtful young fellow named Brown
Spread sawdust on Main Street in town.
　　To his girl he said, "Dear,
　　You have nothing to fear,
We'll have fun when the chips are all down."

2478

A lady with asthma, from Bruce,
Was nursing the cutest papoose.
　　She said, "Kids I adore
　　And I would have had more,
But they're awfully hard to produce."

2479
There was an old fellow named Brynner
Whose wife would swear like a mule skinner.
    He said, "What you call me
    Will never appall me,
But don't call me, my dear, late for dinner."

2480
There was a fruit peddler of Buckingham
Who wrote about quinces and sucking 'em.
    Sometime later this work
    Was eclipsed by a Turk
With a treatise on apples and plucking 'em.

2481
There was a sheep-shearer named Bull
Who sheared all the sheep, one bag full.
    He got caught on a snag
    And fell into the bag,
And the poor fellow died in the wool.

2482
Since the corpse was a heel and a bum,
To his wake the whole nation will come,
    So that people can spit
    On his coffin and shit,
And we'll slide him to hell on the scum.

2483
Inventions devised by young Bunky
Did render the factories junky.
    All the men, out he chased 'em,
    And with apes he replaced 'em,
And machinery was wrenched by a monkey.

2484
There was an old smoker named Burse;
His smell all his friends did accurse.
    He gave up cigarettes
    Which no person regrets,
But he started cigars and smelled worse.

2485. ESPECIALLY RADIOACTIVE DUST*
Man's life on this earth is a bust;
His symbols corrode and they rust.
    To improve his life's term
    He must husband his sperm,
And must work without raising a dust.

2486. UDDER NONSENSE

The prominent dairyman Butters
Worked hard as a youth in the gutters
 And he purchased one cow—
 He has ten thousand now,
But he swears that he owes all to udders.

2487

The waiter came hurrying by;
He slipped and spilled soup on the thigh
 Of a man in full dress
 Who looked down at the mess
And said, "Boy, there's a soup in my fly."

2488. THE STRADIVARIUS

A maestro by name of Calhoun
Was wed to a withered old prune.
 When his friends did deride,
 With a smile he replied,
"On old fiddles I play a fine tune."

2489

There were two ballplayers, Carruther,
Who both of them had the same mother.
 They played such a fine game
 And they gained so much fame,
That they stood in great awe of each other.

2490

A feeble young moron was Carter
And his brains were dashed out by a Tartar.
 With incredible pains
 They assembled his brains;
He recovered to be a lot smarter.

2491. THE ARCING OF JOAN

The king's men were pleased with their catch;
To a stake they tied Joan with dispatch.
 She exclaimed as she stood
 In the twigs and the wood,
"I'm afraid that I've just met my match."

2492
The wife of a fellow named Chape
Could talk the rear end off an ape.
 Once he tried to record it
 But he could not afford it,
For it cost him too much for the tape.

2493*
A thinker whose visions are cheery
Said waiting for new thoughts is dreary.
 Many monkeys he sees
 Pounding typewriter keys
Who in time will produce a great theory.

2494
A wealthy physician named Cheevers
Was lauded by hosts of believers.
 He was asked to explain
 How his wealth he did gain.
"I am grateful," he said, "for small fevers."

2495. THE SAUCY ISOSCELES
Beggs sampled the chef's treat Chinese;
Lee's sauce with two eggs—it did please.
 "This angle," said Beggs,
 "With the two equal eggs,
I believe is a nice sauce o' Lee's."

2496. THE CATHOLIC SHARK
The sharks are a frightening clan—
Their forces the seven seas span,
 But some sharks are selective
 Or perhaps they're defective,
For on Friday they never eat man.

2497
There was an old lady named Clark
Who rose from her bed — to bark
 — they say 'twas a trauma
 When a dog bit her,
Now can you tell me why?

2498. THE NEGATIVE PERSONALITY
Such a negative fellow was Cleft,
And of charm and of wit so bereft,
 That his friends he annoyed,
 And he brought such a void
When he came, that they asked who had left.

383

[2499]
His brother, it seems, was so dumb
That his presence would leave people numb,
    And there was such a void
    All around him deployed,
When he left, people asked who had come.

2500
A recluse who lived in Cologne
Explained why he lived all alone,
    "I have no use for ladies,
    They can all go to Hades—
I'm accustomed to holding my own."

2501
There was a young fellow named Clift
Who gave a young lady a lift,
    And he marvelled the sight
    Of her teeth shining bright,
So she gave him her teeth as a gift.

2502
The soldiers of Custer were clustered;
When mustered they never got flustered.
    They were scared but declared
    They were always prepared
The same as the Boy Scouts or mustard.

2503. DEADLY FRESH AIR
There was an old smoker named Clyde
Whose lungs were all rotten inside.
    He was saved by Doc Schink
    But he had such a stink
That the doctor got sick and he died.

[2504]
So this heavy old smoker named Clyde
Who in pipes and cigars took great pride,
    Took a trip to Gruyère
    To smell Swiss mountain air—
He inhaled a deep breath and he died.

2505
There was a young lady of Clyde
Who lost young McBryde when he died.
    Not too long did she tarry
    And McBrydesmaid did marry—
So McBrydesmaid she was, not McBryde.

2506
There was a young fellow named Clyde
Who fell on a stove and he fried.
    The doctors rushed through
    And they patched him like new,
And when he recovered he died.

2507
There was a young man of Cologne;
To give good advice he was prone.
    He could manage affairs
    Of his friends and confreres,
But he never could manage his own.

2508
There is an old maid of Cologne
Who bad words in print won't condone.
    When she hears of a new one,
    A most sordid and blue one,
She has sculptors engrave it in stone.

2509. SMELLOPHONE
A pipe-smoking man of Cologne
Had lived his whole life all alone,
    For so raunchy he smelled
    That all men were repelled,
And he smelled when he called on the phone.

2510
A man to his dentist complained
That his dentures fit poorly and pained,
    But the dentist said smugly,
    "Though your pains may be ugly,
Nothing dentured, my boy, nothing gained."

2511
To earn a good life is complex
And many young lads it does vex,
    But the way to gain fame
    And establish your name
Is design for the bathroom or sex.

2512
To problems of great complication
Administer digitization.
    The increased luminosity
    Will reduce the verbosity
And result in eschewed obfuscation.

2513. ADVANCE TO THE REAR

Some men are so full of conceit
That they cannot accept a defeat.
 To get out of a mess
 They must needs acquiesce
And indulge in a glorious retreat.

2514. FANCY FOOTWORK

A sculptor named Hand, in concrete
A sculpture produced, fine and neat.
 By his feet it was made
 And in public displayed
As the marvelous handwork of feet.

[2515]

The King saw this sculpture so grand,
And he praised it throughout the whole land.
 The Queen handed a treat
 To young Hand for his feat,
And she called it the feetwork of Hand.

2516

A man, one time wealthy, confessed
What led to his status depressed.
 He spent money on cars
 And on women in bars,
And he foolishly wasted the rest.

2517

There's one thing that we can construe—
If men carry on as they do
 Then the facts we must face,
 Men will soon take their place
With the animals caged in the zoo.

2518

Anti-matter will travel content
Throughout space, and will cause no event,
 But on meeting with matter
 It creates such a splatter
That one asks, not what came, but what went.

2519. IS THE QUESTION A QUESTION?
In college young lads are convening
And answers to questions are gleaning.
    But there's one thing I fear—
    Though the answer is clear,
Does the question itself have a meaning?

2520
A studious lady convincible
That her studies would make her invincible,
    In her courses in banking
    She maintained the top ranking;
Her main interest, of course, was the principal.

2521
A famous old speaker named Costral
Was noted for outpourings rostral,
    But he gained all his fame
    And established his name
For extensively probing his nostril.

2522
There was an old rotter named Cotter
Who drank till he started to totter.
    One man water did pour him
    To attempt to restore him,
But he drowned like a fish out of water.

2523
To make statues is easy, of course—
On a large block of granite use force
    And you chisel away
    Through the night and the day
The material which is not a horse.

2524
The auditor schemes and he counts
As he enters the sums in accounts,
    And he juggles so clever
    That no person can ever
Tell what's his or is mine or amounts.

2525
In the morning the village was creepy;
The squaws and the braves, they were weepy,
    For their poor chief, you see,
    Had drunk gallons of tea,
And they found he had drowned in his tea pee.

2526

A well-traveled lady of Crete
Was sunning herself with young Pete.
    He said, "Tell me, Irene,
    Why your back is so green."
She said, "Grass never grows 'neath my feet."

2527. THE HONEST BANKER*

We have strange ways of judging a crime
And our justice lacks reason and rhyme,
    For the robber of banks
    Goes to jail for his pranks,
While the founder of banks serves no time.

2528. THE SPELLBINDER

The self-styled old clergyman Crist
To speak at a wake would insist,
    And the corpse, we should mention,
    Sat erect at attention,
For no person his speech would have missed.

2529

What old widow Agnes crocheted
Was put on a shelf and displeted
    So beginners could view,
    And the knit-pickers tew,
What wonders with needles are meted.

2530

A minor offender named Dale
Thought lawyers would help without fail,
    But when faced with the rates
    Charged by old lawyer Bates,
He said, "I'll take the ten years in jail."

2531

There were two young men of Damascus
Who said, "There's no problem can task us.
    We are both very smart—
    If there's doubt in your heart
We can settle your doubts if you ask us."

2532. LOOK UNDER THE HOOD
The car that was purchased by Dawes
Was fully inspected because
    He bought only the best,
    But his wife he bought dressed
And neglected to check her for flaws.

2533
The scientist works night and day
The deadly disease to allay.
    For his work he's indebted
    To the man who can spread it
With a coughing and sneezing display.

2534
The baker lay down as if dead—
They say he was struck on the head,
    But this tale was not so
    For some men needing dough
Hit him twice in his basket for bread.

2535
A general who faced a defeat
Had called it *Strategic Retreat,*
    But the enemy's version
    Of this tragic excursion
Was a massacre, plain and complete.

2536
The people say missiles deject 'em
For billions were spent to erect 'em,
    But the cost to detect
    What the foe did erect
Plus the tax for defence is what wrecked 'em.

2537. WHICH WAY IS UP?
If three billion souls in dejection
Point up in symbolic reflection
    And in reverence they plead
    To fulfill some great need,
Then each points in a different direction.

2538
There was a young gambler named Denny
Who lost all his cash to the penny.
    Said the winner with gall,
    "You can not win them all."
Said the loser, "I have not won any."

2539

It seems that our leaders deplore
The threat from the power plant core,
    So they build in devices
    For preventing a crisis,
While preparing for nuclear war.

2540

There was a young man who deployed
The Bible to fill a great void.
    Though he learned how to read,
    Yet this fact we concede:
In the process his mind was destroyed.

2541

A young man, newly rich, still despaired
The good fortune and fame that he fared.
    Said the income tax chief,
    "For your fame I'm no thief,
But your fortune, I fear, must be shared."

2542

In a land where the folks were devout
Came a spell of dry weather throughout,
    So they prayed for some rain
    But to pray was in vain,
For some bastards, it seems, prayed for drought.

2543

Our country is gone to the dickens
And nothing is left but lean pickin's,
    Since our leaders inane
    Leave the rats to guard grain
And the foxes are guarding the chickens.

2544

A young enterpriser named Diggs
Lost all of his cash raising figs,
    But he balanced the sheet
    When he planted no wheat,
And made millions by not raising pigs.

2545

An old millionaire dignified,
In saving up cash took great pride.
    The more money he made
    The more taxes he paid,
And the louder he moaned and he cried.

2546*
With critics one need not dispute;
Like asses they are not astute.
      When asses are roused
      And on fruit trees have browsed,
Then the trees will bear much finer fruit.

2547
Of this there can be no dispute—
Young ladies that blossom to fruit
      Must surely be tasted
      Lest their lives will be wasted
And they rot on the ground destitute.

2548. NO PIT TO HISS IN
There was a rich snake name of Diss
Who lived in a state of great bliss,
      But he went all to hell
      When misfortune befell;
He was left with no pit where to hiss.

2549
The delay to the duke was distressing
For his buttons came off during dressing,
      So he asked tailor Sutton
      If he'd sew him a button—
Said the tailor, his work was more pressing.

2550
When the doctor examined Miss Donder,
He discovered her time she did squander
      To sew clothes and to cook,
      So he gave her a book
On *The Habits of Rabbits* to ponder.

2551
A valley, in case you have doubt,
Like a mountain has rocks strewn about.
      Though it's built of same stuff
      There is difference enough—
It's a mountain that's turned inside out.

2552
The governments waste all their dough
And the tax bite continues to grow.
      The way they are headed
      Once their teeth are imbedded,
Don't expect them to ever let go.

2553
While placing another bet down
The gambler remarked with a frown,
    "Yes, I know the wheel's fixed
    But my feelings are mixed
For there's no other wheel in this town."

2554
The surface of Venus I dread;
It's heated so high it melts lead.
    I'm so glad, I declare,
    That we do not live there,
For I fear that we all would be dead.

2555
There was once a fat man of Dundee
Who was weighing himself constantly.
    Said his wife, one fine day,
    "Tell me, what do you weigh?"
He replied in surprise, "I weigh me."

2556
A clever young fellow named Durbin
Invented a novel gas turbine.
    But the thing would not start
    Until primed with a fart—
A procedure both foul and disturbin'.

2557
There was an old man from the East
Who prayed at the holy day feast
    When the last king's tongue dangled
    After he had been strangled
With the robes of the very last priest.

2558
A plaintiff with dogged endeavor
Had won, for his lawyer was clever,
    But it wasn't for real
    For there was an appeal,
And the case through the courts dragged forever.

2559
For our leader, an old engineer
A lever installed in his ear.
    Its purpose was plain—
    For engaging the brain
Before putting the mouth into gear.

2560
The calm sea, say sailors, enticeth us,
And sailing the salt sea doth spiceth us.
    When the wild wind surceaseth
    And the seething sea ceaseth,
We can say that the sea thus sufficeth us.

2561
A city decay we envision—
The time is now ripe for decision.
    It appears that the answer
    Is the same as for cancer,
And cancer is cured by incision.

2562
From duty we cannot escape
And TV our children must shape,
    But all that the boobs
    Get in front of the tubes
Are some courses in violence and rape.

2563
We've gone to unusual expense
To thwart any Russian offence,
    And our fortress won't falter—
    We are firm as Gibraltar—
But we'll never survive our defence.

2564
A lady desirous of fame
A magician's assistant became.
    He remarked with a laugh
    As he sawed her in half,
"You can see I am new at this game."

2565
A wealthy old widow named Fannic
Was torn by great torments and panic,
    For she lived without hope
    And with life could not cope
Till she married a factory mechanic.

2566
A youth with hair long and fastidious
Was trapped in a circumstance hideous.
    By mistake in the park
    He was grasped in the dark
By a man with intentions insidious.

2567. THE MONKIES WRENCH
Ingenious indeed was old Feenery;
In factories he changed all the scenery.
    He replaced all his men,
    At least nine out of ten,
And used monkeys to wrench the machinery.

2568
When Freddy, the shoemaker, fell,
His output of shoes fell as well.
    Said a customer, "Freddy,
    Will my shoes soon be ready?"
But Freddy said, "Awl is not well."

2569
To pray for some rain, tried Miss Fenster—
When rain failed to come, it incensed her,
    And what made it so tragic,
    She had not studied magic,
Or perhaps a lot more prayed against her.

2570
Unlucky indeed was young Fife
For nagging made misery of life.
    He was terribly fraught
    And a mistress he sought,
But the mistress nagged worse than his wife.

2571
A seamy old surgeon was Fitches;
His patients he patched without hitches.
    When asked how did it go,
    He replied, "Sew and sew,
And I leave all my patients in stitches."

2572
There was a young fellow named Floyd
Who wanted to fly like a boid,
    So he entered the race
    To be first into space,
But he soon was annoyed by the void.

2573
A financial advisor named Flynn
Said investment in sex is a sin.
    Your substantial accretion
    Will suffer depletion
For you never get out what went in.

2574
Down the street walking backwards went Flynn,
To dissuade him no man could begin,
  For it's senseless to know
  Where you're going to go
Just as long as you know where you've been.

2575
The rats that were raised by old Flynn
Were trained like no others had been.
  When a rat learned to speak
  He proceeded to shriek,
"Oh my God, what a man-race I'm in!"

2576
A limburger lover was Fox;
He kept a supply in a box.
  But his wife could not tell
  Any difference in smell,
So she made him a lunch from old socks.

2577
A sage old observer named Frankton
Predicted what man had not banked on.
  When the planet was plundered
  By a race that had blundered
There was naught left for eating but plankton.

2578
There was an old smoker named Fred
Who smoked in his bed while he read,
  And he burned down his house,
  Lost his kids and his spouse,
While his corpse smoked away on the bed.

2579
The newlywed wife of young Fred
Called up at the office and said,
  "I have carpets on stairs
  And remodelled the chairs,
And I have a new spread on the bed."

2580
Up the ladder went Celsius in fright,
And he shook in great fear at his plight,
  For the more he went higher
  Why the more he'd perspire—
He did not very well fare in height.

2581
There was an old dentist named Frindem
Who knew how to pull and to grind 'em.
 His methods were new
 And his false teeth were true
For he burned all his bridges behind him.

2582
There was an explorer named Frost
Who many new frontiers had crossed,
 But there was no recovery
 From his frightful discovery
When he found he was hopelessly lost.

2583
There was a young pilot named Fry;
His plane at great speeds he did fly.
 He had salad at home,
 And the main course in Rome,
And at noon he had pie in the sky.

2584
There was an old lady named Fry
Whose man was just dirt in her eye,
 So his motto, he said,
 While his wife slept in bed,
Was to simply let sleeping dogs lie.

2585. DIEHARD
"The die has been cast!" shouted Fry,
Then fell on his knees and did cry,
 "Now I'll die in great shame,
 As I've sullied my name,
For I know I must never say die."

2586
By friends that you keep you are gaged;
Do not over words be enraged,
 And avoid as a rule
 A dispute with a fool,
Lest you find he is likewise engaged.

2587
So bitchy a wife had old Gelling,
It was rugged to live in one dwelling.
 When she died he was merry
 But he made sure to bury
Her deeper to drown out her yelling.

2588
There was an old lady named Gert
Who cried and she cried till it hurt,
    For her house was so clean
    With her vacuum machine,
She no longer could find any dirt.

2589
There was an old man named Gilhooly,
So vulgar, uncouth and unruly,
    And so full of deceit
    And with hate so replete
That he would not sign letters *Yours Truly.*

2590
A headstrong young athlete named Gillies
Had ankles that gave him the willies,
    But his elbows and wrists
    Were still good for some twists—
His trick knee was his heel of Achilles.

2591
A patient of old Dr. Gilmore
Asked, "Why, when you charge, do you bill more?"
    The old doctor replied,
    "They can't pay when they've died,
And lately I find that I kill more."

2592. DOG'S BEST FRIEND
There was a small man named Girard
Who walked with his big St. Bernard.
    When he felt a great need
    He would stop and he peed,
While his canine stood nearby on guard.

2593
The lion that roamed in the glen
Was hunted by prosperous men.
    If the truth we must tell
    He did not fare as well
As the Christians thrown in the lions' den.

2594
A handsome young fellow named Glover
An ugly old hag did discover.
    Though this girl was a horror
    He did love and adore her—
He did not judge a book by its cover.

2595

A terrified lady named Gnauss
Was scared by a gmauss in the ghauss.
    When she screamed in despair
    No one much seamed to cair,
So she frightened the gmauss with her gblauss.

2596

The housewives to garden stores go
To purchase a rake and a hoe
    And a bushel of feed
    For the lawn, and some seed
So that husbands have fine lawns to mow.

2597

There was a comedian named Gobel
Who claimed he was stalwart and noble,
    But the quips from his lips
    Were but buffalo chips,
For he knew how to fib and to throw bull.

2598

The building of architect Gore
Was built with a ceiling and floor,
    Surrounded by wall
    With no windows at all.
What it needed, of course, was a door.

2599

There was an old farmer of Gosham
Who would spray on his crops and would slosh 'em
    To leave no bugs alive,
    But if some did survive
He would stomp on the beasties and squash 'em.

2600

There was a young lady named Grace
Who put her young beau in his place,
    For she said to him, "Dear,
    If you smoke, don't come near,
For I'm apt to spit full in your face."

2601

There was a young man of Gran Chaco
Whose brain was as hard as quebracho.
    He smoked like a mule skinner
    With his family at dinner
So that all could enjoy his tobacco.

2602
"Oh my," said the ostrich, "it's grand
To live in this wonderful land,
    For when trouble appears
    I just plug up my ears
And I bury my head in the sand."

2603
Said the hunter of game to Miss Granger,
"To the feeling of fear I'm no stranger.
    I respect the big cat
    In his wild habitat,
But a pussy that's small is no danger."

2604
There was a composer named Granoz;
They say that this man went bananas.
    He composed a great symphony
    For the flute and the timpani
And three horses on player pianos.

2605. PEACE IS NOW A THREAT
A scientist working in Greece
A wondrous report did release.
    He developed at last,
    A big bomb with a blast
So great, it was used just for peace.

2606
The cities are now filled with grief,
And are havens for killer and thief.
    They're designed in a way
    So that half of us pay
To maintain all the rest on Relief.

2607
An arrogant fellow of Guelph
Would brag of his conquests and pelf.
    He left no job undone—
    He'd complete every one—
And he made a full ass of himself.

2608
A man grinding lenses in Guelph
Reached up for some tools on the shelf.
    He fell down in between
    The lens-grinding machine,
And a spectacle made of himself.

2609
The dog is a creature of habit;
When he sees running game, he will grab it.
    But the dog, fine and fit,
    If he stops for a shit,
I'm afraid he will not catch the rabbit.

2610
A hard-working fellow was Hame
Who struggled and gained himself fame.
    In Society's eyes
    He was noble and wise,
But his parents both beatniks became.

2611
A non-smoking student named Hartz
Penned a thesis for Doctor of Arts.
    He proved in his studies
    That none of his buddies
Could get cancer from smelling his farts.

2612
An addict of smoking named Haskett
Smoked fags and cigars by the basket,
    So he soon met his fate,
    But the urge was so great
That he asked for a light from his casket.

2613. DEADLINE TAMER
Said the boss, "I'll end up in a hearse,
For this deadline I find is a curse."
    Said a hunter named Harry,
    Who'd been on a safari,
"You will find that a live lion is worse."

2614. LASTING IMPRESSION
A skilled maker of shoes was young Hearst;
When he entered a contest, men cursed,
    And they all were aghast
    When first prize was for last,
For young Hearst for his last came in first.

2615
After fishing all day, Mr. Heldt
Was thrilled with the pride that he felt.
　　He collected a catch
　　That few anglers could match,
For two mermaids he caught, and one smelt.

2616
There was a young fellow named Hilary
Who drank like he owned a distillery,
　　But his wife soon corrected
　　His behaviour dejected,
When she sobered him up in a pillory.

2617
It's hard to find good men and hire 'em;
It seems that all work will soon tire 'em,
　　And their work they will shirk
　　While the coffee does perk—
You no longer can threaten or fire 'em.

2618
A frustrated man without hope
With tension no longer could cope.
　　When they found the poor wreck
　　He was hung by the neck,
With his tension transferred to the rope.

2619
There was a sharecropper named Hopper
Who had a nice wife but did swap her
　　For a sexy show-stopper
　　Whose attire was improper,
And she left poor old Hopper a pauper.

2620. THE HORSE REIGNS
What a valuable asset the horse is;
I'm amazed at his strength and resources.
　　Though we ride everywhere,
　　I am left in despair,
For I'm never too sure what his course is.

2621. CARRYING BRIDGE TOO FAR

While playing at bridge, Mr. Hubbell
Was stung when his wife passed his double,
    So he killed her with glee
    And the judge set him free
For a passed take-out double means trouble.

2622. THE BLUFFER

A despondent young fellow named Huff
Found his problems were getting too tough,
    So he said, in a tiff,
    "I will jump off a cliff."
But they found it was only a bluff.

2623

There was an old chef name of Hugh
Who cooked up an animal stew,
    And this may not be relevant
    But he added an elephant,
Yet the diners all asked, "Is this gnu?"

2624

At eighty an old man named Hugh
Began to chase ladies anew.
    He went out and caught one
    And he found it great fun,
But forgot what he next had to do.

2625

A footloose young fellow named Humburd
With wife and a child was encumbered.
    Though he strove and perspired
    He soon found he was mired
And discovered his days were all numbered.

2626*

The professor proceeds to instruct
How the nature of storms we deduct,
    And he states winds will blow
    From high pressure to low,
But the wind doesn't blow—it is sucked.

2627. THE STEAKOUT
A hungry young thief name of Jake
Asked the judge if he'd give him a break.
    Said the judge, "You must pay
    For your crime—choose the way."
So he asked to be tied to a steak.

2628
A hard-working butcher named Jake
Would never take time for a break.
    He would toil endlessly
    Like the busiest bee,
For he knew that his job was at steak.

2629
There was an old dentist named Jake
Who most perfect of false teeth did make,
    And according to queries
    They would even get caries,
And he made them so good they would ache.

2630
There was a young fellow named Jake
Who feared that he'd make a mistake.
    When the boss said, "Let's go
    On the road with the show."
He would press with his foot on the brake.

2631
So beat was a fellow named Jake
That his bones and his muscles did ache.
    He was almost half dead
    As he crawled into bed,
Then he lay there completely awake.

2632
There was a young lady named Jill
Whose husband smoked so much until
    Like some garbage he stunk,
    But this lady had spunk
For she practiced by sleeping with swill.

2633
A chaplain who came from Kamloops
Invented a game for the troops
    Which was not too complex
    And was more fun than sex
And was moral when played by large groups.

2634
There was an old spinster named Kay
Who carried a chain night and day.
    In her mind was a plan—
    If attacked by a man
She made sure he would not get away.

2635
The scientist, Wernher von Keating
Told how to save fuel at a meeting.
    To get gas, we must leach
    A political speech
And consume it for cooking and heating.

2636. GILTY!*
In court, a young fellow named Kell
Found matters did not go too well.
    Though the jury agreed
    That he should have been freed,
They found *Innocent* too hard to spell.

2637
A sturdy young fellow named Kell
When born had a bad sickly spell.
    He improved right along
    To be robust and strong;
When he died he was healthy and well.

2638
When Cesar was dating Miss Kelter
His manner so charming did melt her.
    She disclosed what would please her:
    To be conquered by Cesar—
But he came when he saw and he smelt her.

2639
There was a young lady named Kessel
Who knew how to box and to wrestle.
    When a druggist one night
    Made remarks impolite,
She subdued him and mortared his pestle.

2640*
For the poor man who steals but a kettle
The hangman his fate soon will settle,
    But a pirate, so bold,
    Steals a shipload of gold,
And he's honored and given a medal.

2641
There is a magician of Kew
Who claims he can cut a canoe
    Into four halves alike,
    But his lies I dislike,
For three halves is the best he can do.

2642. I AM THE GREATEST!
A fanciful dreamer named Kiam
Did fancy himself King of Siam.
    He said, "I never bumble
    And it's hard to be humble
When you find that you're great just like I am."

2643
An expert at sprinting, Miss Kitt,
Would challenge all men fast and fit.
    In a closely matched race
    One young lad set the pace,
But she beat the young lad by a tit.

2644
There was a young fellow named Klaupt;
His head with a hammer he bopped.
    When his friends asked him why,
    It was hard to deny
That it felt very good when he stopped.

2645. WOODEN YOU KNOW?
A poplar young woodsman named Kline
A laurel received fir work fine.
    On the beech he got lit,
    Then did spruce up a bit,
And proceeded to balsam and pine.

2646
"My daughter is drowning, I knew it!"
Hysterically cried Mrs. Hewitt.
    Said a man who was brave,
    "Your dear daughter I'll save."
She said, "Don't take your clothes off to do it."

2647. THE BARK BITES

A badly skinned fellow named Knight
Was chased up a tree in a fright
    By a dog that just nipped him,
    But the tree badly stripped him,
And the bark was much worse than the bite.

2648

There was a young lady named Knight;
The mess that she smoked was a fright.
    Her newborn had innate
    A compulsion so great,
On emerging he asked for a light.

2649. MICKEY MOUSE IS SAVED!

The mousetrap invented by Krauss
Caught all of the mice in the house—
    An ingenious device
    That threatened all mice
Till biologists bred a new mouse.

2650

A sparkling young fellow named Krauss
Had feelings no person could douse.
    His aim and desire:
    "Set the whole world on fire."
He was caught when he burned his first house.

2651

A thoughtless young fellow named Kress
Had tumors that caused him distress.
    He was smoking much more,
    Each day more than before,
And enjoying it daily much less.

2652

Said the puppeteer's helper, Miss Krings,
To a sailor who knew many things,
    "It will increase my hopes
    If you show me the ropes,
And I'll teach you how best to pull strings."

2653

There was an old man of Lahore
Who came home as drunk as a boar.
    He put his dog Fife
    Into bed with his wife
And he threw himself outside the door.

2654
To die by the rope, tried young Lang;
Goodbye to the world, then he sang.
 He had bought some rope strong
 But they cut it too long—
If they gave him less rope he would hang.

2655
The doc warned a fellow of Lansing,
"You must cease your excessive romancing.
 Too much wine, maids and song
 And you will not live long."
So he eased up on part of his dancing.

2656
A beer-drinking man of Lapeer
To water would never come near.
 He claimed men at great cost
 In the water were lost,
But not one ever foundered in beer.

2657
There was a young hot-rod named Larkin
Who asked a young girl to go sparkin',
 But her mother said, "No,
 I will not let you go
Till you promise that there'll be no parkin'."

2658
To the sickly young smoker Larocque,
The doctor some bad news had broke,
 "Although you're very young
 We must take out your lung."
Said Larocque, "Do you mind if I smoke?"

2659. STUDY THE ROACH
Man's term on this earth cannot last—
By the cockroach he will be surpassed.
 Too much credence he places,
 And his future he bases
On improbable tales from the past.

2660
There was a young fellow named Last,
So thin that all folks were aghast.
 He had width so concise
 That he had to try twice
In order a shadow to cast.

2661

Time was when all news traveled late
And for lies every man had to wait,
But inventions by Bell
Have been used very well
To spread lies at an increasing rate.

2662

Cried mother, "Why children, you're late!
You know I serve dinner at eight,
So get into your seat
And be sure that you eat
Every carrot and pea on your plate."

2663

The art works of Toulouse Lautrec
The walls of museums do deck,
But he gathered them all
From the urinal well
Of the Parliament House in Quebec.

2664

A man should not search out a lay
At the place where he's earning his pay.
He should not get his honey
Where he's making his money,
And should not let his meat loaf all day.

2665. HE SAW THE SEA

On the shore an old woodsman named Lee
Cut the waves with his saw into three.
Said his wife in disdain,
"On the sea he won't gain,
And it looks like a seesaw to me."

2666

An avid chess player named Lee
Played chess with his dog with great glee.
But his dog was not smart
For he oft fell apart,
And the dog was beat two out of three.

2667

A mouse scared a lady named Lee;
She died from the fright—plain to see.
But the mouse was scared more
And it fell to the floor,
And it died much more deader than she.

2668
A young scuba diver named Lee
From a mermaid one time had to flee,
 For she wanted to marry,
 But the diver was wary—
There were plenty of fish in the sea.

2669
An animal trainer, Miss Lee,
Taught her doggie to speak fluently.
 Her boyfriend, who missed her,
 Paid a visit and kissed her,
And her doggie said, "What about me?"

2670
There was a zoo keeper named Lew
Who knew every beast in the zoo,
 The rhinoceros and elephant,
 Preposterous, though relevant,
But he never knew what was a gnu.

2671
The office that's run with limpidity
Is due to the boss's timidity.
 He remains thus secure
 And a threat does abjure
By surrounding himself with stupidity.

2672. SPLITSOPHRENIC
One will find that in every locality
There's a man with a morbid mentality
 And a habit distressing
 To view ladies undressing—
He's a man with a split personality.

2673
In each and in every locality
Are men with that agile mentality
 Who are simply terrific
 In the thing non-specific,
And are expert in vague generality.

2674. TOOT YOUR FLUTE
A concert pianist named Lorne
A minor position did scorn.
    "Don't put me in the middle;
    I'll not play second fiddle
If I play, I will blow my own horn."

2675
There was a young lady named Lottie
Who won a Black Belt in karate.
    She met a fine youth
    Who had not been uncouth,
And she forced the young lad to be naughty.

2676
A frisky young girl named Louise
Said walks in the woods made her freeze.
    She would rather instead
    Spend more time in bed;
Besides, money did not grow on trees.

2677. THE NIXON TAPES*
Cryptographers said, "We're in luck,
On transcripts we're no longer stuck.
    The solution is here:
    It is perfectly clear
That the expletive missing is [expletive deleted]."

2678
A gentle, sweet lady named Lyme
By hoodlums was ravaged one time.
    Said her lawyer, "Disgrace!
    It's an open, shut case,
But we must reconstruct the whole crime."

2679
A dieting lady named Mabel
Bought food with a low-calorie label.
    She consumed with great zeal
    A nutritionless meal
And was too weak to rise from the table.

2680. WHAT COULD BE WORSER?
The heavy pipesmoker MacBeth
Was wheezing to draw one more breath,
    But no air could he get
    And the fate that he met
Was far worse than the fate worse than death.

2681. ALAS—STRAW!
A sturdy young fellow was Mack;
His camel with straw he did pack.
 As he placed the last straw
 He fell down on his jaw
And he broke every bone in his back.

2682
Said a women's-lib girl named MacPherson,
"For an insult to gals, there's no worse 'un
 Than the preachers who say
 Ah-men through the day;
We must teach them to change to *Ah-person*."

2683
A thrifty old Scot was MacSligh;
He said, "Though it's time I should die,
 Since with illness I grieve,
 Yet I can't take my leave
On account of the cost, which is high."

2684
There was a young man of Madras
Who smoked such a terrible mass
 There was not room enough
 In his mouth more to stuff,
So he shoved a cigar up his ass.

2685. RAPE OF THE HARLOT
While making deposits, Miss Mape
Did tender a bill of bad shape.
 Said the teller, "Hold still,
 It's a counterfeit bill."
"Holy smoke," said Miss Mape, "this is rape!"

2686
There was a young fellow named Mapes
Who ate just bananas and grapes.
 He would swing through the trees
 Like the flying trapeze,
And he lived in a cage with the apes.

2687
There was a young sculptor named Marvin
Who found that his work left him starvin'.
 If he only had known
 He would not have carved stone—
For it should have been meat he was carvin'.

2688
A helpless taxpayer was Mazey,
His income tax form left him hazy,
    And the greatest perversion
    Was the simplified version
Which he tried to fill out and went crazy.

2689. À LA AMBROSE BIERCE*
To catch all the mice, old McFry
Cut cheese into cubes like a die,
    Then he baited the traps
    And he waited for snaps,
But the traps only yielded a mie.

[2690]
Discouraged, McFry told his spouse,
Who cut up the cheese into douse.
    When the traps were all baited
    They waited and waited
But the traps only yielded a mouse.

[2691]
They hired for a prouse, expert Price,
Who fashioned the cheese into dice,
    Then he set all the traps
    And they heard many snaps,
And they caught all the mice in the hice.

[2692]
So men, give advouse to your spice,
Don't cut like a die, but like dice
    When you're cutting up cheese
    To bait traps, if you please,
And you'll catch every mie in the hice.

2693
To old supervisor McBiddle
The office, he found, was a riddle.
    It was filled with musicians
    Without any ambitions,
For they all seemed to know how to fiddle.

2694. INSPECTOR SUSPECTED
The eyes of inspector McGore
A downward direction did bore.
    Said the boss, "I suspect
    That you cannot inspect."
Said McGore, "I'm inspecting the floor."

2695
There was a young girl named McGraw
Whose morals were wretched and raw.
    She was queried at times
    To account for her crimes,
But she said she did not know the law.

2696
On trial for his life was McLung;
The neck of his wife had been wrung,
    But they could not agree
    What the verdict should be,
So McLung and the jury were hung.

2697. GO ON A DYE IT
While mother dyed clothes, young McLung
In a tantrum the dye bottle flung,
    And the room was a mess.
    Said his ma, "I confess
I have heard that the good ones dye young."

2698
A pipe-smoker name of McLure
Smoked a mix that his friends could endure.
    To a man they did savor
    The delightful new flavor
Made of cherry pie mixed with manure.

2699. TRY IT FROM THERE
A man who was lost asked McNear,
"Tell me how do I get to Lapeer?"
    But McNear scratched his head
    And in puzzlement said,
"There is no way to get there from here."

2700
A fisherman name of McNish
Could not catch the fish he did wish.
    He was told he should not
    Simply fish in one spot,
There was plenty of sea where to fish.

2701. THE PROCTOLOGIST

When I go to the doc, he does me seize,
And I hope he enjoys that which he sees
    As over I turn
    And he looks with concern,
But I fear that he only the fee sees.

2702

Two parallel lines have been meant
To travel divided content,
    And they gain no affinity
    Though they go to infinity,
Unless one toward the other is bent.

2703

Of all of the problems that meet us,
There is one that I fear will defeat us.
    It is not the big bomb
    Which we'll face with aplomb—
It is: What shall we do with the fetus?

2704

So ugly a face had Miss Merrick
That she only was screwed by a cleric.
    She had her face lifted
    By a fine surgeon gifted,
With the help of a crane and a derrick.

2705

Man's habits must alter, methinks;
He's treading on dangerous brinks.
    He must exercise care
    Not to foul up the air,
Or to piss in the water he drinks.

2706

In Boston, for just millionaires,
Society gathered in pairs.
    From their finest cuisines
    They served Boston Baked Beans,
And, oh my, how they all put on airs.

2707

Neurotic was old lady Mills,
Dependent on nostrums and pills.
    They were not injurious
    For the whole lot was spurious,
But so was her gamut of ills.

2708
Our gold is a subject for mirth—
Men dig it for all that they're worth,
    And right after it's mined,
    Into bars it's refined
And then buried right back in the earth.

2709
A lady not up to modernity
Remarked of the driving fraternity,
    "If you don't watch your feet
    While you're crossing the street,
They will blast you right into maternity."

2710
A compulsive young smoker named Moffin
Was subject to coughing too often.
    Though he died from the strain,
    Yet his death was in vain—
He continued to cough in his coffin.

2711
A young sulky driver named Morse
Was thrown as he rounded the course,
    So he rode for a while
    In the hospital aisle
In a wheelchair attached to a horse.

2712*
A studious fellow named Mose
The grindstone applied to his nose.
    When his nose wore to hell
    They asked how does he smell.
He said, certainly not like a rose.

2713
There was a nose-picker named Mose,
An expert at picking his nose.
    He extracted a clinker,
    A prizewinning stinker,
For it dangled right down to his toes.

2714. BOOS & HRS.
A cautious young fellow said, "Mrs.,
I'd love to partake of your krs.,
    But your husband, I fear,
    Is a little too near.
Any thoughts that I have, I dismrs."

2715
Computers, said scientist Muller,
Would pick a fine bride for young Tuller.
  The machine took his data
  But it spewed out errata,
For he got the wrong size, sex and color.

2716. THE RULES OF THE GAME
There is in this world multiplicity
Or beings with strange eccentricity
  Who connive in collusion
  To distribute confusion
And complexity make of simplicity.

[2717]
A typical one is the lawyer,
Purveyor of words and deployer,
  Who discovers porosity
  In the law with velocity,
And of sense is the crafty destroyer.

[2718]
Political men with verbosity
Propound their beliefs with pomposity.
  They mendacities shout
  And throw shadows of doubt
On such matters as need luminosity.

[2719]
The preacher, word monger superb,
Is expert in double-talk verb.
  He's the cunning confuser
  And the able abuser,
And the devious dispenser of blurb.

[2720]
The wily old pope is loquacious,
A genius in matters fallacious.
  He disgorges duplicity
  With apparent felicity
While retaining an image sagacious.

[2721]
While claiming to practice perception
The newspapers spew misconception.
  With righteous pretense
  They falsehoods dispense
And they daily deliver deception.

[2722]
Though the doctor has talents so varied
Yet his patients are worried and harried,
    For their cure is protracted
    Till their cash is extracted,
And mistakes are conveniently buried.

[2723*]
The criminals flooding all nations
Are engaged in the wrong occupations.
    They are wily, rapacious,
    With an instinct predacious,
But lack credit to start corporations.

2724
Phil Attily came dressed up nattily
To speak to the group on philately.
    What he talked about mostage
    Was new use for old postage,
And he gave them their fill, did Phil Attily.

2725*
The elm tree inspector, dressed neat,
Advised a young fellow named Pete
    No dead wood should he store,
    So Pete opened the door
And he threw his wife out on the street.

2726
There has been a considerable noise
On the difference between men and boys—
    But close observation
    Reveals the causation—
It is merely the price of their toys.

2727
At the zoo, an old keeper of note,
Crossed a baboon, a parrot and goat.
    The offspring, unique,
    Soon learned how to speak,
And it asked for its rights and a vote.

2728. SIMPLE AS APPLE PI
A circle is certainly neat;
It starts with a line length discreet,
    Then by grasping each end
    'Round a pi plate you bend—
When the ends touch, the circle's complete.

2729
There was a young couple named Newsome
Who looked like a well-balanced twosome.
    They were peas in a pod,
    But the thing that was odd
Was that each thought the other was gruesome.

2730
A noted stargazer nocturnal
Behaved in a manner infernal
    From the first night in June,
    When there shone a full moon,
Until after the equinox vernal.

2731
A bishop whose station was nominal
Developed a belly phenomenal.
    He was famed on this earth
    Not for oversize girth,
But eruptions and rumblings abdominal.

2732
Beware of the poems of Ogden;
Unwary old folks have been fogden.
    There's so much balderdash
    It will make your teeth Nash,
And your ears will get mired down and bogden.

2733
If you puff on those fags by the pack,
Your lungs their pink color will lack.
    The demented don't mind
    For they say, you will find
That a beautiful color is black.

2734
A student of science named Parker
In annals of fame has a marker.
    In his lab it was where
    He made studies on air,
And discovered that night air was darker.

2735
A smoker who smoked with a passion
Was spit in the face and turned ashen.
    Though he showed some concern
    It was thus he did learn
That spitting was now back in fashion.

2736
The wife of a miner named Paul
Would knit only picks on her shawl.
    She would knit with fine care
    And was known everywhere
As the greatest pick-knitter of all.

2737
A sign was observed by old Paul:
"Don't spit on the floor, not at all."
    With a chew of tobaccy
    He formed one that was tacky
And he fastened a slug on the wall.

2738
The drinks that were purchased by Paul
Had failed to affect Miss McCall.
    Sometime later he groaned,
    "Have you ever been stoned?"
She said, "Yes, but the rocks were all small."

2739
In his lab, an old doctor named Pease
Produced a new serum with ease,
    And to all did expound
    That a cure he had found
For which there was no known disease.

2740
A studious fellow named Pease
Took courses to get Ph.D.'s,
    But the courses got tougher
    And the sledding got rougher,
And he killed himself off by degrees.

2741
A three-pack-a-day man named Pease
One day said, "I'm all done with these."
    So the habit he threw
    And on toothpicks did chew,
And was felled by the Dutch Elm disease.

2742
A near-sighted hunter named Pease
Could not see the wood for the trees.
    He would miss the barn door
    By a mile or much more,
And was expert at shooting the breeze.

2743
A learned young couple pedantic
Debated till they were both frantic.
　　To dispute was endemic
　　For this couple polemic,
But their difference was simply semantic.

2744
A sadistic old fellow was Perce;
And his antics in bed were perverse,
　　Then he wrote poems erratic
　　Of his exploits traumatic,
So from bed the old man went to verse.

2745
There was an inventor named Percy
Who labored amidst controversy
　　To convert, he did state,
　　The gnarled finger of fate
To the wand of the angel of mercy.

2746
A pugilist name of Persimmon
Gave all his opponents a trimmin'.
　　But not one could compare
　　To the way he did fare
With the trimmin' he got from his women.

2747
A salad was fashioned by Pickett
From greens that he picked in the thicket.
　　There passed a grasshopper
　　Right through the food chopper
And Pickett said, "That is not cricket."

2748
There was a nit-picker named Pitts
Who picked every trifle to bits.
　　He spent efforts immense
　　On most trivial events,
And he even found nits on the nits.

2749. 1776–1976
In two hundred years of hard plugging
We've arrived at a fine state of bugging,
　　And ahead, I'm construing,
　　There is simply more screwing,
So I hope there's some kissing and hugging.

2750*
A bashful young man of Podunk
Had a date with a girl but did flunk.
  Since he used the wrong soap,
  He was left without hope,
And he stood in the doorway and stunk.

2751
A bashful young girl of Podunk
Her very first dance she did flunk.
  With her soul full of hope
  She had used the wrong soap,
So it seems that she sat there and stunk.

2752
When oil on rough water is poured
A measure of calm is restored.
  If by man oil is spilt
  We establish his guilt,
Since this action by all is deplored.

2753
A repulsive old fellow was Price
Who never said anything nice.
  When his coffin was nailed
  He still ranted and railed,
So they buried the poor bastard twice.

2754
There was a young fellow named Pringle
With cash in his pocket to jingle.
  Said his girl, "We'll have fun—
  Two live cheaply as one."
But he said, "It's worth more to be single."

2755. LESSER OF TWO WEEVILS
Two weevils sat on the professor—
The small one became the aggressor.
  When it bit through his hide,
  The professor, he died—
Though it was of two weevils the lesser.

2756
There was an old lawyer proficient
In wisdom to all, and efficient.
  His advice to the brave
  Was to work hard and save,
And his word to the wise was *Sufficient.*

2757
If Malthus in his propositions
Was right about crowded conditions,
    Then for sex, we must say,
    We will screw in one way;
There'll be no room to change our positions.

2758
There was an old man named Purnell
Whose fame will remain immortel.
    He devised an emporium,
    A most wondrous sexorium,
And entitled the place a motel.

2759*
Though man may be proud of his race,
And medals his bosom does grace,
    Yet he should not soft-pedal
    That he should pin a medal
On the dog who was first into space.

2760
While fighting the Indians, old Raft
Was pierced through the chest by a shaft.
    He could manage to smile
    Only once in a while,
For it hurt very much when he laughed.

2761*
There was an old fellow who ranted
Till his TV receiver was canted
    At a forty-five angle
    So that he could untangle
The news he received that was slanted.

2762*
The clear-thinking man is a rarity,
For man has such mental disparity
    That illusions appear
    And confusion looks clear,
While he's fully confounded by clarity.

2763. BALLPOINT PEN ROBBERS
Our rights we must now reassess,
For grafters have gone to excess.
    Though their lawyers can't buy
    Any guns, they apply
The old laws of the West with finesse.

2764
A man in outlandish regalia
Mixed a drink with some wax and a dahlia.
    Said the doc, "In an hour
    You'll be sick from the flower,
But do not let the paraffin ail ya."

2765*
It's said that *Cease Fire* means release
Of tension, and hostile acts cease,
    But it's not, we deplore,
    A cessation of war,
So it must mean cessation of peace.

2766
The poor people offered resistance
To things the rich kept with consistence,
    And for goods they all cried,
    But the rich just replied,
One thing you can keep—that's your distance.

2767
When you find that it's time to retire,
It isn't the end of desire.
    Though there's snow on the roof
    You can still provide proof
That the furnace has plenty of fire.

2768
The lawmakers started reviewing
The laws that related to screwing.
    They have lifted the lid
    From what blankets had hid;
It's now legal to do what you're doing.

2769
There were two old scholars of Rhodes,
Both experts in noblums and nodes.
    They debated at length
    On the strength of the wength
And the gordum of garbitall godes.

2770
There was a conductor named Rhodium
Whose concerts were played with such odium
    That he got no ovation
    Though he held a high station,
Till the time that he fell off the podium.

2771. THE GRAVE DIGGER*

If in Congress a Congressman rigs
A system, wherein, just like pigs,
    At the trough his help feeds
    And he skims the proceeds,
Then it seems that his own grave he Diggs.

2772

An ape taught to speak by old Ritter
Became a most talkative critter.
    He was told how his clan
    Was related to man;
His complaint of the insult was bitter.

2773

A fanciful dresser from Rome
Wore socks that caused people to groan.
    One red and one blue,
    Each bright in its hue,
And a pair he had like it at home.

2774

An artless young fellow named Rose
Was given some work to dispose,
    For he lacked any vision
    For a simple decision,
So he stood there just picking his nose.

2775

To bring up a child with good rules,
The parents should study at schools.
    To raise pigs, one needs knowledge
    Which you get at a college,
But most families are raised by damn fools.

2776

Whenever the butcher drank rum
He'd end up as tight as a drum,
    Then the orders for meat
    Would go out incomplete,
But he promised the wurst was to come.

2777

Great men should have fame for sagacity—
Instead they are known for mendacity,
    For their violent obsession,
    For their hateful aggression,
And diversified forms of rapacity.

2778
There was an old squaw named Sarubin
Who said to the chief, "Where have you been?"
    He said, "Gathering canoes
    From the mud and the ooze,
And I've put them all in the canoe bin."

2779. EQUAL FOR A MOMENT*
Grandiloquent orators say,
With tongues in their cheeks hid away,
    That all men are born equal,
    While ignoring the sequel,
That disparity starts the first day.

2780
There were two young hunters named Sayers
Who divided their catch in two shares.
    Many rabbits they shot
    And they piled up the lot
And they spent the whole night splitting hares.

2781
There was a musician named Scarp
Who taught many lads to play harp.
    He enlarged his department
    In a rented apartment
And the flats that he rented were sharp.

2782
There was a young fellow named Schink
Who said, "I am thirsty, I think."
    So his wife got the car
    And they drove to a bar,
And they say that she drove him to drink.

2783. WITH BOXING GLOVES
Ingenious, inventive young Schlepper
In things electronic was hepper.
    He produced an extensor
    With tubes and condenser
Which would pick out the flyspecks from pepper.

2784
A shoddy old butcher named Schust
Insisted his meat was a must,
    But a maid did complain
    And she clobbered his brain,
Which was meet and most certainly just.

2785
An innocent lady named Scott
Was taught to be righteous in thought.
    It's a terrible waste
    To remain pure and chaste;
It's more fun to be chased and then caught.

2786
When asked, a young fellow named Sears
Rejected professional careers.
    "I'll not work to the bone,
    I'll just get me a loan
And I'll spend my whole life in arrears."

2787
A henpecked old man of Seattle
Indulged with his wife in some prattle.
    "That's my answer," she said
    As she nodded her head,
But he claimed he did not hear the rattle.

2788
An option one time man did seize
To live on the ground, if you please.
    From the progress he's made
    And the talents displayed,
It is time to go back to the trees.

2789
There was a pipesmoker named Seth
Who said, "I am all out of breath!"
    But his breath was so tainted
    That ten people fainted,
For his breath had a smell worse than death.

2790
When the bridge-builder blunders, he shakes;
There is no way to hide what he makes,
    For the wreckage is seen—
    But the surgeon is clean—
If he blunders, he buries mistakes.

2791. THE SHOPKEEPERS
When Richard and Spiro kept shop
No man their conniving could stop.
    They were forced to resign
    But they're still doing fine,
For the scum always floats to the top.

2792

Though sick and diseased was old Shrife
He lived ninety years with this strife.
    When he dropped dead from dropsy
    They performed an autopsy
To determine the cause of his life.

2793

A ruffled bridge player named Slade
Was trumped by his wife and dismayed.
    With her heart she did mess
    A sure diamond finesse,
So he clubbed her, but good, with a spade.

2794

The government took a big slice
In taxes that squeezed like a vise.
    But the Senate astute
    Made them fun to compute,
And so some people paid the tax twice.

2795

There was a car dealer named Slickbach
Who sold a big car to young Rickbach.
    Then from goodness of heart
    A bank loan he did start,
And the bank gave dear Slickbach a kick back.

2796

The office informer is slinky
With conduct repugnant and stinky.
    He will point without shame
    To the man who's to blame,
While the snot hangs in strands from his pinkie.

2797

The dentures produced by Doc Sloan
Were finer than heretofore known.
    No man better could do,
    And he made them so true
That they hurt and decayed like our own.

2798

The bankers so neat and dressed smart,
As servants do play a fine part.
    They give thoughtful advice
    And make great sacrifice,
And they all have our interest at heart.

2799*
An object which travels in space
A circular orbit will trace.
 Yet notions persist
 That a force does exist
Which makes a straight path commonplace.

2800. NOTHING DEFINED
A vacuum's defined as a space
Which objects of some sort did grace.
 They've been taken away,
 Just to where, I can't say,
And nothing was put in their place.

2801
A nutty old poet named Spence
Nonsensical verse did dispense,
 But when he was delirious
All his poems were serious,
Yet his nonsense was what made most sense.

2802. THE PROOF IS IN THE PUDDING
To avoid being trapped by a spoof,
A man must seek adequate proof.
 To be certain the broth
 Is composed of whole cloth
He must needs know the warp from the woof.

2803. $VER, MIF, ORM. 00
Abdominal misery had Spurgeon;
His pains from appendix did burgeon.
 To most men on this earth
 No appendix has worth,
But it's priced very high by a surgeon.

2804. THE WORM'S TURN
The worm 'neath the table did squirm,
And turned so that he could confirm
 If the bird was still there—
 To his utter despair
The table was turned on the worm.

2805
In Fairbanks there blew a big storm;
The temperature dropped below norm.
    To his car ran young Mose
    With hot water, which froze,
And so quickly, the ice was still warm.

2806
Some men will endure all the stress
To climb to the heights of success,
    But on reaching the pinnacle
    You will find they turn cynical—
There is nobody left to impress.

2807. ELECTION EAR MUFFS
The public should not be subjected
To speeches, unless they're protected
    And their ears are both bound
    And impervious to sound,
Lest their brains become badly infected.

2808
It shouldn't cause any surprise
That newspaper strikes are not wise,
    For the people soon dread
    If they are not misled,
And they seek other sources for lies.

2809
The *Elephish* lives in a swamp,
And there in delight he does romp.
    On peanuts he feeds
    In the rushes and reads
How the king and the queen live in pomp.

2810
A commonplace fellow named Sy
To life on this earth said goodbye.
    When they buried his bones
    There was moaning and groans
On account of the cost, which was high.

2811. CONDITIONED RESPONSE
Said a man to his dog, "Can you tell
Who had stayed here last year for a spell?
    It was Einstein, I'll bet."
    But the canine said, "Nyet,
It was Pavlov—does that ring a bell?"

2812
A hopeless illiterate was Tex;
He was not too sure of his sex.
    His check for Relief
    Brought him nothing but grief,
He could not even sign a full X.

2813
Young lads who in college learn things
Are told that in life they'll be kings.
    It is fine to have hopes
    When you know all the ropes,
But it's best if you start pulling strings.

2814
There was an old butcher named Thistle
Who sent to young lads this epistle:
    "Don't cut meat for a living,
    It's a job unforgiving.
It's no pleasure to wrestle with gristle."

2815. BOY SCOUT CROSSES STREET
A Scout helped a lady go through
A busy street crossing in Kew.
    She said, "Thank you, my dear.
    I was shaking with fear."
Said the Scout, "I was more scared than you."

2816. RETROACTIVE?
A lad his dear parents had thwarted
And with hoodlums and harlots cavorted.
    Said his mother, so stern,
    "You have caused me concern;
'Twould be better had you been aborted."

2817
The simple man sweats and he toils,
And his hands at his labor he soils.
    Millionaires are unseen
    But their fingers are clean,
As they gather to divvy the spoils.

2818
Now everyone knows what's a torus—
A pastry decorous but porous,
    Just a sausage of dough
    Wrapped around a big *O*.
Any further discussion will bore us.

2819
A fed-up young fellow named Trevor
Decided his marriage to sever.
    "Thirty years," said the judge
    And from this would not budge,
"You must not use the knife, no not ever."

2820. THE GALLUP POLL
The pollsters assemble their trivia
Contorting the facts that they give ya.
    For some sinister deed
    They intend to mislead,
And we Gallup along to oblivia.

2821
The housewife around the house trudges
Removing the filth and the smudges
    Which she finds with eye keen
    In a house that is clean,
While she wonders why men can't be drudges.

2822. AND THE LAMB SHALL EAT MEAT
I believe that the Bible is true
Where the lion will lay down with the ewe,
    And it shall come to pass
    That the lion will eat grass
And the blackbird with pigeons will coo.

2823. SUCKERS & CHISELERS*
A wealthy old fellow named Tuckers
Claimed all of us could be big-buckers.
    But if all of us chisel
    Then the whole thing will fizzle,
For who will be left to be suckers?

2824
The scientist, Hermann von Twist,
In his lab at his work would persist.
    He boldly declared
    He had answers prepared
To solve problems which did not exist.

2825
There was a nosepicker undaunted
By threats of his parents who taunted.
    They proposed it be cured
    And a gift they procured,
But he said it was snot what he wanted.

2826. NO BULL!
A Russian success was unfurled
As dogs into space they had hurled.
    But they took many bows
    When they sent up ten cows—
'Twas the herd that was shot 'round the world.

2827
To rhyme *orange* you'll find is unreal,
So the effort is lacking appeal.
    You'll do well, I deduce,
    If you rhyme with the juice,
Or perhaps find a rhyme with the peel.

2828. WORD TO THE WIVES: SUFFICIENT
With words one must not be too venty;
For children use not over twenty.
    By dispensing with verbiage
    You get rid of disturbiage,
And one word to the wives should be plenty.

2829
A stolid young fellow of Vichy
Was asked if for girls he was itchy.
    He said, "No thank you, dear,
    For I already fear
That I have one that's grouchy and bitchy."

2830. NO SPARK—NO FLAME
An insecure fellow was Vince;
When ladies would smile, he would wince.
    As a youth in the park
    He had plenty of spark,
But of late he was all out of flints.

2831. THE WHITE HOUSE LAUNDRY
As one day through the White House they wandered,
Old Spiro and Richard both pondered
    How to pull in the green
    And yet keep their hands clean,
So the money they handled was laundered.

2832
The atom bombs dropped in the war
Destroyed ninety thousand or more,
    But the Japs attacked slyly
    With their stratagem wily,
And with Hondas they bettered the score.

2833
A pauperized fellow named West
With living in slums was distressed,
    So he went on to college
    To acquire more knowledge
And a beatnik became like the rest.

2834
While he worked on the job, Mr. Wheeling
Held his head toward the sky with great feeling.
    When his boss asked him why
    He was facing the sky,
He replied, "I'm inspecting the ceiling."

2835
There was a young fellow named Whiting
Who spent with his wife much time fighting.
    She said, "We're in a bind,
    We must act more refined."
He said, "Dear, can you put that in writing?"

2836
Though the lady in math was a whiz
Yet she failed in her very first quiz.
    She made a good try:
    "It's a function of pie,
But I can't tell what flavor it is."

2837
While stirring tomatoes, chef Willie
Got dizzy and felt a bit silly.
    He complained he felt hot
    As he fell in the pot;
When the kettle boiled down he was chili.

2838
An avid young novice named Wings
Was eager to learn a few things.
    He said he had hopes
    If they'd show him the ropes,
But they told him to first pull some strings.

2839
Though man at his future has winked,
The answer is clear and distinct,
    And the smart thing to do
    Is put two in a zoo
To preserve them before they're extinct.

2840*
The language of English I wish
Were phonetic, and not mash and mish,
    And according to Shaw
    There's no order or law,
Because *GHOTI*, it seems, sounds like *FISH*.

2841
Some men are renowned for their wonders
And others well known for their plunders,
    And some stand apart
    For their fine works of art,
While some have gained fame for their blunders.

2842
The car that was purchased by Wood
Was checked and inspected but good.
    But when Wood picked a wife
    He disrupted his life
For he failed to check under the hood.

2843
The book peddler, Simon from Worcestershire
Once tickled a lady and goosed her,
    Whereupon she lost poise
    And she made a great noise
"Please be quiet," said Simon and shooshed her.

2844*
Though dying, a man of great worth
Went to heaven with feelings of mirth.
    When he asked for the Lord,
    Said St. Peter, so bored,
"He is busy with smiting on earth."

2845
When man fails to grasp his own worth
And increases by uncontrolled birth,
    He will die, I do think,
    In a terrible stink,
For there'll be no fresh air on this earth.

2846
Said Fisk to a lady named Yates,
"When I see you, my heart palpitates."
    But she said to him, "Fisk,
    I have no*,
Which is why I do not go on dates."

2847
A famous magician of yore
Engaged a young girl for a chore.
    She said, "I can work steady;
    You can saw when you're ready."
He said, "Haven't I sawed you before?"

19

Chamber of Horrors

2848
A terrorist Palestine ace
Was killed by a Jewess named Grace.
    Her masterful plot
    Was a bomb in her twat,
And she blew up her cunt in his face.

2849
A fastidious old man of Alsace
Was fucking a girl on the grass,
    When he noticed a sign:
    "If you litter—pay fine,"
So he shoved his cigar up her ass.

2850
The coveted Duchess Award
Was won by a man who was bored,
    And he sharpened his teeth,
    Ate a whore underneath,
Then he finished her off with his sword.

2851. VIRGO INTACTO DECOFFINATO
A girl of strong will was Miss Baker;
She swore that no fellow could make her.
    She expired, in fact,
    With her hymen intact,
But was fucked by the old undertaker.

2852. ANCHOR MAN
A horny old captain named Banker
Hung a whore by the ass on an anchor,
    Then he gave her a screw
    And likewise did the crew,
So they wrote her a letter to thank her.

2853
A whore on vacation, Miss Barr,
Was stopped by six men in a car.
    Their minds were on rape
    And there was no escape,
So she stayed and outfucked them by far.

2854
There was an old fellow named Baynes
Whose dear wife was sick and in pains.
    When she died on the bed
    He did not lose his head,
For he managed to fuck the remains.

2855
There was a young fellow named Beggs
Who took his girl down a few pegs.
    He said she was unclean
    And the foulest he'd seen,
So she left with her tail 'tween her legs.

2856
A madam who came from Belgrave
Kept all her dead whores in a cave,
    For she said with some smiles,
    "They have plenty of miles
And they do me no good in a grave."

2857
There was a young girl of Belgrave
Who kept a dead man in a cave.
    She said, "Though he is old
    And he's terribly cold,
Yet he's better than my husband Dave."

2858
The train struck Miss Senter and bent her.
At the morgue they reviewed what did dent her.
    Said old coroner Skinner,
    "It is now time for dinner,
But first I must get off dead Senter."

2859
A Frankenstein surgeon named Bloom
Arose from a period of gloom
    To distort the vagina
    Of a dead whore from China,
And he fell to his doom in her womb.

2860
One look at the whore of Bombay
Would turn a man ashen and gray,
       For the sag of her tits
       Would give strong men the shits,
And she carried her cunt in a tray.

2861
There once was a soldier named Brylent
Who fought in a battle so violent
       That his ass was struck dumb
       By the bombs that had come,
And henceforth his farting was silent.

2862
An old undertaker named Carriere
Prepared a cadaver to bury her.
       They brought four more that night
       And he cried in delight,
"The more that they bring in, the merrier!"

2863
A tolerant man named Carruther
Claimed one man was good as another,
       But he soon changed his tune
       When he saw a buffoon
A-fucking away with his mother.

2864
A girl that smoked heavy had Chase;
Her breath stunk all over the place,
       But her pussy smelled sweetly
       So he kissed it discreetly
And he fucked her tobacco-stained face.

2865
When the plumber was fucking Miss Croylett,
She was thrilled as he'd twist it and coil it.
       It was not simple luck,
       For he learned how to fuck
By plunging the turds from a toilet.

2866
Her ass, said a lady named Claribel,
To greatest of queens was comparibel,
       But a fellow named Bower
       Fucked her only an hower,
For he said that the stench was unbaribel.

2867
A quick-thinking fellow named Clark
Once picked up a slut in the park.
    She was ugly and crude
    And a horror when nude,
But was good for a fuck in the dark.

2868
A solemn gravedigger named Dave
Some remnants of dead whores did save.
    He fucked with delight
    The assemblage one night,
Though it still had one foot in the grave.

2869
There was a young fellow named Dave
Who tackled a whore in her cave.
    There was not much to pay,
    And the reason, they say,
Was one foot which she had in the grave.

2870
A necrophile fellow named Earse
Once kissed an old corpse in the hearse.
    He drew back in a shiver
    Which threw chills down his liver,
Then he tried something more and fared worse.

2871
There was an old pimp from the East
Who kept some old harlots deceased.
    Their ass was for rent,
    Not to any old gent,
But the bishop, the pastor and priest.

2872
In the winter a strumpet named Flo
Fell dead when a blizzard did blow.
    She was fucked by Count Rumford,
    But she gave him cold comfort—
She had lain for too long in the snow.

2873. THE BROWN-NOSER
To a pipe-smoking suckhole named Flock,
The death of his boss was a shock,
    So he chiseled a bowl
    From the corpse's asshole
And he fashioned a stem from his cock.

2874. SURROGATE SUBTERFUGE

An old undertaker named Flock
Once lifted a young lady's frock.
    She was fucked without strife
    For the time of her life,
But he fucked her with grandfather's cock.

2875

A practical welder named Forch
Was fucking his girl on the porch.
    Her pussy was tight
    But he set it aright
By enlarging her twat with his torch.

2876. LONG LIVE NECROPHILIA!*

On the night of the wedding, young Fred
Told his bride, before getting to bed,
    To please take a cold shower
    For at least half an hour,
Then to lie on the bed as if dead.

2877. A HERCULEAN TASK

There was a young fellow named Gable
Who picked up a whore dressed in sable,
    But her filth made him shiver
    So he looked for a river
Which would flush out the Augean stable.

2878. COLD COMFORT

The coroner's daughter, Miss Gail,
Was having a cold piece of tail.
    She preferred her men dead,
    And the reason, she said,
Was that heads which are cool will prevail.

2879

A repulsive old floozie of Gander
Had boasted that no man could brand her.
    She was ravaged by Blanding
    An old cowboy at branding,
Who convulsed, but he managed to stand her.

2880
So smelly a lady was Gorth
That for screwing no man would come forth,
     But a man got the best of her
     As he stayed to the west of her,
While there blew a stiff breeze from the north.

2881
There was a young GI so glum—
From Vietnam with medals he come.
     He received in the mail
     Both his arms in a pail.
"It's a good place," he said, "to be from."

2882
At Auschwitz, the Nazi, von Hainz,
In cutting up corpses took pains.
     All the pussies were saved
     For his cohorts depraved—
In the ovens he threw the remains.

2883
When dead, an old harlot named Hayes
Received from devotees much praise.
     She was kept in behalf
     Of the coroner's staff,
For her pussy kept twitching for days.

2884
Observed old philosopher Hearst:
This one is by far the world's worst.
     It does not cause surprise
     To see so many flies,
But I think I must scrape her off first.

2885
There was a young beatnik named Howard
Whose girl for a month had not showered.
     When there blew a slight breeze
     She would smell like ripe cheese.
He backed off and she called him a coward.

2886
The embalmer's apprentice, young Jack,
Said, "I fondle each dead lady's crack.
     Though they're cold on the dick,
     Yet they sure do the trick,
For they never complain or fight back."

2887. STILL, YET AND AGAIN
Said a man to a widow named Jill,
"Tell me, why don't you bury poor Bill?"
    She replied, "Though he's dead,
    I will keep him in bed.
He's my darling and I love him still."

2888
A baker's apprentice was Jock;
He pissed in the dough in the crock.
    His false teeth he would take
    To trim icing on cake,
While the doughnuts he made on his cock.

2889
An old undertaker named Jock
A corpse on the slab did unfrock.
    In a coffin he tucked her
    And he laughed as he fucked her,
But he fucked her with grandfather's cock.

2890
A pensive young man of Khartoum
Considered with gloom his girl's womb.
    Though he fucked the great cavern
    Of the maid at the tavern,
He had never observed such a tomb.

2891
On viewing the harlot from Kootenay,
The soldiers had threatened a mutiny,
    But it came out all right
    When she turned out the light,
For she could not withstand a close scrutiny.

2892. FLYSWATTER INCLUDED IN PRICE
To the madam went money-short Kyes;
His fifty-cent piece he thought wise,
    But felt something was queer
    When he patted her rear
And from out of her asshole flew flies.

2893
There was an old man of Lapeer
Who fucked an old whore from the rear.
    It squeezed on her sprat
    And there jumped out a rat
Which had lived in her twat for a year.

2894
The girl that I find the best lay
Is one without arms name of Fay,
 It is true she can't hug me
 But I find it don't bug me
For she never has pushed me away.

2895. CAN'T LIVE WITH URNINGS
A henpecked old man of Lucerne
No peace in his life could discern.
 When his bitchy wife died
 He cremated her hide,
But he still heard her shouts from the urn.

2896
Poor Charlie was struck with bad luck;
His dear friend was crushed by a truck.
 When he viewed the departed
 He exclaimed as he farted,
"I must give his poor widow a fuck."

2897
A crippled old man of Manila
Was screwing a whore named Priscilla,
 But he thrashed with his crutches
 To get out of her clutches,
For she grasped like a hairy gorilla.

2898
A miserly man named McKnight
Had manners which gave men a fright,
 For he cooked all his grub
 In the large thunder mug
Which he kept in his bedroom at night.

2899. FREEDOM OF CHOICE
There was a young fellow named Moffin
Who said to his dear wife so often,
 "You don't know what you're missing—
 It is not just for pissing—
And it's no goddam good in a coffin."

[2900]
But the old undertaker named West
Remarked with much candor and zest,
    "Though I find I'm confused
    By a cunt that's not used,
Yet a fuck in the coffin is best."

2901
There was an old barber named Moffin,
While shaving a corpse for the coffin,
    Did embrace it profuse—
    But he had an excuse—
He did not get this chance very often.

2902
There was an old lady named Mopsy
Who died of a bad case of dropsy.
    But the old undertaker
    Said he'd not try to make her
Until doctors performed an autopsy.

2903
"As for women," said old hermit Mottsum,
"In the past, I must say I have bought some,
    But I don't pay no more;
    I go down to the shore
And I search through the jetsam and flotsam."

2904
An arsonist hailing from Natchez
Was also a voyeur of snatches.
    To fulfil his desires
    To see snatches and fires
He ignited some snatches with matches.

2905
The old undertaker named Niven
A fuck to a lady was givin'.
    He said to her, "Jill,
    Lie perfectly still,
For I never have fucked with the livin'."

2906
"What price for a whore, cheap and old?"
Requested a man without gold.
    Said the madam, "One buck,
    And it's not for the fuck,
But the scraper to scrape off the mold."

2907. THE BEEKEEPER

A man who feared insects, named Paine,
From fucking a girl would abstain
  Till he looked, if you please,
  For hornets or bees
By poking her twat with a cane.

2908

A horny old bastard was Perce;
He buggered a corpse in the hearse.
  He arose from the dead
  With a smile and he said,
"This day I forever shall curse."

2909

A thrifty old Scotsman named Perce
Encountered a matter adverse.
  While he screwed an old whore
  She fell dead on the floor
So he finished her off in the hearse.

2910

There was a young fellow named Perce
Whose antics were somewhat perverse,
  For he cried and he cried
  When his grandmother died,
But he buggered her corpse in the hearse.

2911. FIRST THINGS FIRST

Said the old undertaker named Pete,
As the corpses he studied, discreet,
  "Though I know I can't tarry
  And the dead we must bury,
But first thing, I must bury the meat."

2912. THEREBY HANGS A TAIL

A wily old butcher named Pete Cook
Was fucking a whore with a beat look.
  She dropped dead with a twitch
  So he finished the bitch
As she hung by her ass on the meat hook.

445

2913. ASK NO QUARTER

There was a young fellow named Porter
Whose wife was blown up by a mortar.
    All his nephews and nieces
    Helped him gather the pieces
So he gave each young helper a quarter.

[2914]

He studied the pieces, did Porter,
Then labeled each piece and did sort her,
    And this fellow, so foxy,
    Had her glued with epoxy,
And he fucked her but had to support her.

2915. SIMPLE INTEREST

A practical fellow named Prater
Wed a quad amputee of Decatur,
    And the poor girl was blind,
    But he said, "I do find
The percentage of twat is much greater."

2916

The embalmer a corpse did prepare—
On the hard granite slab she lay bare.
    Then he started with screwing
    And he said, "How'm I doing?"
But she gave him a cold, glassy stare.

2917

There was an old whore with proficiency
Who gave a good fuck with sufficiency.
    Though her left tit was shot
    With a cancerous rot,
Yet her right tit made up the deficiency.

2918. THE LAST RIGHTS

In the hospital bed lay Miss Proctor,
Debauched by the rapist who socked her.
    As she cursed her abductor
    Seven orderlies fucked her,
And the interne, the priest and the doctor.

2919. AN URN SAVED IS AN URN EARNED

The new wife of widower Raines
Caused nothing but misery and pains.
    She was not worth a durn—
    He got more from the urn
In which rested his late wife's remains.

2920

An old undertaker named Rand
Once screwed a dead whore in the sand.
    He performed his rendition
    In the finest tradition;
An embalmer conducted the band.

2921

A thirsty old bum in Rangoon
Went into a scummy saloon.
    There he begged for a beer,
    But they turned a deaf ear,
So he drank from the slimy spittoon.

2922

In a whorehouse in central Rangoon
The harlots were slimy by noon.
    One man who was slick
    Got a much better kick
By fucking the half-filled spittoon.

2923

A man with his cock on the rise,
A tart on the street did apprise.
    He raised up her kilt
    But his pecker did wilt,
For on patting her ass, out flew flies.

2924

If bargains are what you are seeking,
A madam has harlots from Peking.
    She has dead ones on ice,
    And some covered with lice,
And some with foul odors are reeking.

2925. PAYMENT IN SERVICES

For a harlot, old carpenter Slade
A partition installed, and conveyed
    A bill for the labor,
    But the harlot said, "Neighbor,
You can take out your payments in trade."

[2926]
He accepted the harlot's condition
She lay down and he took the position
    With his finger and thumb
    In her cunthole and bum
And said, "Pay or out comes the partition."

2927
There was a young fellow named Skinner
Who worked in the morgue, the poor sinner.
    His mind had some warps
    For he'd pull out a corpse
And he'd have a few fucks before dinner.

2928
There was an old fellow named Walker
Who froze a dead whore in a locker,
    And on Christmas and Easter
    He would thaw out her keester,
And the way that he fucked her would shock her.

2929
While screwing a harlot, old Waring
Did not like the way she was staring.
    She was not very spriteful
    But he thought it delightful
Till he found she was dead as a herring.

2930
In the snow, an old recluse named Watt,
Found a whore, well-preserved, and no rot,
    And her tits were still firm,
    So he pulled out his worm
And he dusted the snow from her twat.

2931. OPPORTUNIST
There was an old fellow named Wills
Whose dear wife had so many ills
    That he nearly had fits,
    Till he turned to his wits
And he fucked between fevers and chills.

2932
"What we need," said a non-smoker wise,
"Is to give men who puff a surprise.
    We must give them a smoke
    So they'll gag and they'll choke,
And they'll drop down around us like flies."

2933
There was a young lady named Wise
Whose ass would have won a *First Prize,*
    But you needed a swatter
    And an oversize blotter
Just to get past the juice and the flies.

2934. DOWN IN FLAMES!
Young Moses, it seems, had a yearning
To pursue a strange method of learning.
    He ignited the hair
    Of a lady's affair,
And he talked to the bush that was burning.

2935
The coroner sliced with great zest
Of the corpse which lay prostrate undressed.
    He won honors and fame
    For he studied the game—
And he did it by keeping abreast.

20
Addenda

2936
A man with a prick like Apollo
A buxom young maid once did follow.
  She succumbed to his wiles
  And it brought him big smiles,
Till he found that his victory was hollow.

2937
A young man with a tone of assurance
Made a date with a girl of allurance.
  As he parted her hair
  He exclaimed in despair,
"But I do not have sinkhole insurance!"

2938
The elegant swan does attract us
Though sometimes his manners distract us,
  Like his action so crass
  With his bill up his ass—
It's a trick that a doctor should practice.

2939
In Iran, a young man Bani-Sadr
Would drink Ayatollah's foul water,
  Then he'd turn facing Mecca
  And he'd pull out his peckah
And he'd fuck with his mudr and fadr.

2940
Ron Reagan for missiles now begs—
Take care for we're treading on eggs.
  So beware of his charms,
  If we vote for his arms
It may cost us a couple of legs.

2941
To a girl said old carpenter Bing,
"Let us go to the woods for a fling.
  With the tools of my trade
  You'll be properly laid,
And a wood screw will be just the thing."

2942

By the rule of clear thinking be bound;
Speak with reason and logic profound.
    One must never defile
    With the epithet vile,
For a man who throws dirt loses ground.

2943

Asked a girl of young astronaut Brad,
"What excitement in space have you had?"
    As he fondled her thigh
    He said, "Feelings run high
At the moment I lift off the pad."

2944

With a telephone pole Mr. Bream
Rammed the cunt of a girl of broad beam.
    Fourteen hours of bliss
    And she said, " 'Nough of this,
If you touch me once more, I shall scream."

2945. PYTHAGOREAN THEOREM*

On three hides sat the chief's three new brides
And he saw, as they lay on their sides,
    That the one named "Big Bottom Ass,"
    Squaw upon hippopotamus,
Equalled squaws on the other two hides.

2946

A soft-hearted harlot named Bryce
Was fucking a gentleman nice.
    He was ready to blow
    When she let the man know
She expected an increase in price.

2947. WHITE HOUSE CAPER*

In the kitchen poor Richard was caught,
And he said, with his hand in the pot,
    "Though I did bake a cake,
    What I miss—I miss steak—
But a cook—this for certain I'm not!"

2948

The professor was fucking Miss Claire
On the floor, on the bed, on the chair.
   Though he graded her poor,
   He admitted for sure
The potential for learning was there.

2949

For dinner the soldiers were clustered—
To a man they complained and they blustered.
   They accepted the soup
   Which was made of elk's poop,
But the moose turds were lacking in mustard.

2950*

A colostomy patient, Miss Clyde,
First despaired, then she took it in stride.
   She still peddled coition
   In the supine position,
But she made a lot more on the side.

2951*

There was a young fellow named Clyde
Who fell in the privy and died.
   Along came his brother
   And he fell in another,
And they both were interred side by side.

[2952]

To the morgue they brought both brothers Clyde
And the coroner had to decide
   How to write the reports—
   A dilemma of sorts—
Disinterred and *In Turd* both applied.

2953. WHEREVER THERE'S SMOKE . . .

In the village the maids did conspire
With a monk who aroused their desire
   To send signals of smoke
   When they needed a poke—
Now wherever there's smoke there is friar.

2954
Said the convert to Pope Constantine,
As he knelt at the Vatican Shrine,
　　"Please advise your position
　　On connubial coition."
Said the Pope, "I find dog-fashion fine."

2955
A senile old hunter named Cotter
Observed a nude girl by the water.
　　When he asked, "Are you game?"
　　She said, yes, without shame,
So he raised up his rifle and shot her.

2956
The police dog of Officer Cotter
Was trained as a copulate spotter.
　　He would sniff with cognition
　　An illicit coition,
And would douse it with buckets of water.

2957
At the bird zoo, a man from Crimea
Said, "It seems like a brilliant idea
　　To have all these birds dyed,
　　But what bothers my pride—
How the devil does one dye a Rhea?"

2958
To the doctor a lady of Dallas
Showed her cunt with an oversize callus.
　　Said the doc, "It appears
　　You have spent a few years
With a man with a very hard phallus."

2959
An old man of good breeding from Dallas
Was berating his girl friend so callous.
　　"When you're down on your knees
　　You must learn to say 'Please,'
And don't speak with a mouthful of phallus."

2960
Our national aim I deplore—
A future most bleak is in store
　　Since more funds we release
　　For maintaining the peace
Than we ever spent fighting a war.

2961

When man his good senses deployed
Then smallpox no longer annoyed.
    There's a much better plan
    Which will benefit man—
When the last atom bomb is destroyed.

2962

A lady well-bred and discreet
Was sucking a fire fighter's meat.
    It was not for the paste,
    But she relished the taste
Of the hickory smoked sausage treat.

2963. MORE WHITE HOUSE CAPER

Said the president, somewhat distraught,
When surprised at a young lady's twat,
    "There were times, I'm afraid,
    When mistakes have been made—
But a voyeur for certain I'm not."

2964

A Victorian young lady named Ewing
Had suppressed any passion for screwing,
    But one day, feeling chipper,
    She unzipped a man's zipper,
Which promoted a virgin's undoing.

2965

The death notice ads I forbear—
They fill me with grief and despair.
    I avoid them completely,
    Turning pages discreetly,
For fear that I'll find my name there.

2966

Said the president, hiding a frown,
"In a sea of inflation we'll drown,
    But I see a bright light,
    Some relief is in sight—
I hear panties are still coming down."

2967

The noted economist Gaines
Divulged after racking his brains,
    That the rich always share
    All the wealth that is there,
While the poor folk divide what remains.

2968
When we play at the politics game,
We kick out the scum that's to blame.
    Yes—the rascals are out—
    But it still leaves some doubt
For it seems that the stench is the same.

2969
On his bride a young fellow named Gene
Saw the very first cunt he had seen.
    He could not comprehend
    How to start or to end,
Nor what things he should do in between.

2970
A cautious young fellow was Ginnit;
Any water he drank had gin in it.
    It seems water alone
    He would never condone
After learning that fishes fuck in it.

2971
A young lady depressed was Miss Glick
For her paycheck so small made her sick,
    Till she found a good way
    To mix pleasure with pay,
And a fly-by-night job did the trick.

2972
A lonely old salesman named Gore
Met a pimp as he walked on the shore.
    "I am homesick," he said,
    "Send a girl to my bed—
A decrepit, irascible whore."

2973
The buffalo hunter named Grange
Was courting a lady so strange,
    For he kissed what was hairy
    'Neath the stars on the prairie,
Then he fucked her at home on the range.

2974. THE LONG RANGER
On the range, a young cowgirl named Granger
Was seduced by a copper-skinned stranger.
    It was Tonto, no less,
    But he lacked the finesse
Of the man in the mask—The Long Ranger.

2975. LEAVE NO LEAF UNTURNED
In the Garden of Eden, in grief,
There sat Eve with a need for relief,
 Likewise Adam, so blue,
 Knowing not what to do—
It was time to turn over a leaf.

2976
In the haystack a lady named Grimes
Recollected her fun in past times,
 But her quest inconclusive
 Found no needle elusive,
Though she did feel the prick several times.

2977
While biking, a whore name of Gump
Sucked the seat up her cunt with a whump.
 She was thrilled with delight
 So she rammed it up tight
With the end of a bicycle pump.

2978
Let us pity a fellow named Heep—
He was spurned by all harlots as cheap.
 Then the ultimate blow
 Which the Fates could bestow—
While he jacked off his hand fell asleep.

2979
There was an old plumber of Hocking
Who took off a young lady's stocking,
 Then he raised up her dress
 And he said, "I confess
That your cunt is in need of some caulking."

2980
The wife of a doctor named Hong
Spread her legs and said, "Slip in the dong."
 Said the doc, "I am beat;
 There's no life in my meat.
I've been looking at cunts all day long."

2981
A hard-up young fellow named Hood
Once took an old whore to the wood.
 He remarked, so forlorn,
 "It is festered and worn,
And it smells pretty bad but it's good."

2982. FAST FOOD JOINT
To *MacDonald's* would go young Miss Hopper—
Quarter Pounders were in and were proper,
    But she soon had an itch
    For a *Burger King* switch—
For where else can you get the *Big Whopper*.

2983
To all nations, the pope in a huff
Gave his speech with the same crap and stuff.
    "Our new plan we'll release
    For promoting the peace.
We've promoted the war long enough."

2984
For his daughter named Kate, horny Hugh
Was searching to get him a screw,
    But his son was on Kate,
    So old Hugh had to wait
Twenty minutes before Son was through.

2985
To her boss said a typist, Miss Hyatt,
"I am through—take a kite and go fly it,
    For I seek a transition
    To a better position."
Said her boss, "Please undress and let's try it."

2986. THE RULES OF IRAN
Ayatollah Ruhollah Khomeini
Published rules for his followers zany:
    Wipe your ass with a bone
    Or a fine polished stone,
And fuck sheep, not with lions, if you're brainy.

[2987]
Ayatollah did further instruct—
And this from his works we deduct—
    You can fuck on demand
    Any beast in the land,
But you can't eat the sheep that you fucked.

2988. HOLEY CANDLES
At the abbey, the Cardinal knocked
And the Mother Superior was shocked.
    She had cause to suspect
    That he came to inspect
In the room where the candles were locked.

2989. ONCE A CORK SOAKER ...
A young man who sacked coke in Fort Knox
Lost his job so he worked tucking socks.
    Then he moved to Grand Forks
    Where he tried soaking corks,
But he quit and he's now sucking cocks.

2990
A well-hung musician was Kropps;
On a scale one to ten he was tops.
    When his tool came in view,
    Said his girl, "Let us screw;
What an organ—please pull all the stops!"

2991
A fag bumped a truck in Laporte
And the fender did slightly distort.
    Said the irate old trucker,
    "Suck my cock, you dumb fucker!"
And they settled the case out of court.

2992
To the doctor a fellow named Long
Said his wife had objections so strong—
    Though he fucked her first class
    'Twas a pain in the ass.
Said the doc, "You are doing it wrong."

2993
When dining, a man named McNish
Had trouble selecting the dish.
    Said his wife, "You're amusing,
    You have trouble in choosing—
Take the bull by the horns and choose fish."

2994
A patrolman who beat on his meat
Wed a girl who was not too discreet,
    So he felt no dismay
    When she left him one day,
He was glad to be back on the beat.

2995
The old etymologist Metters
Said that four-letter words have no betters.
    To establish conformity
    For a grievous deformity,
He proposed to spell PRIK with four letters.

2996
Dear Abby advised every Miss
On the blessings of virginal bliss—
    Do not fondle man's meat,
    Keep his hands off your teat—
Cross your legs when he gives you a kiss.

2997
Said the president, "I am mistook,
For I entered the kitchen to look.
    It appears that I'm caught
    With my hand in the pot,
But for certain I am not a cook."

2998
Toward men, an old virgin named Moffin
Her attitude never would soften.
    She was laid out in grace
    With a smile on her face—
At the end she was screwed in her coffin.

2999
A starving young fellow named Moffin
Ate his brother and sister to soften
    His intense hunger pains.
    To respect the remains
He committed his turds to a coffin.

3000
A busy Afghanistan moll
From Russians was making a haul.
    Warned old Boris the colonel,
    "Cease this fucking infernal."
So she promised a token withdrawal.

3001
A man who knew cheese to perfection
Advised how he made his selection:
    It must smell like a cunt
    And I'll put it up front
If it gives me a first-class erection.

3002
An old engineer name of Pete
Was giving a lady a treat.
    She could not understand
    What made fucking so grand,
So he showed her a sketch of his meat.

3003
For the mailman a lady named Pickett
Dropped her panties, exposing her thicket.
    Said the mailman, "This box
    Can be used to mail cocks,
But the stamps will not stick till I lick it."

3004
So long was the tongue of young Pickett
That right up his ass he could stick it,
    And he dreamed, so discreet,
    Of the ultimate treat—
If his ear were a cunt he would lick it.

3005
Of the madam asked pro golfer Pine,
"What's par for nine whores all in line?"
    She said, "Eighty-five strokes,
    Plus or minus two pokes."
But he scored for nine holes—sixty-nine.

3006
A young sailor who stopped at all ports
Got in trouble with girls of all sorts,
    So a new leaf he turned
    And his britches he burned,
And he now walks around in his shorts.

3007
With a dollar a man did presume
To approach an old whore of Khartoum,
    So his dollar she took
    And she gave him a book,
Then she showed him the self-service room.

3008
To all nations the pope spoke with pride,
The world's future they now must decide.
    He sought help to release
    His new plan for the peace,
And old whores by the hundreds applied.

3009
In his lab sat old scientist ˙Schmidt,
And a problem reviewed with brows knit.
    His own fart to his nose
    Smelled as sweet as a rose,
While another man's fart smelled like shit.

3010
The sheep that I fucked last September
Within me has left a hot ember.
    Though I look every day
    I can't find the same lay;
Her vagina is hard to remember.

3011. CUBAN CLEANUP
The refugees fled Cuba's shore—
To America's coast they did pour.
    They were happy to leave—
    Said Fidel, "Though I grieve,
If you want them, we'll fuck and make more."

3012
The hand surgeon's pecker was sick;
A tendon transplant did the trick
    Which he took from his hand.
    His erection is grand
But he can't get a hold of his prick.

3013
To his squaw said the chief with eyes sleepy,
"There is wampum all over my tepee!"
    Said the squaw with eyes bright,
    "Why, I earned it last night,
And I did the whole thing with my peepee."

3014
Contraceptives are high-priced, and this
Could result in disruption of bliss.
    If the cost is too steep,
    You'll find rhythm is cheap,
But the price will be high if you miss.

3015
To an African hunter named Tim
Said the dentist with visage so grim,
    "In your teeth there's a plaque
    From the balls of a yak,
Or the hair of an antelope's quim. "

3016

What a strange-looking bird is the toucan
With his odd-looking beak and his blue can.
    He can shove his red beak
    In a place I can't speak—
It is much more than I can or you can.

3017

To heaven went Christ on his trip,
But someone had made a bad slip.
    From the cold earthly prison
    Of the tomb He had risen,
But the rabbi was left with a tip.

3018

A thoughtful young widow, undaunted,
By her husband's demise she was haunted.
    The remains of her man
    She exposed to a fan,
For a blow job was what he had wanted.

3019

For his cabinet, Reagan so vague
Chose a man who would let loose a plague,
    So we sit and we pray
    And we long for the day
When the last atom bomb blows up Haig.

3020

"I like men of the sea," said Miss Violet.
"They have fine points, the way I compile it.
    For example, the mate
    Is a fucker first rate,
And the captain, he knows how to pile it."

3021

At the abbey, a monk name of Wells
Studied hard to advance from the cells.
    After learning the ropes
    He was filled with high hopes,
But they gave him a job tolling bells.

3022

A big-bosomed lady named Whipple
At Olympic events caused a ripple.
    She took on all competers
    In the one hundred meters,
And she beat the young lads by a nipple.

[3023]
She challenged a sprinter named Jacques;
To distract him she raised up her smock.
　　But he moved out in front
　　When he glanced at her cunt,
And he won by the knob of his cock.

3024. TOPOLOGY APOLOGY
The English prof eating Miss Young
Had thoughtlessly licked at her bung,
　　So he said, in apology,
　　"I know naught of topology—
Please exculpate this slip of the tongue."

Bibliography

This bibliography lists the books and publications that have in-fluenced my efforts in this field. For a comprehensive listing of limer-ick literature, the reader is directed to Gershon Legman's The Lim-erick *and* The New Limerick.

Baring-Gould, William S. *The Lure of the Limerick: An Uninhib-ited History,* New York: Clarkson N. Potter, Inc. 1967. A fine introduction on the history of the limerick, followed by an ex-cellent collection of limericks, extensively expurgated, many of which are to be found in Legman's *The Limerick.*

Billington, Ray Allen. *Limericks Historical and Hysterical: Pla-giarized, Arranged, Annotated, and Some Written by R.A.B.,* New York/London: W. W. Norton & Co. A collection of 275 limericks, some old, many new, and some composed by the au-thor and his wife. Footnotes are liberally used throughout to provide a historical background. This publication is the most re-cent addition to the field.

Crist, Clifford M. *Playboy's Book of Limericks,* edited by C.M.C. Chicago: Playboy Press, 1972. A collection of 655 limericks, sev-eral hundred new and the rest from printed sources. Many of the new limericks are originals of C. M. Crist.

Legman, Gershon. *The Limerick: 1700 Examples With Notes, Vari-ants and Index.* Paris, 1953; New York, 1964, 1969. The bible of limerick aficionados, with an excellent introduction and a com-prehensive index.

———— *The New Limerick.* New York: Crown Publishers, Inc., 1977. An additional 2,750 limericks, all recent—a superb collec-tion. This volume contains 200 selected items from Crist's col-lection, and 200 items from Chaplin's published and unpub-lished works.

Pepys, J. Beauregard [Roy W. West]. *Limericks for the Main Line, or The Art of Social Descending Made Easy.* Philadelphia, 1973. Sixty original limericks focused on the Philadelphia scene.

———— *The Lilt in his Kilt, or The Flasher in the Rye.* Limericks in the spirit of Robert Burns. Lahaska, Pennsylvania, 1978.

Bibliography

Society of the Fifth Line, Chicago. The author has attended the 1978 through 1981 meetings of the Society and wishes to acknowledge that some fifty limericks appearing in this volume were the result of ideas that were prompted by these meetings. The Society of the Fifth Line is, to the best of the author's knowledge, the most prolific producer of quality limericks at the present time. Some of these are to be found in R. Billington's *Limericks Historical and Hysterical* and in C. Crist's *Playboy's Book of Limericks.*

Notes

Numbers refer to the number of the limericks, not *to the page on which they may be found.*

2. Little Romances

32. The Volkswagen *Rabbit* is a small, popular car introduced circa 1975. The bucket seats fold back in the same manner as in the *Mercedes.* The results should be the same in either car.

36. *Make Peace—Not War.* This was the slogan of the college students in the United States in the sixties and the seventies, especially pronounced during the Vietnam War period.

47. *Lissajous Figure.* The series of plane curves traced by an object executing two naturally perpendicular harmonic motions, forming a distinct pattern when the ratio of the frequencies of the motions is a ratio of small integers.

79. Ralph Nader is a well-known consumer advocate in the United States. His criticism of the General Motors *Corvair* was an instrumental factor in the cancellation of this model. Nader's cliché in regard to the *Corvair* was "Unsafe at any speed!"

87. Men are aroused by visual stimuli, and in general they prefer sex with the lights on. Joke: Little Johnny asked mother if people can eat light bulbs, and mother said, "No—why do you ask?" Johnny replied, "Father had the maid upstairs, and he said: Put the light out and I'll eat it."

122. *Batman* was a syndicated comic strip in the United States in the 1950s and the 1960s. It was made into a popular television show.

123. *Wrigley's Doublemint* chewing gum is advertised with the slogan "Double Your Pleasure, Double Your Fun."

125. In the early days of television, one of the common faults was a distorted picture that came in at 45 degrees.

155. Formula for secretarial advancement: If you wish to succeed, get under a good man and work your way up.

161. What is the difference between an epileptic cornhusker and a lady with diarrhea? The epileptic cornhusker shucks between fits.

186. This limerick is dated by the horse-drawn vehicle for delivery of milk, hence it refers to the pre-1935 period.

198. "Super Glue" is a registered name for a fast-setting Cyano-acrylate Ester. The label carries a warning to use with extreme caution and to avoid getting the material on fingers or eyelids.

206. It is customary for a toolmaker to prepare a piece of steel with coating of a blue dye before starting his layout. The blue dye is made of *Gentian Violet* dissolved in alcohol.

255. "Which Twin Has The Toni?" was an advertising slogan in the 1950s and 1960s for a hairdo kit sold for home use.

270. World War II Joke: Russian colonel sits next to WAC on U.S. train. Nothing is said for an hour, then WAC says, "Nice day." Russian colonel says, "Enoff ov dees lovemaking—let's fock."

281. The mother of buxom Miss Claire
Discovered her secret affair.
    She admonished her child
    For her antics so wild,
"This is something we both have to share!"

286. A TV show, *World Adventure Series,* hosted by George Pierrot, showed a travelogue in Africa. The females in one African tribe smeared dung on their faces to attract greenbottle flies, which settled thereon, making them appear more attractive. From a distance the flies sparkled like jewels.

3. Organs

404. From *Playboy,* February 1980, p. 237: 1565—Erotic paroxysms sweep the Convent of Nazareth in Cologne, Germany. Hundreds of nuns stretch out on their backs, eyes shut, moaning and thrusting their torsos heavenward. It is later explained that they have had erotic seizures caused by sexual frustration.

410. *Dentyne* chewing gum contains oil of cloves, which is used for relieving toothache. It is advertised for freshening the breath and for keeping the teeth clean and healthy.

418. A Study in Contradictions: If the penis is soft, it is a bone of contention. If the penis is hard, it is not a bone of contention. Modern surgery can repair faulty erectile valves or can supply hand-operated pumps for erecting the penis.

421. Grandfather observed little Johnny driving worms into the ground with a hammer.
"How do you do that?" asked grandfather.
"I put the worms in this chemical and they stiffen right up, then I can drive them into the ground."
"Let me have that solution," said grandfather, "and you will find five dollars under your pillow tomorrow morning."
Next day, Johnny came running to grandfather, saying, "I found two five-dollar bills under my pillow!"
"The other five dollars was from your grandmother."

443. In *The Limerick*, this is #1204. In *The Lure of the Limerick*, this appears on page 6. The author has added a second limerick to this well-known classic. The *Fitzgerald-Lorentz Contraction* hypothesis postulates that a moving body exhibits deformation in the direction of motion. This was later corroborated by Einstein's *Special Theory of Relativity*. The author submits his hypothesis in the second limerick: If a body moves with sufficient velocity, it can occupy two or more places at one time.

482. The deposed Shah of Iran came to U.S. from Mexico for a cancer operation. The Ayatollah Ruhollah Khomeini, the new religious leader of Iran, permitted the seizure of the American Embassy staff in Teheran by Iranian students. The Americans were held as hostages for the return of the former Shah and his fortune, which was estimated at several billion dollars. Mexico refused to take back this hot potato, and the dying Shah finally found refuge in Panama.

515. Pencil leads used by draftsman and artists commonly vary from *6H*, the hardest, to *6B*, the softest.

518. In *The Limerick*, No. 313:
There was a young fellow of Kent
Whose prick was so long that it bent,
    So to save himself trouble
    He inserted it double,
And instead of him coming, he went.

542. In *The Limerick*, No. 255:
A pious old woman named Tweak
Had taught her vagina to speak.

It was frequently liable
To give quotes from the Bible,
But when fucking—not even a squeak!

552. *The Lady of Natchez.* This delightful set of three limericks in
italics is taken from *The Limerick*, Nos. 201–3. The author has
felt that someday the Lady of Natchez must meet Locke and
therefore, with this end in view, has taken the liberty of adding
four limericks, which now provide this series with a happy
ending.

559. *The Saga of Corkscrew Dick.* This is a new twist on the story
of that unfortunate gentleman who was born with an organ
with a helical twist. Following is one version of this story.
Readers may recall other renditions.
This is the story of Screwy Dick
Unfortunately born with a corkscrew prick.
Around the world he went to hunt
To find a girl with a corkscrew cunt,
And when he found her, he fell down dead,
For the son-of-a-bitch had a left-hand thread.

582. There was a young fellow named Fritz
Who planted an acre of tits.
They came up in the fall,
Pink nipples and all,
And he leisurely chewed them to bits.
See No. 775, *The Limerick*.

642. During the height of the Watergate scandal, President Nixon
made a special TV appearance to explain his position. He proclaimed, "I may have made mistakes, but I am no crook."

683. *What Is Done Is Done.* In this series, originally consisting of
four limericks, the author has made some improvements. An
interested reader had sent the author a letter suggesting that
the last line of No. 686 be revised to read "I am Dunn! Opus
Four." This was a worthy suggestion and it was promptly in-
corporated. At this point the author received a Divine Revela-
tion, that although Dunn was done in by his dastardly deeds,
his digit, increasingly rigid, could be dunned to do what must
be done, this action being described in No. 687, where Dunn
done what he done unto death, and even after.

4. Oral Irregularity

809. *No Apples in Eden.* The Garden of Eden was bare country in a tropical paradise. It is unlikely that apples would grow in this climate. No doubt this is an error in the myth—which leads one to suspect that the myth originated in a more northerly clime. From *Playboy,* July 1971: On one segment of TV's *The Galloping Gourmet,* Graham Kerr told his audience that he had determined, after considerable research, that Eve had been tempted by the banana—not the apple.

821. In *The Limerick,* No. 56:
A pansy who lived in Khartoum
Took a Lesbian up to his room,
    And they argued all night
    About who had the right
To do what, and with which, and to whom.
G. Legman notes that this limerick is based on an Oscar Wilde joke.

824. *Popsickle:* Frozen fruit-flavored water on a stick.
Popesickle: Frozen holy water on a stick.
Poopsickle: Shit on a stick.

849. In the 1950s, a Swedish citizen sued the estate of the King of Sweden for the equivalent of a widow's rights.

878. A *Playboy* article was based on the notion that a man's creative abilities were enhanced by sexual intercourse or fellatio.

6. Buggery

903. In *The Limerick,* No 1087:
There was a young lady of Chester
Who said to the man who undressed her,
    "I believe you will find
    It is better behind,
For the front is commencing to fester."

7. Abuses of the Clergy

974. *The Bishop of Birmingham.* This series is one of the great classics in limerick lore. The original series contained three limericks. A later version expanded this to six. The author has added two limericks to make this series a total of eight. Nos. 974–976 appear in *The Limerick,* in *The Lure of the Limerick,* and in *Playboy's Book of Limericks,* The author has added Nos. 977 and 978. No. 979 is from *The Limerick.* Nos. 980–81 were first noted in *Playboy's Book of Limericks.*

993. In *The Limerick*, No. 617:
There was an old Scot named McTavish
Who attempted an anthropoid ravish,
    But the object of rape
    Was the wrong sex of ape,
And the anthropoid ravished McTavish.

1003. Rhythm Roulette is a parody on Russian Roulette, a game of chance wherein each player in turn, using a revolver containing one bullet, spins the cylinder, then points the muzzle at his head and pulls the trigger. Rhythm Roulette is more dangerous for it ends in life, not death.

1027. In California (and also other states) irrigation wells have been dug deeper and deeper. As a result, the water table has fallen and the salt water from the ocean is flowing in, thus making the well water brackish. This is a typical example of man's inability to work with nature.

1075. The author was advised by a reliable friend that, when he was a youth, the local priest had slipped his hand into his trousers pocket to be certain that he was not entertaining evil thoughts!

1086. The Catholic Church has been most remarkable in procrastination when progressive ideas are proposed. The following excerpt, under the heading "Cutting the Bonds of Acrimony," is taken from *Life Magazine*, February 11, 1966, page 4: The subject is divorce laws.

> As New York legislators tried to draft their law, a Catholic spokesman asked that the whole matter be sent back for further study. New Yorkers, who have lived for 179 years under a law that is archaic, discriminatory and unworkable, might answer that the subject has already been pretty well studied.

Another typical example of Further Study by the Catholic Church is given in the July 2, 1968, issue of the *New York Times*. The article, under the heading "Vatican May Lift Censure of Galileo," is datelined Bonn, July 1, and it states that the Vatican may lift its censure of Galileo Galilei, who lived from 1564 to 1642. Galileo was declared a heretic for asserting that the earth moves around the sun. At this rate, the Catholic Church will take 340 years to consider the settlement of the divorce and birth control issue. When the issue does surface again, the Church, no doubt, will request more time. It appears that the Church is interested in a further study of *Further Study!*

1098. Excerpt from the *Detroit News,* January 8, 1967, page 19A:

Spellman Home, Urges Viet Victory
NEW YORK—(UPI)—Francis Cardinal Spellman returned Saturday from his annual Christmas pilgrimage to U.S. servicemen overseas and said there can be no peace in Vietnam "until we have victory."
Spellman's airport remarks to newsmen were certain to raise eyebrows again in the Vatican. . . .

The prelate was seventy-seven years old, and we can dismiss his remarks as being simply due to congenital senility in a reactionary.

1100. This limerick was prompted by the following bit of doggerel:
The Frenchmen are a funny race,
They fight with their feet and fuck with their face.

8. Zoophily

1139. In the U.S., oleomargarine has gradually displaced butter in the last forty years. The dairy interests, in an attempt to maintain their position in the market, initiated an advertising campaign with the slogan: *Real Butter Is Better.*

1185. In the 1930s, the Camel Cigarette Company advertised their cigarettes with the following slogan: *Nine Out of Ten Doctors Prefer Camels.* It wasn't long before the sequel was added: . . . the other one prefers women.

9. Excrement

1186. There was a young lady of Niger
Who smiled as she rode on a tiger.
They came back from the ride
With the lady inside,
And the smile on the face of the tiger.

There is obviously more to this limerick than merely a transportation of smiles.

1187. News Item, *Detroit News,* Jan. 13, 1980, p. 9A: Bert Lance, the one-time confidant of President Carter, goes on trial Monday in Atlanta on bank fraud charges. Lance, who was Federal Budget Director for eight months in 1977, is charged with twenty-two counts of bank fraud and conspiracy. In a long-drawn-out defense of his friend, President Carter failed to obtain a continuing federal appointment for Lance.

1200. Clark Gable and Vivien Leigh had the major roles in the classic movie *Gone With the Wind*, circa 1939. In the movie, Gable departed from the morality code (imposed by the Catholic Church) when he said, in the closing scene, "... Frankly my dear, I don't give a damn!"

This was the first straw that led to the breaking of the back of the censorship program in the movie industry, which was under the direction of the *Hays Office*.

1202. See Limerick No. 2952 for the classic "There was a young fellow named Clyde."

1224. In *The Limerick*, No. 745, The Farter from Sparta farts the complete oboe part of a Haydn Octet in B-Major.

1232. In *The Limerick*, No. 733:
There was a young man of Rangoon
Whose farts could be heard to the moon.
When you least would expect 'em
They would burst from his rectum
With the force of a raging typhoon.

1237. Compare to *The Limerick*, No. 1368, "There was a young man of Australia."

10. Gourmands

1282. In *The Limerick*, No. 22:
A lady while dining at Crewe
Found an elephant's whang in her stew.
Said the waiter, "Don't shout,
And don't wave it about,
Or the others will all want one too."

1287. This is the joke in the X-rated movie *Deep Throat*, starring Linda Lovelace.

13. Prostitution

1460. Riddle: What is the difference between a troupe of acrobats and a row of chorus girls? Answer: The acrobats show some fine cunning stunts.

Riddle: What is the difference between a bunch of thieving midgets and a girl's basketball team? Answer: The thieving midgets are a bunch of cunning runts.

1586. Compare with No. 1649. Also *The Limerick*, No. 917:
There was a young man of Cape Horn
Who wished he had never been born,
    And he wouldn't have been
    If his father had seen
That the end of the rubber was torn.

1633. *Jolly Green Giant* is the trademark of a brand of canned and fresh-frozen garden vegetables.

14. Diseases

1699. Rudolf Bing, noted opera impresario, was the head of the Metropolitan Opera of New York until his retirement in the late 1970s.

1701. Joke: A man rushes into a restaurant and he orders breakfast, "Give me two eggs, and I want them bad."

1704. In *The Limerick*, No. 1087:
There was a young woman of Chester
Who said to the man who undressed her,
    "I believe you will find
    It is better behind,
For the front is beginning to fester."

1705. The 4-D's—You Get What you Vote For. See also Nos. 1739–40. This limerick was prompted by newspaper reports in the *New York Times*, dated November 9 and 29, 1967. The articles were devoted to filth found in meat packing plants. "Government meat inspectors testified before a Senate Agriculture subcommittee at the time that the Administration endorsed a *compromise* meat inspection bill to provide *more adequate* protection for the public from the so-called "4-D meat—that derived from dead, dying, diseased, or disabled animals. . . . "

"The House [*always on the lookout for the public interest*] rejected an attempt to speed into law a meat inspection bill designed to guarantee consumers wholesome meat."

Following are some additional mouth-watering morsels from the articles:

sick meat to consumers; additives which are not permitted; flies were abundantly present; mold throughout the plants; filthy clothes; abscessed beef; parasitic infested livers; vermin droppings on floor; rodent harbors.

Need we say more? This is just another case of "The Public Be Damned!"

1713.   Joke: At the office, a fellow took off his shoe, and he tickled the snatch of the girl who sat at the desk opposite him. A week later his toe swelled and he went to the doctor, where it was diagnosed as *Gonorrhea of the Big Toe.*
"I'll bet you don't get many strange cases like this," said the man.
"Oh, I don't know," said the doctor. "Just the other day a lady came in here with *Athlete's Foot of the Pussy.*"

1720.   A good example of this would be the late senator of the 1950s who conducted "The Great American Inquisition."

1737.   The United States has been the haven for despicable, repressive dictators who have been violently ejected from their home countries. These dictators know many years in advance that they will be forced out, so they steal all that they can, and they transfer their wealth to foreign countries. The Shah of Iran was forced to leave Iran in 1978, and he found a haven in Mexico. In 1979 he came to the United States for cancer treatment. The aroused people of Iran seized the U.S. embassy personnel and held them in ransom for the return of the Shah.

15. Losses

1785.   In *The Limerick*, No. 1132:
There was a young sailor named Bates
Who tried the fandango on skates,
　　But he slipped on his cutlass
　　And it rendered him nutless,
And it made him quite useless on dates.

1794.   Similar to *The Limerick*, No. 1133.

1796.   Circa 1950(?) a spray had been advertised that would make old cars smell like new, thus enhancing used-car sales.

17.　Assorted Eccentricities

1932.   The much-publicized change-of-sex operation in Denmark where George was changed to Christine.

1940.   "Oh my God!" the doc swore,
          "I can see to the floor,
And your cunt is in need of repair."

1954. This is another version of a limerick heard at a Society of the Fifth Line meeting. See *Limericks Historical and Hysterical,* p. 92.

1992. In the 1920s and 1930s there was no union in the automotive industry. The story came out, probably based on fact, that, when a workman at the Ford Motor Company went to the toilet, a security guard would, on occasion, check the toilet for feces to make certain that the workman did not take out time for a rest.

1993. Riddle: What can a swan do that a doctor should do? Answer: Shove his bill up his ass.

2005. Church architecture is said to be traced back to the phallic symbols of heathen worship.

2019. At the end of World War II, Mussolini was captured by Italian partisans, killed, and then hung by his heels in a public display.

2021. In 1978 incumbent Mayor Mike Bilandic of Chicago was defeated by Jane Byrne—a notable upset of the well-known Chicago Machine.

2023. See note on No. 1586.

2107. Circa 1977, the author overheard a Canadian radio broadcast wherein an announcer gave his views on the detestable habit of smoking. He especially attacked pipe-smokers, and he berated his fellow announcer for smoking a *cherry pie and horseshit mix.*

2191. From an article in the *New York Times,* datelined Rome, June 26, 1968: Pope Says Bones Found Under Altar Are Peter's. [Thank God for the fortunate apostrophe] In *The Limerick,* No. 166:
There was a geologist Jossyl
Who found a remarkable fossil.
          He could tell by the bend
          And the wart on the end,
'Twas the peter of Paul the Apostle.

2251. See note on 2191, above. This series of two limericks is based on the following joke: The archaeologist was digging for fossils in the Mideast. He sent back an unusual find to the British Museum, with the following note: Have Found the Petrified Penis of a Prosperous Persian Prince. A reply came back by telegram: Have Studied Fossil and Conclude That Some Creep Crept Into Crypt Crapped and Crept Out Again.

2261. In the 1960s a U.S. oil company advertised their gasoline with the slogan "Put a Tiger in Your Tank."

2313. The Great Cheerleader Controversy of 1979. Some cheerleaders of the Dallas Football Club posed for nude pictures in *Playboy Magazine.* Football Commissioner, pious Pete Rozelle, requested that the girls be dismissed from activities with the Dallas Club.

2331. Dow and Dupont are busy manufacturing explosives and chemicals, whereas they should be spending their major effort on producing contraceptives—then there would be no need to kill people through war.

2349. Vice-President Spiro Agnew was caught with his hand in the till and was forced to resign his office.

2378. Common expression heard in public schools: If you were dying of thirst, I wouldn't give you the sweat off my balls.

2385. The cheesemaker wanted to make limburger cheese, but he forgot whether he should take two pails of milk to the shithouse, or two pails of shit to the milkhouse.

2391. *Simoniz* is a well-known brand of automotive polish.

18. Weak Sisters

2414. Thalidomide, $C_{13}H_{10}N_2O_4$, was used as a tranquilizer and sedative in the 1950s and 1960s. When taken during pregnancy, it was discovered to affect the normal growth of the fetus and it resulted in abnormally shortened limbs of the newborn. It is estimated that there were 5,000 to 8,000 grotesquely deformed babies born worldwide to mothers who had taken the drug during the early weeks of their pregnancy. In a number of cases, illnesses caused by tobacco are more prevalent, deadly, and insidious, but the results are not as dramatic as thalidomide.

2419. In the 1960s and 1970s, Detroit was known as the murder capital of the United States. In 1974 the city recorded 714 homicides. The year 1979 was a good year—only 416 recorded murders by the end of November.

Notes

2427. After the assassination of John Kennedy, William Manchester wrote a book, *The Death of a President.* Jacqueline Kennedy received a good portion of the profits. This procedure is known as *Capitalization on Calamity.*

2439. This limerick was prompted by an item in *The Devil's Dictionary,* written by Ambrose Bierce.

2465. See note above.

2473. Arson in the United States is a very popular and profitable pastime.

2475. From *Gulliver's Travels* by Jonathan Swift: In the Grand Academy of Lagado, Gulliver recounts his visit to one of the rooms wherein a projector (inventor) was busy at work in "an operation to reduce human excrement to food ... by separating the several parts, removing the tincture which it receives from the gall, making the odour exhale, and scumming off the saliva." The 1979 version is the proposal of scientists in the United States to feed cow dung to cattle.

2476. In Jonathan Swift's *Tale of a Tub,* Section IV, Peter, in a rage, attempted to convince his two brothers of the validity of his argument: "Such a thundering proof as this left no further room for objection. ..."

2485. Man's existence on earth is being threatened by overpopulation, chemical waste, and radioactive garbage.

2493. Dr. Gamow proposed that all letter combinations of one line of a newspaper could be printed, thus covering every possible line ever written or ever to be written in the future. Dr. Gamow also calculated the amount of paper that would be required to print all these combinations—it would cover the earth for many thousands of miles in depth.

2527. *The Honest Banker,* Washington (UPI) [circa 1976]: 6 New York Banks, Mayor Knew of City's Collapse.
Six major banks and top New York City officials, including Mayor Abraham Beame, knew the city was on the verge of financial collapse in early 1975 but still arranged the sale of $4 billion in municipal bonds to an unsuspecting public, the Securities and Exchange Commission said yesterday.
It cited Bankers Trust, Chase Manhattan, Chemical, Citibank, Manufacturers Hanover and Morgan Guarantee and the nation's largest brokerage—Merrill Lynch—as institutions that had "knowledge of the crisis" but still underwrote a $4 billion New York bond offering.

Notes

2546. In Jonathan Swift's *Tale of a Tub*, Section III, A Digression Concerning Critics: "The Nauplians in Argia learned the art of pruning their vines by observing that when an ASS had browsed upon one of them, it thrived the better, and bore fairer fruit. So it must be with Critics."

2626. In physics, students are taught that bodies of air flow from high pressure to low pressure. Buckminster Fuller says that it is the other way around—the wind doesn't blow—it is sucked.

2636. The author at one time found himself on a jury where at least one member could barely read or write.

2640. A wayward president or vice-president also make out very well when they are caught stealing.

2677. This is in reference to the Watergate scandal and the infamous Nixon Tapes, which were expurgated when reviewed for the public.

2689. This series of limericks is patterned after a similar thought in *The Devil's Dictionary* by Ambrose Bierce. Here Bierce reviews the inconsistencies of the English language in regard to pluralizing similar words. George Bernard Shaw was also a strong proponent of the simplification of English.

2712. In the 1930s, on the *Jack Benny Show*, the joke about the goat without a nose was played to death over a period of several months. When Benny was asked, how did the goat smell, he replied, "Awful!"

2723. Howard Scott, Director of Technocracy, Inc., defined a criminal as a human being with predatory instincts but insufficient capital to form a corporation.

2725. In the United States during the height of the disastrous elm tree disease people were advised not to store elm trees for firewood, since this provided a breeding place for the beetles that carried the Dutch Elm fungus. To date, no method of stopping the spread of the disease has been successful, and it appears that the elm tree is doomed along with the American chestnut, which was exposed to a similar fate.

2750. Polish Joke: Did you hear about the new Polish doll? You wind it up and it stands there and stinks.

480

2759.   The first mammal in space was a dog, which was sent into orbit by the USSR.

2761.   In the 1950s and 1960s a common fault of TV reception was an image displayed at a 45° angle. Slanted news broadcasts should theoretically clear up when recieved at this angle.

2762.   It has been the author's experience that many people cannot understand simplicity, claiming that it is incomprehensible. A typical example is when people refuse to try to understand simple addition under the pretext of not being versed in mathematics.

2765.   *Cease Fire.* Almost weekly throughout the Vietnam War, the newspapers stated that a "Cease Fire" had been implemented, but that did not stop the shooting. In an article from the *Detroit News*, dated November 21, 1966, p. 3A, headlined "Catholics Back Viet Action" comes the following excerpt: The American Catholic bishops, in a strong statement on peace, have defended United States military intervention in Vietnam. . . .

2771.   Congressman Diggs of Michigan was convicted in 1978 of skimming the payroll of his employees in his Washington office. He was sentenced to three years in prison, but the sentence was reduced to ten months. A government suit for $240,000 in back taxes was eventually dropped as uncollectible. His fellow congressmen debated long and hard before evicting him from Congress, many of them, no doubt, realizing that a similar fate could be bestowed upon themselves. While in prison, Diggs was reelected to office, which shows the mentality of the voters, and points out weaknesses in the system that permits felons to run for office.

2779.   This is one of the many myths that are presently taught to our unsuspecting youth.

2799.   Sir Isaac Newton said: An object travels at a uniform velocity in a straight line unless acted upon by an external force. He should have said: All objects always travel in varying velocities in ever-changing curved lines, since they are acted upon by external forces at all times.

2823.   *Suckers & Chiselers.* The country is made up of suckers and chiselers in the ratio of 1,000 to 1. If you are in doubt as to which class you belong to, examine your bank accounts.

2840.   According to George Bernard Shaw, *GHOTI* is pronounced *FISH*—"GH" as in *laugh;* "O as in women; "TI" as in *nation.*

2844. On arriving in heaven, old Spear
Asked St. Peter, "Is God somewhere near?"
Said St. Peter in mirth,
"He is smiting on earth—
How the heck do you think you got here?"

19. Chamber of Horrors

2876. *Long Live Necrophilia!* This limerick is based on a letter
written by a frustrated bride to *Dear Abby*, wherein the bride
described the disconcerting events that took place on her
wedding night.

20. Addenda

2945. The story is told about the Indian chief who had three
squaws—one on a deer hide with one papoose, one on a bear
hide with one papoose, and one on a hippopotamus hide with
two papooses. One day the chief entered the teepee and made
a sage observation: Sons of squaw on hippopotamus equal
sons of squaws on other two hides.

2947. When Richard Nixon was faced with impeachment, he
stated, "I may have made mistakes, but I am no crook!" See
also limericks 2963 and 2997. As fate would have it, Richard
Nixon was not impeached. He maneuvered the appointment
of Gerald Ford as the next president. Spiro Agnew, the vice
president, was not available on account of his legal troubles.
Gerald Ford, upon receiving the country's highest office, im-
mediately proceeded as the first order of business, to pardon
Nixon, who had never been tried or found guilty of any
wrongdoing—a first in American jurisprudence: Pardon Before Charges Are Laid. Gerald Ford must now live the rest of
his life with Nixon's shadow hanging over him—no one par-
doned him for pardoning Nixon! This episode deserves to be
commemorated:

Nixon's tenure was naught but a thread
As impeachment hung over his head,
But there came a bright light
Like a star in the night,
"There's a Ford in my future!" he said.

"There's a Ford in my future" is the advertising slogan of
the Ford Motor Company.

2950. This limerick is based on a theme from Ray Billington's marvelous example:

Colostomy victims, they say,
Pose problems for friends who are gay,
For they now must decide
Is the bottom or side
The preferred pederastical lay.

2951. The classic Clyde limerick is No. 709 in *The Limerick*. It also appears in Langford Reed's *The Complete Limerick Book* (1925), p. 210. Legman states: It is the only off-color specimen Reed allows himself—possibly out of sheer misunderstanding.

I have taken the liberty of adding a sequel.

Index

Numbers refer to the limerick number, not the page number on which the limerick appears.

Abdu, 2409
abduction, 27
Abdul-Hissun, 1917
abhor, 2410
ability, 28, 1425
abject, 1918
abound, 2411, 2412, 2413
absurd, 960, 1186, 1919
accounting, 961
accrue, 2416
ace, 2848
acquire, 2415
acrobatic, 1117, 2414
action, 29
Adair, 1118
admire, 1921
admit, 565, 1920, 2417
adore, 2418
adroit, 2419
adventure, 786
advice, 1327
affinity, 30, 962
affront, 2420
aflame, 1303
aghast, 1242
aglow, 2421
agog, 1119
Akeem, 1829, 1924
Alas, 2400
Algiers, 1304, 1426, 1750, 1926
Alice, 1925
alive, 687
all-fired, 1427
alliance, 1830
allow, 1428
allurance, 2422, 2423
allurin', 787
alluring, 1751
aloof, 1305, 1306
Alphonse, 383
Alsace, 2849
Alsatian, 384, 963
amass, 1147, 1928
amends, 898
amiss, 981
Andes, 1429
anew, 1929
Annabel, 1752

Anne's, 2275
annoyed, 385
annoys, 2424
ano, 1699
Apollo, 2936
appalled, 1430
apparent, 1402
appeal, 964
appears, 965
appraise, 2425
apprehend, 386
arise, 1930
aroma, 2426
arrive, 1187
art, 899
arts, 1753
assortment, 966
assurance, 2937
Astor, 31, 967, 1307, 1431, 2427
astute, 1931
attacked, 2428
attract, 1432
attract us, 2938
auspicious, 1308
autumn, 1932
averred, 1933
avoids, 1433
Award, 2850
Azores, 387, 1239, 1934

Babbitt, 32, 968, 969
Babbs, 1700
Bach, 1754, 1935
Backshun, 2429
Bacon, 2430
Baghdad, 388, 1701
Baird, 970, 1434, 1755, 1936
Baker, 1309, 2851
Bangkok, 1403
Bani-Sadr, 2939
Banker, 2852
Banks, 389, 1435, 1831
Banner, 1937
Barbados, 1939
Barden, 33
bare, 1940, 2398
Barents, 390
Barger, 1436

Index

Barm, 1832
Barr, 391, 392, 1941, 2431, 2432, 2853
Barrett, 1756, 1833, 1942, 1943
Barrie, 393
Bart, 971, 1188, 1189, 1240, 1437, 1944, 2433, 2434, 2435
Basle, 900
Bassett, 1438
Bate, 34, 2436
Bates, 1310, 1439
Bayer, 1834, 1945
Baynes, 2854
Beach, 2437
Beakley, 35, 2438
Beard, 901
beasts, 972
Beatty, 36, 37
beauty, 394
because, 2439
Beecher, 902
Beedle, 395
began, 1120, 2440, 2441
Beggs, 38, 39, 396, 1946, 2855
begs, 2940
beguiled, 788
begun, 1190
Behring, 649
Beirut, 397, 789, 1311
Belfast, 398
Belgrade, 40, 903, 1702, 1757, 1835, 1836
Belgrave, 2856, 2857
Belle, 1964
Ben, 1312, 1538, 2443
Benares, 399
bench, 2401
bend, 2367
Bend, 342, 760
Bengal, 1241, 1440
Bennett, 2444
Benny, 1121
bent, 1947
bent her, 2858
Bentley, 1243
Beque, 1441
bereft, 41
Berlin, 973, 1442, 1758
Berne, 42, 904
Bernice, 1948
Bernice's, 1443
Bert, 44, 1244, 1837, 1949
Bertie, 400
beset, 1759
Bess, 45, 401, 1445, 1760
Bessie, 1950
Beth, 2445
Betty, 402
bewilders, 2446

Bickly, 2447
Biddle, 46
Bierce, 2448
Bierley, 1951
Biggar, 47
Billings, 650
Bing, 1952, 2941
binge, 403
Binks, 48, 1446, 2449
Birch, 404, 982, 983, 1447
Birmingham, 974, 979
Bister, 49
bit, 2450
bitchin', 1953
Black, 478, 790, 1448, 1954
Blaine, 1955
Blaining, 405, 984, 2452
Blair, 2453
Blake, 1404, 1449, 2451
Blanc, 1613
Blanding, 1450
blew, 666
bliss, 2230, 2454
Bliss, 791, 1191, 1703, 1761, 1956
Blissit, 792
Block, 986
Bloom, 2859
Bloor, 50
blotches, 2455
Blue, 793
Blugg, 794
Blunt, 1957, 1958
Bobby, 1451
Bodim, 1615
Bogg, 1313
Boker, 1314
Bokum, 651
bold, 652, 1452, 1959
Bombay, 2860
Bonctor, 2456
bones, 2457
bonnet, 51
bony, 1324
Boocher, 1453
Booth, 653
Bordeaux, 53
bore, 1454
Boris, 654
Borum, 1960
Bostick, 2458, 2459
bound, 2942
Bounter, 655
Bounting, 1455
bout, 1043
Bower, 54, 55
Bowles, 905, 906
Box, 987
boy, 52

Boyce, 2460
Boyd, 1315
Boyes, 56, 1961
Boyle, 1704, 2463
bracket, 2461, 2462
Brackett, 57, 1962
Brad, 2943
Brady, 1122
Bragg, 1762
braves, 2464
Brazilian, 406
Bream, 2944
Brechtly, 988
bred, 2465
Breech, 1456, 1963
Breethaus, 2466
Brenda, 407, 989, 990
Brent, 1970
Brest, 991, 1969, 2467
Bret, 2468
Bricker, 1245, 2469
Brickley, 58, 408, 1838, 2470
bride, 907
brides, 2945
Bright, 59, 795, 992, 1123, 1971, 2471
brightening, 2472
bright one, 2473
Brimbles, 656
bring, 60, 1972
brink, 2474
Brinkage, 61
Brinker, 62
brood, 2475
Brook, 63, 64, 65, 1973, 1974
Brophey, 66, 657
Browder, 67, 2476
Brown, 409, 410, 908, 1246, 1247, 1248, 1975, 2477
Broze, 796
Bruce, 68, 658, 2478
Bryce, 1316, 1457, 1458, 1459, 1976, 2946
Brylent, 2861
Brynner, 2479
buck, 1977
Buckingham, 2480
Bud, 69
Bull, 2481
bum, 2482
Bunce, 1460
Bunche, 70
Bunky, 71, 1124, 1978, 2483
Bunny, 1461
Burgess, 659
Burke, 72, 1462, 1839, 2060
Burl, 1979
Burrage, 1463
Burse, 2484

bust, 2485
Bustard, 73
Butte, 411, 1192, 1193, 1405, 1464, 1465
Butters, 2486
buying, 1705
by, 2487
Byron, 74, 1980

Caesar, 660, 661
Cahalan, 412
Calais, 75, 413, 797, 1125
Calhoun, 1981, 2488
Campbell, 76
Capper, 77
Cappy, 1764
caprice, 1466, 2248
care, 977, 1249
Carr, 78, 1126
Carrie, 414
Carriere, 415, 2862
Carruther, 909, 1467, 2037, 2489, 2863
Carruthers, 910
Carson, 1765, 1982, 1983
cartel, 416
Carter, 1194, 1195, 2490
Case, 1250
Cass, 1317, 1406, 1766, 1984
Castle, 798, 1196, 1985
catch, 2491
caught, 2947
Cavage, 993
cavernal, 417
Chaco, 2601
chafe, 79, 1318
Chape, 80, 1319, 2492
charts, 1986
Chase, 81, 418, 799, 1840, 1987, 2170, 2864
cheery, 2493
Cheevers, 2494
Chesapeake, 995
Chester, 1468, 1706, 1707
chic, 1988
chick, 419, 994
Chinese, 2495
choice, 82
choir, 978
Chris, 662
Christine, 996
Christopher, 420
chubby, 1469, 1708
Chuck, 663, 1989
churn, 1841
Claire, 83, 800, 1081, 1648, 1649, 1990, 2948
Clairwell, 84
clamor, 421
clan, 2496

Index

Claribel, 2866
Clark, 85, 86, 87, 1320, 1991, 2497, 2867
class, 801, 911, 997, 1127, 1197, 1992, 1993, 1994
Claude, 422, 1709
Cleft, 88, 89, 2498
Clif, 1995
Cliff, 1470
Clift, 1471, 2501
Clive, 1472
clothes, 423
clustered, 2502, 2949
Clyde, 664, 667, 668, 912, 1842, 1843, 1996, 1997, 2503, 2504, 2505, 2506, 2950, 2951, 2952
coast, 1321, 1473, 1998
coition, 90
Cole, 424, 913, 1322
collected, 998
collegian, 669
Cologne, 91, 92, 1999, 2000, 2500, 2507, 2508, 2509
colonel, 670
comb, 1844
Commer, 673
compassion, 1474
complained, 2510
complex, 2511
complication, 2512
concrete, 2514
conceit, 2513
concern, 802, 918
conclusion, 999
condition, 2926
confessed, 2516
confinement, 425
confronts, 1251
Conne, 803
connived, 1252
consent, 2358
consortion, 1407
conspire, 2953
Constantine, 2954
construe, 2517
content, 2518
contented, 2001
convening, 2519
conversed, 671
convincible, 2520
Coombs, 93
cope, 2360
Cord, 94
Corning, 1198, 1475, 1710
Costral, 2521
Cottam, 1476, 1711
Cotter, 95, 1477, 1478, 2002, 2522, 2955, 2956
Cotton, 1712

Coulsom, 96
counts, 2524
course, 2423
Coxsaxie, 97
crap, 1767
Crassar, 98
Crassus, 804
Cratchet, 426
creepy, 2525
crept, 99
Cretchmore, 914
Crete, 427, 2526
Crewe, 490, 491
crime, 2527
Crimea, 2957
Crist, 2528
Critchit, 428
crocheted, 2529
Crockett, 1323, 1325
Croft, 1479
Crowe, 1329
Croylett, 1845, 2865
Cruse, 1480
Cumbo, 2003
Cummer, 100
cunts, 444
cure, 1341
curled, 2004
Curry, 1481
curse, 1408
Cushing, 1768

Dades, 1482
Dag, 101, 1769
Dale, 2530
Dali, 674
Dallas, 1330, 2005, 2958, 2959
Damascus, 2531
Damatur, 676
Dan, 1199, 2006
dance, 1846
Danius, 2007
Danny, 429
Danville, 675
Dare, 102, 1770, 2008
Darius, 677
dash, 103, 104, 2374
dashes, 1000
date, 430
Daucus, 1483
daughter, 105
Dave, 1966, 2868, 2869
David, 915
Dawes, 1484, 2532
Dawson, 106
day, 431, 2533
dead, 1485, 2009, 2534

dear, 1771, 2010
debase, 1331
Decatur, 1128, 1253, 1486
decay, 1001
Decker, 2011
decorous, 488
Dee, 678
deep, 1254
Deever, 1002, 2012
defeat, 2535
Defiance, 1773
defrayment, 1487
deft, 806, 1772
dejected, 2013
deject 'em, 2536
dejection, 1332, 2537
delight, 2014
demented, 2015
demure, 1409
Denny, 2538
deplore, 2539, 2960
deployed, 2640, 2961
depravity, 107
Depter, 679, 680
despair, 432, 1129
despaired, 2541
Detroit, 108, 433
devout, 1333, 2542
Dewald, 109
Diana, 805
dickens, 2543
Dickinson, 110
Diggs, 2544
dignified, 2545
Dimmage, 1488
Dintage, 2016
discerned, 1489
disciplined, 1200
discover, 434, 2017, 2018
discreet, 1490, 1938, 2019, 2962
discretion, 2020
discuss, 111
disgrace, 2021
disgusted, 2023
dismay, 645
displayed, 112
dispute, 2546, 2547
Diss, 2548
distraction, 1491
distraught, 2963
distressed, 1847
distressing, 2024, 2549
divest of it, 113
divulge, 1410
Dix, 1492, 1848, 2205
Djibouti, 1493
do, 1003
doc, 435

Dockery, 1004
Dodd, 2025
Dokks, 681
dollar, 436
Dome, 1005
donation, 1967
Donder, 2550
Donna, 2026
Dorgan, 682
Doris, 437
Dotty, 2027
doubt, 2551
Dougal, 114
dough, 2552
Douglas, 1494
Dover, 115, 116, 117
down, 2553
Dr., 1334
Draper, 1499
dread, 2554
Drew, 118, 1849
Dreyoss, 1500
Drife, 1255
droll, 807
drudge, 2028
Druid, 1006
Dubuque, 1495
Ducharme, 1130
duchess, 119
Duckworth, 1496
due, 1411
Duff, 1850
Duluth, 2029
dumb, 2499
Dumore, 120
dunce, 808
Dundee, 121, 688, 689, 1497, 1498,
    1774, 2555
Dunder, 122
Dunn, 123, 683, 690, 1007
Dunway, 124
Durante, 125
Durbin, 2556
Durham, 1256
Dutch, 126
duty, 2405

Earse, 2870
earth, 1008
East, 691, 1009, 1131, 1258, 1335, 2557,
    2871
Easterner, 2030
Eiffel, 438
Eire, 127
Elaine, 439
elastic, 1851
elation, 1775
Eleanor, 2031

Elias, 1010
Elliot, 1502
Ellis, 692
embarks, 1011, 2032
embossed, 1503
endeavor, 2558
endure, 1012
enduring, 1776
engineer, 2559
enlist, 561
ensconce, 2033
entice, 1504
enticeth us, 2560
enured, 1852
envision, 2561
erected, 128
erection, 558
escape, 2562
Esther, 129
Eve, 130
Ewing, 131, 693, 1013, 1505, 1777,
    1853, 2034, 2035, 2964
excesses, 132
excite me, 133
excuse, 1854
exhibition, 2357
expansion, 2249
expect, 1014
expense, 2563
explorer, 134
express, 917

Fabia, 1778
faced, 2036
face it, 1779
fails me, 2038
fair, 135
Fairless, 1506
fall, 1015, 2039
fame, 2564
Fanchion, 440
Fannic, 2565
far, 2040, 2041
Farber, 1507
Farlet, 1508
fart, 1201
fastidious, 2566
fate, 809
feared, 2022
feel it, 1259
feels, 441
Feenery, 2567
fell, 2568
fellow, 1260
Fenchter, 1509
Fender, 916
Fenster, 2042, 2569
Fern, 442, 694, 1510

Fern's, 1511
Ferrer, 695, 1016, 1017
fickle, 2043
Field, 2044
Fife, 136, 137, 138, 1132, 2570
filed, 160
Finches, 139, 1336
Finnegan, 140
Fisk, 443
fisted, 1236
fit, 1018
Fitch, 1512, 2045
Fitches, 1019, 1337, 2571
Flanagan, 141
Flavey, 142
Fleckers, 445
Fleegle, 1133
Fletcher, 696
flew, 2046
flexing, 446
flinches, 447, 449
fling, 1513
flipped, 1338
Flo, 143, 448, 919, 2047, 2872
Flock, 144, 450, 1134, 1261, 2873, 2874
floor, 157, 686
floored, 1020
Florrie, 2048
Flossa, 145
Flounce, 1514
Floyd, 2572
flushes, 2372
Flushing, 1515
Flynn, 1516, 2573, 2574, 2575
foam, 2049
focked her, 2050
focus, 146
Fogg, 1135, 1136, 2051
foggy, 1517
Fong, 2052
fool, 975
foot, 1713
forbear, 2965
Forch, 2875
Ford, 147, 2053
Fordham, 2054
foreigner, 148
forgotten, 149
forlorn, 1780
form, 2055
Forrer, 150
forum, 2056
fossilology, 151
Foster, 152, 1021, 2057
Fot, 451
found, 2058
fount, 153
Four, 2059

Fox, 811, 1137, 1339, 1781, 2062, 2063, 2576
Fran, 2064
France, 1340
Frances, 1342
Frank, 1855, 2066
Frankton, 2577
Franktum, 1023, 1024
freckle-faced, 2065
Fred, 154, 156, 452, 1025, 1782, 2068, 2069, 2070, 2578, 2579, 2876
free, 2071
Freeman, 1856
French, 1519, 1857
Fretter, 155, 453, 920, 1138, 1139, 2072, 2073
friar, 1026
Frick, 812, 1343, 2235
fright, 2580
Frindem, 2581
Fritz, 161, 454, 1714, 2074, 2075
Frommes, 1858
Frood, 921, 1262
Frost, 455, 2076, 2582
frown, 2966
Fry, 162, 697, 1263, 2077, 2583, 2584, 2585
full, 749
Funks, 1520
funnel, 1521
funny, 1522
Furze, 1523

Gable, 2877
gaged, 2586
Gail, 1524, 1526, 1715, 2878
Gaines, 698, 2967
gaining, 1527
Galion, 1140
Galions, 1141
Galt, 163
Galt, he, 1027
game, 2968
Gander, 2879
gaped, 1344
Garrity, 1528
Gary, 1264
Gast, 164
Gastard, 1028
Gaynor, 165
Gellicut, 2078
Gelling, 2079, 2587
Gene, 166, 456, 457, 1265, 2080, 2081, 2969
gentle-hearted, 167
Geraint, 1029, 1859
Gert, 1266, 2588
Gertie, 1345

Gibraltar, 1030
Giles, 168, 2083, 2276
Gilhooly, 2589
Gillies, 2590
Gilmore, 2591
Gimbel, 458
Gimp, 922
Ginnit, 2970
Girard, 2592
Girk, 2082
glances, 1031
Gleason, 1530
glee, 685
Gleek, 1529
glen, 2593
Glick, 813, 1860, 2971
Glim, 1531
Glitz, 2084
Glock, 814
Glosting, 169
Gloucester, 170
Glover, 171, 1532, 2594
Gluck, 459, 1346, 1914, 2085
glum, 2881
Gnauss, 2595
go, 2596
Gobel, 2597
Goff, 1783
Gog, 2086
Goggs, 1142
Gold, 172, 699
gone, 1326
Good, 700
goods, 1533
Goozie, 173
Gophet, 174
Gord, 701
Gore, 175, 176, 177, 1032, 1784, 1785, 1786, 1787, 1863, 2087, 2088, 2598, 2972
Gorse, 178
Gorth, 2089, 2880
Gosham, 1788, 2599
Goss, 2090
Gossage, 1267
gout, 1534
gown, 672
grace, 555
Grace, 179, 180, 181, 460, 815, 816, 817, 818, 819, 2091, 2092, 2600
grand, 461, 2515, 2602
Grange, 702, 1535, 2973
Granger, 2603, 2974
Granoz, 2604
gravity, 820
Gray, 821
Greece, 2605
Greenery, 462

Greer, 703, 1536
greet, 2362
Gression, 1033
grief, 1347, 2606, 2975
grieves, 1034
Grimes, 2093, 2976
Groatwell, 463
Grogg, 1143, 1144
groove, 1537
Grout, 1539
Grover, 182
Grunday, 822, 1540
grunt, 2365
grunts, 464
Gwen, 467, 468, 823
Gubb, 465, 2094
Gudget, 1541
Guelph, 183, 1542, 1543, 1789, 2095, 2607, 2608
Gulcher, 2096
Gump, 184, 185, 2097, 2977
Gus, 1716, 1717
Gusty, 466
guy, 891

habit, 2609
Hadl, 704, 705
Hadley, 1348
Hagan, 1035
Haines, 186
Hainz, 2882
Hall, 706
haltered, 1202
Hamal, 1145
Hambler, 707
Hame, 469, 718, 2098, 2610
Hammer, 923
Hamp, 470
Hample, 188
Hans, 824
Hap, 1719
Harold, 924
harass, 2099
harried, 1146
Harriet, 708, 1864
Harris, 709
Harrow, 2100
Harte, 1203
Hartley, 189, 710
Hartz, 1204, 1205, 1206, 1793, 2611
Haskett, 2101, 2612
haste, 1865
Hasting, 1349
Hatch, 711, 1544, 2102
Haver, 1720
Hayes, 190, 2883
heard, 980

hearse, 2613
Hearst, 191, 1545, 1546, 1721, 2103, 2104, 2614, 2884
Heather, 1547
heat with, 1866
Hector, 471, 925
Heep, 2105, 2978
Heeper, 1148
Heldt, 2615
Hensley, 1149
Herm, 1548
Hewitt, 1350, 1867
Hicks, 192, 825, 826, 1790, 2106, 2107
Hilaria, 472
Hilary, 2616
Hill, 1794
Hinches, 2108
Hind, 193, 194
Hiram, 2109
hire 'em, 2617
hit, 2110
Hite, 195
Hoboken, 196, 1351, 1722
Hocking, 2979
hole, 1827
Hollow, 827
Hong, 2980
Hood, 197, 299, 2981
Hooper, 198
Hoover, 199, 200
hope, 926, 2113, 2618
Hope, 1861, 1862, 2112
Hopper, 1795, 2619, 2982
Horn, 1763
horse is, 2620
Horton, 201
hot in, 202
Howard, 2885
Howe, 474
Howell, 1207
Hubbell, 1549, 2621
Huck, 2114
huff, 2983
Huff, 828, 2115, 2622
huffing, 203
Hugh, 204, 205, 206, 207, 1796, 2116, 2623, 2624, 2984
Hughes, 208, 209
Humburd, 2625
Humphrey, 927
hunt, 477
Hunt, 210, 211, 475, 476, 480, 829, 830, 1036, 1550, 2117, 2118
Hurd, 1037, 1208, 1209, 2119
Hussey, 1723
Hutch, 831, 2121
Hyatt, 2985

492

Index

Ignatius, 1038
ill-lucked, 2122
ill-treated, 481
implored, 1039
impressions, 2123
inch, 712
incited, 212
inept, 1150
Inge, 1082
inhibited, 2124
Innsbruck, 2125
installs, 2364
instruct, 2126, 2626, 2987
instructor, 213
inveigle, 1551
invincible, 214
Iran, 482, 928
Iraq, 483
Italian, 1040

Jack, 215, 216, 484, 485, 486, 832, 1352, 2127, 2128, 2129, 2886
Jackson, 217
Jacques, 1041, 2130, 3023
Jake, 2627, 2628, 2629, 2630, 2631
Jane, 218, 1353, 1552, 1553, 2131, 2132
Janus, 2133
Jay, 219, 1151, 1797
Jean, 833, 1354
jeep, 1355
jerk, 220, 2134
Jesus, 1554
Jewett, 1555
Jill, 2632, 2887
Joan, 487, 1152, 1868
Jock, 221, 489, 492, 1044, 1798, 1799, 1869, 1870, 2888, 2889
jocular, 713
Joe, 222, 493, 834
Joel, 1268
John, 715
Jones, 1556
Joy, 223
Juba, 494
Jude, 224, 495
Junction, 985, 1042, 1095
June, 835

Kamloops, 2633
Kane, 225
Kant, 1412
Kapps, 1724
Kate, 226, 227, 836, 1725, 1871, 2135
Kay, 229, 230, 496, 497, 1557, 1558, 1726, 2136, 2634
Keating, 498, 837, 1045, 2635
Keaton, 838, 929
Keats, 1872

Keitel, 499
Keith, 500, 839, 840, 841, 842, 843
Kell, 844, 2636, 2637
Kelly, 1413, 1414, 1873
Kelter, 2137, 2638
Kent, 1046, 1559, 1560, 1561, 2138, 2139
Kentucky, 1047
Kessel, 2639
Kett, 231
kettle, 2640
Kew, 976, 2641
Keyes, 1210
Keynes, 1211
Keys, 1563
Keyser, 716
Khartoum, 930, 2140, 2890
Khomeini, 2986
Kiam, 2642
Kibbel, 1269
Kieful, 1356
Kiefer, 1564
Kiel, 1565
Kim, 714
Kimball, 501
Kimber, 502
Kimmen, 717
King, 232, 1800, 1874
Kings, 503
Kippers, 2141
kissed, 1153
Kissel, 504, 1801
Kitchener, 505, 718, 1566
Kitt, 506, 2643
Kitty, 1567
Kivel, 1270
knees, 508
knew it, 2646
knife, 1154
Knight, 1357, 1358, 2647, 2648
Knightley, 234
knocked, 2988
known, 235
Knox, 509, 810, 2061, 2989
Klatsch, 2142
Klaupt, 2644
Kleering, 507
Kline, 233, 1568, 1727, 1802, 2645
Klotz, 2143
Klutz, 1569, 2144
Kong, 473, 2111
Kootenay, 2891
Koppers, 845, 1570
Koppler, 2145
Krantz, 1212
Krauss, 1359, 1578, 2649, 2650
Kregg, 1875
Kreitzon, 236

Krepp, 1048
Kress, 2651
Krings, 2652
Kropp, 510, 1271, 1360, 2146
Kropps, 1571, 2990
Krupp, 511, 1155, 1572, 1573
Kubik, 2147
Kudents, 2148
Kurd, 931
Kurtew, 2149
Kyes, 2892

LaBlunt, 846
lack, 512
LaFarge, 1575
Lahore, 1049, 1576, 2653
laid, 1579
Laker, 720, 2150
Lakme, 1361
lamas, 2151
Lancet, 237, 1728
land, 2152
Lang, 2654
Lansing, 2655
Lapeer, 513, 932, 1156, 1157, 1272,
    1577, 1803, 1876, 2656, 2893
Laporte, 2991
Larket, 1580
Larkin, 2657
Larocque, 2658
last, 2659, 2660
late, 2661, 2662
Latrobe, 2153
Laurel, 514, 847
Lautrec, 238, 721, 2663
Lauzon, 239
lawyer, 2717
lay, 1818, 2664, 2894
Lear, 2154, 2155
learner, 933
learning, 240
LeClaire, 1581
led, 2156
Lee, 241, 515, 722, 848, 934, 1050, 1051,
    1052, 1158, 1877, 1878, 1879, 2157,
    2158, 2665, 2666, 2667, 2668, 2669
Leeds, 516
Leedy, 2159
Leith, 1880
Lemann, 1582
Levant, 2160
Lew, 517, 518, 1583, 2161, 2670
lick, 849
lifted, 519
Lillian, 242, 1159
limpidity, 2671
Linkter, 937
Linnet, 2162

Linning, 243
Linus, 1273
Linz, 244, 723, 2163
Lipe, 245
Liskeard, 566
Liskers, 850
Lissing, 1274, 1362
List, 560
Lister, 935
Liston, 520
Livonia, 1584
Lize, 1585, 2164
Lizzie, 521
Lloyd, 2165
locality, 2672, 2673
Locke, 553, 1053, 1054
Long, 2992
looking, 2167
loquacious, 2720
Lord, 1364
Lorne, 1213, 1586, 2166, 2674
Lottie, 2675
lots, 522
Lou, 246, 523
Louise, 2676
Lourdes, 2168
Lucerne, 2895
luck, 1275, 2171, 2368, 2677, 2896
Lucknow, 1587, 1588
Luigi, 247
Lumming, 524
Lundy, 1055
Lunt, 851, 1589
Luntz, 525, 852, 1276, 1729, 2172
lusting, 1056
Lute, 724
Lutz, 2173
Lyme, 2174, 2678
Lynch, 248, 249, 526, 1590, 1881
Lynd, 1160
Lynn, 725, 1363
Lyriad, 1415, 2175

Mabel, 250, 2679
MacAllister, 2176
MacBeth, 2680
McBiddle, 2693
MacBird, 251
McCarty, 2185
McCawdel, 1883
McCord, 731, 1600, 1601
MacDilts, 726
MacDubbers, 252
MacDuff, 1591
McFink, 1730
MacFogg, 1365
MacFrost, 1592
McFry, 2689

Index

McGavity, 263
McGirk, 534, 535
McGivery, 1804
McGore, 2694
McGraff, 1416
McGraw, 264, 732, 1163, 2186, 2695
MacGregor, 1593
McHugh, 1602
Mack, 2681
McLoud, 537, 2187
MacLout, 1594
McLoutch, 538
McLouth, 539, 540, 856, 857, 2188
McLung, 2696, 2697
McLure, 733, 858, 1603, 1731, 1884, 2698
MacMaddit, 2177
MacMeech, 853
McNair, 541, 1216, 1604, 2189
MacNeal, 527, 1366, 1882, 2169
McNear, 2699
McNight, 2898
McNish, 1164, 2700, 2993
McNull, 734
McNurd, 542
MacNurd, 2178
MacPherson, 727, 2682
MacSligh, 2683
McWade, 1885
Madder, 728, 1161
Madras, 253, 528, 938, 2179, 2180, 2181, 2684
Madrid, 1367
magazines, 1368
Magoo, 254
Mahler, 1595
Mahoney, 255
Mahooty, 256
maid, 257, 529, 1057
make, 854
males, 939
Mallory, 1596
Malone, 729
Mame, 530, 1214, 1215, 1597, 2182
man, 1277
maneuver, 258
Manila, 2897
Manion, 531, 532
manor, 730
Mape, 2183, 2685
Mapes, 2686
Marge, 259, 1162
Mario, 260
Marvin, 2687
Mary, 1278
Mason, 855
match, 1279
Matthews, 1598

Mattis, 1369
May, 2184
Mays, 261
Max, 262, 533, 940, 1599
Mazey, 2688
meant, 2702
Measick, 1605
meat, 2994
meet us, 2703
Mel, 1170, 1217, 1218, 2190
Mellin, 859
Merrick, 2704
Merritt, 543, 860
me seize, 2701
met, 554
meters, 2191
methinks, 2705
Metters, 1606, 2995
Meyer, 1518, 1607, 2192
Meyers, 1059
Mick, 544
Mickel, 1060
Mickey, 1608
Middlesex, 1501
Milan, 267, 1165
millionaires, 2706
Mills, 2707
Milt, 2193
Milwaukee, 1609
Minnie, 268, 1370
Minter, 269, 1732
mirth, 2708
Miss, 2996
mission, 1061, 1062
mistook, 2997
Moak, 1083
Mobile, 1610
modernity, 2709
Moffin, 735, 2710, 2899, 2901, 2998, 2999
Molder, 2194
moll, 3000
monasterial, 1219
Moncrieff, 1886, 2195
Mongolia, 2196
Montbello, 270, 736
moor, 1611
Mopsy, 2902
more, 1612
Morse, 545, 1166, 1167, 1805, 2711
Mort, 546, 1614
Mose, 547, 2712, 2713
Moses, 2197
Motch, 2198, 2199
mother, 2200
motivity, 2201
Mott, 271, 548, 941, 1371, 2202
Mottsum, 2903

Index

Mrs., 2714
Mudge, 549
Muller, 2715
multiplicity, 2716
Munich, 1806
Murray, 272
musician, 2203

name, 273
Nantucket, 1807, 1923
Nash, 861
Natchez, 550, 552, 557, 559, 737, 1280, 1616, 2204, 2904
Nate, 274, 738, 862, 2206
nations, 2723
nattily, 2724
Neals, 942
neat, 275, 2725, 2728
need, 2207
Nell, 276, 1733
Nellie, 1734
nerve, 1617
Nettie, 1417
Neville, 277
Newman, 1220
Newsome, 2208, 2209, 2729
Newt, 1419, 1808, 1809, 1810
Nick, 1281, 1282, 2210, 2211
Nicky, 279
night, 280
Nile, 1618
Niven, 2905
Nixon, 551, 2212
nocturnal, 2730
noise, 2726
nominal, 2731
note, 1168, 2727
nuder, 739
numb, 2213
numerical, 1063

oath, 281
obsolete, 2214
Occupation, 1619
occurred, 1620
O'Connor, 1621
O'Dare, 740, 1283, 2215
O'Dirk, 282
Ogden, 2732
O'Hare, 283, 741
O'Hart, 2216
O'Hunt, 1064
O'Keefe, 1372, 1622
old, 2906
O'Malley, 284
oration, 1065
Oregon, 285, 1066
oriental, 567

Orillia, 568
Orleans, 1623
Ostend, 1373
outclassed her, 1067

Pace, 286, 2217
pack, 2733
Pagonia, 287
Paine, 2907
Pakenham, 569, 1887, 1888
palace, 943
Pam, 2218
Papp, 1284
par, 2219
Parches, 1068
pardon, er, 288
Park, 1624
Parker, 2734
Parr, 1285
part, 1221
parts, 1222
Pask, 1374
pass, 2359
passion, 2735
Pat, 570
Patch, 1735, 1889, 2220
path, 289
Patterson, 2221
Paul, 594, 944, 1176, 1625, 1650, 1651, 1652, 2736, 2737, 2738
Pauline, 1626
Peak, 571, 1375, 1376
Peaks, 1420
Pearl, 2222
Pease, 572, 1286, 1736, 1811, 2223, 2739, 2740, 2741, 2742
pedantic, 2743
peers, 43
Peking, 2224
Perce, 573, 2744, 2908, 2909, 2910
perception, 2721
Percy, 2745
perfection, 574, 3001
Perkins, 290, 1627
perplexed, 936
Persimmon, 2746
persistance, 1377
Perth, 742, 1421, 2225
Peru, 575, 576
Pete, 291, 863, 1287, 1288, 1289, 1628, 1812, 1813, 1817, 1890, 2226, 2911, 3002
Pete Cook, 2912
Peters, 292
Pflugge, 578
Phelps, 1169
Phil, 293, 1629
Philippe, 743

496

Index

Phipp, 1630
Phipps, 294, 864, 2227, 2228
Phlitte, 2231
Pickett, 577, 865, 2747, 3003, 3004
pickle, 228
Pict, 866
Pierre, 295, 2229
piety, 1069
Pine, 1171, 3005
pines, 1172
Pink, 296
pissed, 579
Pitt, 580, 1223, 1631, 1632, 2232
Pitts, 581, 2748
plan, 1173
plastered, 2233
please, 582, 2067
Pleasure, 583
pliant, 1633
plugging, 2749
Plum, 297, 298, 584, 867, 945, 1891
pocket, 665
Podunk, 2750, 2751
Pola, 744
Polk, 2234
Polly, 1634
pope, 1070
Porter, 2913, 2914
portrayed, 2236
ports, 3006
position, 1071
Post, 1072, 1635
Potter, 2237
Potts, 868, 1636, 2238
Pound, 745
poured, 2752
Powell, 746
Prater, 585, 2915
Pratt, 1378
pray, 1637
Preakness, 1379
precision, 586
Prentiss, 1638
prepare, 2363, 2916
Presk, 747
presume, 3007
price, 2239
Price, 2691, 2753
prick it, 869
pride, 870, 1257, 2240, 3008
priest, 1073
Pringle, 2754
Proctor, 1380, 2918
professional, 1074
professor, 2755
proficiency, 2917
proficient, 2756
propositions, 2757

protect, 1075
Prude, 300
Pryor, 1639
Purdue, 302, 303, 2241
Puritan, 301
Purnell, 2758
Pursall, 304
purveyor, 2250
Pyle, 305, 306, 587, 1640, 1641

quaint, 1076, 1642
Quatorze, 2242, 2243
Quebec, 307, 1381, 1643
Queen, 871
quick, 1737, 1738
quo, 308

race, 2759
Racine, 748, 1290, 1644
Radwan, 1174
Raft, 2244, 2760
rail, 1922
raiment, 2246
Raines, 2919
Rainey, 1645
raised, 1814
Ramon, 309
Rand, 310, 1892, 2245, 2920
Randall, 1893
Randitt, 311
Rangoon, 1224, 1646, 2922, 2921
ranted, 2761
rapt, 2251
rarity, 2762
Rassity, 312
Rasting, 588
Ravenna, 2253
Ray, 1225, 1739, 2254, 2255
reassess, 2763
reckless, 1791
Reepie, 1895
Reese, 589, 750, 2256
refined, 313, 946
reflection, 314
regalia, 2764
Regina, 590
Reichert, 2257
release, 2765
remorse, 158, 751, 1077, 1226
repented, 1291
replete, 2399
resistance, 2766
resource, 647
resources, 2258
Restroke, 2259
retire, 2767
Retwun, 1227
Reuben, 752

497

Index

reveal, 872
reviewing, 2768
Rheims, 1815
Rhodes, 2769
Rhodium, 2770
Richters, 1382
Richurr, 2260
ride, 2261
Rideout, 1383
Riffer, 873
Riggs, 2262
right, 563
rigs, 2771
Rinky, 1741
Rinnish, 2263
Ripley, 2264
rise, 2923
Ritter, 772, 1422, 2772
River, 1894, 2442
roach, 1022
roam, 2247, 2265
Roarch, 2266
robust, 315
rocks, 2267
Roma, 874, 1228
Rome, 1647, 2773
Rootes, 1384
rootless, 1385
Rory, 1078
Rose, 591, 1896, 2268, 2269, 2774
Rote, 1175
rotund, 2270
Rousseau, 316
Royster, 1079, 1080
Rube, 2271
Ruggling, 2272
Ruhr, 592, 1386
rules, 2775
rum, 2776
Runshawn, 317
rural, 593
Russell, 2273
Ryerson, 2274

sagacity, 2777
said, 318
Salome, 875
Salonika, 319
Sam, 320, 1177, 1178
Sands, 595, 2277
Sarubin, 2778
Saskatchewan, 1653
Sasso, 2278
Savoy, 1654
Sax, 1655
say, 753, 876, 2779
Sayers, 2790
scandal, 2279

Scarp, 2781
Schartner, 321
Scheering, 1229
Schick, 596, 877, 1387, 2280
Schickel, 1897, 1898
Schiller, 1656
Schilling, 322
Schink, 597, 598, 947, 2782
Schippers, 599
Schirring, 323
Schleft, 324, 1084
Schlepper, 2783
Schlock, 878
Schmidt, 325, 326, 600, 3009
Schroeder, 2281
Schule, 601
Schust, 602, 2282, 2784
Schwartz, 327, 604, 605, 606, 879
science, 2283
scoff, 607
scoop, 2402
score, 948, 2284
Scott, 608, 609, 610, 611, 612, 754, 880,
    1085, 1292, 1293, 1294, 1295, 1657,
    1819, 1899, 2285, 2286, 2287, 2288,
    2289, 2290, 2291, 2785
Scotten, 1742
scowl, 2366
Scringe, 755
script, 2292
Scroll, 1086
Sears, 613, 881, 1927, 2786
Seattle, 1900, 2787
Sebastian, 949
secure, 2293
seeking, 2924
seize, 2788
seized, 1388
Sentry, 2294
September, 3010
Seth, 2789
Seward, 1389
shakes, 2790
shame, 1390, 2295
Shaver, 603
Shaw, 614
sheep, 1179
Shevor, 328
Shield, 1658
shirk, 329
Shirley, 1391, 1901
shock, 615, 2369
shook, 719
shop, 2791
shore, 1659, 1743, 3011
Shore, 330, 2296, 2297
Shorter, 756
Shorty, 1744

shove, 2298
Shrife, 2299, 2792
Shutes, 616, 617, 883, 1660, 1820
sick, 882, 2300, 3012
Sid, 1902
sights, 2301
Simms, 757
sin, 1087, 2302, 2303
Sinbad, 331
sisters, 1392
sit, 1230
Skilling, 1661
Skillings, 2304, 2305
Skinner, 332, 758, 2306, 2307, 2927
Skokie, 950
sky, 1231
slacks, 1662
Slade, 333, 1903, 2793, 2925
Slatter, 334, 1745, 2308
sleepy, 3013
slice, 2794
slick, 479, 1088, 1904
Slickbach, 2795
slinky, 2796
Sloan, 335, 2797
slob, 1393
slumming, 1663
smart, 1232, 2798
Smith, 336
Smither, 1394
Smitty, 2309
smocks, 2310
Smutches, 1664
Smuts, 1089
Snaith, 1090
Snood, 759
Snyder, 337
so, 338
sobbin', 1423
sod, 618
Sommer, 2311
sordid, 2312
sorrow, 339
sought, 340, 619, 1965, 2313
South, 341, 1905, 2314
sown, 343
space, 2799, 2800
Spain, 620, 761, 1665
spark, 344
spasm, 621
Speers, 2315
Spence, 1091, 1666, 1667, 1821, 2801
Spencer, 2316
Sperling, 1395
spice, 2692
Spicer, 1816
spilt, 1092
spoof, 2802

spouse, 2690
spree, 1668
Springer, 622, 1792, 1822, 1906, 1907,
   2317
spry, 1396
Spurgeon, 1397, 2803
squid, 1296
squirm, 2804
Stan, 345
star, 2318
stare, 2373
start, 2319, 2320
started, 1093, 1233
Stein, 762
Steiner, 623, 1297
Stella, 346
sternest, 951
Steve, 347
stew, 1298, 2370
stick it, 2371
stir, 763
stirred, 1234
Stockholm, 348
Stokes, 764
stooped, 2252
storm, 2805
Stott, 2321
Stottam, 1746
stout, 765
straining, 624, 1094
Strand, 625, 766, 1096, 2322, 2323
Strensall, 1671, 2324
street, 349, 1699, 1670
stress, 2806
strong, 1672
Stubby, 1673
Stuttgart, 2325
subjected, 2807
subsistence, 1908
success, 1444
suffer, 884
superb, 2719
surprise, 2808
Susie, 1674
Sutter, 767
swami, 627
swam in her, 626
swamp, 2809
sweeper, 952
sweet, 885, 886
Swincombe, 1675
Sy, 2326, 2810
Symes, 1823
symmetric, 564

Tacoma, 1747
taste, 1676
Tateful, 350

taught, 2327
taut, 2328
tea, 2329
Tealing, 1097
team, 2330
Tedder, 1824
tell, 1968, 2811
tender, 953
tent, 351
Tex, 2812
Thant, 2331
Thatcher, 768, 769
there, 556
thigh, 352
things, 2813
think, 2404
this, 3014
Thistle, 2814
Thomas, 887
Thor, 353
thought, 2332
Thrace, 628, 888, 1100, 1677, 1909, 1910
Thrasher, 1180
Thresher, 1678
throngs, 1098
through, 684, 2333, 2815
thumbs, 2334
thwart, 159
thwarted, 2816
tilt, 1328
Tim, 3015
Tinder, 1825
tired, 2335
tires, 2336
Tish, 629
Titehouse, 2337
Toal, 630
Tobruk, 354, 1679
today, 2338
Todd, 1099
toils, 2817
Toni, 1181
Toole, 1235
Toronto, 355
torus, 2818
Totum, 2339
toucan, 3016
tower, 357
town, 1101
towns, 1680
Towser, 358
toy, 356
tractor, 359, 770
tray, 1299
treasure, 2340
treat, 2341
tree, 2342

tremble, 1826
Trent, 2343
Trevor, 2819
tricks, 360, 1748, 2344
Trieste, 361
trip, 3017
tripped, 1102
trivia, 2820
Trout, 890
trudges, 2821
true, 2822
trusting, 362
Tuck, 889
Tuckem, 1103, 1681
Tucker, 631, 2345
Tuckers, 1682, 2823
Tudder, 2346
Tudor, 1398
Tuller, 363, 632
Tully, 364
Tunney, 2347, 2348
Tuppet, 1911
Turk, 892
twat, 2388
Tweed, 365
Tweek, 954, 1399, 1683
Twickenham, 1104, 1105, 1106, 1107
Twinning, 1684
Twist, 2349, 2824
twister, 562
twist it, 1912
Twitting, 1685, 2350

Umberto, 633
unaware, 955, 2351
undaunted, 634, 2825, 3018
undaunting, 1686
undertook, 1182
undressed, 1787
unfurled, 2826
unknowing, 893
unobtrusive, 2352
unperplexed, 2361
unreal, 2827
unrefined, 366
unwitting, 2389
Utrecht, 2353

vague, 3019
Vail, 1913
Vance, 2354, 2355
Vancouver, 367, 1108
Vandyke, 635
vapours, 2375
varied, 2722
Veep, 1183
venty, 2828
Venus, 368, 636

Index

verbosity, 2718
Verdun, 1109
Vetch, 369, 370
vexed, 644, 894, 1688
vicarial, 1110
Vichy, 2829
view, 2356
Vince, 371, 2830
Violet, 637, 771, 3020
virtuosity, 1400
Visser, 2376
votes, 372

Wacker, 373
Wade, 374
wag, 2397
Wage, 375
waist, 2377
Wales, 1689
Walker, 2928
Wallace, 1690
Walls, 773, 2378
Walt, 638
Walter, 774, 1111
wandered, 2831
Wapping, 956
war, 2832
Warbocks, 2379
Waring, 2929
warns, 2380
Watson, 775, 776, 957, 1691
Watt, 1184, 2930, 1300
Waugh, 895
Wayne, 1915
wedding, 958
Weeks, 1401
Weiss, 1692
Welch, 2381
well-fed, 2382
Wells, 777, 3021
Wertz, 778, 779, 1693
west, 1694
West, 376, 639, 1113, 1185, 1562, 1695,
    2383, 2833, 2900
Westminster, 377
Whaling, 1696
what, 646
Wheatley, 1237
Wheeling, 378, 640, 1112, 1916, 2834
Whipple, 379, 3022

whirled, 641
White, 380, 959, 1301
Whithouse, 2384, 2385
Whiting, 2835
Whitney, 2386
whiz, 2836
whore, 1740
Wigger, 1238
Wilford, 381
Willet, 780, 1114
Willie, 2837
Wills, 2931
wince, 382
Wings, 781, 2838
Winifred, 1697
winked, 2839
Winkle, 782
wise, 642, 2403, 2932
Wise, 896, 1302, 1698, 2387, 2390, 2391,
    2933
wish, 2840
wish you, 1749
Woking, 1115, 2392
wonders, 2841
Wong, 2394
Wood, 2393, 2842
Woodhaven, 2395
woods, 643
Worcestershire, 2843
word, 1116
worth, 2844, 2845
wrangle, 2396

yak, son, 897
Yale, 1828
Yates, 2846
yearning, 2934
years, 2406
yen, 2407
yore, 2847
York, 278, 1418, 1424
Yost, 783
Young, 3024
Ypsi, 784

Zeeter, 648
Zend, 2408
zest, 2935
Zimmer, 785